THE COMPLETE COURSE FOR DRAWING

MANGA

THE COMPLETE COURSE FOR DRAWING MANGA:
LEARN TO WRITE AND ILLUSTRATE YOUR FIRST MANGA
KURU

TEXT & ILLUSTRATIONS: MANON BORDES

PROJECT EDITOR: JOCELYN HOWELL
PROJECT MANAGER: LISA BRAZIEAL
MARKETING MANAGER: KORYN OLAGE
LAYOUT: MAUREEN FORYS, HAPPENSTANCE TYPE-O-RAMA
COVER PRODUCTION: MAX MARCIL
GRAPHIC DESIGN: SONIA BLANCHARD
TRANSLATION: MARIE DEER

ISBN: 979-8-88814-322-3
1st Edition (1st printing)

English language edition © 2025 Rocky Nook, Inc.
Authorized translation from the French edition
Original French title: *Cours complet de dessin manga*
© First published in French by Fleurus, Paris, France – 2024
(French ISBN: 9782215180609)

Rocky Nook Inc.
1010 B Street, Suite 350
San Rafael, CA 94901
USA

www.rockynook.com

Distributed in the UK and Europe by Publishers Group UK
Distributed in the U.S. and all other territories by Publishers Group West

Library of Congress Control Number: 20249477 0

This book is printed on acid-free paper.
Printed in China

THE COMPLETE COURSE FOR DRAWING
MANGA

KURU

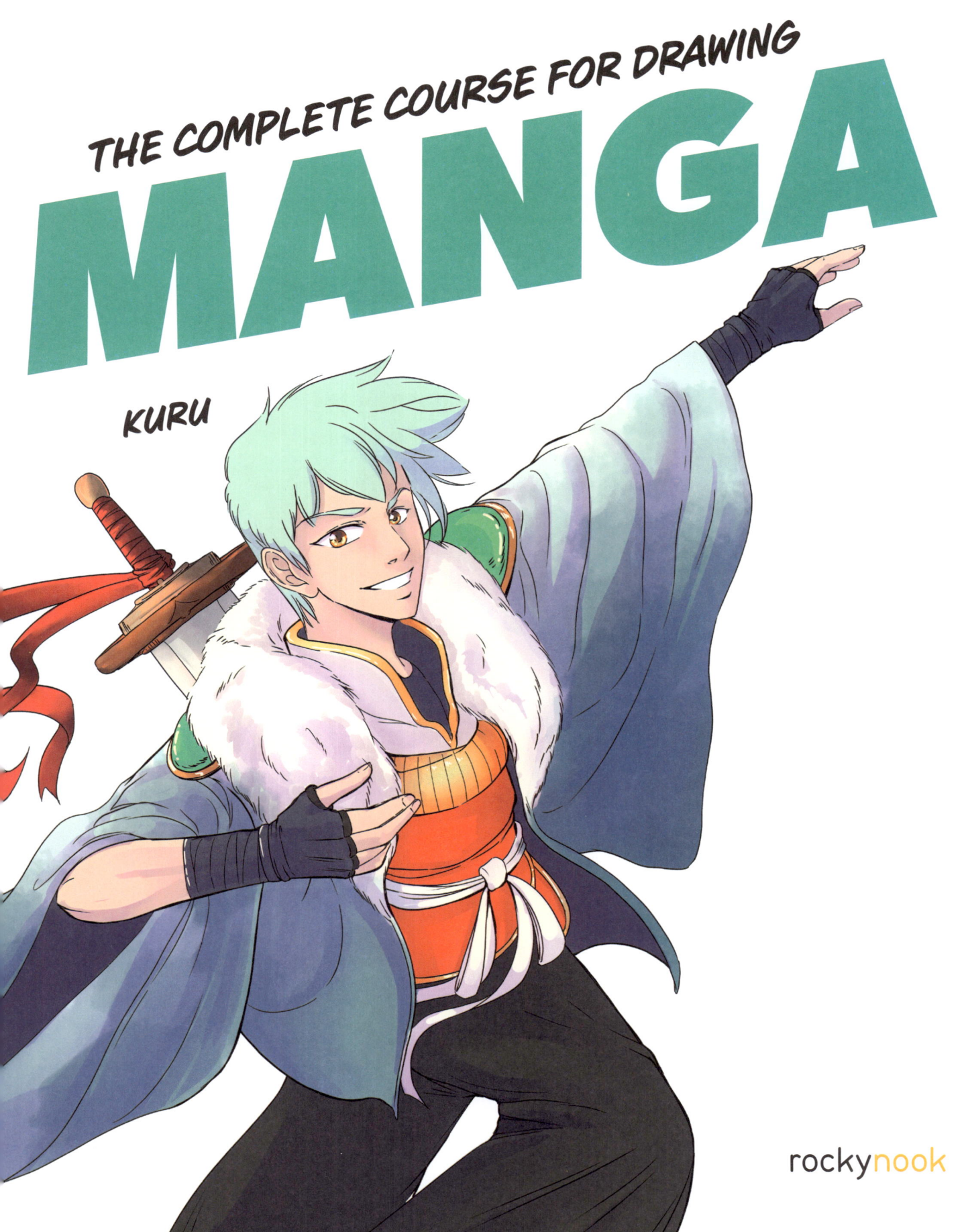

rockynook

CONTENTS

INTRODUCTION

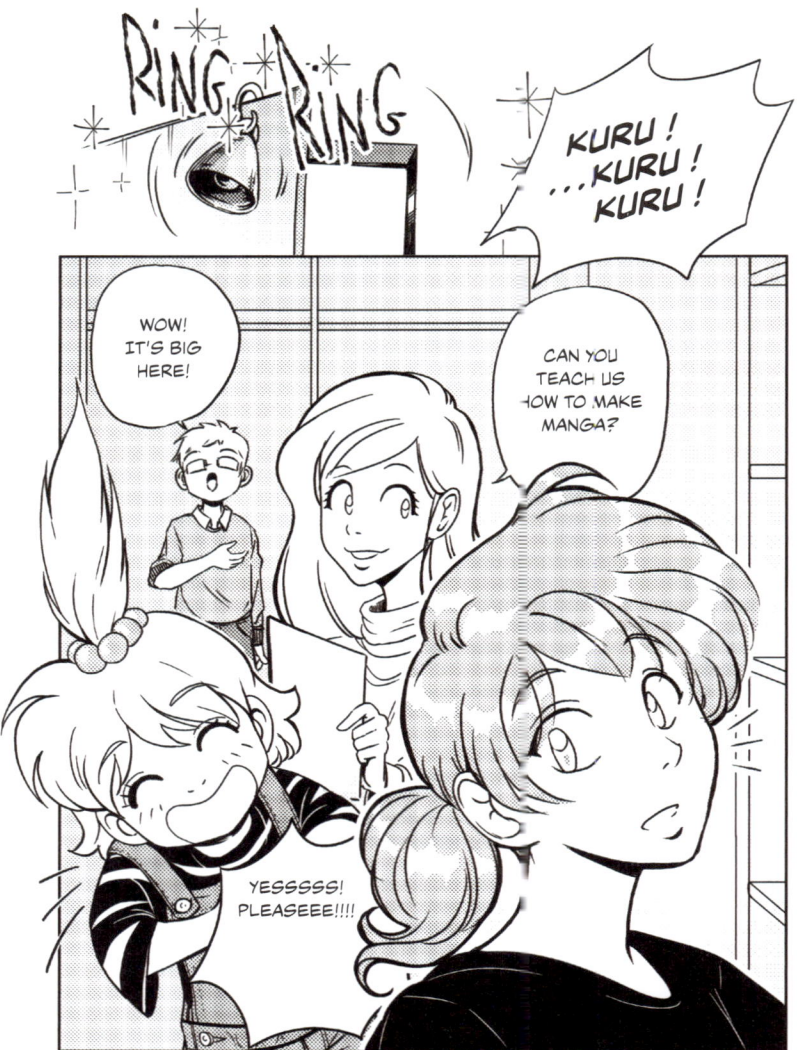

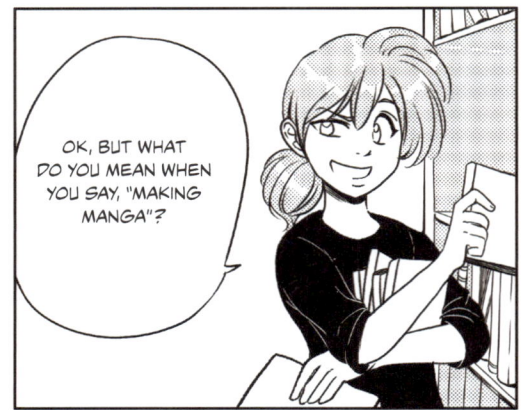

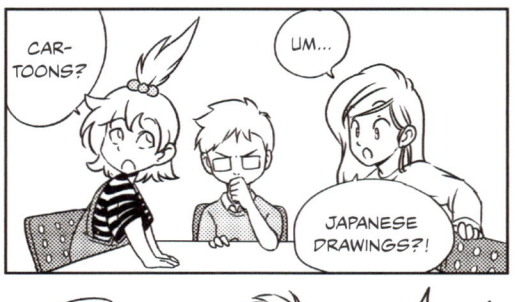

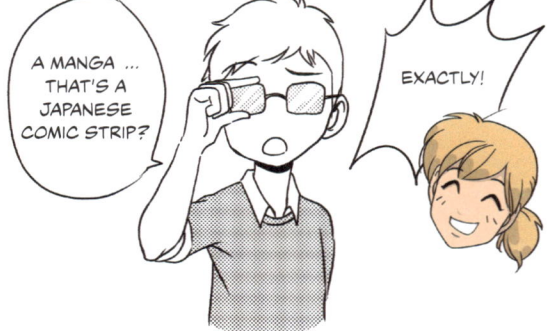

In this book, we will define a **manga** as a book in which a story is told in illustrated sequences, usually from left to right, with black-and-white drawings that use Japanese-influenced graphic codes. Manga will take us on a journey and let us feel a multitude of emotions!

The best-known genres of manga include **shonen** (action and adventure manga), **shojo** (romances), and **seinen** (dramas, thrillers, horror stories). But there are manga for all ages and all preferences.

Some of the important words used in this book are explained in the glossary on page 204.

The word "manga" is also used as an adjective to describe the characteristic style of the drawings in these books. You will sometimes see me using the term "manga drawing" to talk about drawings that come from or are inspired by manga.

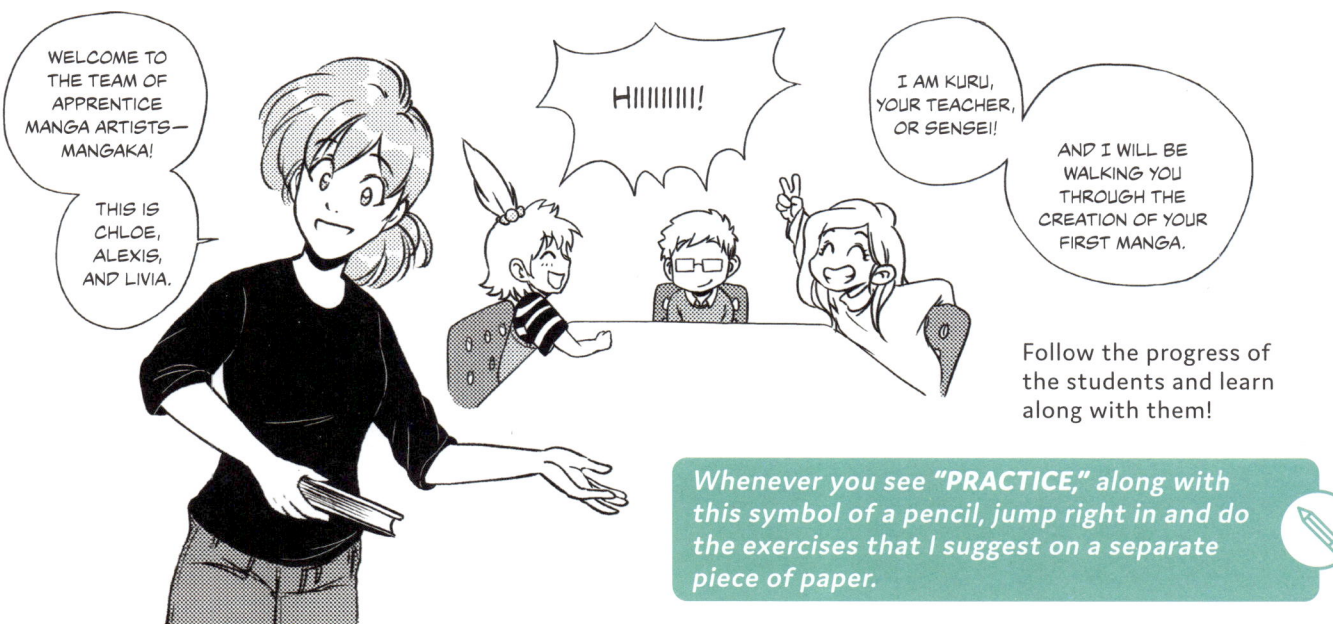

Follow the progress of the students and learn along with them!

Whenever you see **"PRACTICE,"** along with this symbol of a pencil, jump right in and do the exercises that I suggest on a separate piece of paper.

THE STEPS TO CREATE A MANGA

It's a long road from wanting to draw a manga to finishing your first one. What can you do so you don't get lost along the way?

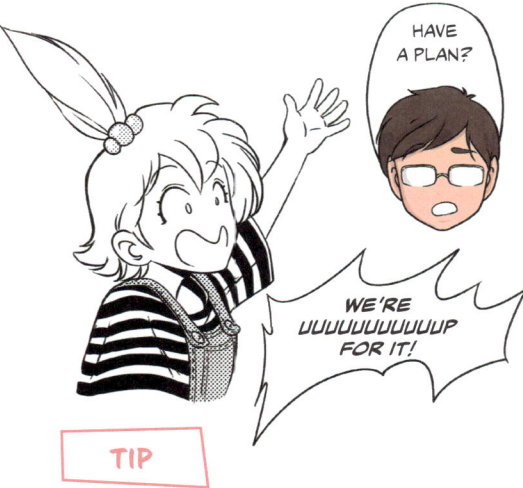

TIP

Whatever level you are at, in order to make rapid progress in your drawing, be curious, read a lot of different things, and experiment on your own with things that cannot necessarily be found in instruction manuals.

Here's the plan I suggest we follow together:

1 GET READY
- **Get Information**: Read manga and specialized books and watch tutorials.
- **Get Organized**: Set small goals and deadlines that are achievable.
- **Get Set Up**: Select and obtain the materials you need.
- **Learn to Work**: Get into the habit of concentrating on the things that will really help you make progress.

2 PRACTICE DRAWING
- **Observe**: Discover the basics of drawing through observation.
- **Understand**: Learn how to draw shapes, proportions, and perspective.
- **Build Endurance**: Practice regularly.
- **Find Your Own Style**: Combine inspiration and imagination.

3 TELL STORIES
- **Create a Script**: Imagine characters and show them acting in stories.
- **Transpose the Text into Images**: Create storyboards.

4 FINALIZE YOUR DRAWING
- **Create the Boards**: Sketch in pencil, add ink, add the screens, and finalize.
- **Create the Color Cover Image**: Synthesize your story.

5 SHARE YOUR STORY
- **Show It**: Share your creation with your friends, your family, or even the pros!

BEFORE YOU START

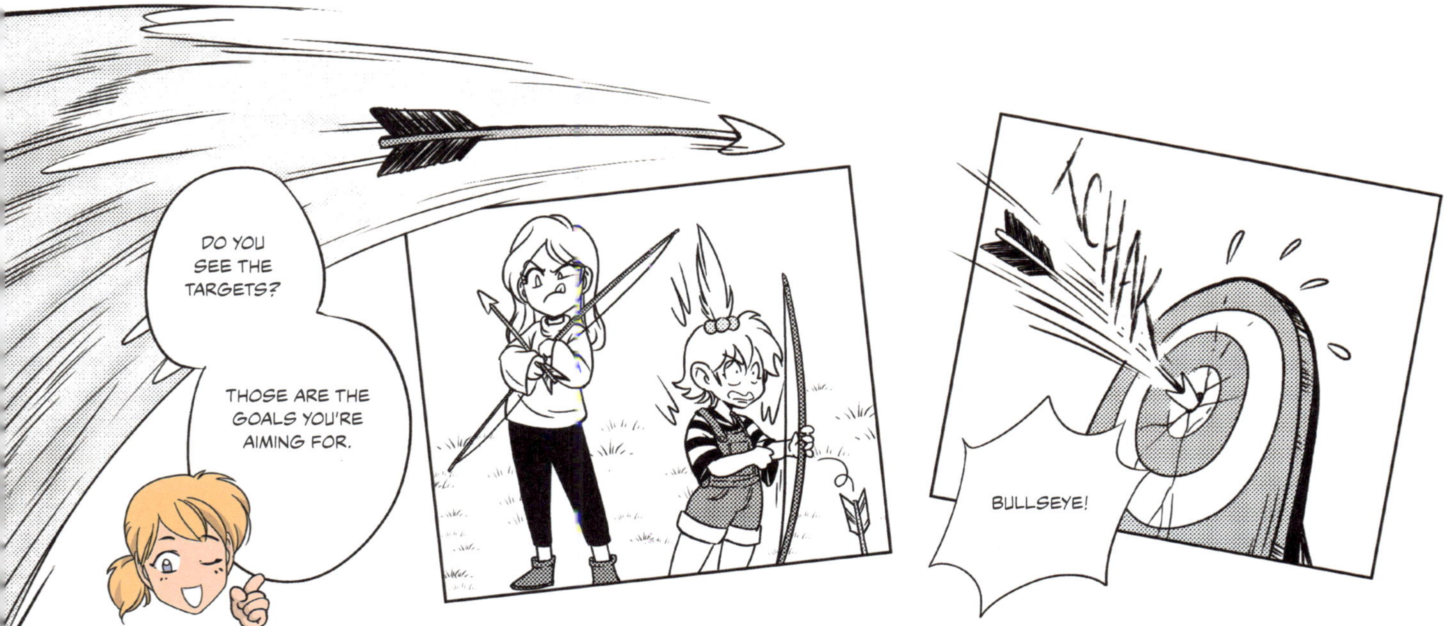

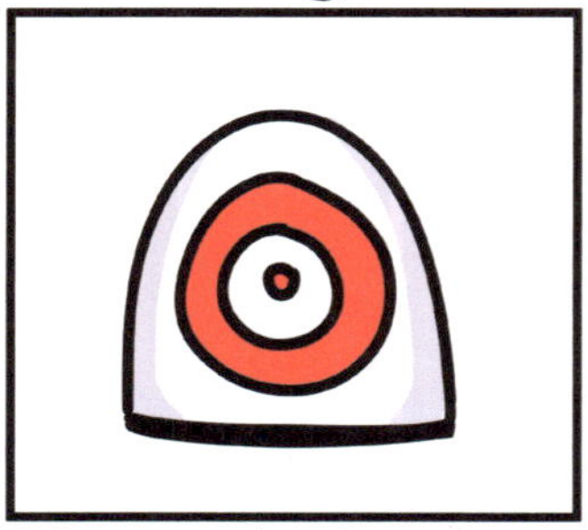

> DO YOU SEE THE TARGETS?
>
> THOSE ARE THE GOALS YOU'RE AIMING FOR.

BULLSEYE!

HIHI !

▲ Some are close by and easy to reach.

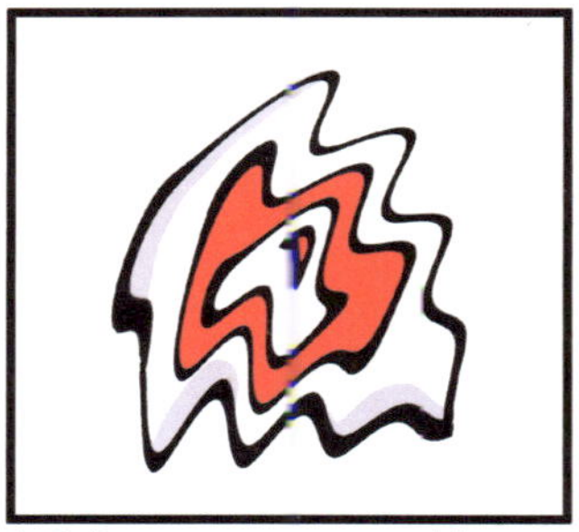

▲ Others are vague and hazy.

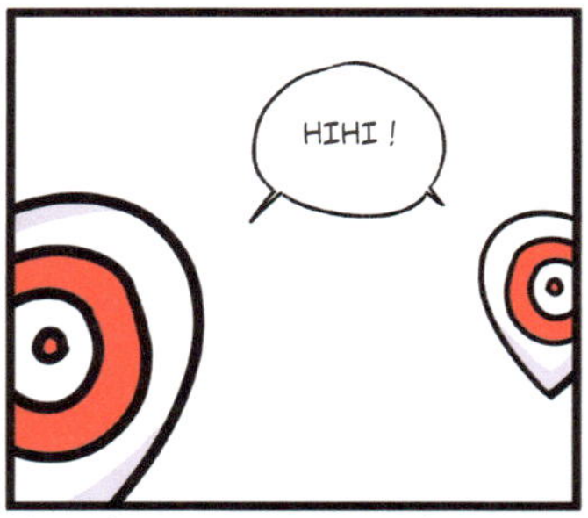

▲ Others are constantly on the move because you keep changing direction . . .

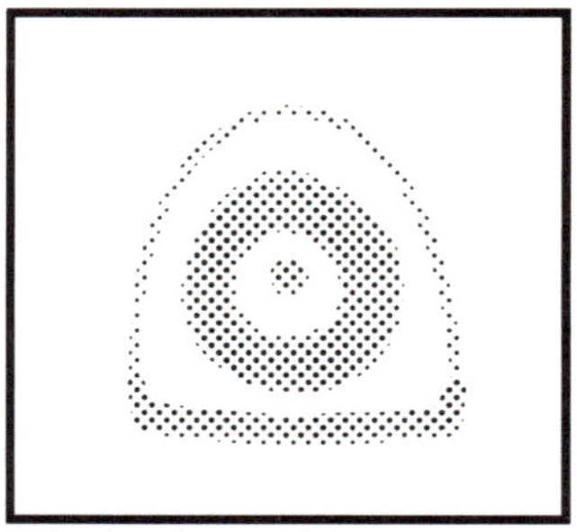

▲ And . . . here, there is no target at all?

A BIT OF METHODOLOGY

In order to make progress, **you need a clear, achievable, and stable objective**.

Let's say your most fervent wish is to know how to draw manga. Do you really know what a manga is? What are the concrete actions you need to undertake to succeed in your manga project?

Drawing a manga like a pro is a very complex undertaking because there are a lot of things to know in terms of drawing, storytelling, and technique . . . You run the risk that your targets will be constantly moving because you will sometimes skip steps as you jump from one to the next.

Writing down your goals is a good way to visualize them, internalize them, and achieve them.

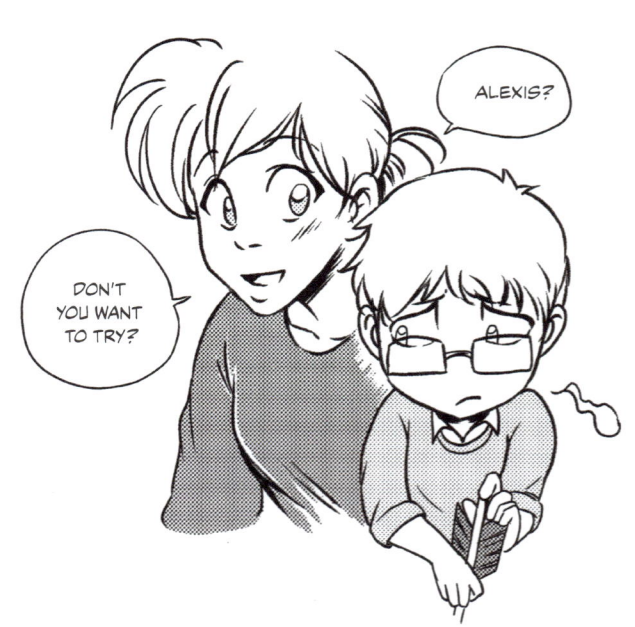

> ALEXIS?
>
> DON'T YOU WANT TO TRY?

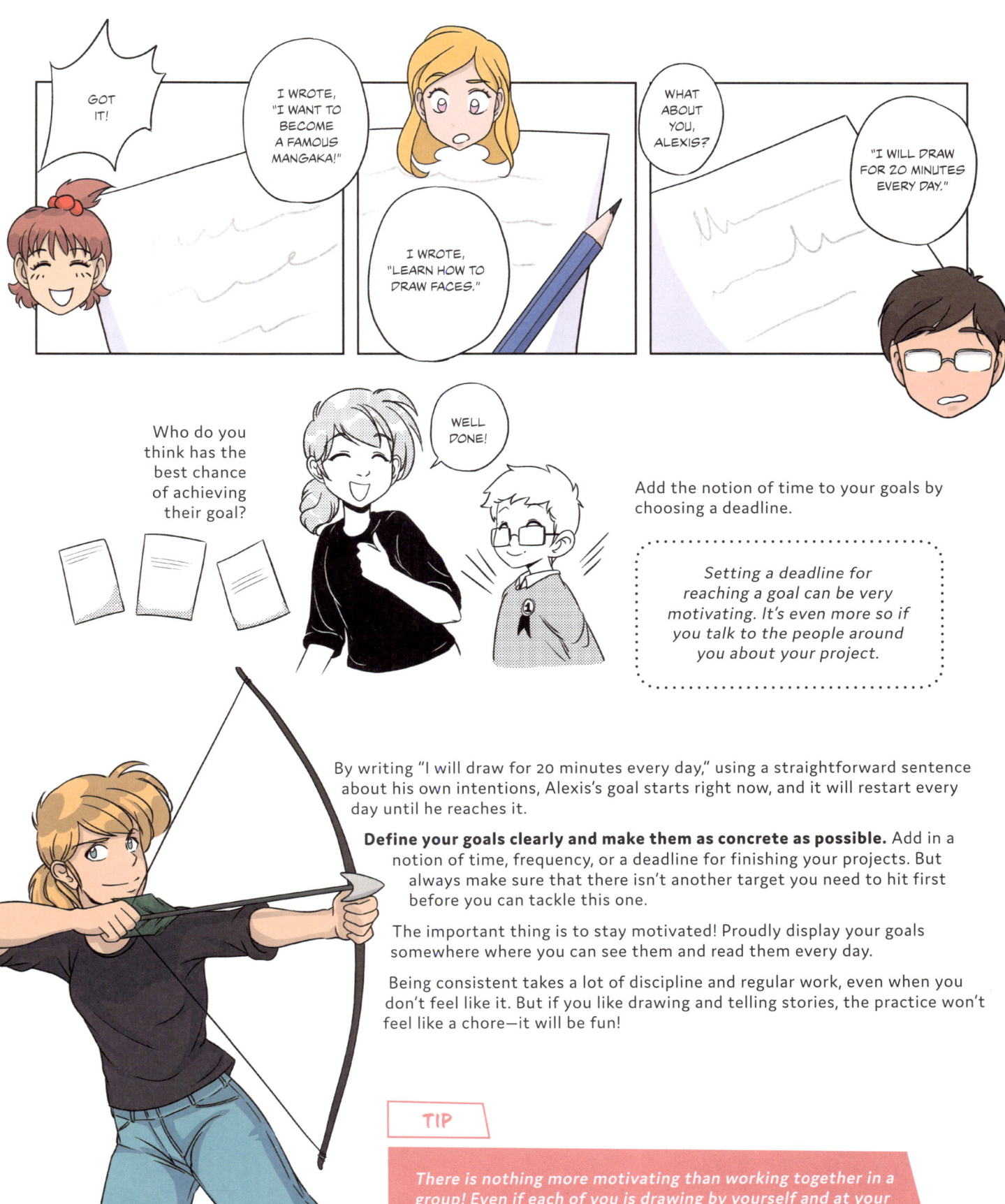

GOT IT!

I WROTE, "I WANT TO BECOME A FAMOUS MANGAKA!"

I WROTE, "LEARN HOW TO DRAW FACES."

WHAT ABOUT YOU, ALEXIS?

"I WILL DRAW FOR 20 MINUTES EVERY DAY."

Who do you think has the best chance of achieving their goal?

WELL DONE!

Add the notion of time to your goals by choosing a deadline.

Setting a deadline for reaching a goal can be very motivating. It's even more so if you talk to the people around you about your project.

By writing "I will draw for 20 minutes every day," using a straightforward sentence about his own intentions, Alexis's goal starts right now, and it will restart every day until he reaches it.

Define your goals clearly and make them as concrete as possible. Add in a notion of time, frequency, or a deadline for finishing your projects. But always make sure that there isn't another target you need to hit first before you can tackle this one.

The important thing is to stay motivated! Proudly display your goals somewhere where you can see them and read them every day.

Being consistent takes a lot of discipline and regular work, even when you don't feel like it. But if you like drawing and telling stories, the practice won't feel like a chore—it will be fun!

TIP

There is nothing more motivating than working together in a group! Even if each of you is drawing by yourself and at your own pace, the journey is more fun if we take it together.

13

HOW DO YOU LEARN TO DRAW?

In this section, we will take a look at the **good habits** we need to adopt when we start drawing manga and at how we can **learn to draw** more generally.

Stylization is the basis of manga drawing: We take inspiration from reality, but then we represent it in a simplified way.

A few lines are enough to draw a face, for instance. But this simplification is what can make the "manga" style of drawing difficult because a good cartoonist or manga artist needs to know which lines to draw, and in which places, in order to making the drawing clear.

So, anyone can learn to draw in manga style, as long as you know and follow these principles:

- Observe the real world.
- Understand what you're drawing.
- Simplify the shapes.
- Create new codes based on the ones that are already established.

Everything you are going to draw will be inspired by something you have already seen. Thus, **learning to observe** is essential for becoming a good illustrator and cartoonist.

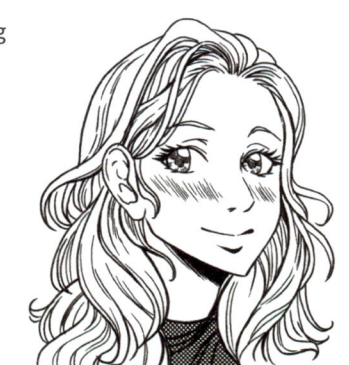
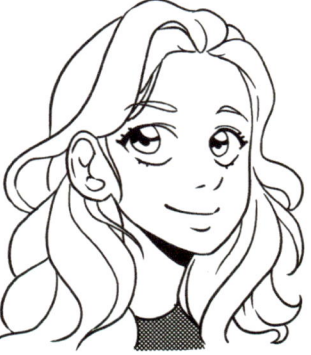

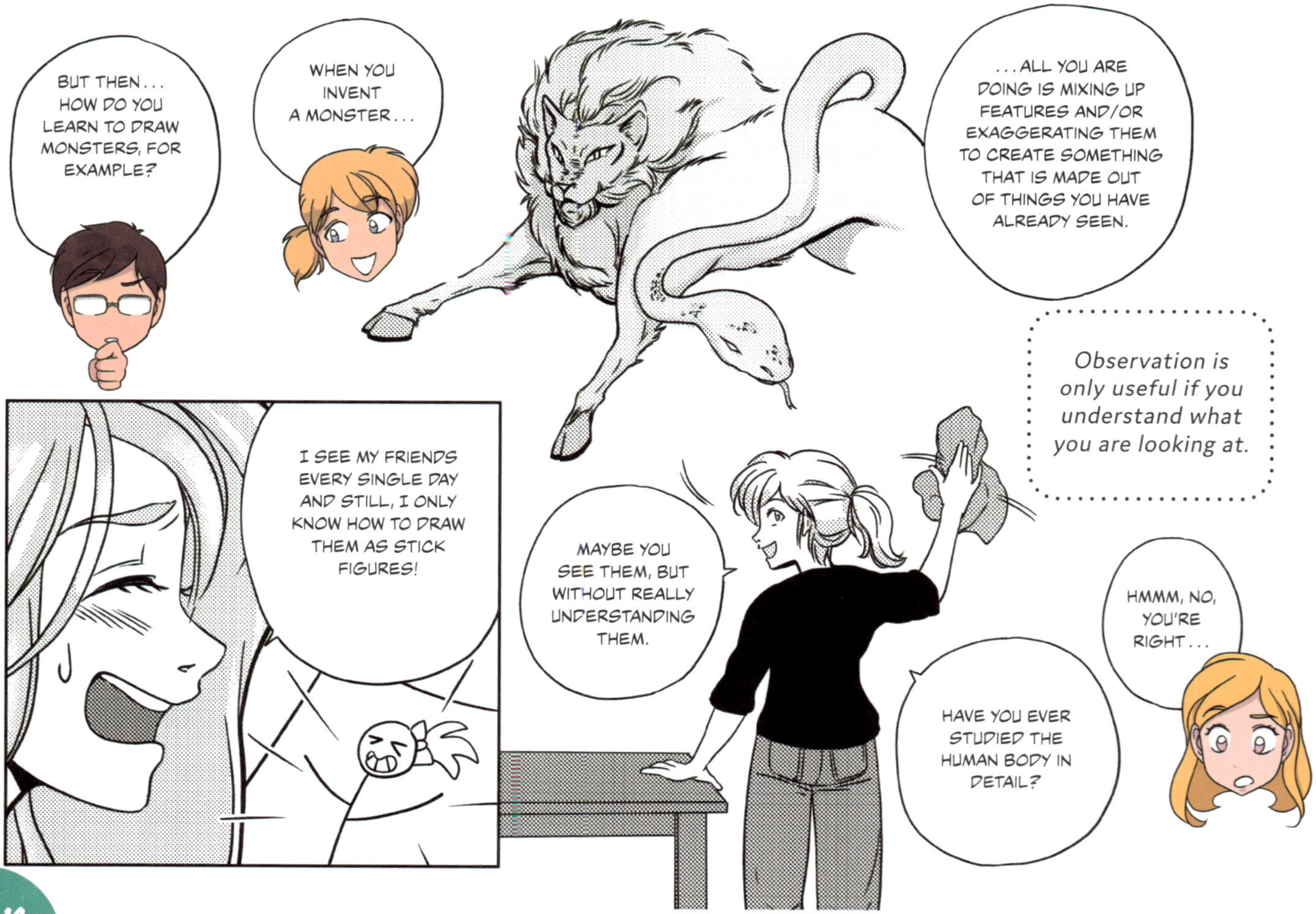

BUT THEN... HOW DO YOU LEARN TO DRAW MONSTERS, FOR EXAMPLE?

WHEN YOU INVENT A MONSTER...

...ALL YOU ARE DOING IS MIXING UP FEATURES AND/OR EXAGGERATING THEM TO CREATE SOMETHING THAT IS MADE OUT OF THINGS YOU HAVE ALREADY SEEN.

Observation is only useful if you understand what you are looking at.

I SEE MY FRIENDS EVERY SINGLE DAY AND STILL, I ONLY KNOW HOW TO DRAW THEM AS STICK FIGURES!

MAYBE YOU SEE THEM, BUT WITHOUT REALLY UNDERSTANDING THEM.

HAVE YOU EVER STUDIED THE HUMAN BODY IN DETAIL?

HMMM, NO, YOU'RE RIGHT...

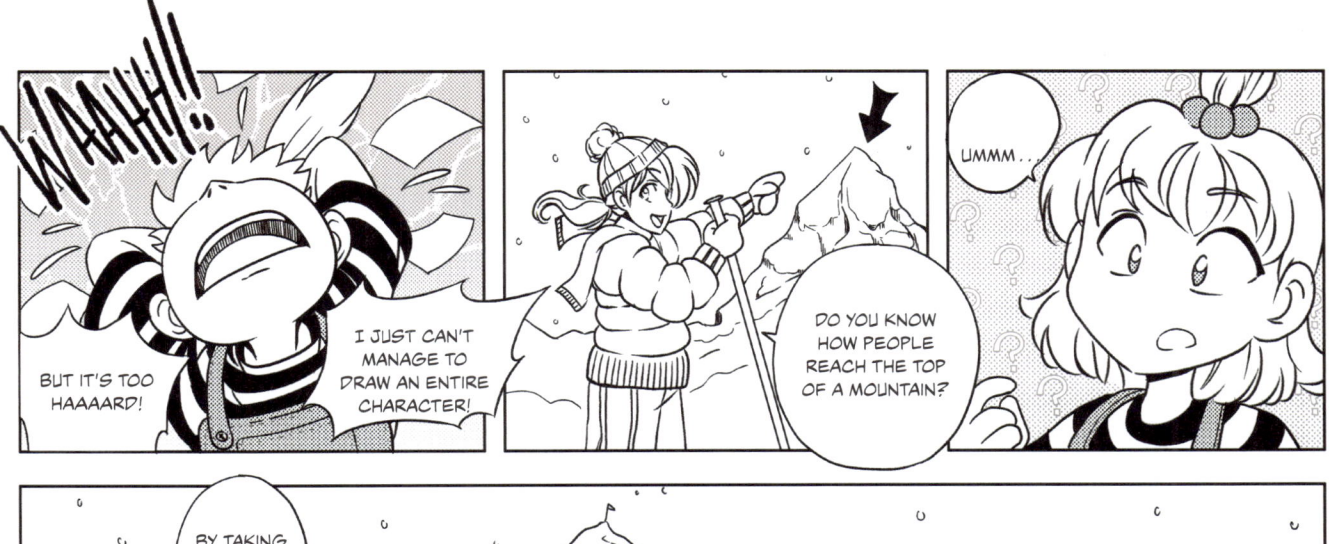

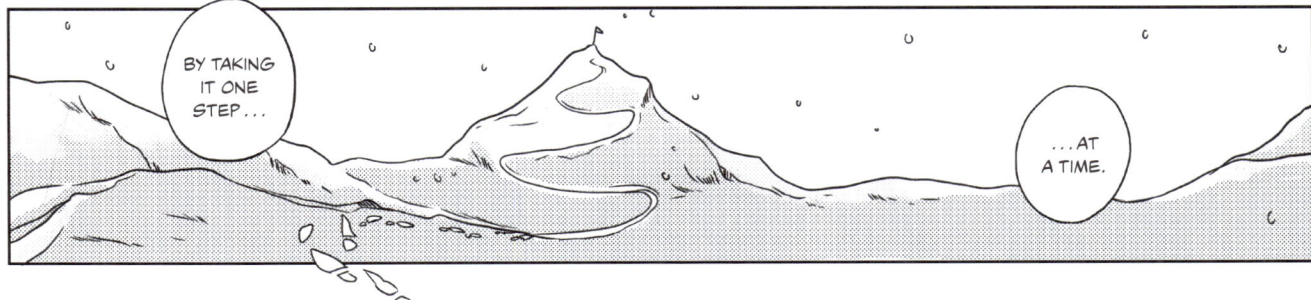

If something seems too hard for you to draw or represent, simplify it.

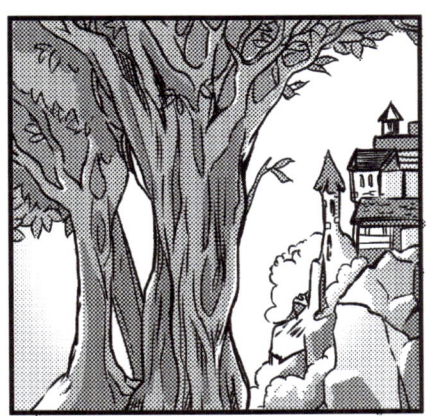 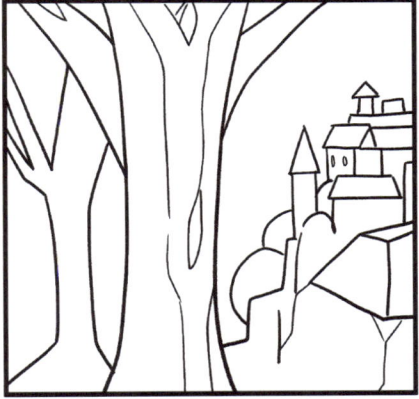 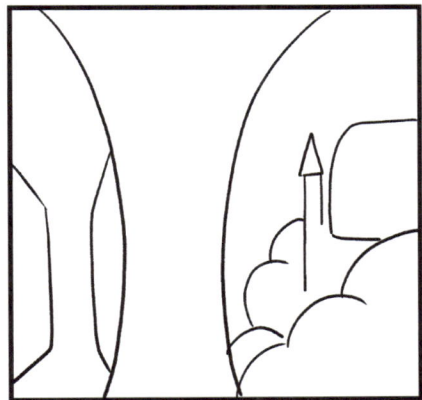

Start with geometric shapes that are easy to produce to get a sense of how much room the various elements of your drawing will take up.

These basic shapes are called **construction lines**. It is important not to press too hard on your pencil at this stage.

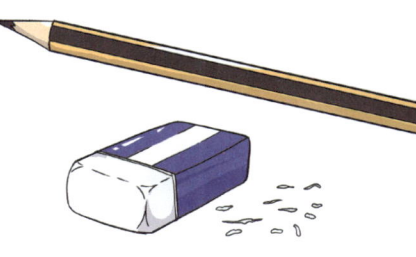

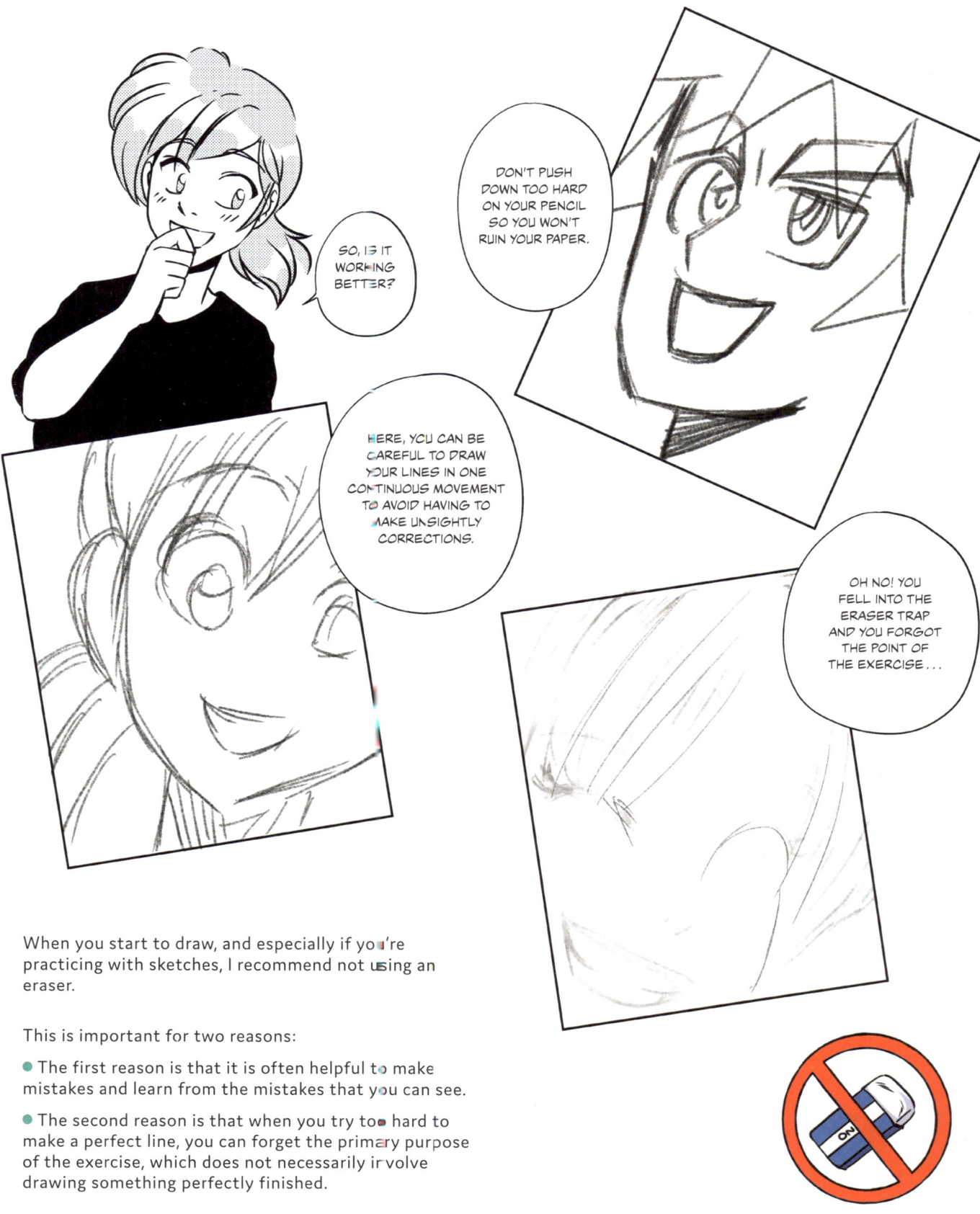

When you start to draw, and especially if you're practicing with sketches, I recommend not using an eraser.

This is important for two reasons:

● The first reason is that it is often helpful to make mistakes and learn from the mistakes that you can see.

● The second reason is that when you try too hard to make a perfect line, you can forget the primary purpose of the exercise, which does not necessarily involve drawing something perfectly finished.

THE MATERIALS OF THE MANGA ARTIST

Choosing the materials for your manga drawing can be a real headache when you're getting started. Let me share my experience with you to help you collect the right materials.

THE MATERIALS DO NOT MAKE THE ARTIST

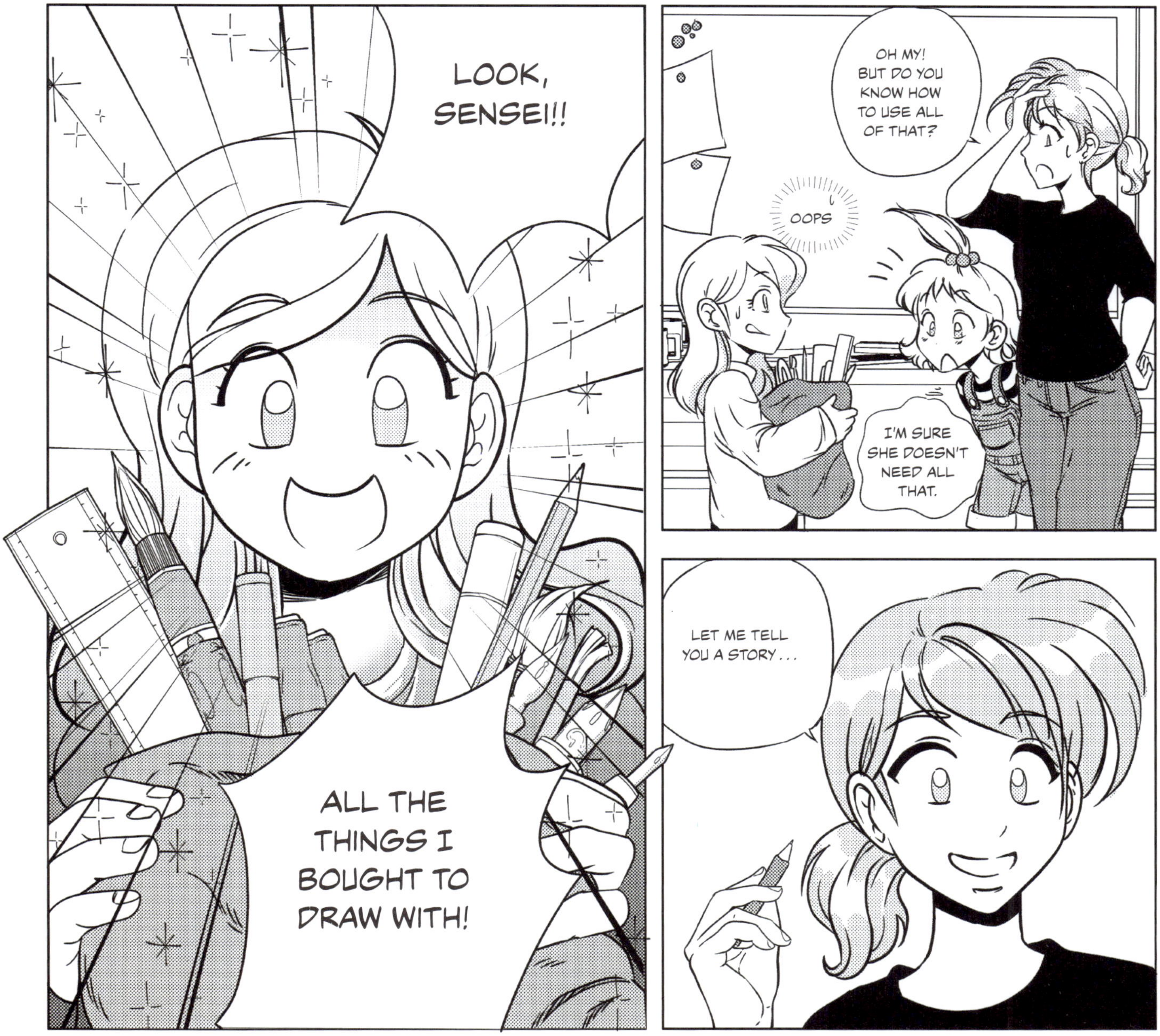

LOOK, SENSEI!!

ALL THE THINGS I BOUGHT TO DRAW WITH!

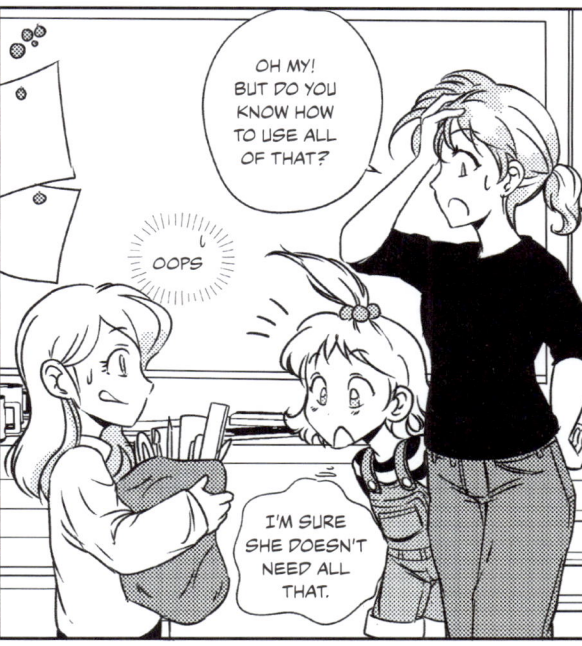

OH MY! BUT DO YOU KNOW HOW TO USE ALL OF THAT?

OOPS

I'M SURE SHE DOESN'T NEED ALL THAT.

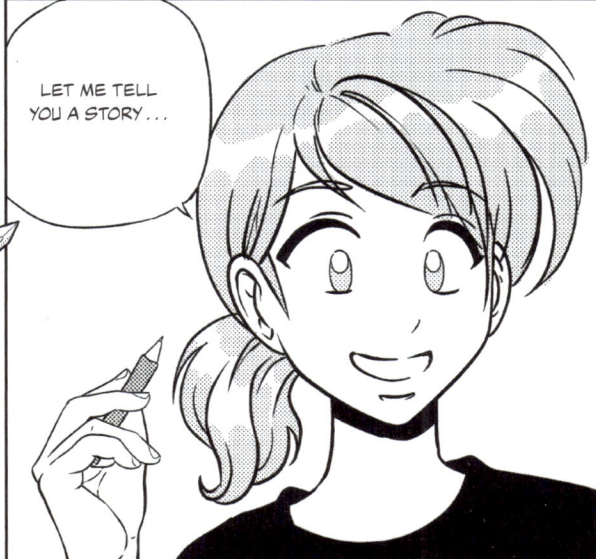

LET ME TELL YOU A STORY...

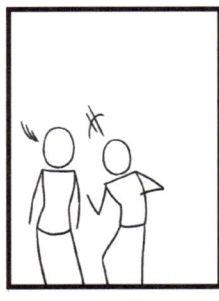 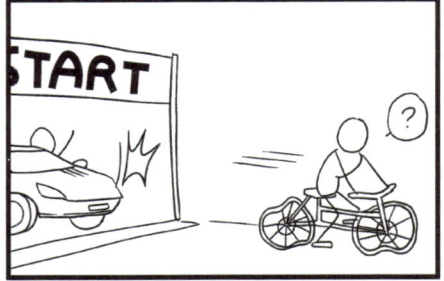 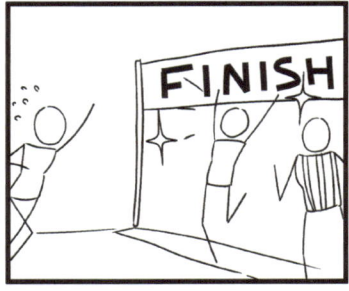

▲ Two friends challenge each other to a race and ask a third friend to be the judge.

▲ Their friend loans them a race car and a shabby little bike that they randomly assign to each of them.

▲ At the starting line, the bike moves forward a little, but the car doesn't move at all. It's impossible to get it started without the keys...

▲ So the slowpoke gets out of the car and finishes the race on foot.

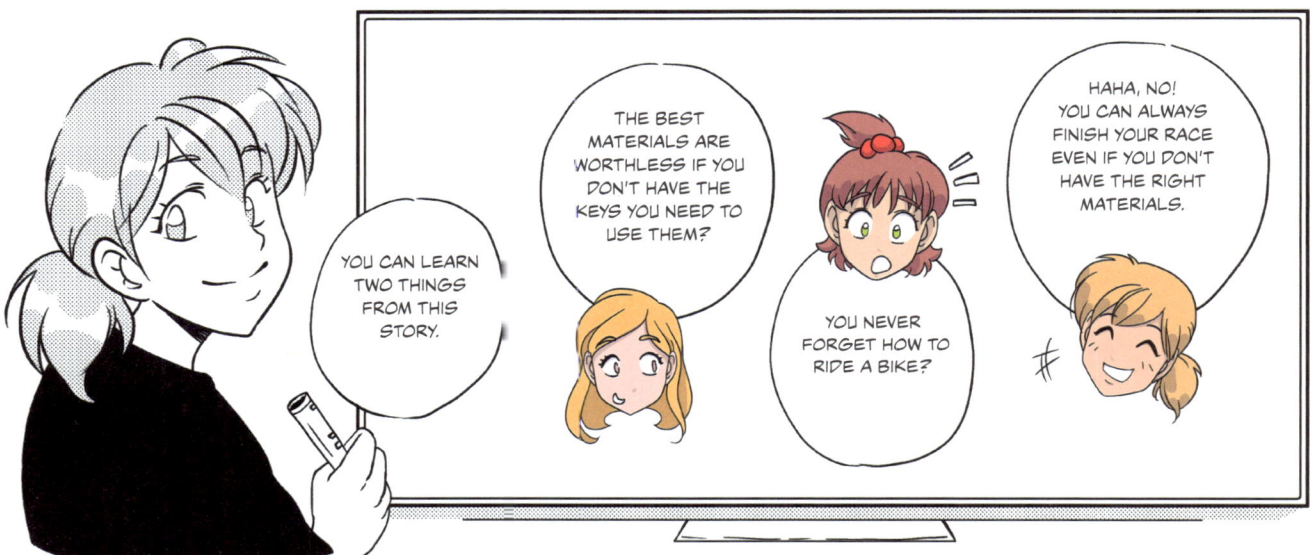

YOU CAN LEARN TWO THINGS FROM THIS STORY.

THE BEST MATERIALS ARE WORTHLESS IF YOU DON'T HAVE THE KEYS YOU NEED TO USE THEM?

YOU NEVER FORGET HOW TO RIDE A BIKE?

HAHA, NO! YOU CAN ALWAYS FINISH YOUR RACE EVEN IF YOU DON'T HAVE THE RIGHT MATERIALS.

The materials don't draw for you and they won't help you to draw "better," either. They are just tools that you choose and that you need to start on your adventure. Whether they are traditional or digital, they help you to get to a particular destination, but it is important to know how to use them in order to move forward effectively.

If you want to make a color illustration, for example, a black pen will not be enough. However, you can choose among several techniques (watercolor, colored pencils, alcohol markers), several palette sizes, and multiple ranges of products to add the color.

Don't forget that even the best materials, if they are used poorly, can produce a catastrophic final product. An excellent pen will not help you to write a high-quality storyline. And conversely, it is possible to create an extraordinary manga with a simple wooden pencil.

Start with a small selection of materials, and then you can add to your collection over time as you progress. Be curious and inventive!

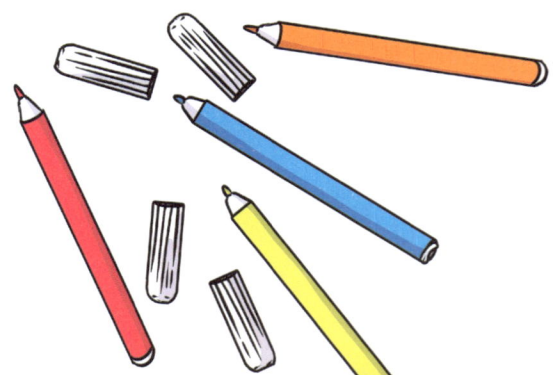

CHOOSING YOUR MANGA MATERIALS

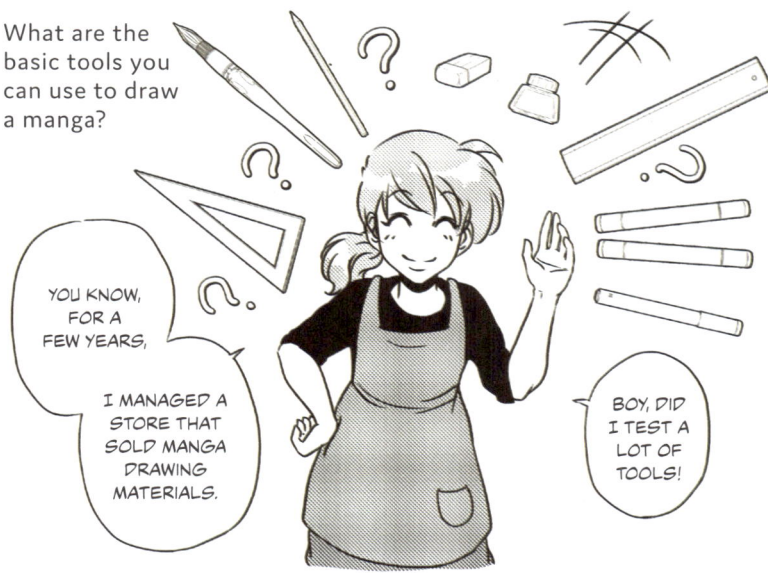

What are the basic tools you can use to draw a manga?

YOU KNOW, FOR A FEW YEARS,

I MANAGED A STORE THAT SOLD MANGA DRAWING MATERIALS.

BOY, DID I TEST A LOT OF TOOLS!

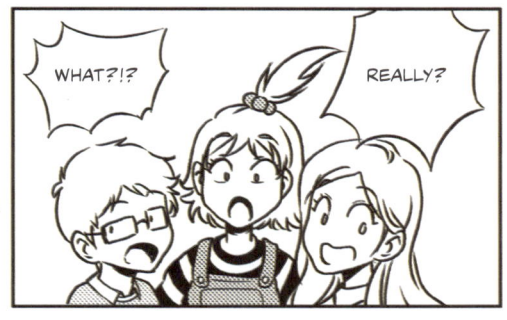

WHAT?!?

REALLY?

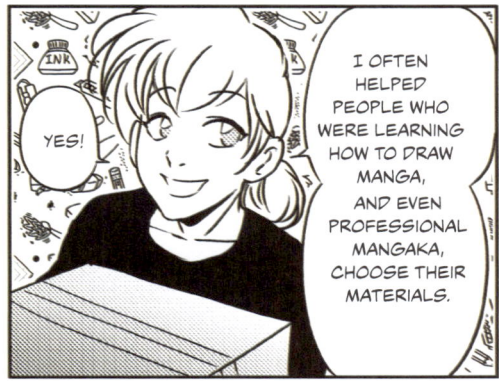

YES!

I OFTEN HELPED PEOPLE WHO WERE LEARNING HOW TO DRAW MANGA, AND EVEN PROFESSIONAL MANGAKA, CHOOSE THEIR MATERIALS.

Here are three tips to help you choose your manga artist materials:

1 DEFINE YOUR NEEDS

Start by clearly defining your project so that you can choose the appropriate materials: What are you going to draw? Sketches, boards, color illustrations? All of the above?

If you're not sure, start with the materials you need for sketching: a notebook or a few sheets of paper, a pencil, and an eraser, maybe even a black fineliner.

2 TRY OUT THE TECHNIQUES

If you are a beginner at manga drawing, you don't know yet what techniques you might want to use: traditional or digital? Black and white or color?

I've often noticed that inking with a drawing pen is a dividing line for students: either they love it or they hate it. This is why it is a good idea to try out different techniques before you start buying all the materials.

3 FIND THE RIGHT TOOL

As soon as you know where you are going and the technique you want to use to get there, all you need to do is to choose the most appropriate tool.

For instance, there are several different sizes of drawing pens, but you might only choose one. In the same way, you may prefer one brand that you like the best.

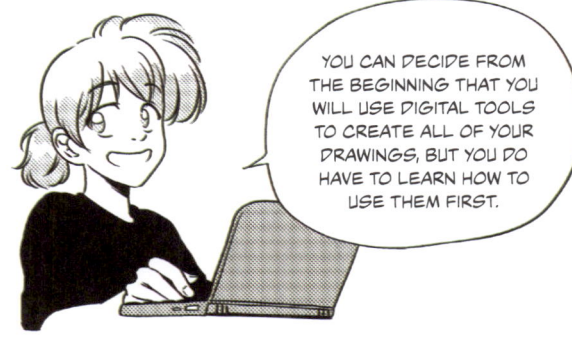

YOU CAN DECIDE FROM THE BEGINNING THAT YOU WILL USE DIGITAL TOOLS TO CREATE ALL OF YOUR DRAWINGS, BUT YOU DO HAVE TO LEARN HOW TO USE THEM FIRST.

There is no one right way to proceed. It's up to you to decide how you would like to draw every day, with what seems most comfortable to you! You can expand your collection of tools as you move along in the process of creating your manga.

In the following pages, I will be showing you a variety of the tools of a mangaka, a manga artist, and how they can be used. This will give you a good foundation to help you become acquainted with all of these materials.

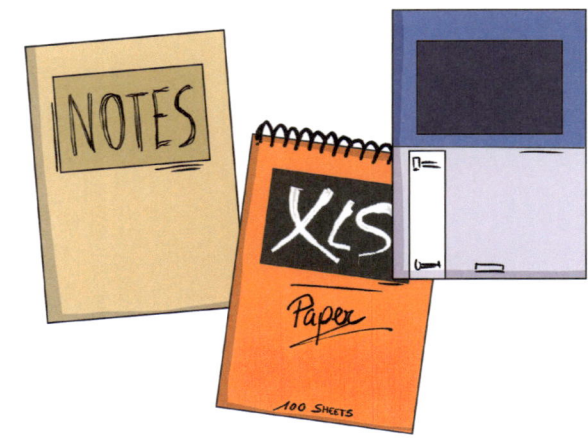

MEDIA AND PAPER

If you opt for traditional drawing, paper will be the pillar of your project because it will support all stages of the project, from the pencil sketch to the screens and the finishes. Choose the type of paper you will use based on your technique and the final result that you want to achieve.

For Sketches

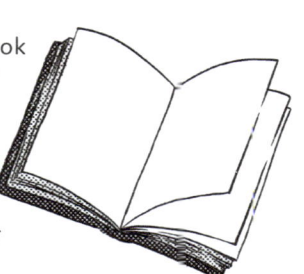

Choose a sketching notebook or inexpensive white paper sheets for your research, sketches, and studies.

If you are not going beyond the stage of the sketch, there is no need for specific expensive paper.

For Boards

Traditionally, manga boards are drawn on smooth, thick paper with fine blue reference markings, which allow you to effortlessly draw uniform panels from one page to the next. I will show you how to use these on page 126. These boards can be size A4 (21 × 29.7 cm) or B4 (25 × 35.3 cm). (A4 and B4 are international paper sizes. A4 is close to but not the same as American letter size. Manga artists use the international paper sizes.)

The choice of paper depends on the technique used. Pay attention to the weight, grain, and composition of the paper.

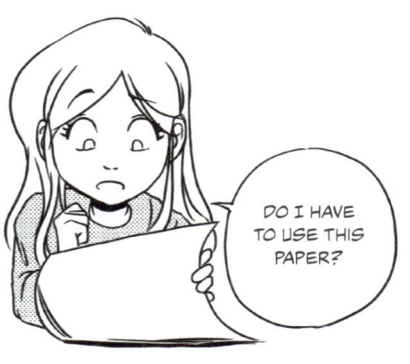

DO I HAVE TO USE THIS PAPER?

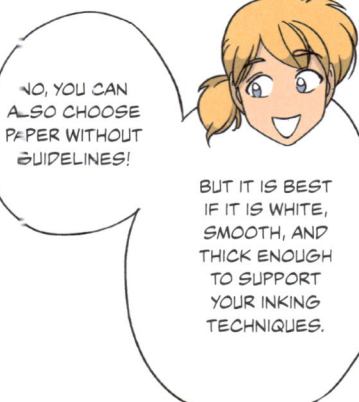

NO, YOU CAN ALSO CHOOSE PAPER WITHOUT GUIDELINES!

BUT IT IS BEST IF IT IS WHITE, SMOOTH, AND THICK ENOUGH TO SUPPORT YOUR INKING TECHNIQUES.

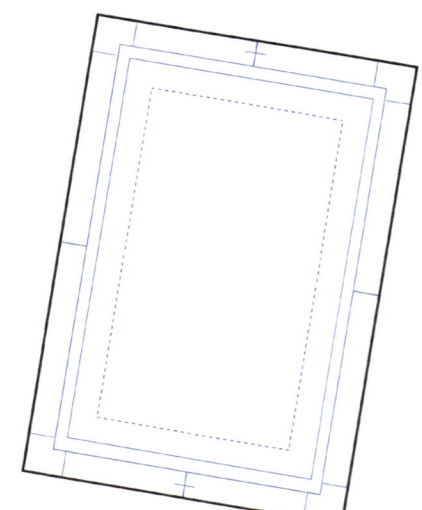

For Color Illustrations

"Layout" and Bristol" style papers, which are very smooth, are compatible with the ink of alcohol markers.

Grained, textured paper is perfect for colored pencils.

Finally, for all water-based painting techniques, I recommend a special watercolor paper with a fine, rough, or satin grain.

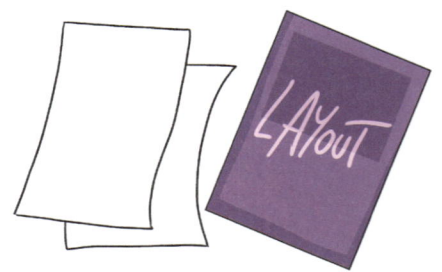

TRADITIONAL PENCILS AND MECHANICAL PENCILS

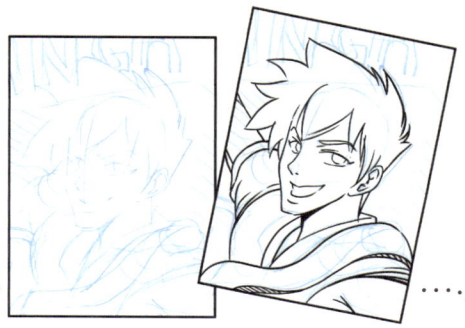

We draw sketches with a traditional (wooden) pencil or a mechanical pencil.

Mechanical pencils allow you to draw finer and more consistent lines than a traditional pencil, whose lead becomes dull over time. But traditional pencils are more versatile because their leads come in different sizes. There are a variety of hardnesses (2H, H, HB, B, 2B, etc.) and sizes of leads for mechanical pencils (0.1, 0.3, 0.5, 0.7, 0.9 mm).

Each of these has its own advantages and disadvantages. Make your choice based on how hard you press down on your paper or on what you are going to draw.

TIP

Softer leads (HB, B, or 2B) are more suitable for drawing characters because they do not require you to press too hard on your paper and they are easier to erase. For details and small decorations, it is better to use a mechanical pencil.

Some artists use blue pencils for their sketches. This allows them to save time because they don't have to erase the boards after inking, as the blue lines won't show up on the image when it is scanned in black and white.

The time it takes to erase the sketch lines from a drawing might seem negligible, but when you are talking about 200 boards, it can become worthwhile to switch to blue pencils.

ERASERS

Erasers come in several textures, shapes, and sizes. In manga drawing, we use different kinds based on the different situations.

A **kneaded** eraser, or **putty rubber**, is pliable and can be used to soften the sketch before inking.

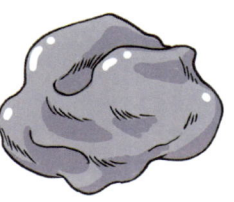

If you're in a pinch, you can use **hard erasers** and **novelty** or **decorative erasers**, but I recommend that you rely on soft, flexible erasers for your sketches. They don't leave marks and won't wear out the smooth surface of your boards.

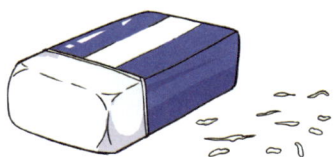

Soft vinyl erasers are used the most for corrections and for removing all pencil lines after inking. You can find them in different sizes and even in eraser holders to allow you to make more exact corrections.

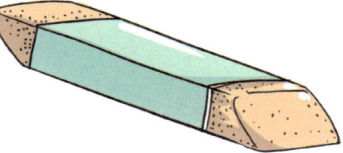

Abrasive erasers are useful for blending and for creating light effects on screens.

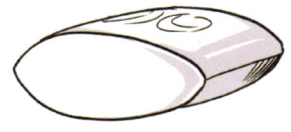

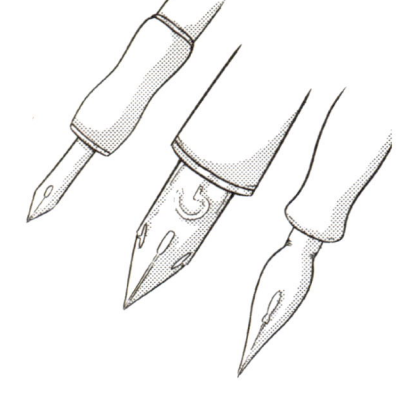

PEN NIBS AND PEN HOLDERS

Drawing Pens allow you to draw lines in varying thicknesses depending on how hard you press down on the page. We will come back to the importance of these differences in the section on inking techniques (page 148).

KABURA

The **Kabura pen**, with its shell shape, has the largest reservoir. It lets you draw even, regular lines. It is generally used for drawing characters or for sketches.

G PEN

The **G Pen** is the most used in manga drawing. It allows a greater variation in the thickness of your lines. You can use it to draw characters.

MARU

The **Maru pen** is tubular. it allows you to draw finer lines, which is perfect for drawing backgrounds, details, or hatching.

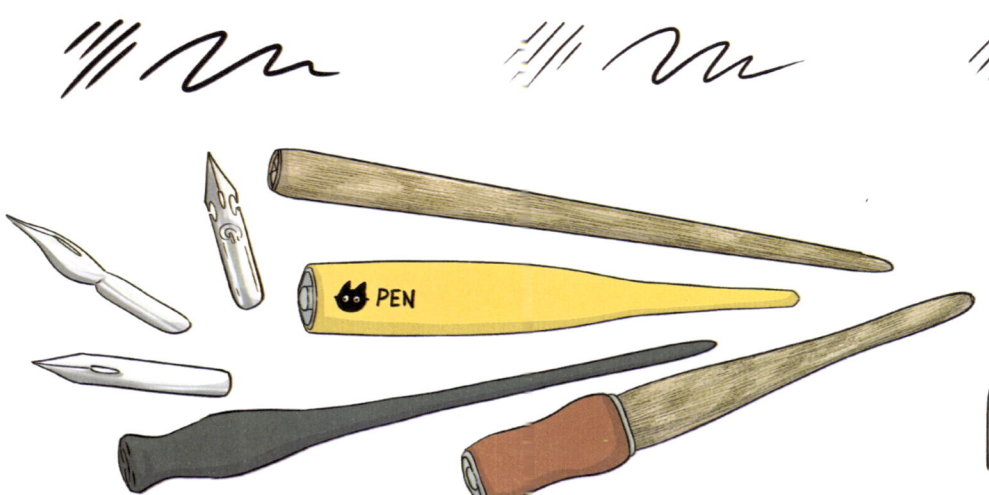

These pen nibs are held in **pen holders**, which are available in a variety of shapes and sizes.

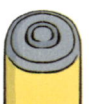
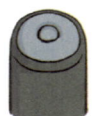

DRAWING INKS AND INDIA INK

When you want to draw with a drawing pen, there are several black inks you can choose from.

India Ink produces an opaque black finish. Its water-based composition means that it requires a fairly long drying time, and it can damage the pen nibs over the long term.

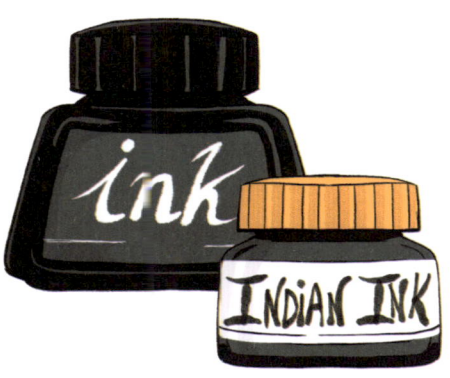

There are also special waterproof drawing inks for comics and manga. These matte black inks work well with techniques for coloring. Thus, you can use the same ink for your black-and-white boards and your color illustrations.

Choose your ink based on the types of projects you want to do. Do you need an ink that is water-soluble? Does it need to be an intense black?

WHITE CORRECTION FLUID AND WHITE INK

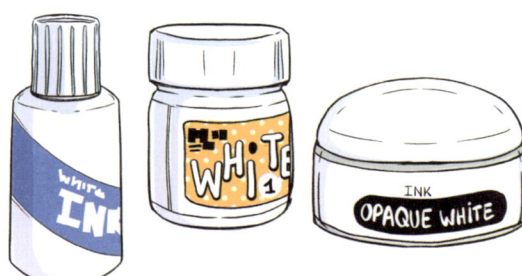

White correction fluid (or **opaque** white) has several uses in drawing. It can be used for correcting small inking mistakes, drawing patterns, or adding lighting effects to your boards.

Finding the right **white ink** can be a real headache because the white has to be opaque enough to cover up the black lines while also being fluid enough to be applied with a pen or a brush.

If you can't find white ink that can achieve these effects, you can always get inventive and use white correction fluid or even acrylic paint.

FINELINER PENS AND BRUSH PENS

Fineliner pens are felt pens with tubular tips, available in several different sizes and colors. In manga, people generally use black-ink fineliners.

The lines that these pens produce are good for drawing the **outlines of panels**, speed lines, decorations using rulers, **lettering**, and **sound effects**. Their points, which range in diameter from 0.3 mm to 2 mm, can also be used to draw characters and backgrounds.

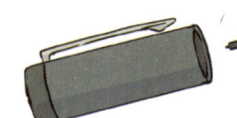

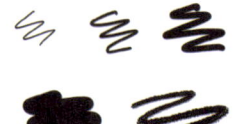

It is possible to create all of your inking lines using fineliners, but it takes a certain amount of practice to be able to give the illusion of three-dimensionality using the different line thicknesses.

I recommend you use permanent fineliners when you are going to be coloring with alcohol markers, watercolors, or colored inks.

A **fude pen**, or **brush pen**, is useful for painting **flat** areas of black. The ones with hairs are easier to use. They look like reservoir paintbrushes with black ink cartridges.

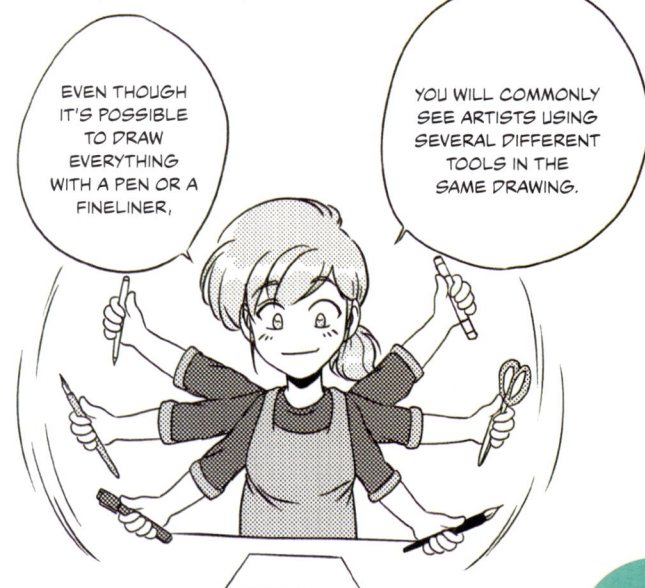

EVEN THOUGH IT'S POSSIBLE TO DRAW EVERYTHING WITH A PEN OR A FINELINER,

YOU WILL COMMONLY SEE ARTISTS USING SEVERAL DIFFERENT TOOLS IN THE SAME DRAWING.

DRAWING TOOLS

Rulers, triangles, French curves, and geometrical templates are tools that allow the manga artist to draw even lines.

I recommend that you draw the lines of your sketch freehand, but when you start to draw your final boards, you can use drawing tools to obtain a cleaner and more precise drawing.

There are different kinds of rulers that meet different needs in manga drawing:

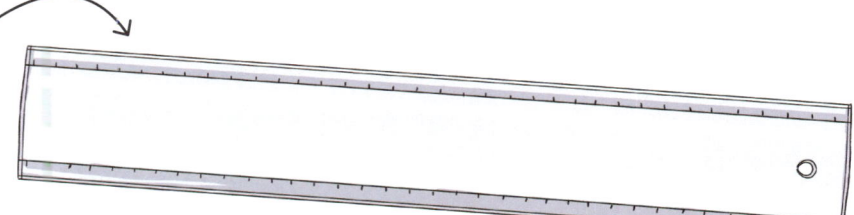

Transparent, squared rulers allow you to more easily draw scenery in perspective.

Beveled rulers are useful for drawing the outlines of panels, objects, and decorative elements, without running the risk of smearing the ink on the page. Choose a ruler to work with the size of your boards: 30 or 40 cm long for A4 sheets or 40 or 50 cm for B4 sheets.

Metal rulers or reglets are preferred for guiding a paper cutter on straight cuts, for example, because steel will not erode, unlike plastic.

If you decide to create your boards on blank paper, **triangles** are essential to allow you to draw straight squares. They come in different angles: 90° and either 30/60° or 45/45°.

Flexible rulers are pliable and allow you to draw all sorts of curves, just like French curves, which are more reliable because they will not lose their shape. French curves are usually transparent and have a beveled edge.

Geometric templates are useful for effortlessly drawing geometric shapes like circles or ovals.

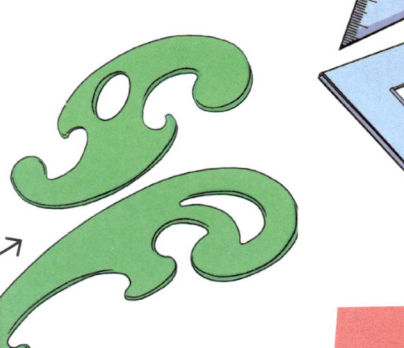

TIP

Draw your speech bubbles freehand so that you can perfectly fit the size of the bubble to the text and the shape of the panel. Your outlines will be livelier and more dynamic than if you drew them using a circle template, for example.

THE LIGHT TABLE

A light table is a surface that is illuminated from behind, which we can use to make our drawing paper transparent. This serves multiple purposes.

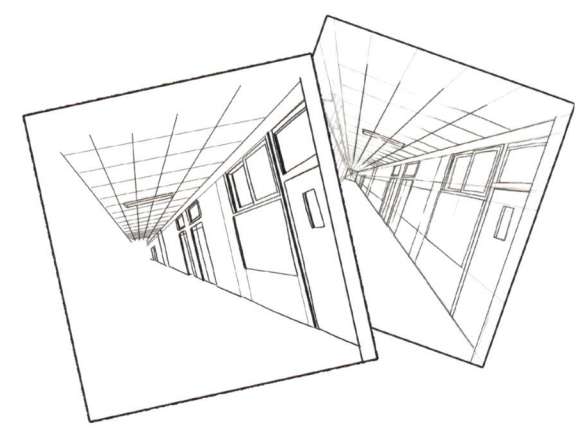

Some artists draw their rough drafts on inexpensive paper and then do their inking on high-quality paper by tracing the main lines, using a light table to make the top sheet transparent. This allows them to keep their sketch intact while also transferring their drawing to a higher-quality paper.

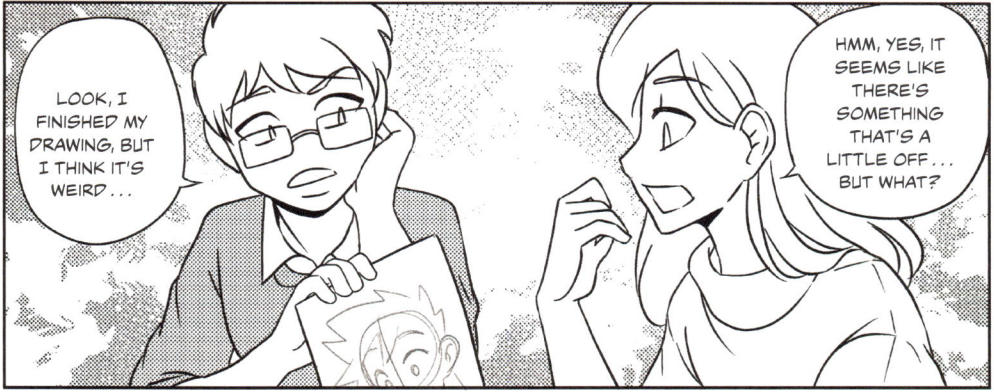

LOOK, I FINISHED MY DRAWING, BUT I THINK IT'S WEIRD...

HMM, YES, IT SEEMS LIKE THERE'S SOMETHING THAT'S A LITTLE OFF... BUT WHAT?

2

The light table is a great tool for beginners because it allows them to correct themselves.

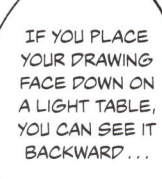

IF YOU PLACE YOUR DRAWING FACE DOWN ON A LIGHT TABLE, YOU CAN SEE IT BACKWARD...

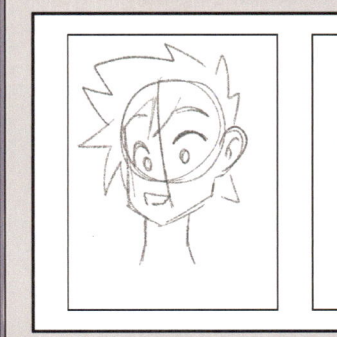

....AND YOU WILL BE ABLE TO SPOT ERRORS IN PROPORTION RIGHT AWAY

You can also use the tracing method to complete a board with a sketch or background that you drew on a separate piece of paper.

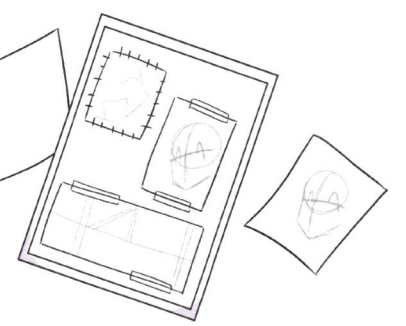

The light table has many advantages, but it is not essential. You can also look at your drawing in a mirror or taped to a windowpane in order to see it backward.

SCREENS AND ACCESSORIES

Screens, or screen tones, are transparent adhesive sheets that are printed with patterns or rows of dots. This tool makes it possible to represent color textures, shadows, and patterns in manga.

You can find screens with all kinds of patterns: hatching, shading, speed lines, textures, and even complete backgrounds. The most common ones are rows of dots.

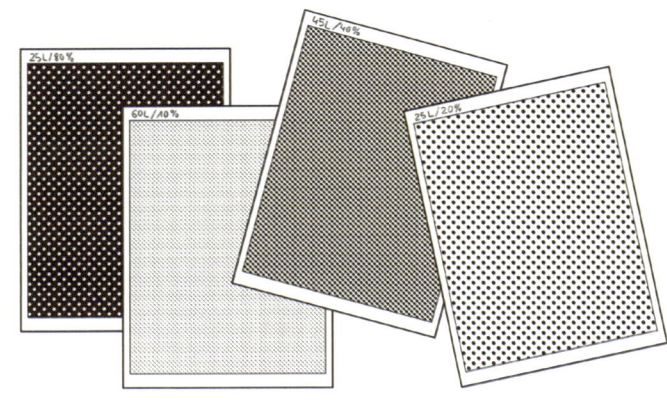

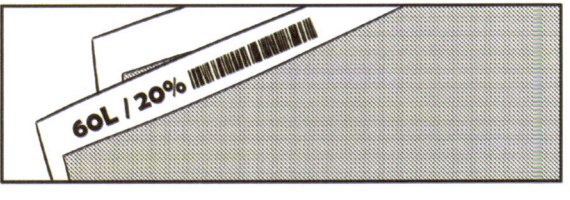

60L is the **screen ruling**. This corresponds to the number of rows of dots per inch (2.54 cm).

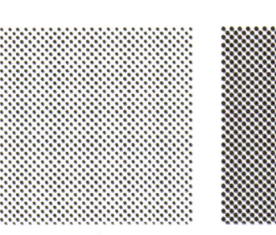

▲ 30L / 20 %   ▲ 30L / 40 %   ▲ 30L / 60 %

20% refers to the **value of the "gray"** and determines the size of the dots.

▲ 30L / 20 %   ▲ 45L / 20 %   ▲ 60L / 20 %

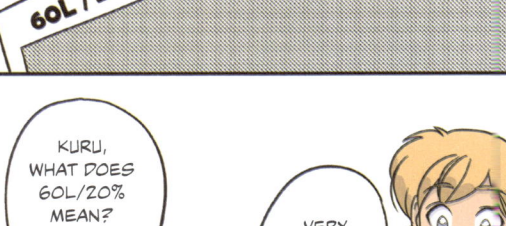
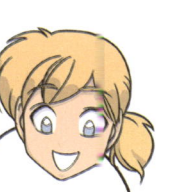

> KURU, WHAT DOES 60L/20% MEAN?

> VERY GOOD QUESTION!

> THAT SHOWS THE CHARACTERISTICS OF YOUR SCREEN TONE SHEET.

> OH, RIIIIGHT! THAT'S HOW YOU MAKE GRAY IN MANGA!

> YES, INDEED. BUT LOOK CLOSELY!

> IT SEEMS LIKE WE'RE SEEING GRAY, BUT IT'S ACTUALLY TINY BLACK DOTS.

The lower the screen ruling, the farther apart the dots will be spaced.

The higher the percentage, the thicker the dots will be.

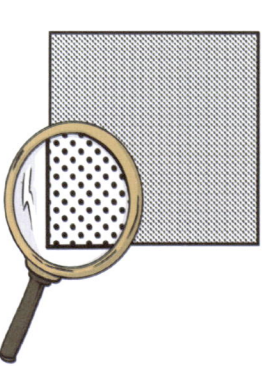

MOIRÉ EFFECT

Screen sheets are transparent. Thus, you can overlay them to enrich your panels, but watch out for the **moiré effect**!

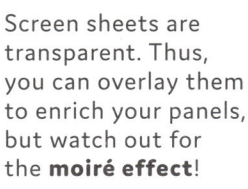
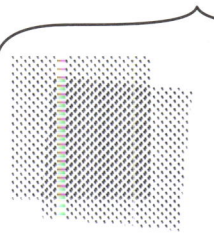
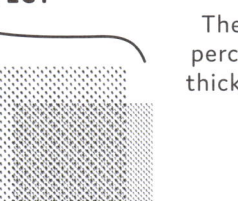

Adding traditional screens requires the use of a box cutter or a scalpel, a spatula, and a cutting mat to protect your worktable. Go to page 170 for more about how to use screens.

Box Cutters and Scalpels

We use scalpels (or precision knives) to cut up the screen sheets following the outlines of the subject, in order to fill it in or keep it open.

The blades of the box cutter are usually used to scratch the surface of the screens and create lighting effects.

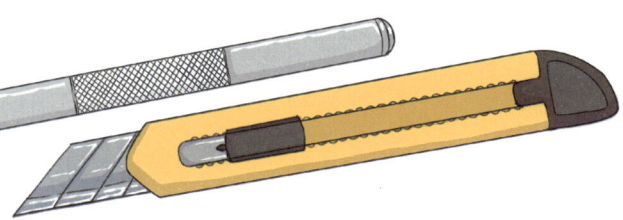

WATCH OUT
Be careful when handling sharp cutting tools!

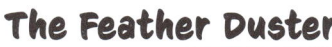

The Spatula

This spatula (specifically the Tone Hera tool) is used to attach the screen sheets onto the boards. It allows you to smooth away any air bubbles and it uses friction to activate the adhesive of the screen sheets.

The Feather Duster

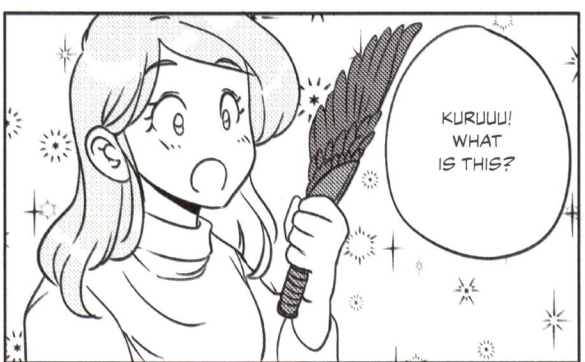

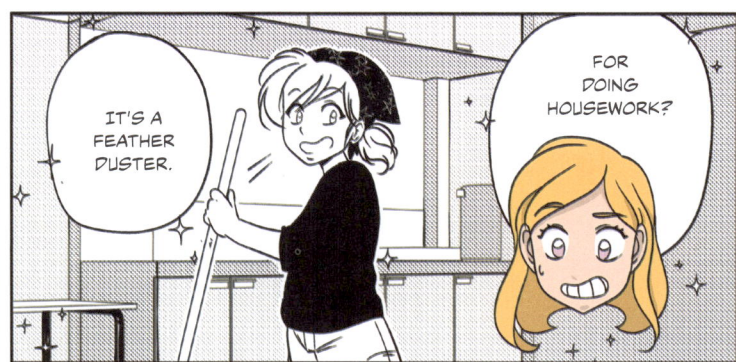

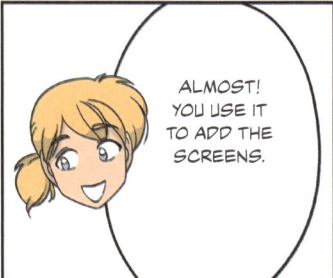

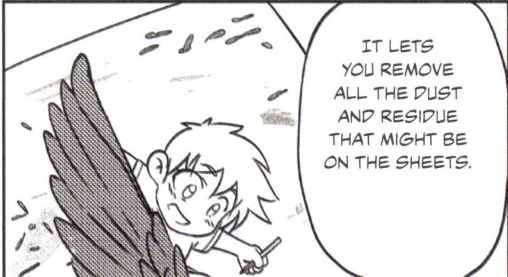

The feather duster can also be used to draw speed lines with one movement. All you have to do is dip the end of the feathers in a little bit of ink and then run them over the page in a quick, light movement.

Manga pages are mostly done in black and white.
You can find color on the covers of the books, sometimes on some
of the introductory pages, and in the attached illustrations.

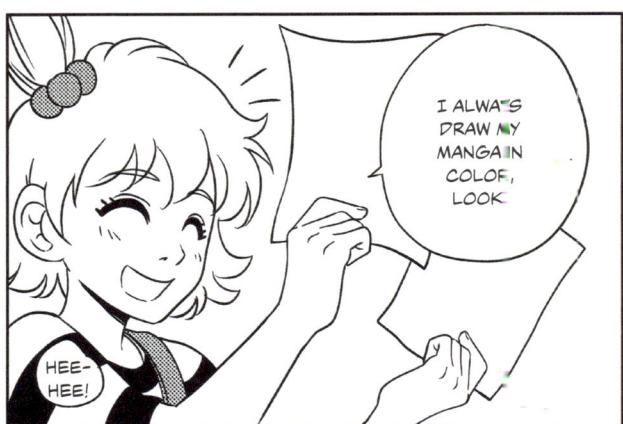
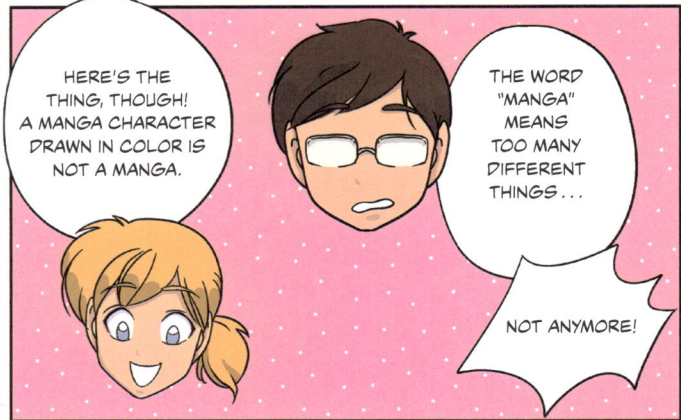

For your coloring, you can choose from a variety of traditional or digital techniques.
All of them will allow you to produce unique and different results.

ALCOHOL MARKERS

There are no rules about the techniques to use
for coloring your drawings, but people generally
associate manga cover art with alcohol markers.

What makes these markers interesting is
their alcohol-based ink. Its longer drying time
compared to classic felt markers allows the traces
of the marker lines on the page to disappear and
lets you shade and mix colors.

Alcohol-based inks are transparent. You can go
over an area several times with the same color to
create different shades, or overlay two colors on
top of each other to create a third color.

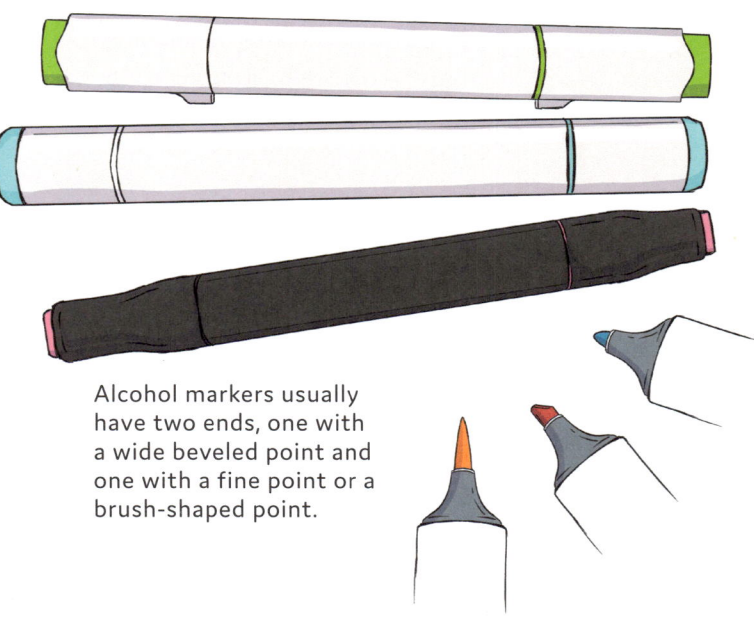

Alcohol markers usually
have two ends, one with
a wide beveled point and
one with a fine point or a
brush-shaped point.

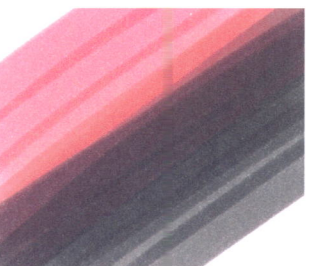

*The ink of these markers can bleed
through certain kinds of paper,
so choose your paper carefully.*

I recommend markers with a brush tip. This type
of tip allows you to make thick and thin strokes in
one movement, which is very useful for drawing
hair, for example.

THE GRAPHICS TABLET

I'm discussing digital tools last because if you are drawing on paper, it is usually toward the end of the process that you will use digital tools.

Even though many manga artists use alcohol markers, more and more of them are turning to digital tools to create their manga covers.

SO YOU DON'T USE IT FOR ANYTHING BUT COLOR?

It is definitely possible to create all of your boards and illustrations digitally with **specialized drawing software**.

HOW DO YOU DRAW ON A COMPUTER?

YOU DRAW USING A GRAPHICS TABLET.

Just like with vehicles, there are graphics tablets for all levels and every budget. You can find them in different formats, with or without a screen, and sometimes with shortcut keys . . .

Whatever model you use, though, you are drawing in a **detection area, using a stylus**. The pressure of the stylus and your movements are instantly transcribed onto the screen.

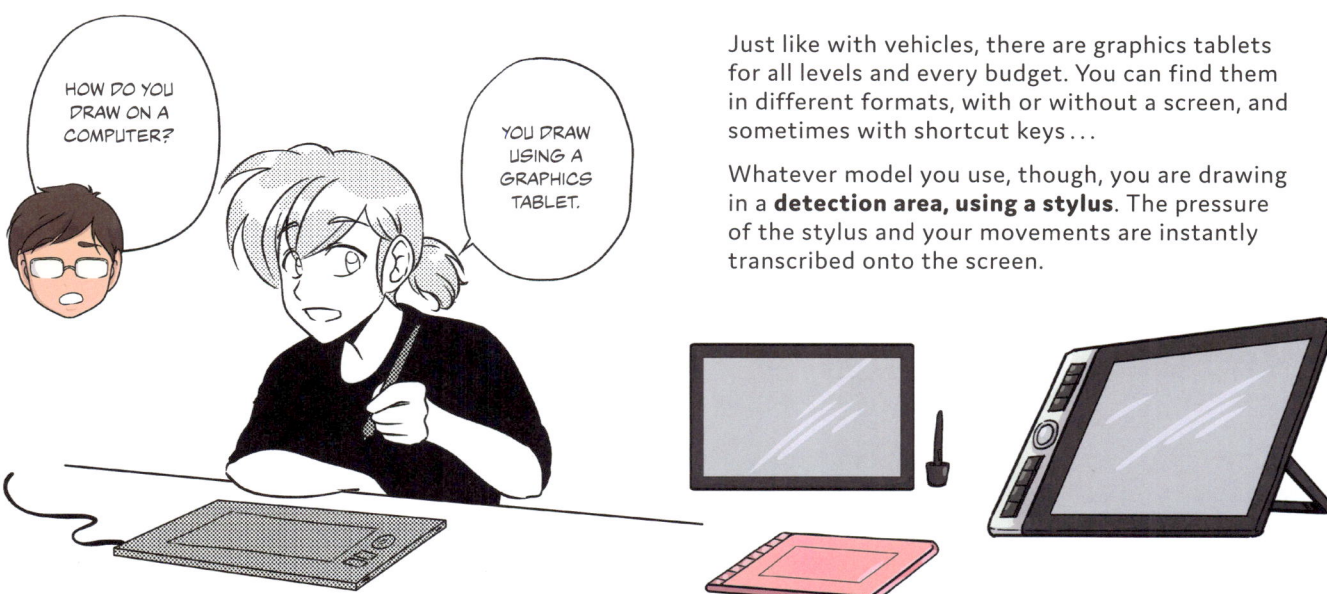

A graphics tablet is a little bit like a super-sophisticated computer mouse. You connect it to a computer, tablet, or smartphone where you have installed drawing software.

Here are some examples of graphics tablets:

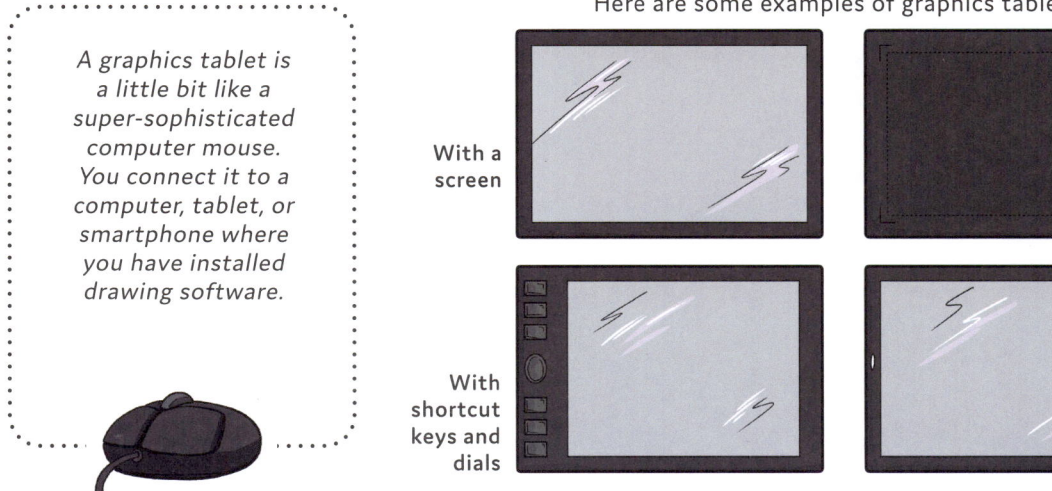

With a screen

Without a screen

With shortcut keys and dials

Independent tactile tablet

And now we have finished our overview of the tools of the manga artist! You are already pros on the equipment.

MAINTAINING YOUR DRAWING MATERIALS

Now that you have chosen your tools, get to know them.
Your materials have enemies: **the sun, humidity, variable temperatures, and settling**.
But to keep them in good condition, you just need to know how to clean them, put them away,
and how often to **maintain them**.

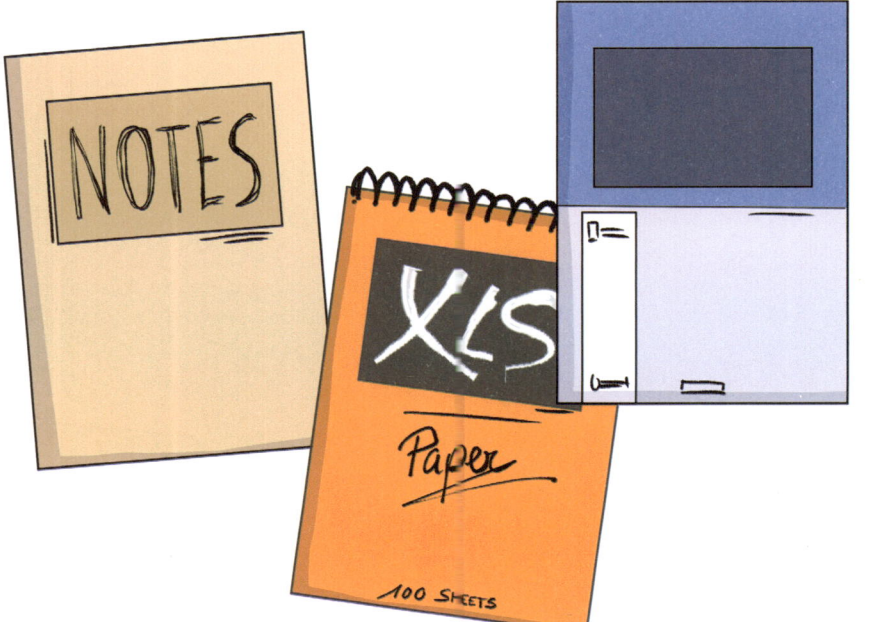

Paper is sensitive to humidity and sunshine. Store it in folders or binders and keep it away from exterior walls.

A dirty **eraser** can leave marks on the paper. Rub it on a piece of scrap paper until it is clean again.

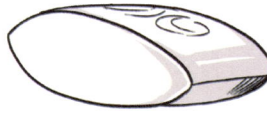

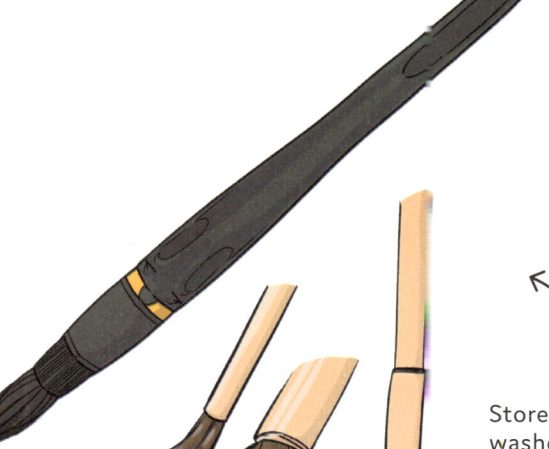

Store your **brushes** flat or with their heads down on a brush washer. If you keep them in a pencil jar, their bristles will be exposed to dust. And as for residual humidity, it can rust the metal ring (or ferrule) that holds the bristles in place.

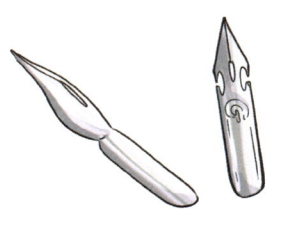

New **pen nibs** are protected by rustproofing, but they become very sensitive to humidity as soon as they are used. Keep your new nibs separate from your used ones.

Do not clean your nibs with water. Rub them with a paper towel and regularly remove ink residue when you use them.

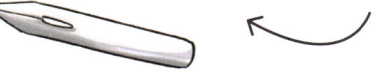

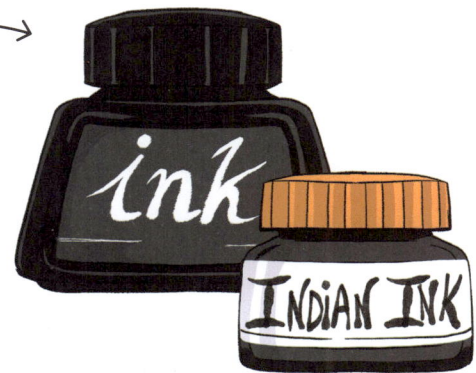

Close your **ink** pots tightly after use and keep them in a drawer. The ink can degrade over time, dry out, or even form lumps.

Is your India ink drying out or getting pasty? Add a little water to it with a dropper. Wipe the rims of the ink pots frequently.

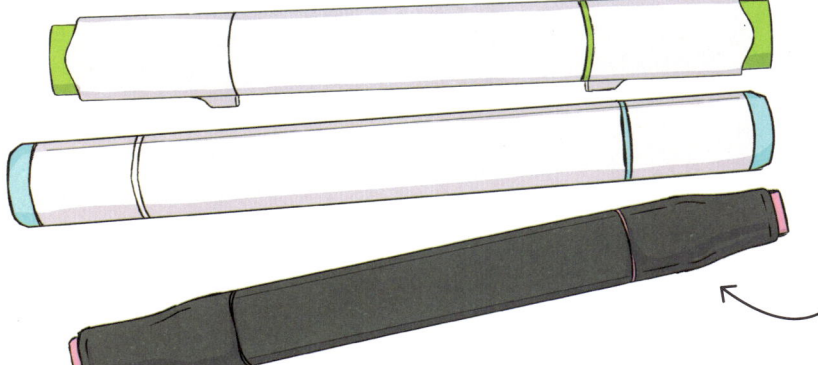

The ink in **alcohol markers** evaporates quickly. Make sure to close your markers after you use them and to store them lying flat.

Are their caps not allowing you to close them completely? Clean them with a paper towel and 70% to 90% alcohol. Wipe around the outside of the points, but without touching them so as not to absorb the ink.

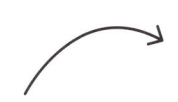

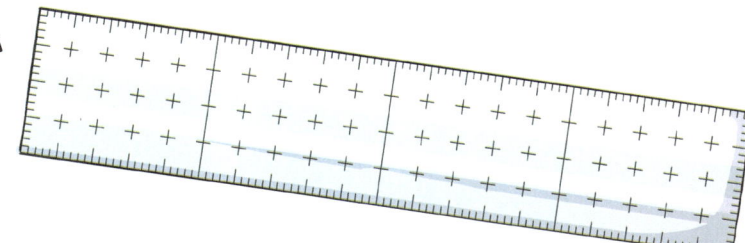

Don't forget to clean the edges of your **drawing tools** with a little piece of paper towel from time to time.

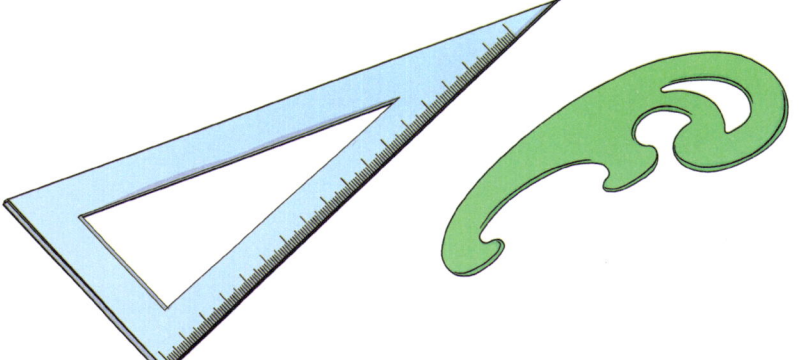

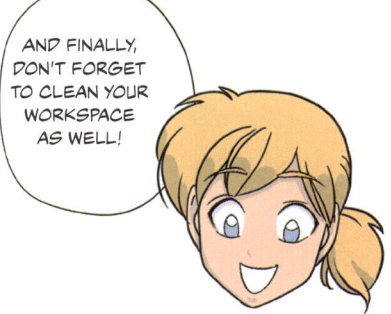

AND FINALLY, DON'T FORGET TO CLEAN YOUR WORKSPACE AS WELL!

REFERENCE IMAGES

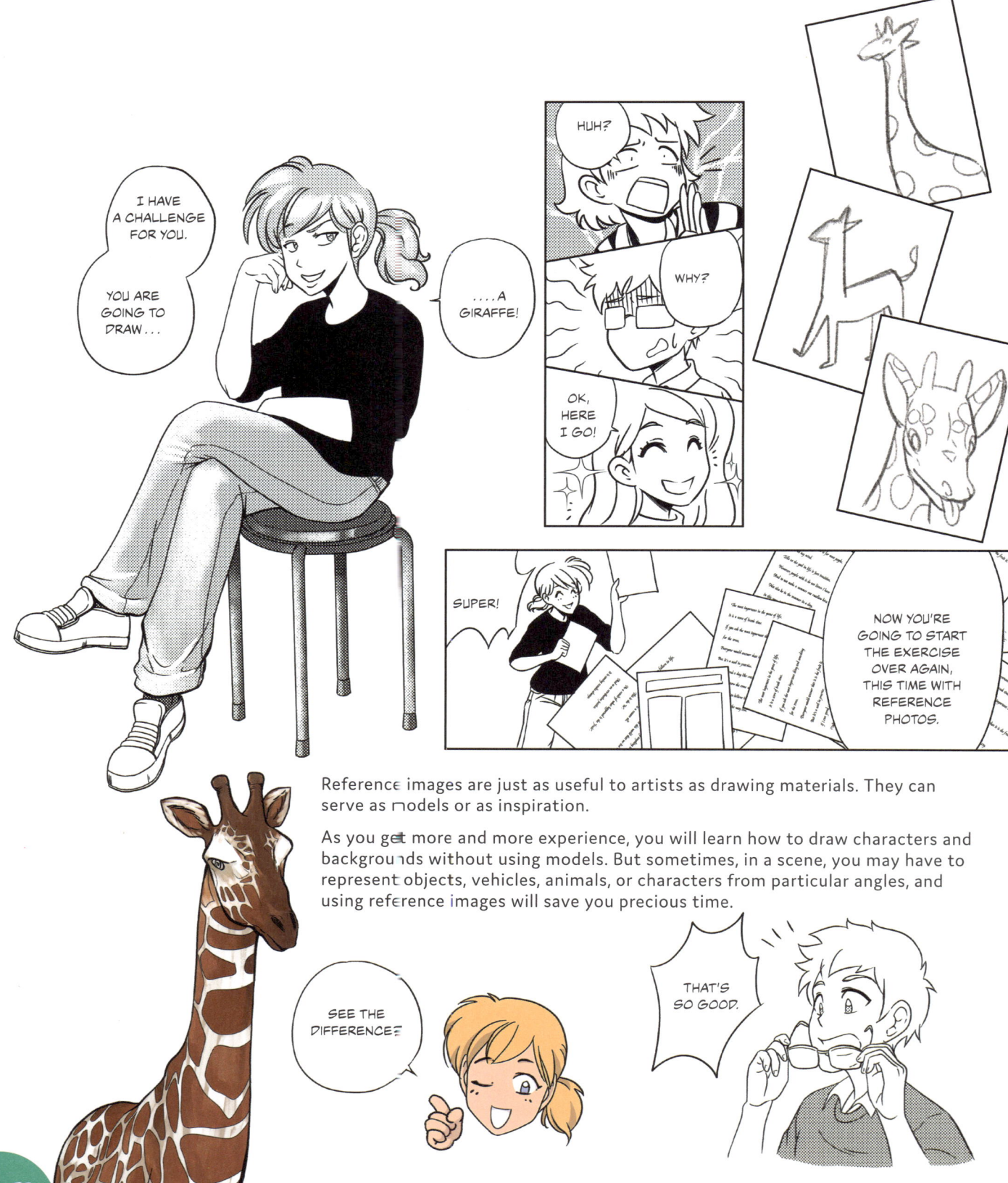

Reference images are just as useful to artists as drawing materials. They can serve as models or as inspiration.

As you get more and more experience, you will learn how to draw characters and backgrounds without using models. But sometimes, in a scene, you may have to represent objects, vehicles, animals, or characters from particular angles, and using reference images will save you precious time.

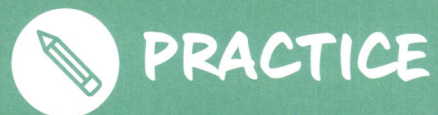 # PRACTICE

*The time has come to move on to practice!
I encourage you to practice using the exercises shown here, starting now and throughout your adventures as a manga artist.*

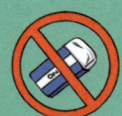 *Try not to use your eraser for now.*

Drawing from Observation

This is a simple exercise, but it's important when you start out. It's about observing a real subject and then transcribing it onto paper. If you prefer to use reference images, then you can choose photos to use.

At first, your drawing will not necessarily be in the "manga" style. You are going to draw what you see using the greatest amount of detail possible—for instance, by adding in shadows and light. When you've gotten more comfortable, you will be able to stylize what you see and draw it in just a few lines.

If you are having a hard time finding inspiration, here are a few ideas for subjects to draw:

- people (portraits, silhouettes);
- settings or scenery (interiors, exteriors);
- objects or pieces of furniture;
- vehicles (cars, motorcycles, bicycles, scooters, buses);
- animals (wild or pets);
- plants (flowers, bushes, trees).

A TRICK

You can give yourself 10 minutes to draw a subject, then redraw it in 5 minutes, then in 1 minute, and finally in 30 seconds. This will cause you to naturally choose the most important lines and you will be training yourself to stylize.

Copying Models

Copying models is a good exercise for observing and understanding the techniques used by the professionals. This will enrich your drawing and manga skills, as a complement to your drawings from observation. Use different styles of models and try to choose drawings, illustrations, and boards.

In this case, we can consider copying to be a process of training and research.

- Copy characters and observe how the artist has represented their eyes, hair, hands, etc.
- Copy entire pages of manga to understand the dynamics and composition of the panels.
- Transpose pages: Copy the scenes of a manga page, but change the characters or the setting.

Once you have figured out how to represent the subjects in a stylized way, concentrate on observation techniques: Look at the thickness of the inking lines, count the frames, find the highlights and shadows in a color drawing.

When you are copying a drawing, you are no longer observing the subject itself, but rather how the artist has stylized it.

TIP

Don't forget the fundamental rule: You are not a photocopy machine!

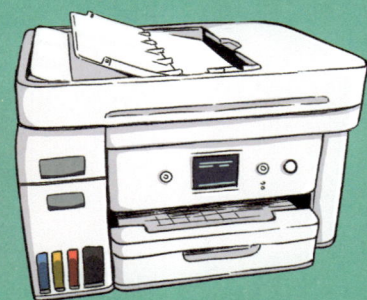

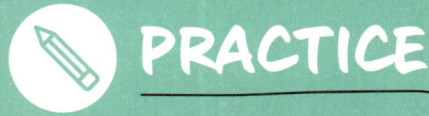

PRACTICE

Drawing Geometric Shapes

We have seen that everything, even the most complex things, can be redrawn if we take the trouble to break the subject down into several parts and subparts.

Geometric shapes are a valuable aid in creating construction lines. But if your foundation is wobbly, your entire drawing will look crooked.

Get into the habit of drawing shapes freehand, without using guides or templates: circles, triangles, squares, ovals, stars, cylinders . . .

Draw them frequently, in different sizes.

As much as possible, limit the number of lines you use.

Finger Exercises

Your eyes are now trained by copying and drawing from observation. You know how to take apart subjects and represent them in a stylized manner, starting with geometric shapes. Now it is time to train your hand to draw clean lines with a single movement.

Transfer this grid to a separate page and fill in the squares with vertical, horizontal, and diagonal lines, in one direction and then in the other, as in the first squares. The lines should be parallel to each other, evenly spaced, and you should draw each one in a single movement, without picking up your pen or pencil or starting over. The lines should also touch the edges of the squares, but without going beyond them.

PLEASE NOTE

Pay close attention to the direction of the lines before you start: in blue if you are right-handed, in green if you are left-handed. No matter what, make sure not to drag your hand over the lines that you have just drawn.

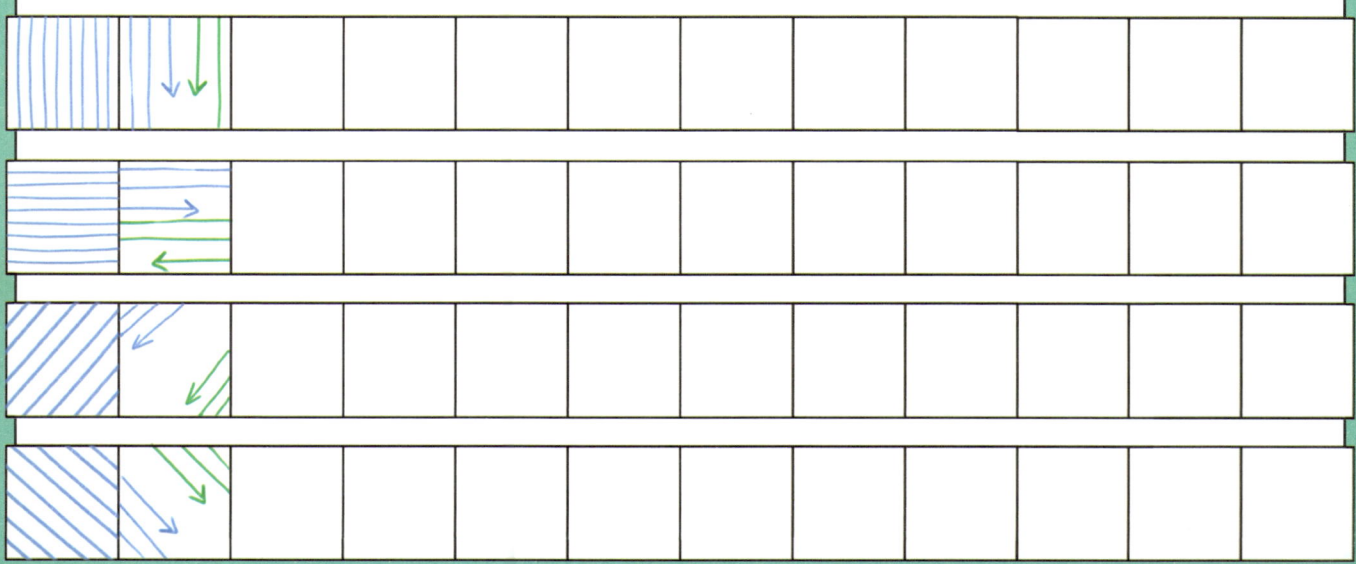

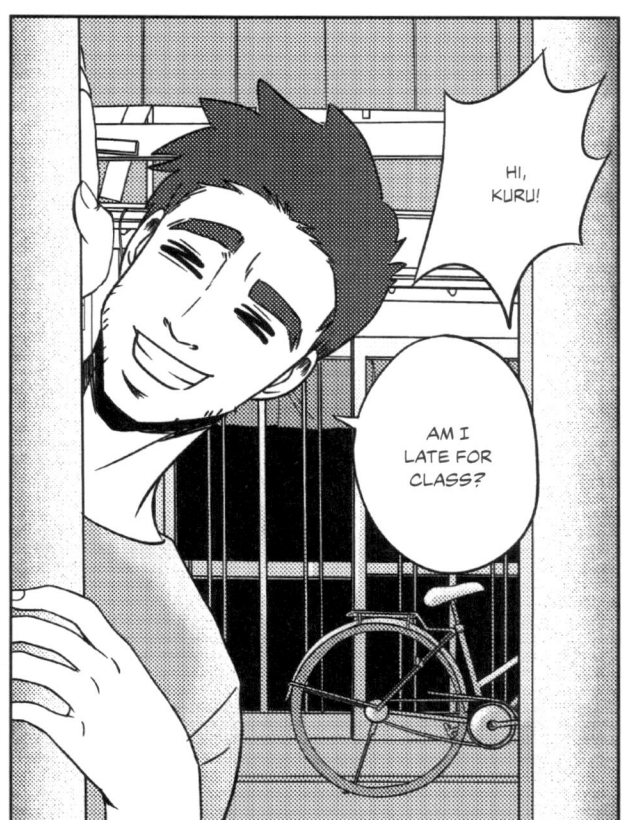

HI, KURU!

AM I LATE FOR CLASS?

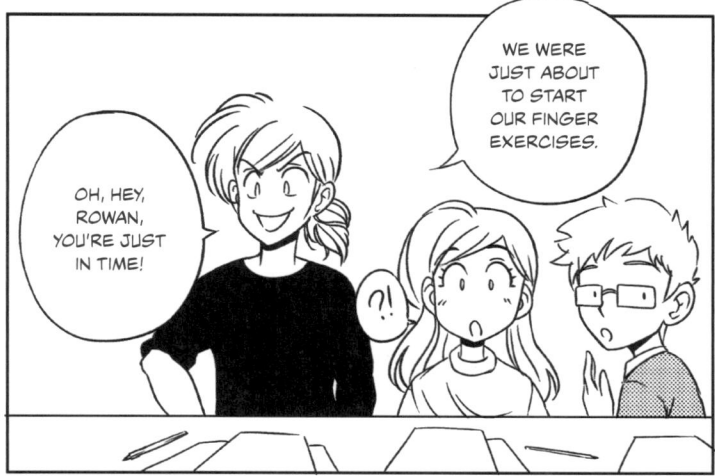

OH, HEY, ROWAN, YOU'RE JUST IN TIME!

WE WERE JUST ABOUT TO START OUR FINGER EXERCISES.

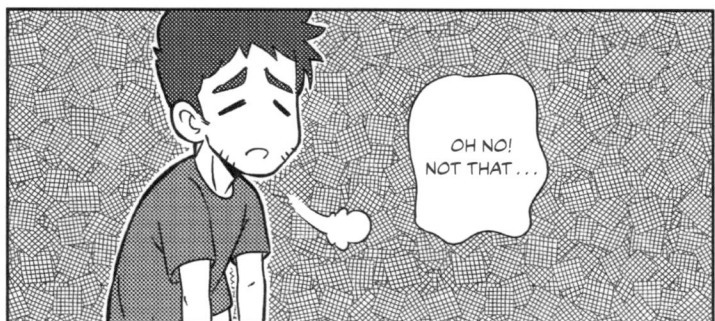

OH NO! NOT THAT...

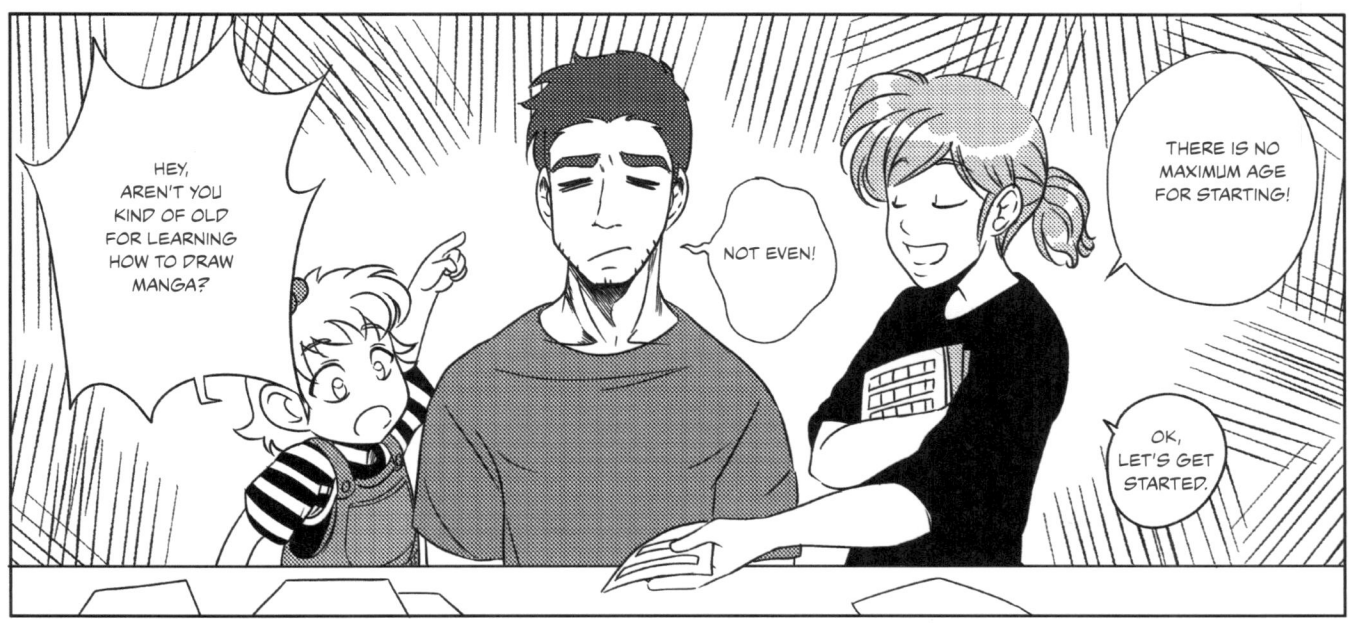

HEY, AREN'T YOU KIND OF OLD FOR LEARNING HOW TO DRAW MANGA?

NOT EVEN!

THERE IS NO MAXIMUM AGE FOR STARTING!

OK, LET'S GET STARTED.

It might seem pointless to draw lines in squares, but by learning how to draw in the right direction, mastering distances, and teaching yourself regularity, you will acquire good habits right away that you can use for the future.

While you are **sketching**, you will learn how to cut down the number of lines on your paper and thus avoid erasing too much. You are already practicing inking techniques without even realizing it. And as you learn to trust your hand, your lines will become smoother.

DRAWING CHARACTERS

Characters are the heroes of your stories. In order for people to understand them, you will have to learn to represent them well.

In this section of the book, which is a little more theoretical, we will be talking about **anatomy, proportions, emotions,** and **different morphologies,** as well looking at how to **dress** and **style the hair** of your characters.

Remember that I advise you to observe and understand what you are going to draw before you get started.

FACES

People often start with faces when they are learning how to draw manga characters, but it is not the simplest element to represent. Faces reflect the protagonists' personalities, convey all kinds of emotions, and bring the protagonists to life. We can become attached to them, or not appreciate them…

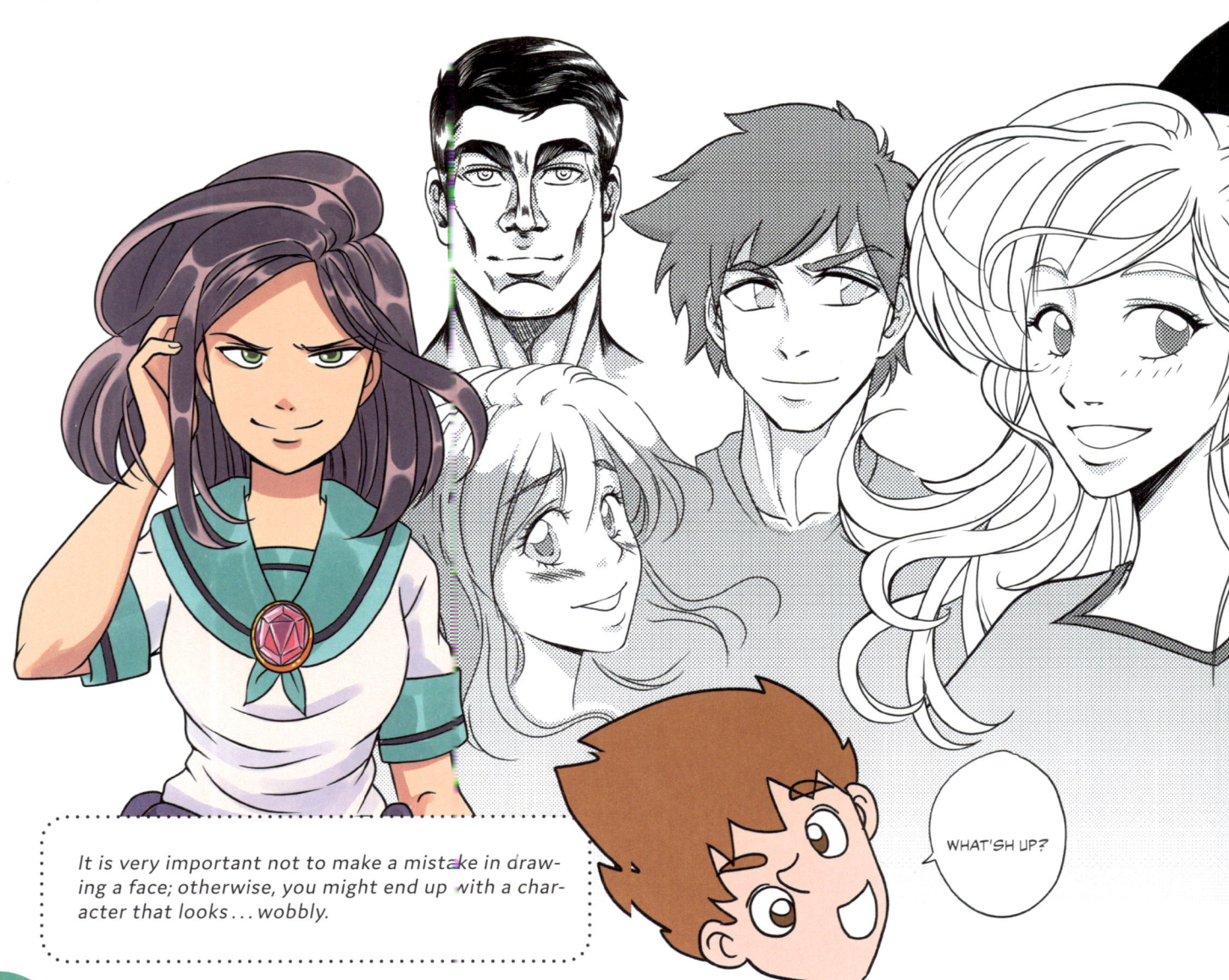

WHAT'SH UP?

It is very important not to make a mistake in drawing a face; otherwise, you might end up with a character that looks … wobbly.

Here are some basics on the anatomy of the human face.

The face presents cavities, bumps, and protrusions.

The brow bone is slightly rounded.

The occipitofrontalis muscle allows us to raise our eyebrows or bring them together, as in a scowl.

The orbit is the cavity in which the eye sits.

The eye can close and open thanks to its orbicularis oculi muscle.

The nasal bone is very short, with an extension of more flexible cartilage. This is why it is easy to bend or twist the nose.

The zygomaticus major and zygomaticus minor muscles connect the corner of the mouth to the zygomatic arch and contract when we smile.

The zygomatic arch is found just below the cheekbones and gives them their rounded appearance.

The mouth's orbicularis oris muscle, also known as the "kissing muscle," surrounds the oral opening.

The jaw is made up of two parts: a fixed part (the maxilla, or upper jaw) and a mobile part (the mandible, or lower jaw).

It is the muscles that give shape to the face and allow it to move.

TIP

If you'd like to dig deeper, I invite you to consult complete works covering human anatomy.

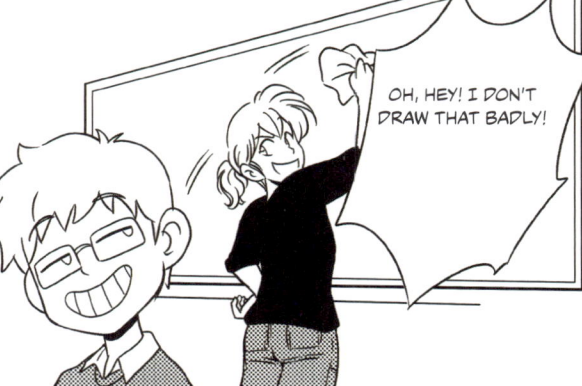

I UNDERSTAND NOW WHAT YOU WERE TRYING TO SAY WHEN YOU TALKED ABOUT MONSTERS INSPIRED BY REALITY.

OH, HEY! I DON'T DRAW THAT BADLY!

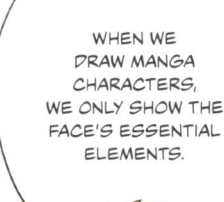

WHEN WE DRAW MANGA CHARACTERS, WE ONLY SHOW THE FACE'S ESSENTIAL ELEMENTS.

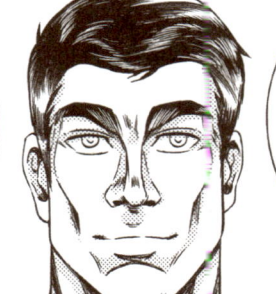

BUT WE STILL HAVE TO PLACE THEM CORRECTLY!

In order do this, it is important to pay attention to **proportions**. They involve a balance, a coherent relationship among several elements of the same whole. There are several methods for studying the proportions of the face. I offer one here that works for all bodies and that makes it hard for you to go wrong. That being said, don't hesitate to try other methods in different books to find out what works best for you.

Here is a stylized face, seen from the front:

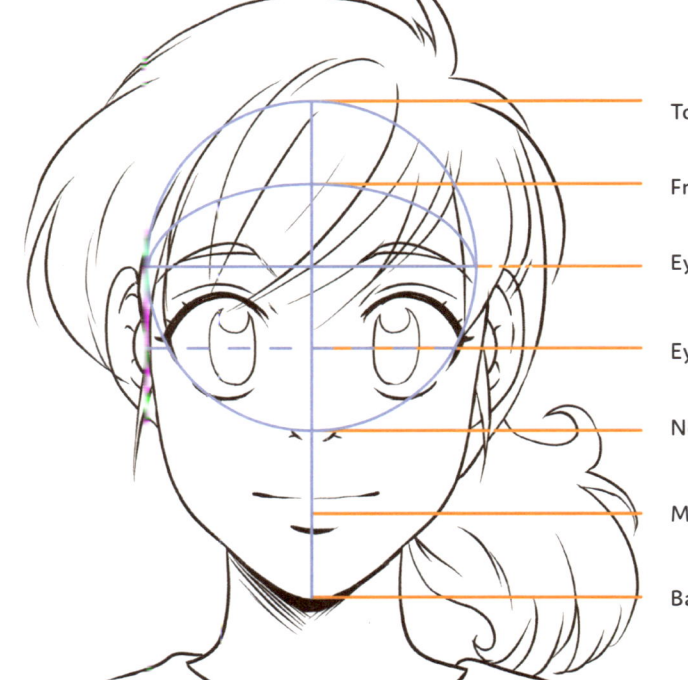

Top of the skull

Front of the forehead

Eyebrows

Eyes

Nose

Mouth

Base of the chin

Along the vertical line that divides the face in half, all of the reference points are spaced the same distance apart.

Seen from the front, the space between the two eyes is exactly the width of an eye.

Using **construction lines** is a good way to draw faces without making mistakes. The vertical line that divides the face into two equal parts is a good reference point for positioning the elements that make up the face.

Depending on the character, the eyes can have different shapes and sizes. Thus, it is important to draw them straddling their line so that they are placed at the right height on the face.

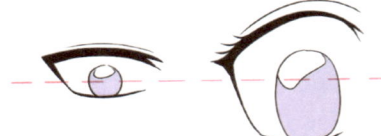

To draw a face in three-quarter profile, keep in mind the same height proportions as we saw for a face seen from the front. As the head turns, the position of the nose with respect to the ears does not change.

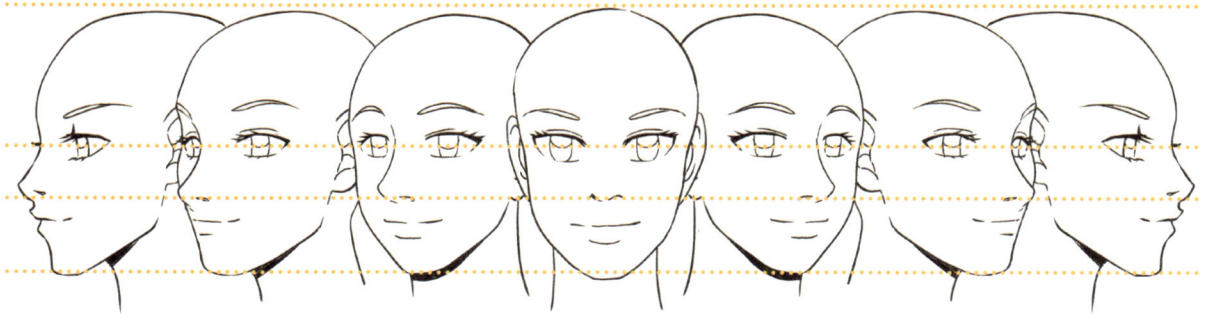

To give a face volume, transform the straight lines of a face seen from the front into curves.

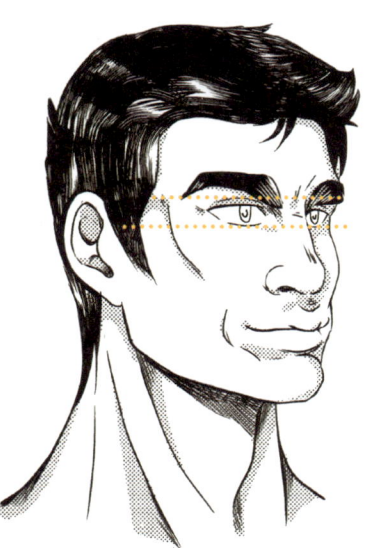

1 The nose is drawn in the same direction as the orientation of the face.

2 The ears can be more or less visible.

3 The height of the eyes stays the same, but their width changes as the head rotates.

4 The shape of the mouth changes as the orientation of the face changes.

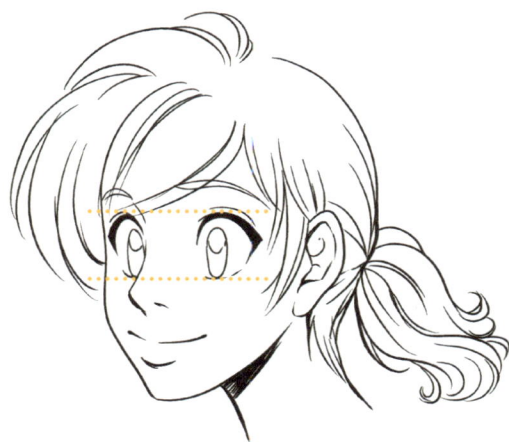

On faces drawn from a three-quarter view, the eye that is closer to us will be wider than the one that is further away.

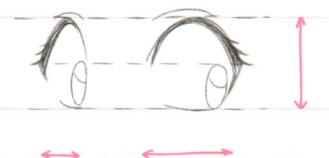

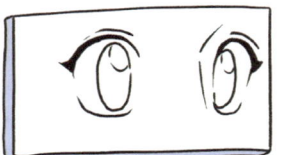
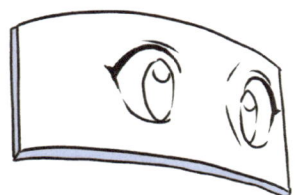

The eyes are positioned along a rounded plane and not on a straight plane. Draw them at the same time, step by step, so that they look similar.

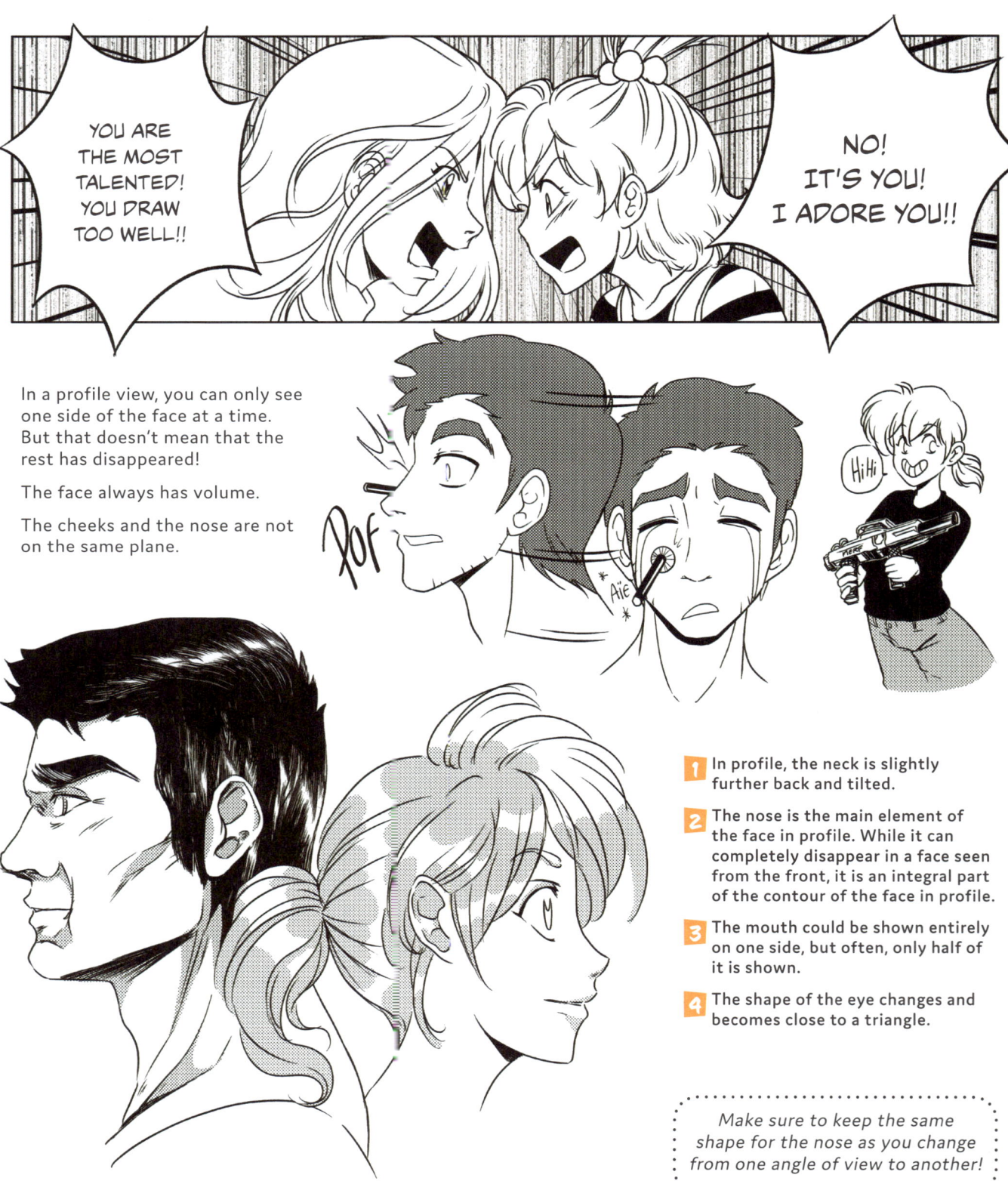

In a profile view, you can only see one side of the face at a time. But that doesn't mean that the rest has disappeared!

The face always has volume.

The cheeks and the nose are not on the same plane.

1 In profile, the neck is slightly further back and tilted.

2 The nose is the main element of the face in profile. While it can completely disappear in a face seen from the front, it is an integral part of the contour of the face in profile.

3 The mouth could be shown entirely on one side, but often, only half of it is shown.

4 The shape of the eye changes and becomes close to a triangle.

Make sure to keep the same shape for the nose as you change from one angle of view to another!

42

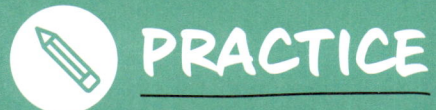

PRACTICE

To draw a face, I suggest you follow the steps shown below, reproducing them freehand on a separate sheet of paper, and not pressing too hard on your pencil.

The Foundation

From the Front

1 Draw a circle with a cross inside it.

2 Extend the vertical line down the same distance as one radius of the circle (half the circle's diameter, or width).

3 Draw the jaw by connecting the horizontal line of the circle with the bottom of the vertical line.

4 Draw seven reference lines spaced equally far apart along the vertical line: the top of the skull, front of the forehead, eyebrows, eyes, nose, mouth, and base of the chin. Draw the neck.

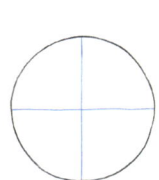
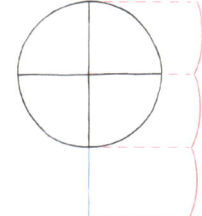
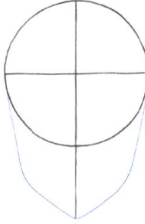
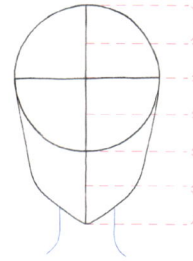

5 Draw the ears: they are positioned between the line of the eyebrows and the line of the nose.

6 Draw an arc on the forehead, as if the character were wearing a swimming cap. Then draw two marks along the line of the eyes.

7 Draw the eyes, leaving a space the width of an eye between the two eyes. Then add the final elements (eyebrows, nose, and mouth).

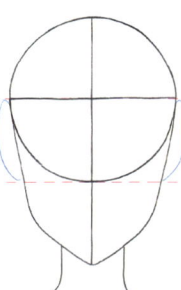
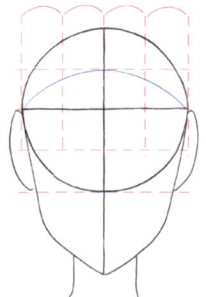
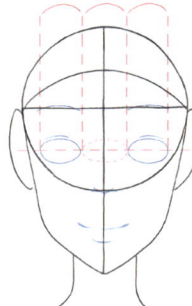

In Profile

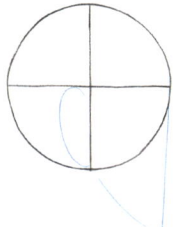
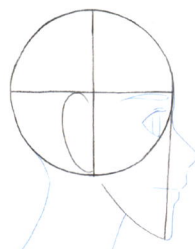

In Three-Quarter View

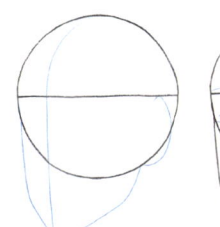
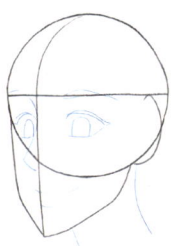

Draw the line that divides the face in half, curving it at the top. Position the visible ear between the line of the eyebrows and the base of the circle.

Still using the same reference points, position the other facial elements.

Starting from the middle of the right edge of the circle, draw a vertical line downward, the same height as the circle itself. Position the ear behind the vertical line within the circle and connect the two vertical lines to draw the jaw.

Keep using the same reference points as in step 4 of faces seen from the front to position the elements of the face.

TIP

For every face, determine the first volumes using geometric shapes, and then draw the elements, adding the details as you go along.

Now that we know where to place the elements of the face, let's take a look at how to draw eyes, noses, mouths, and ears of different sizes and shapes.

Eyes and Eyebrows

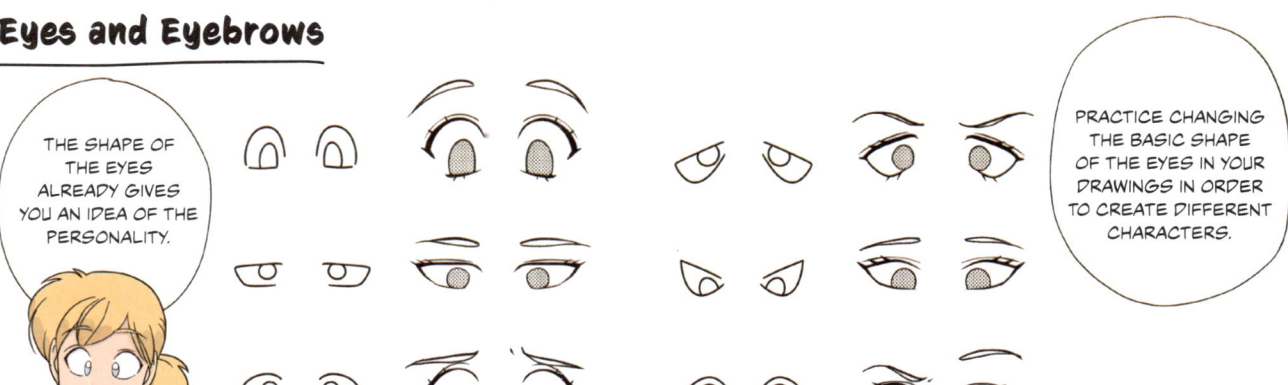

THE SHAPE OF THE EYES ALREADY GIVES YOU AN IDEA OF THE PERSONALITY.

PRACTICE CHANGING THE BASIC SHAPE OF THE EYES IN YOUR DRAWINGS IN ORDER TO CREATE DIFFERENT CHARACTERS.

The eyes are like marbles housed within cavities and protected by two eyelids.

1 Upper eyelid
2 Lower eyelid
3 Iris
4 Pupil
5 Eyelashes
6 Eyelid fold
7 White of the eye

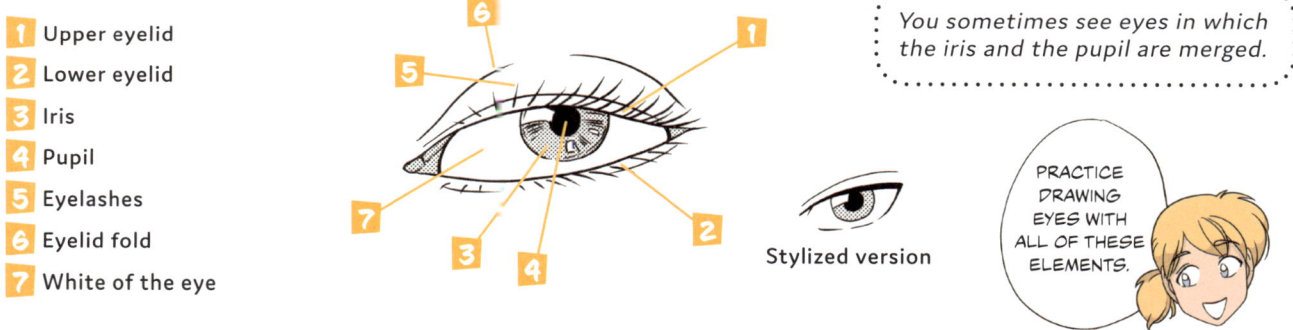

You sometimes see eyes in which the iris and the pupil are merged.

Stylized version

PRACTICE DRAWING EYES WITH ALL OF THESE ELEMENTS.

The eyelashes may be longer or shorter, but they are always longer on the upper eyelid than on the lower eyelid.

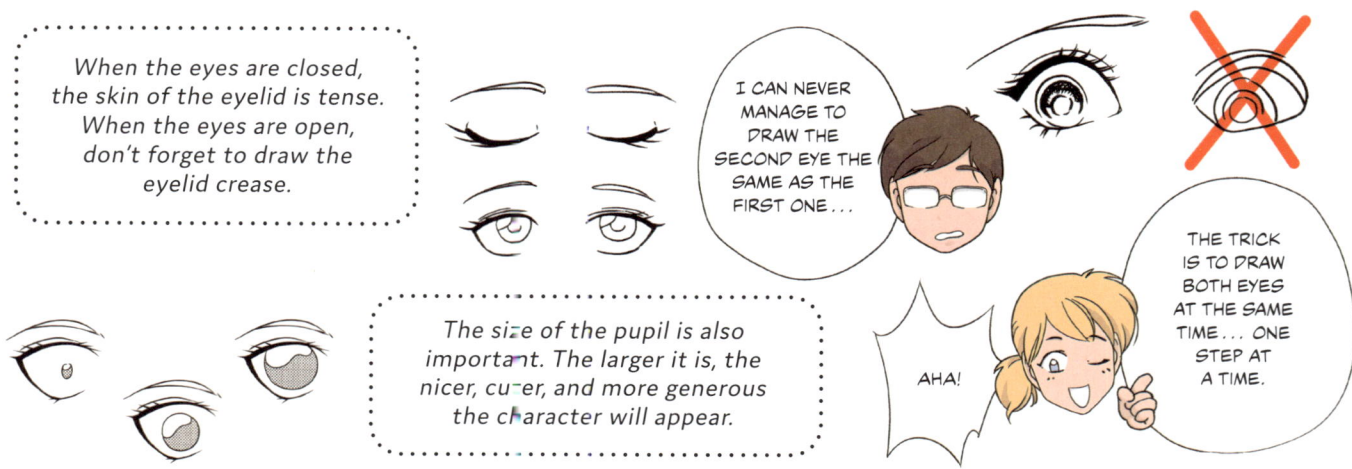

When the eyes are closed, the skin of the eyelid is tense. When the eyes are open, don't forget to draw the eyelid crease.

I CAN NEVER MANAGE TO DRAW THE SECOND EYE THE SAME AS THE FIRST ONE...

THE TRICK IS TO DRAW BOTH EYES AT THE SAME TIME... ONE STEP AT A TIME.

The size of the pupil is also important. The larger it is, the nicer, cuter, and more generous the character will appear.

AHA!

The Nose

The nose can be broken down into several simple shapes: a vertical ridge, a hump at the tip, and two nostrils.

From the front, it is usually drawn as a little bridge, a "U," or a "V."

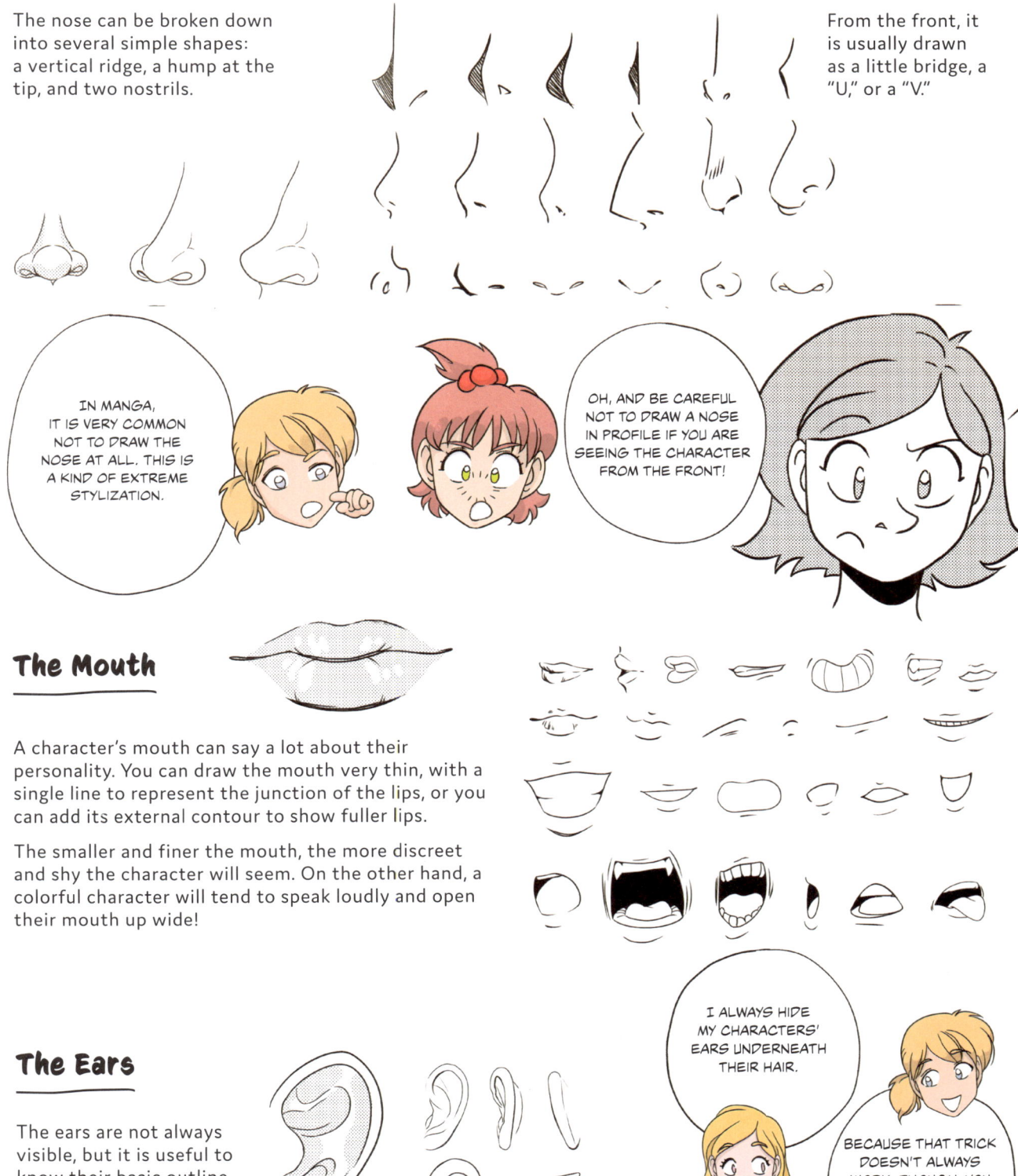

IN MANGA, IT IS VERY COMMON NOT TO DRAW THE NOSE AT ALL. THIS IS A KIND OF EXTREME STYLIZATION.

OH, AND BE CAREFUL NOT TO DRAW A NOSE IN PROFILE IF YOU ARE SEEING THE CHARACTER FROM THE FRONT!

The Mouth

A character's mouth can say a lot about their personality. You can draw the mouth very thin, with a single line to represent the junction of the lips, or you can add its external contour to show fuller lips.

The smaller and finer the mouth, the more discreet and shy the character will seem. On the other hand, a colorful character will tend to speak loudly and open their mouth up wide!

The Ears

The ears are not always visible, but it is useful to know their basic outline in order to be able to draw them better.

I ALWAYS HIDE MY CHARACTERS' EARS UNDERNEATH THEIR HAIR.

BECAUSE THAT TRICK DOESN'T ALWAYS WORK, THOUGH, YOU NEED TO CAREFULLY OBSERVE WHAT IT IS IMPORTANT TO REPRESENT.

DIFFERENTIATING FACES

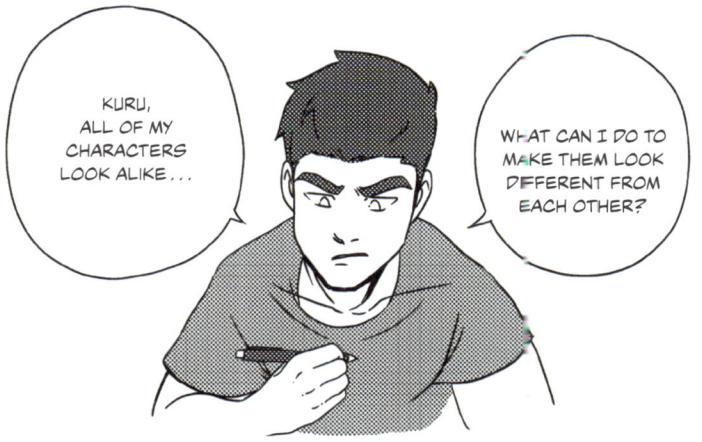

KURU, ALL OF MY CHARACTERS LOOK ALIKE...

WHAT CAN I DO TO MAKE THEM LOOK DIFFERENT FROM EACH OTHER?

Every character is unique, just like you! Once you know how to draw a well-proportioned face, you can have fun with changing some of the shapes in order to change the age, body shape, and sex of your characters.

The shape of the jaw depends on the angle of the face's contour lines.

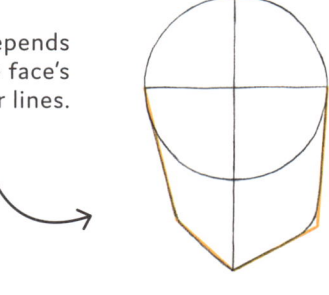

You can change your character's age by changing the length of the vertical line that extends below the circle. The shorter that line, the younger the character will look. And the longer the line, the older they will look.

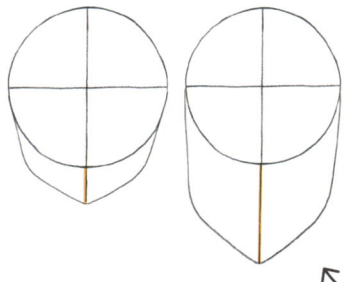

To draw more feminine characters, make the jawlines rounder; to make your characters more masculine, give them a more angular jaw and chin.

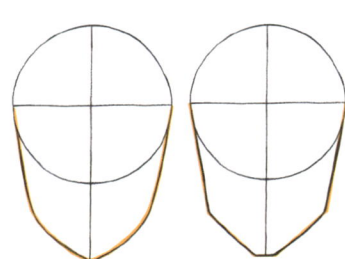

DO YOU SEE THE DIFFERENCE?

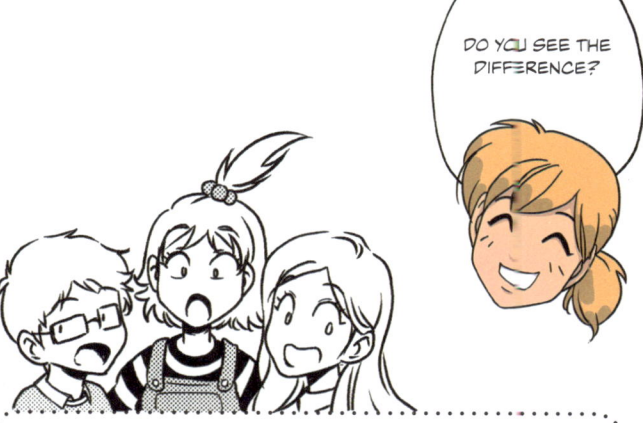

You can also use geometric shapes as a base for the bottom of the face.

I UNDERSTAND, SENSEI!!

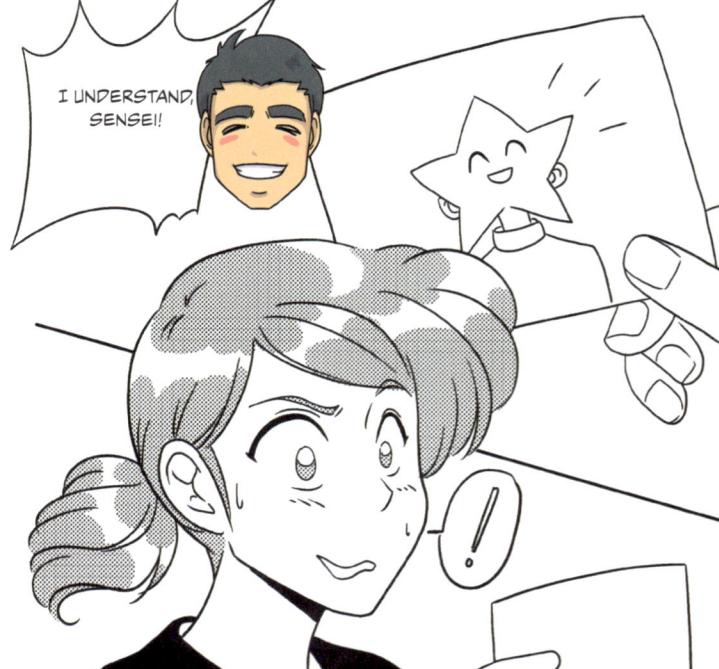

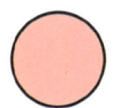
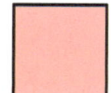
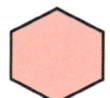

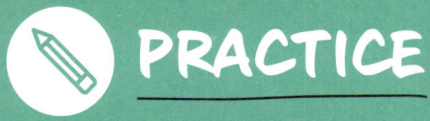

PRACTICE

Drawing Different Faces

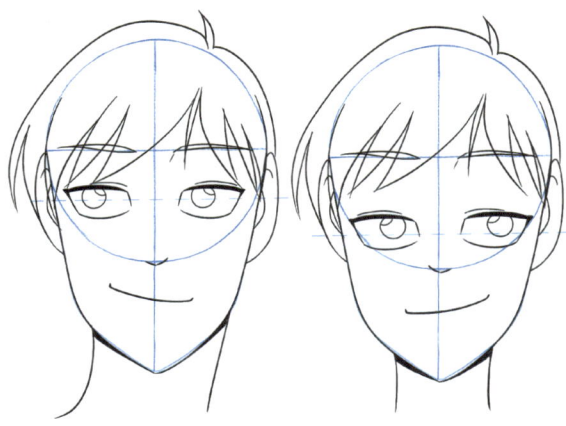

Refer back to page 43, where I had you draw faces from the front, in profile, and in three-quarter profile, and repeat the exercise, this time changing the size of your construction lines and the shape of the facial contours. Put the line of the eyes lower down to make the characters younger, and place them higher up to draw older characters. Try out all kinds of combinations to draw different characters.

Drawing Eyes

To practice drawing eyes, start by drawing boxes, like the ones shown below, on a separate sheet of paper. The eyes should touch each of the four sides of the boxes.

The box in the middle is the distance between them. Don't forget to leave this empty space between the two eyes if you are drawing without using the boxes.

Change the shape of the eyes, their size, and their details to differentiate your characters.

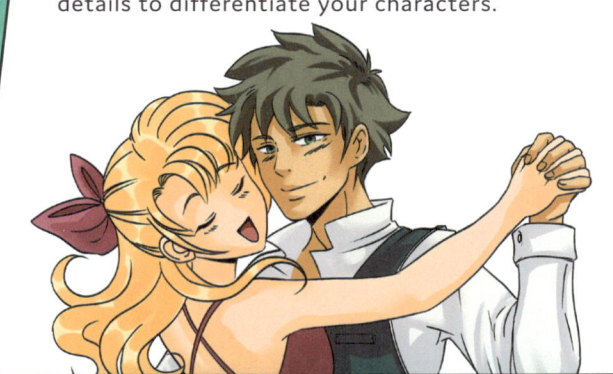

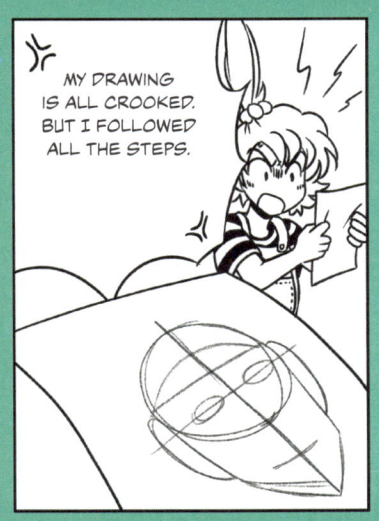

MY DRAWING IS ALL CROOKED. BUT I FOLLOWED ALL THE STEPS.

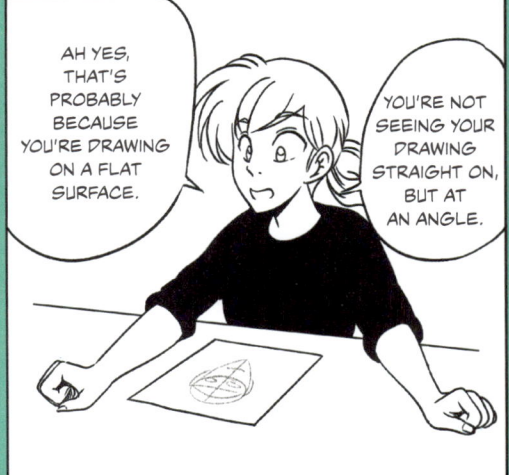

AH YES, THAT'S PROBABLY BECAUSE YOU'RE DRAWING ON A FLAT SURFACE.

YOU'RE NOT SEEING YOUR DRAWING STRAIGHT ON, BUT AT AN ANGLE.

TIP

Take breaks every now and then and lift up your sheet of paper to see the overall look of your drawing.

EMOTIONS

Emotions are essential in manga. They bring us closer to the characters and allow us to understand what they're feeling.

Concretely, in order to draw the emotion of a character, all you have to do is have fun changing the shape, size, and position of three elements: their **eyebrows**, **eyes**, and **mouth**.

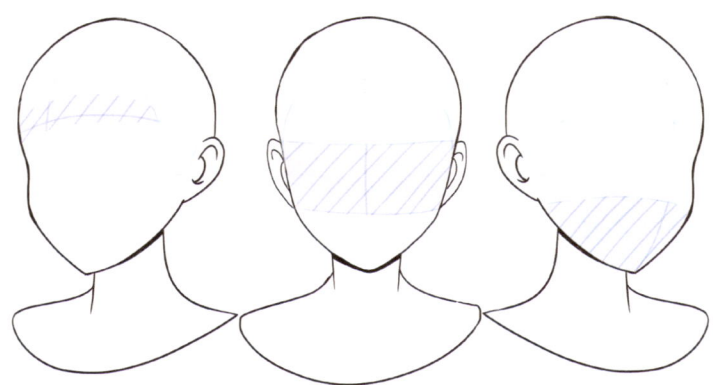

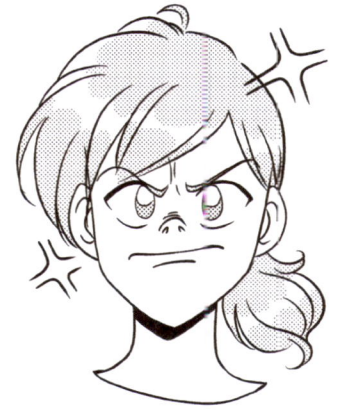

A TRICK
*To create colorful, memorable characters, the **key to success is exaggeration!***

Don't be afraid to deform the elements of the face and push boundaries—for instance, by drawing a face that juts out beyond the outline of the face.

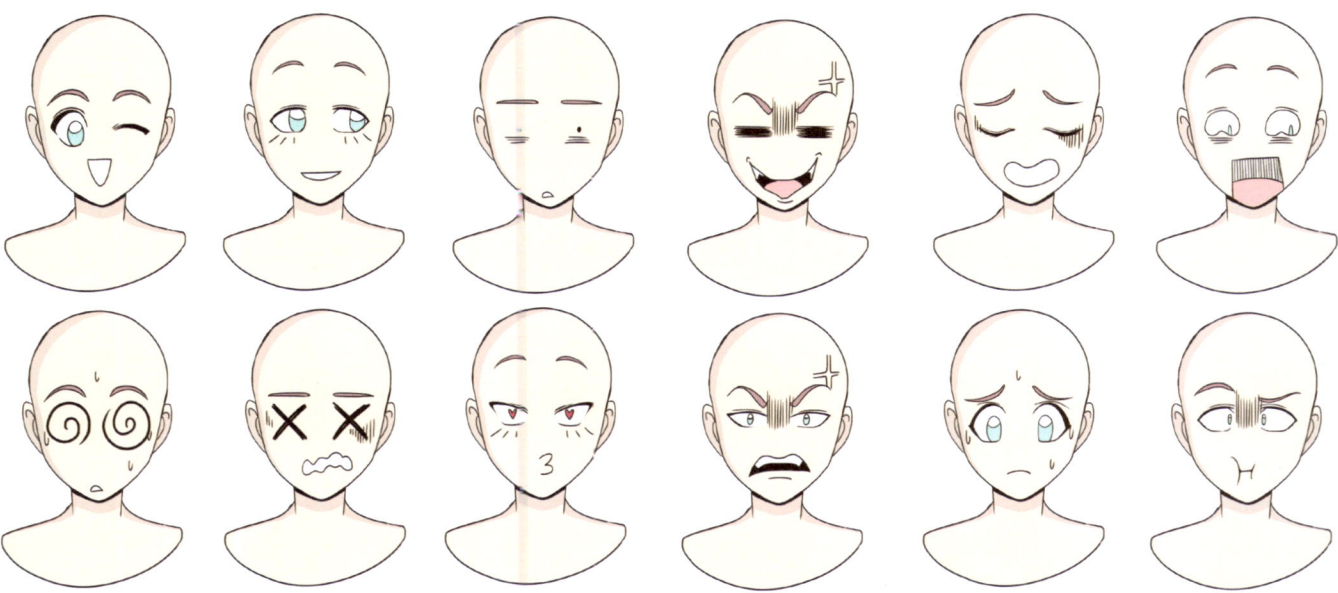

Use the following elements as inspiration for creating unique combinations and bringing your characters to life!

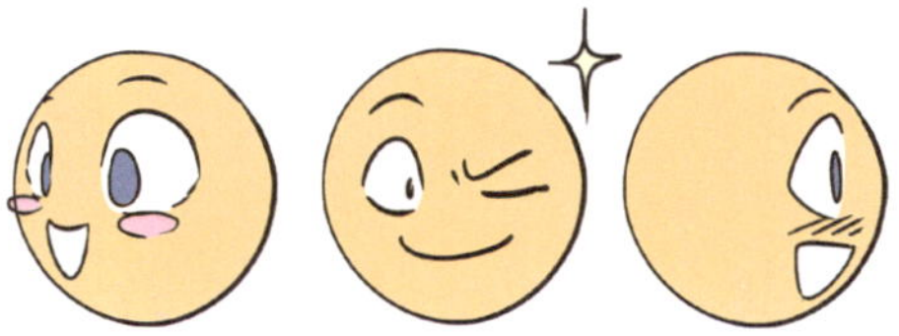

Eyebrows

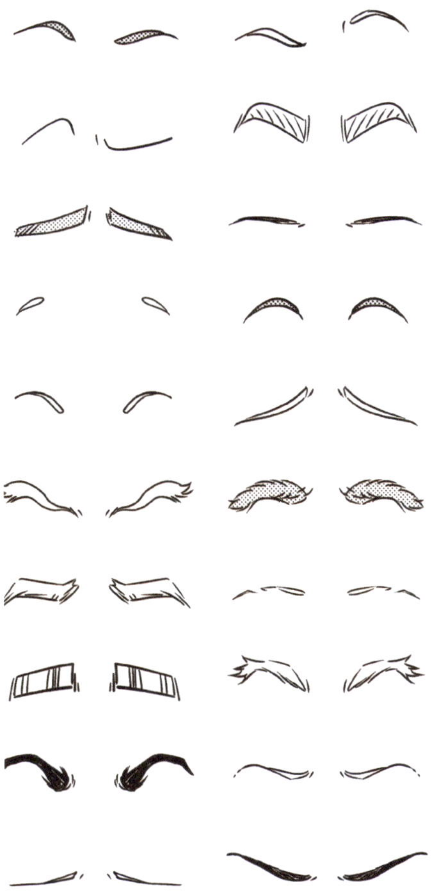

Eyes

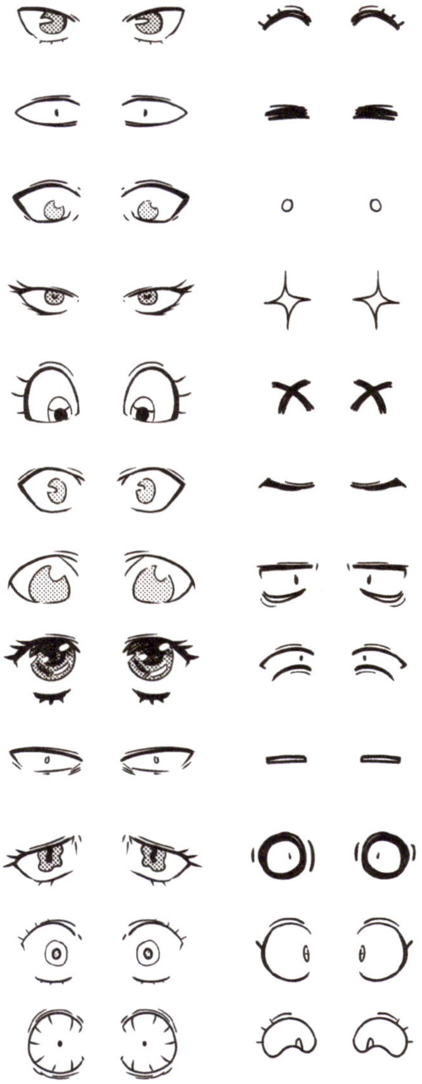

Mouths

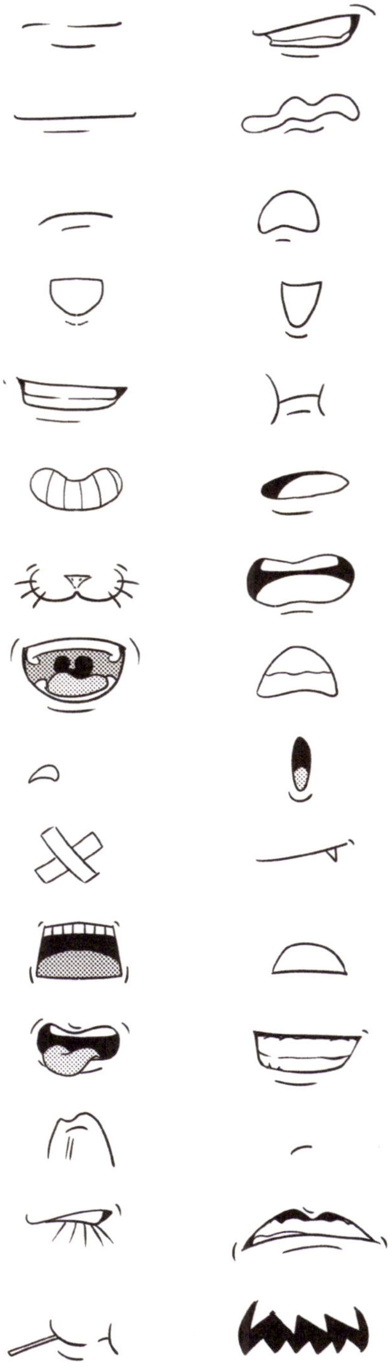

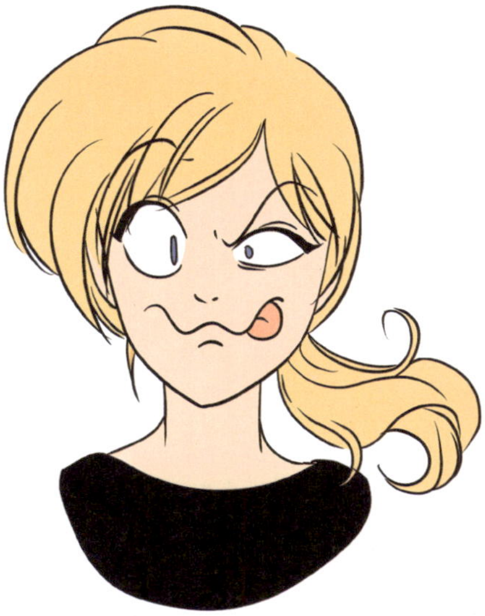

TIP

Practice drawing an emoji of the emotion that you want to represent.

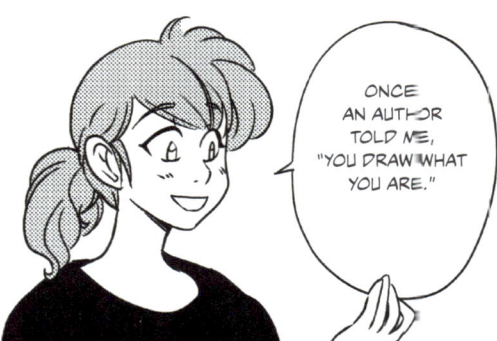

ONCE AN AUTHOR TOLD ME, "YOU DRAW WHAT YOU ARE."

Sure enough, drawing is a form of expression, above all, and beyond the messages it conveys, it also serves to communicate emotions: **your** emotions!

It's not enough to know how to draw well. Experience emotions, make faces, put yourself in your character's shoes and let it all out on paper!

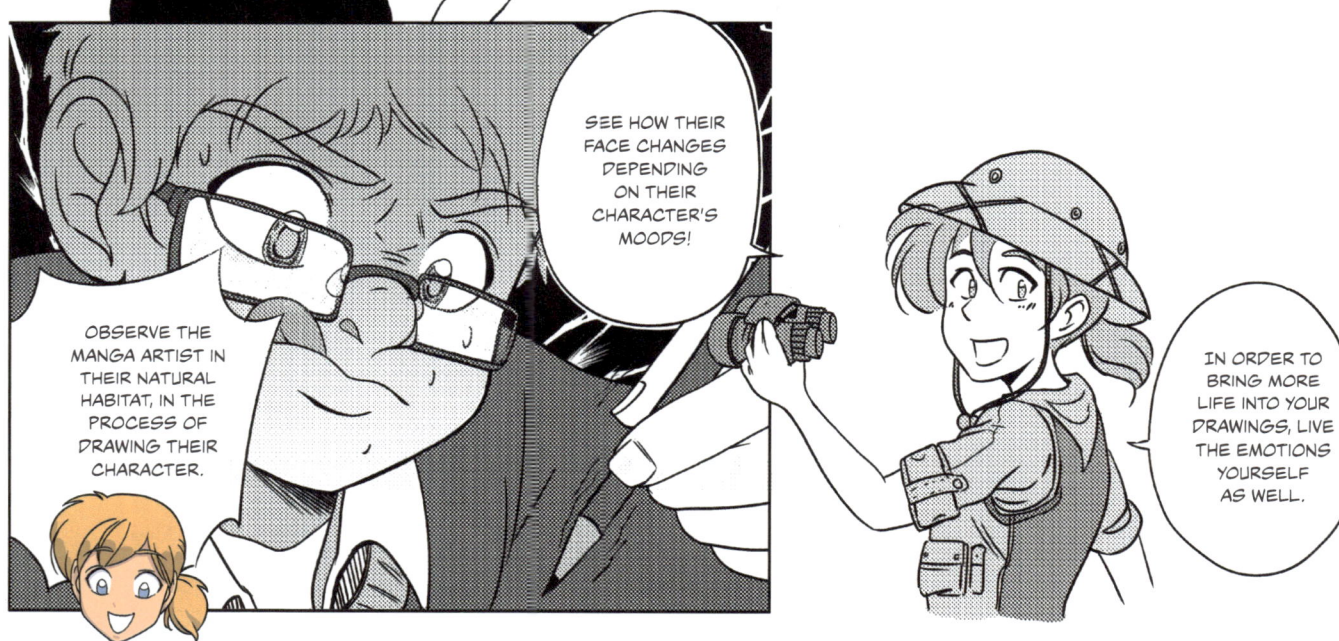

OBSERVE THE MANGA ARTIST IN THEIR NATURAL HABITAT, IN THE PROCESS OF DRAWING THEIR CHARACTER.

SEE HOW THEIR FACE CHANGES DEPENDING ON THEIR CHARACTER'S MOODS!

IN ORDER TO BRING MORE LIFE INTO YOUR DRAWINGS, LIVE THE EMOTIONS YOURSELF AS WELL.

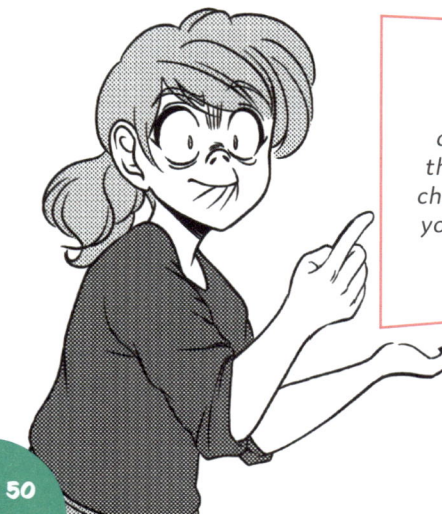

A TRICK
To bring your drawings to life, make the same face that your character is making while you are drawing it. Act it out and make faces.

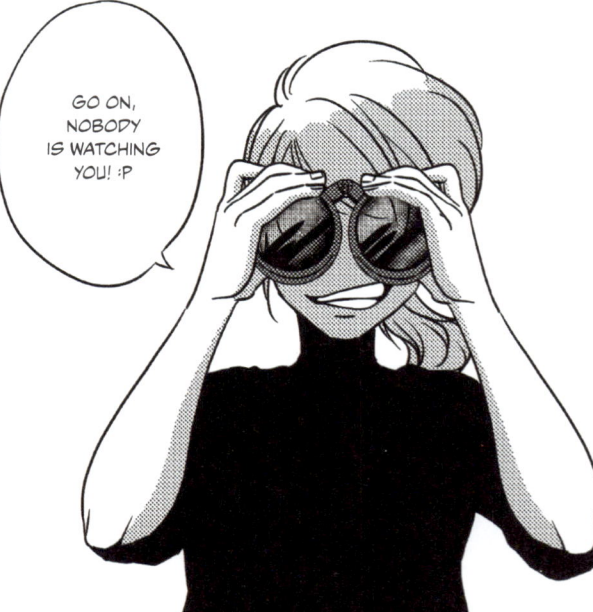

GO ON, NOBODY IS WATCHING YOU! :P

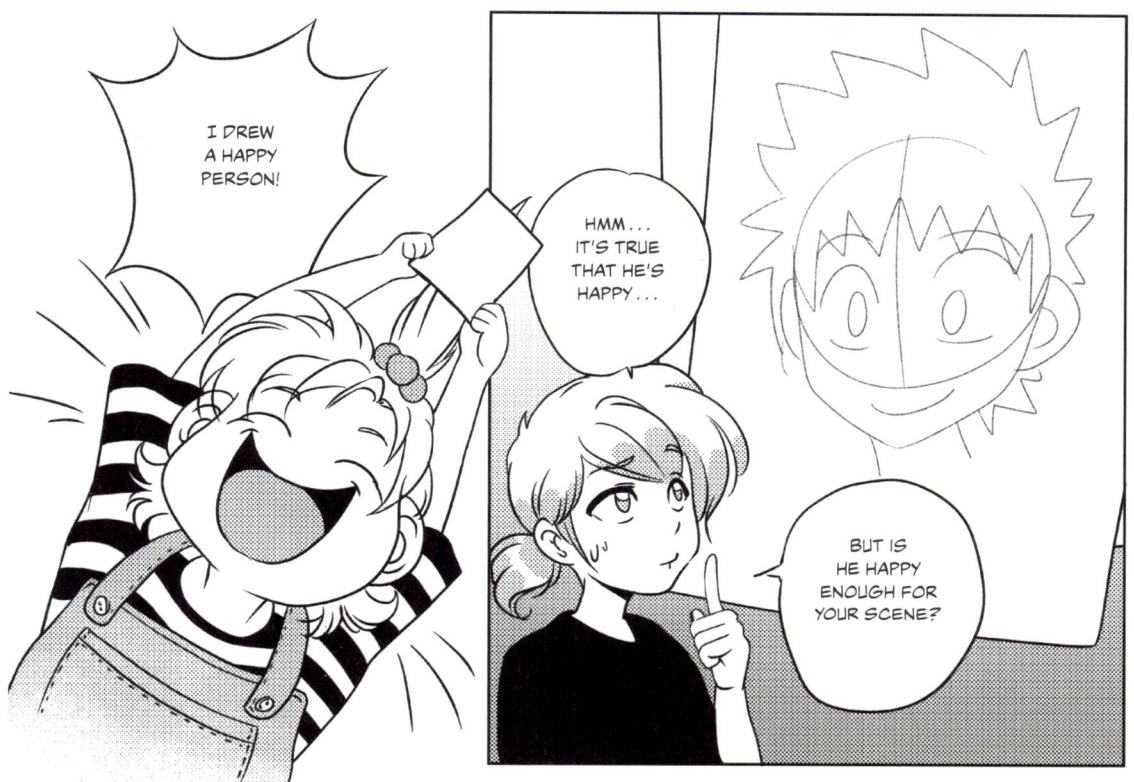

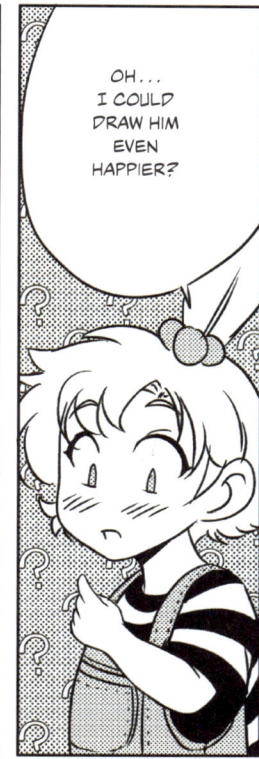

Here is an example of emotions of different intensities. Observe carefully what changes.

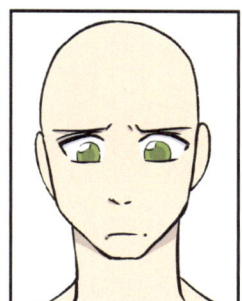 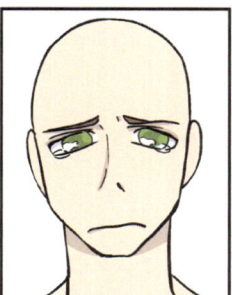 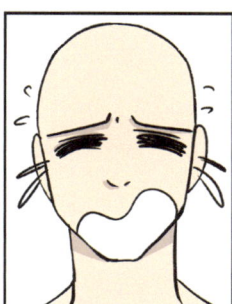

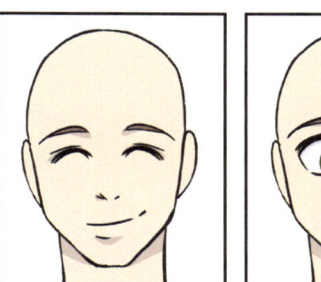 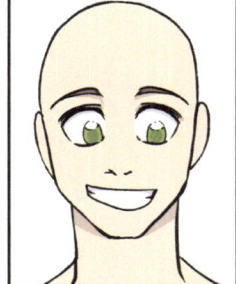 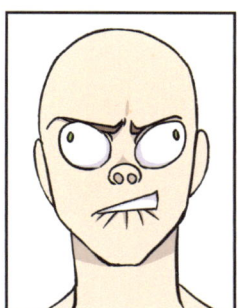

The way in which you choose to exaggerate certain elements can completely change the perception of your work.

Sometimes, the exaggeration is a way to reassure the reader, by introducing a comical aspect to what might have seemed very serious at the beginning.

If you have to draw a particular scene, make sure to choose the right intensity for your characters' emotions.

Adapt your graphic choices to your storytelling.

TIP

When you're going to create a new character, practice showing the character in a variety of situations. Think about the character's personality, including whether they are extroverted or reserved, when you are drawing the character with different emotions.

Here are a few examples of emotions, some more and some less exaggerated, that you can use for inspiration.

Joy

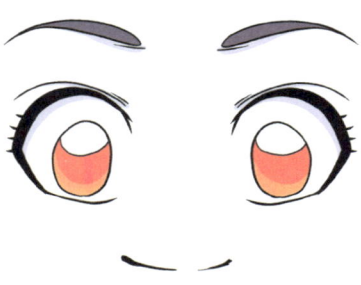 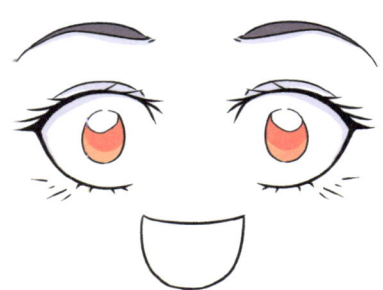 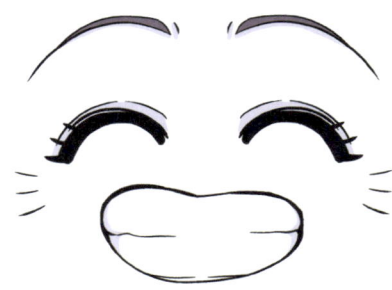

Anger

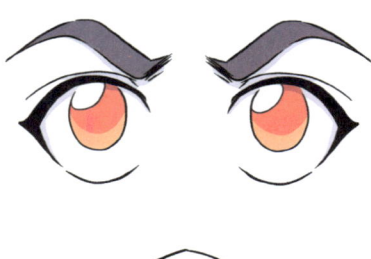 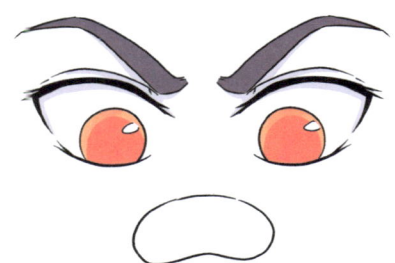 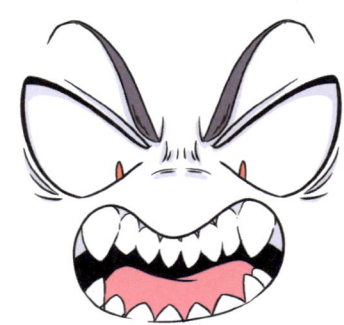

Sadness

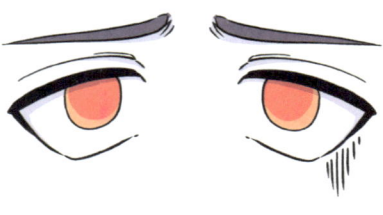 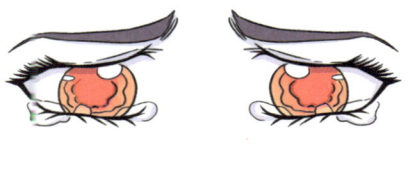 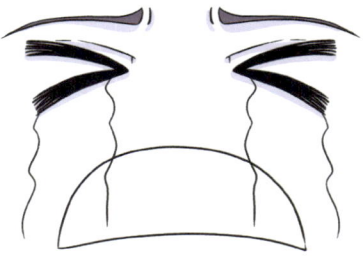

Discomfort

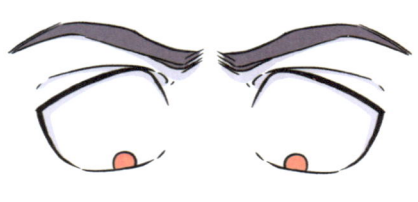  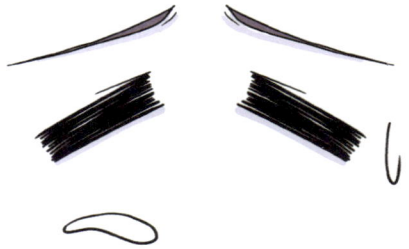

Surprise

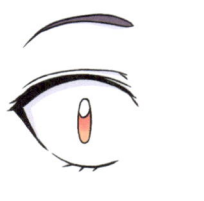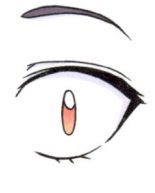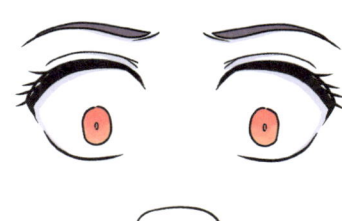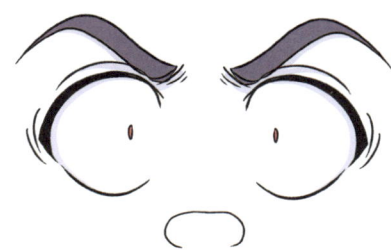

Fear

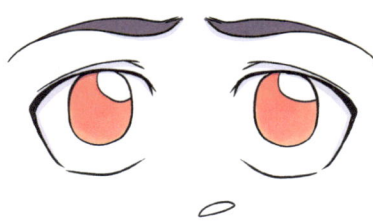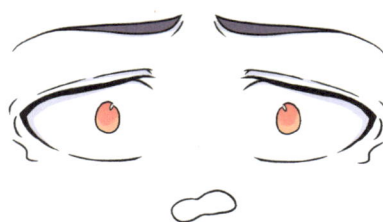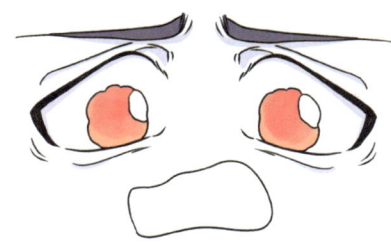

Embarrassment

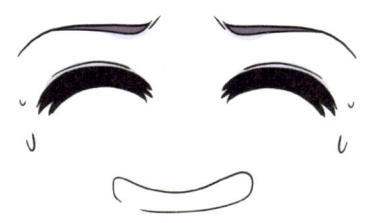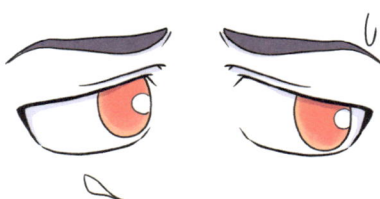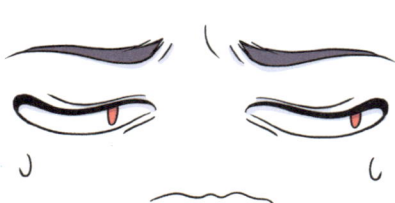

Blankness

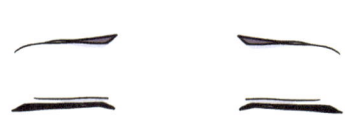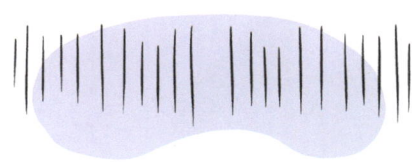

Peacefulness

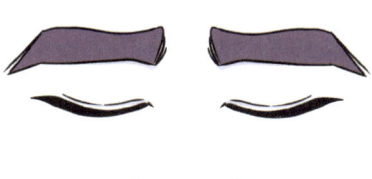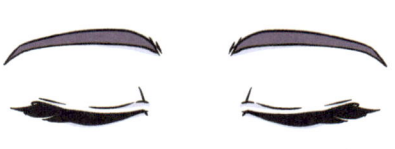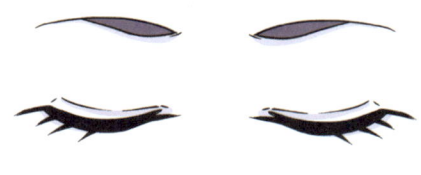

53

In manga, the emotions that are represented by facial expressions are sometimes accompanied by symbols called **manpu**.

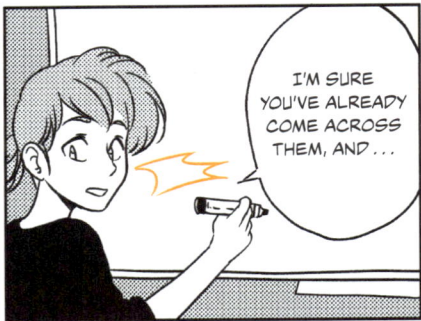
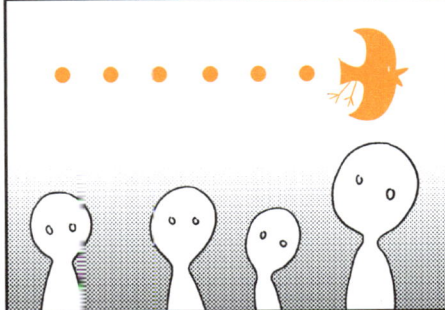
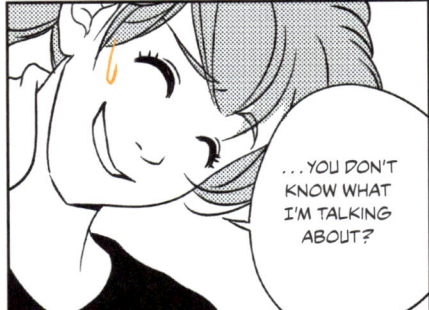
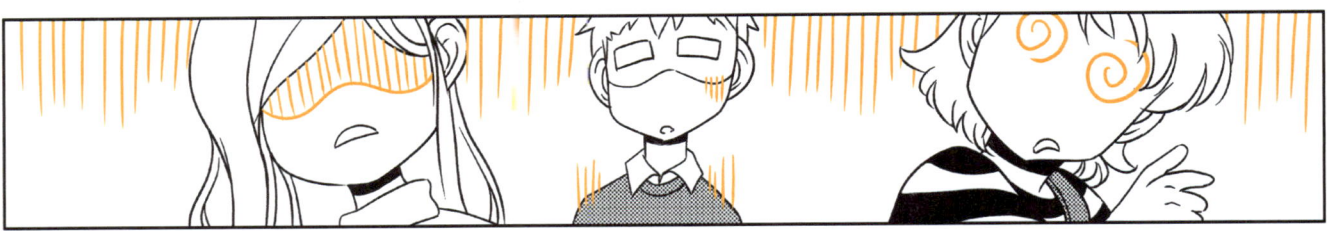
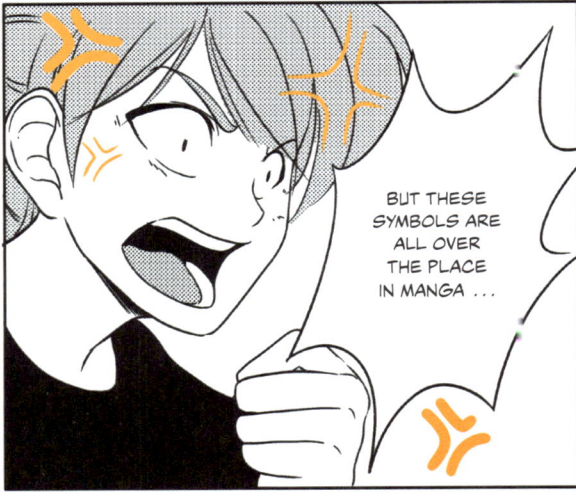
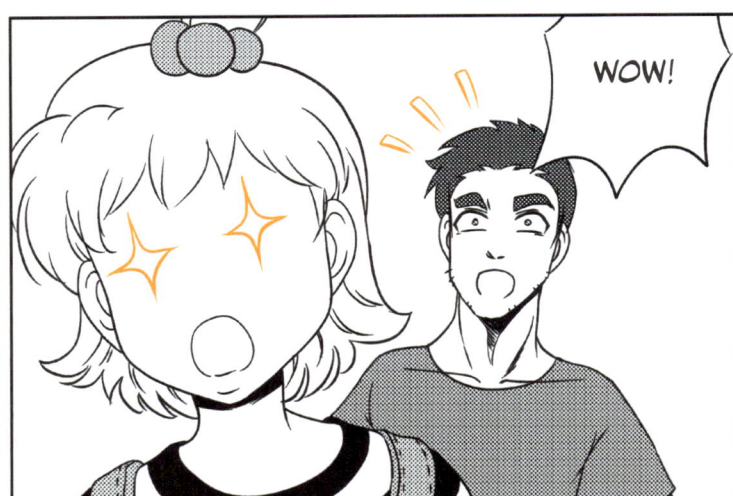

As you can see, the symbols I have presented here serve to reinforce the characters' emotions. The larger the symbol, or the more symbols there are, the more the emotion is intensified. But the absence of any symbols can also be very important in our understanding of a scene. Think about it!

Manpu are universal and everyone can understand them.

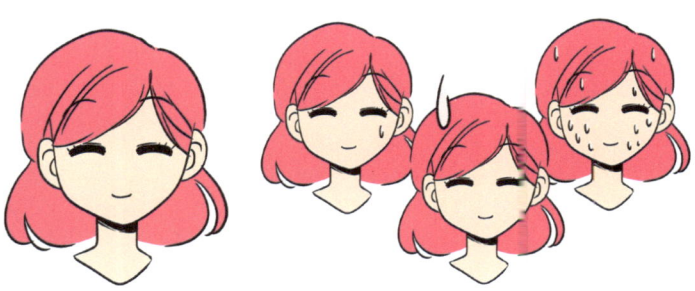

Here are some examples of manpu that you can have fun adding to your drawings.

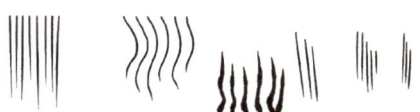 

Lines: tension, unease, pressure

 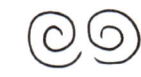

Drops: embarrassment, unease, stress

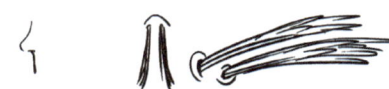

Nosebleed: strong emotion

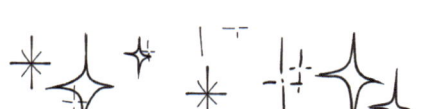

Star-shaped eyes: admiration

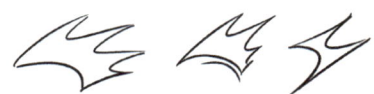

Spirals: unease, dizziness

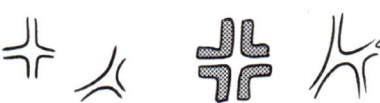

Flashes: revelation, surprise

Veins: anger

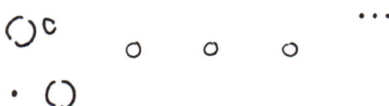

Three small dots: silence, unease, whiteness

Hearts: love, admiration

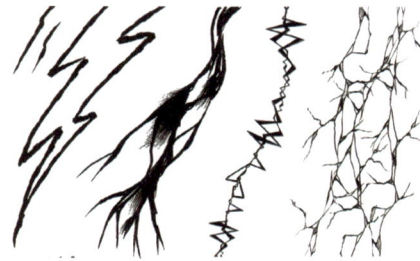

Lightning bolts: tension, action, anger

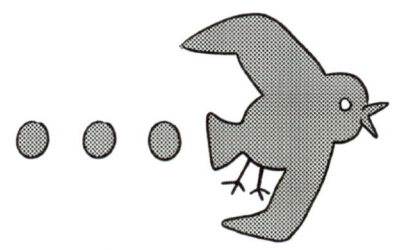

Crow: unease, silence

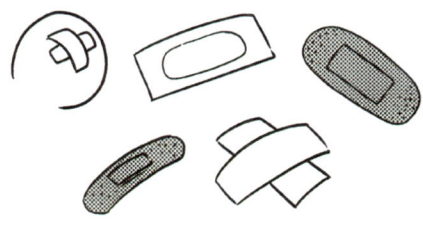

Bandaids: trivial suffering

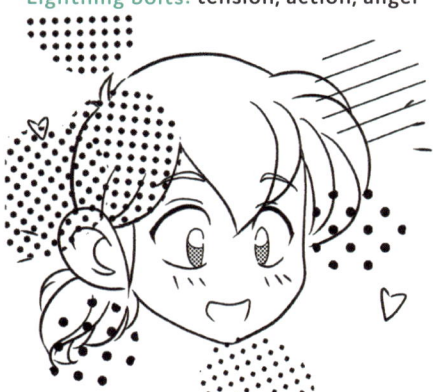

Chibi-style characteristics: caricature of a child

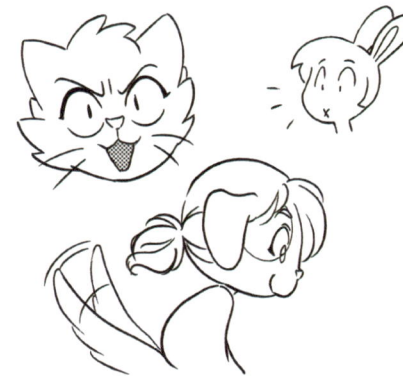

Animal-style characteristics: caricature of an animal

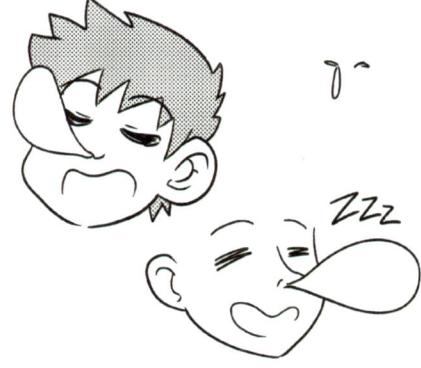

Nostril drop: sleeping character

Don't be afraid to create your own combinations by choosing several different manpu in the same drawing.

PRACTICE

Draw expressive faces by changing the shape of the eyes, the position of the eyebrows, and the shape of the mouth. Add the appropriate symbols to accentuate the emotions and make the graphic codes of manga drawing your own.

HAIR

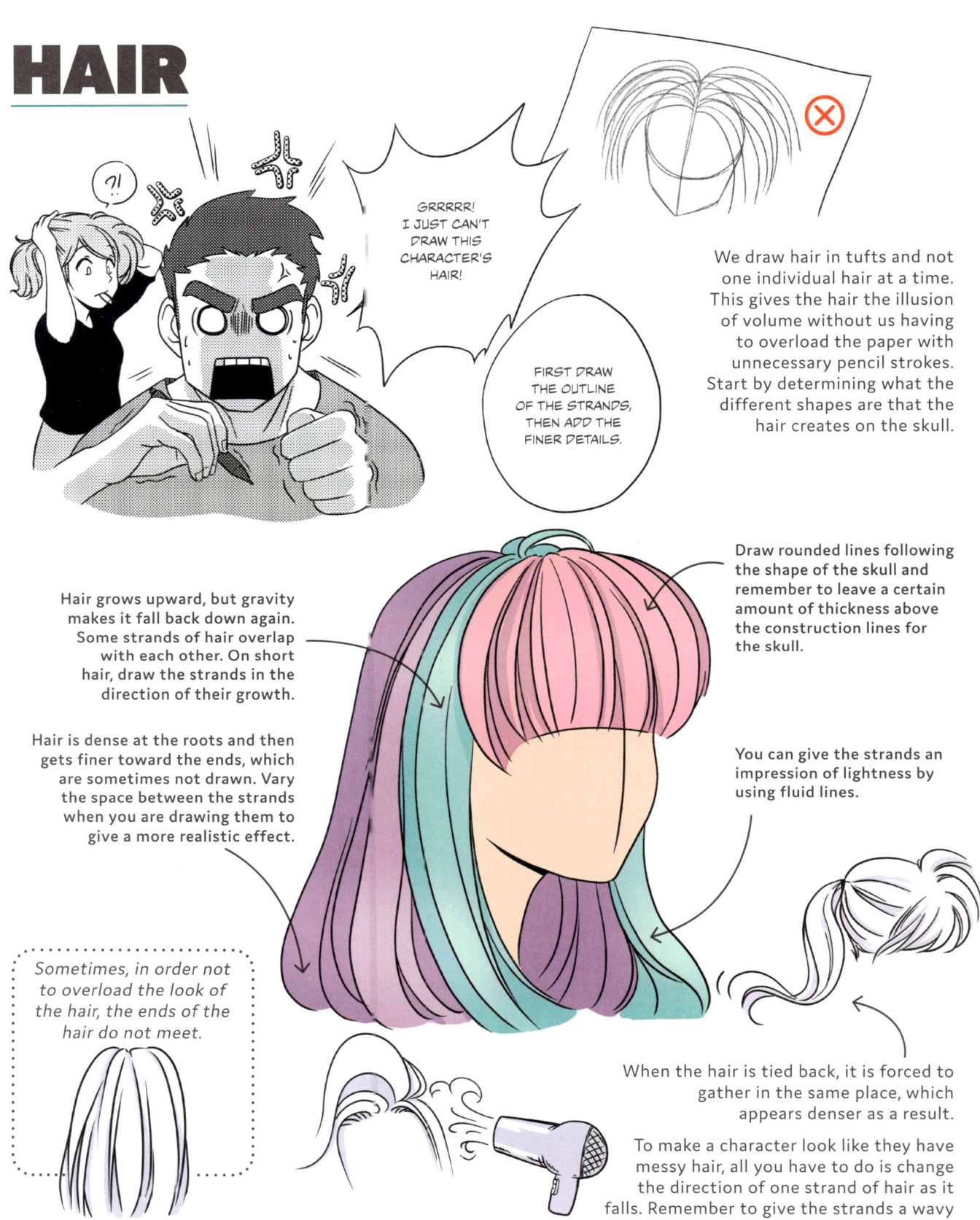

GRRRRR! I JUST CAN'T DRAW THIS CHARACTER'S HAIR!

FIRST DRAW THE OUTLINE OF THE STRANDS, THEN ADD THE FINER DETAILS.

We draw hair in tufts and not one individual hair at a time. This gives the hair the illusion of volume without us having to overload the paper with unnecessary pencil strokes. Start by determining what the different shapes are that the hair creates on the skull.

Hair grows upward, but gravity makes it fall back down again. Some strands of hair overlap with each other. On short hair, draw the strands in the direction of their growth.

Hair is dense at the roots and then gets finer toward the ends, which are sometimes not drawn. Vary the space between the strands when you are drawing them to give a more realistic effect.

Draw rounded lines following the shape of the skull and remember to leave a certain amount of thickness above the construction lines for the skull.

You can give the strands an impression of lightness by using fluid lines.

Sometimes, in order not to overload the look of the hair, the ends of the hair do not meet.

When the hair is tied back, it is forced to gather in the same place, which appears denser as a result.

To make a character look like they have messy hair, all you have to do is change the direction of one strand of hair as it falls. Remember to give the strands a wavy look to make them more realistic and give them the impression of movement.

HAIR SHAPES AND HAIRCUTS

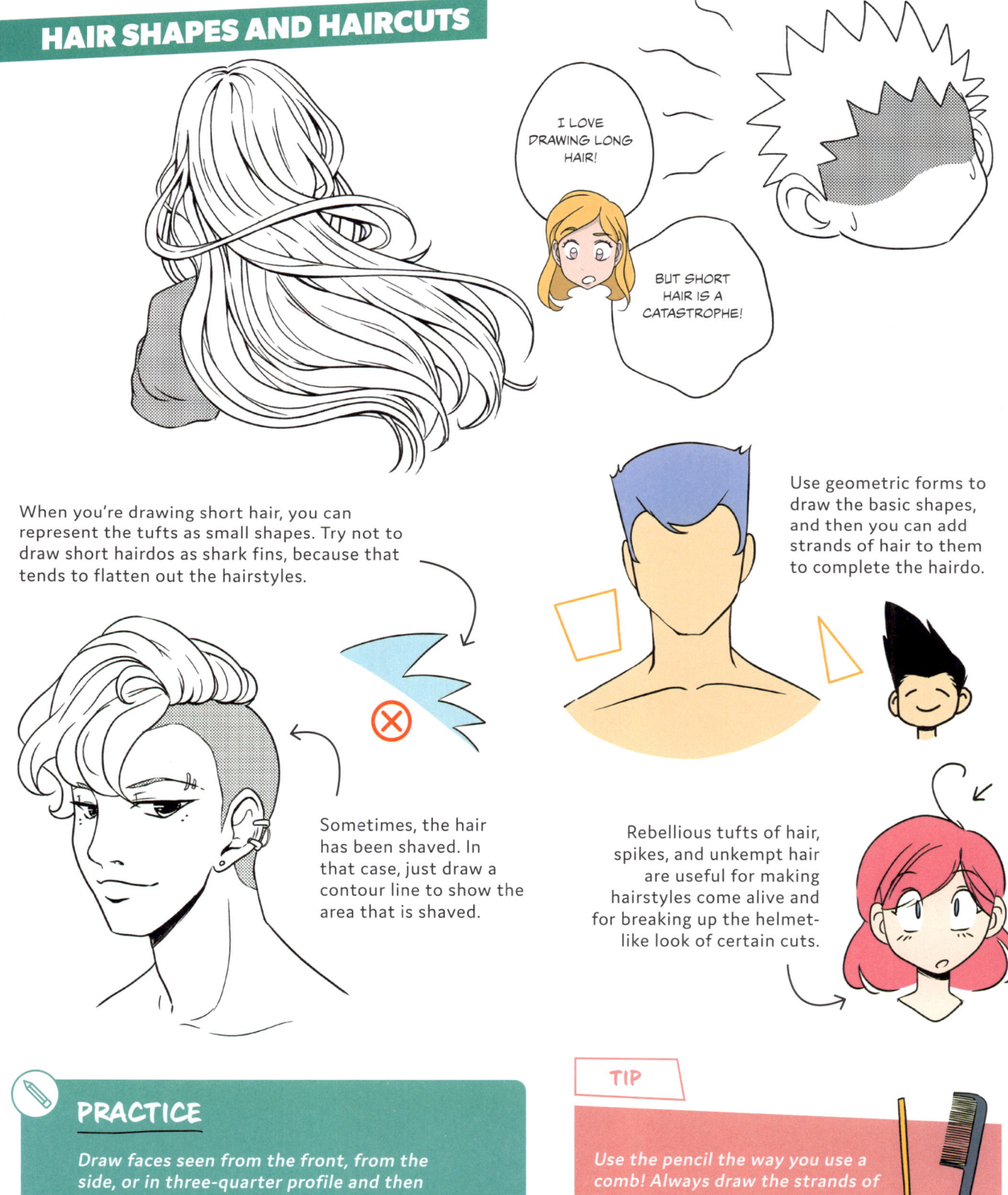

I LOVE DRAWING LONG HAIR!

BUT SHORT HAIR IS A CATASTROPHE!

When you're drawing short hair, you can represent the tufts as small shapes. Try not to draw short hairdos as shark fins, because that tends to flatten out the hairstyles.

Use geometric forms to draw the basic shapes, and then you can add strands of hair to them to complete the hairdo.

Sometimes, the hair has been shaved. In that case, just draw a contour line to show the area that is shaved.

Rebellious tufts of hair, spikes, and unkempt hair are useful for making hairstyles come alive and for breaking up the helmet-like look of certain cuts.

PRACTICE

Draw faces seen from the front, from the side, or in three-quarter profile and then give them hairstyles. Add strands to create unique hairdos.

TIP

Use the pencil the way you use a comb! Always draw the strands of hair starting from their roots and going toward their ends.

THE BODY

Here is a full-length character:

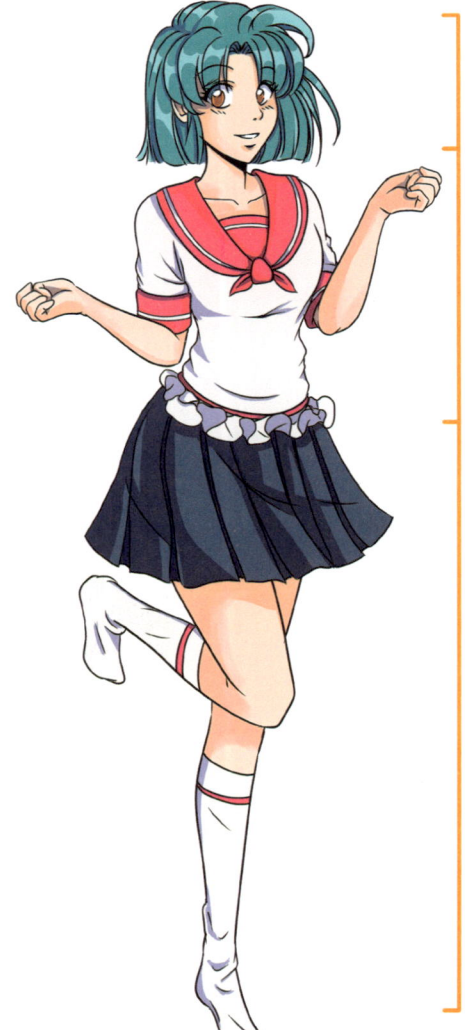

The body is made up of several parts: the head, the torso, and the limbs, whose shape and size vary depending on the character's age, sex, and body type.

If you want to draw a **full-length** character, I suggest that you follow these steps to draw the different parts of the body:
1. The head and neck first
2. Then the torso (the bust and the pelvis)
3. The legs and feet
4. The arms and hands

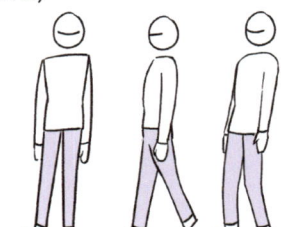

The spine is important because it determines a character's balance and movement.

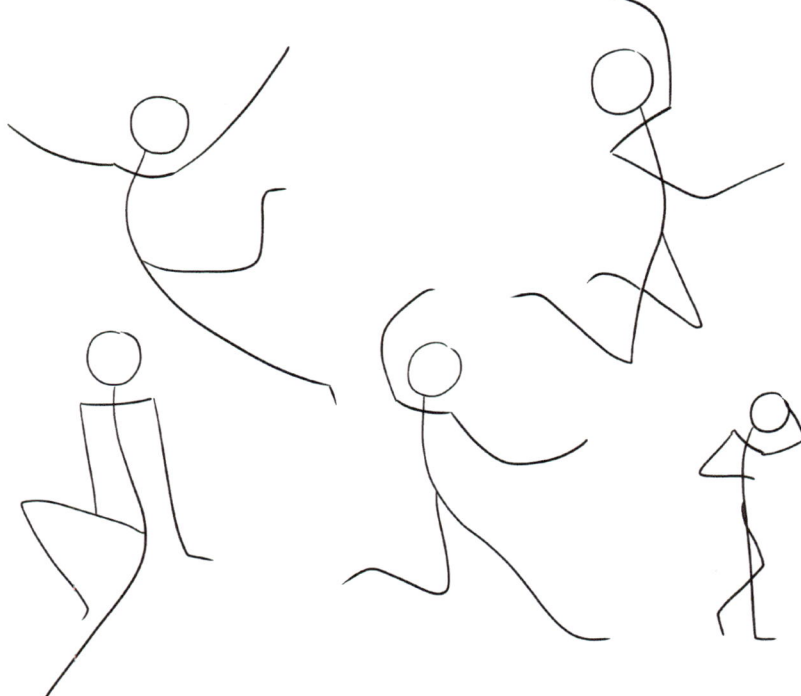

TIP

Are you good at drawing stick figures? Now transform them into string figures! You will find that your characters immediately become more flexible.

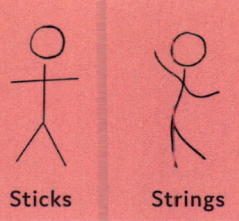

Sticks   Strings

Please Note! Seen from the front, the spine looks straight, but it takes the form of an S-shaped curve when you look at it from the side.

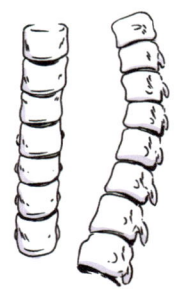

Masculine and feminine bodies have certain morphological differences that allow us to identify them.

Men

- The bones are thicker for a broad stature.
- The rib cage is wide and rectangular.
- The shoulders are 2 times the head height.
- The hips are equal to at least 1 head height.
- The body parts are angular.
- The hips are high and narrow.
- The neck is often as wide as the lower jaw.
- The buttocks are square.

Women

- The bones are thinner.
- The rib cage is in the shape of an upside-down pear.
- The shoulders are 1.5 times the head height.
- The hips are at least 1.5 times the head height.
- The lines of the body are curved.
- The waist is indented.
- The breasts are in the shape of pears.
- The buttocks are rounded.
- The curvature is more pronounced.

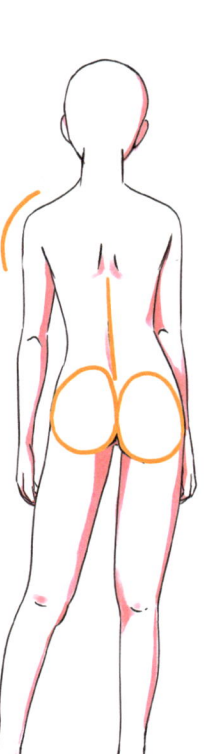
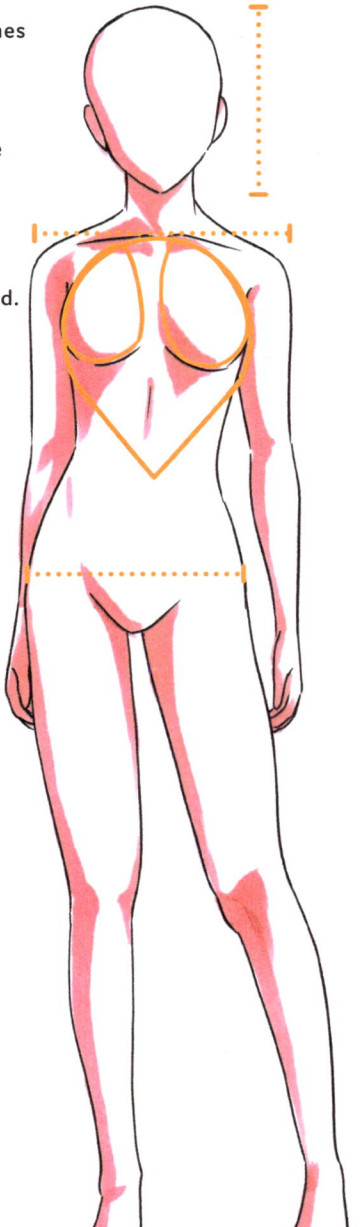
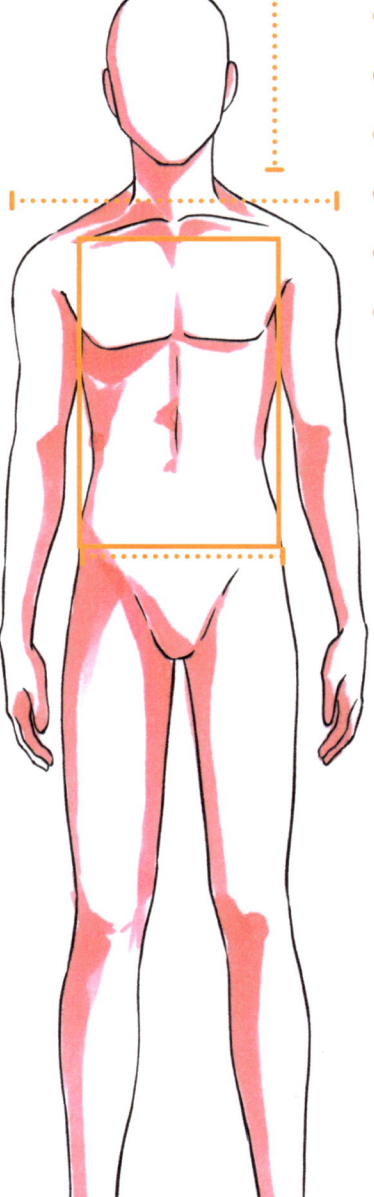
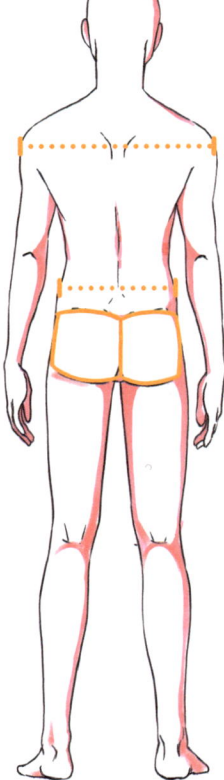

BODILY PROPORTIONS

The head height is most often used as the unit of measurement for determining a person's height based on their age and body type.

As we did with faces, we will first study a body with **canonical** proportions—in other words, proportions that are considered within the norm and aesthetically pleasing. Then we will learn to vary the head-to-body ratio and the size of the limbs in order to draw characters with varied physiques.

Here is a character whose body is 7.5 times the height of his head.

In manga drawings, adult women have a 1:7 head-to-body ratio and adult men have a 1:8 head-to-body ratio. But because the heroes of manga are often younger—for instance, teenagers—their head-to-body ratio is often larger than that.

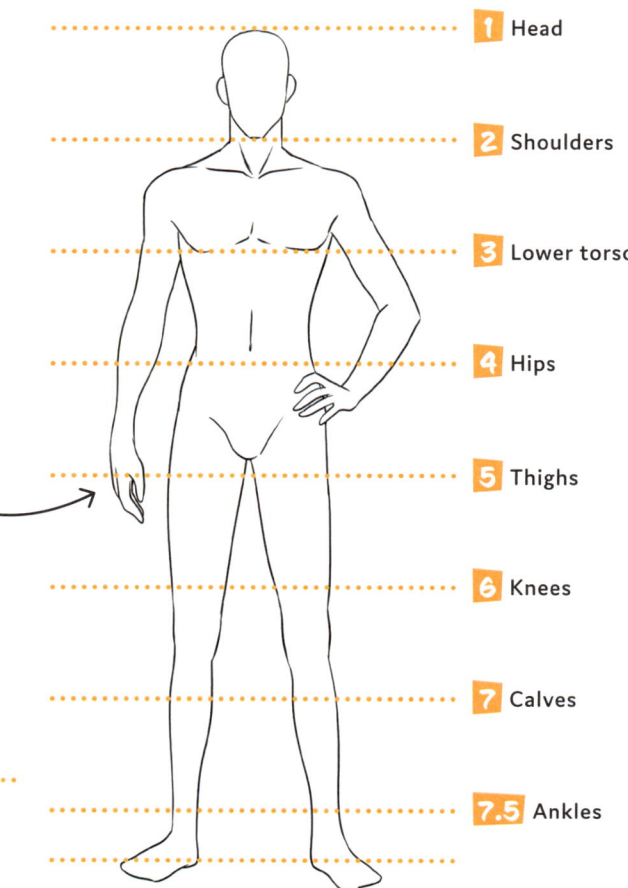

1 Head

2 Shoulders

3 Lower torso

4 Hips

5 Thighs

6 Knees

7 Calves

7.5 Ankles

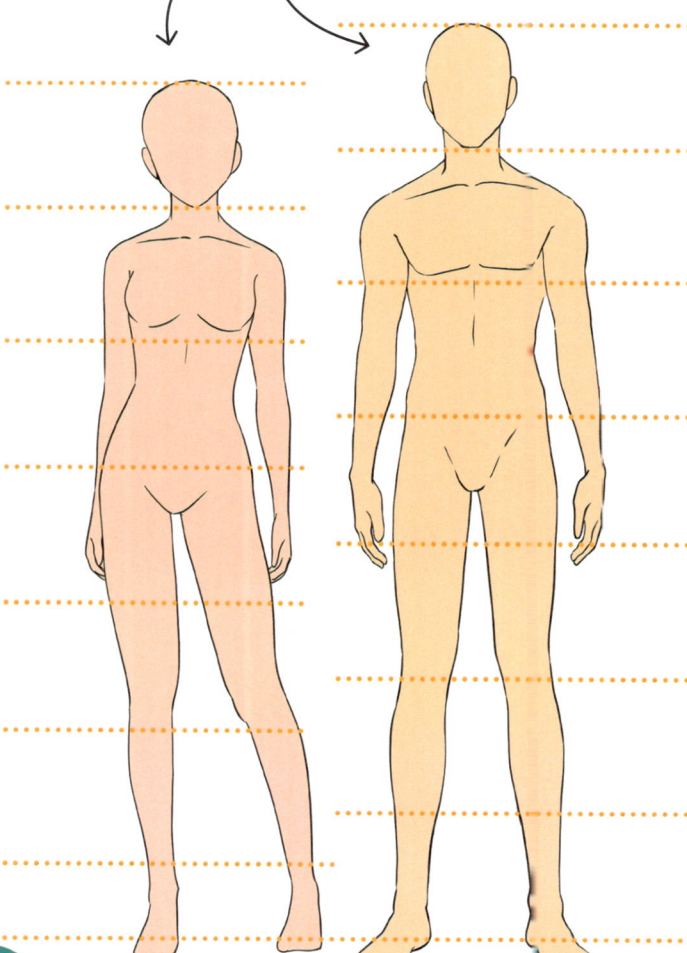

The heads of the characters opposite are the same height, but the woman is represented as being shorter. Her height corresponds to 6.5 head heights and the man's height corresponds to 7 head heights.

You can see that the way to start differentiating your characters is by changing the head-to-body ratio.

> *Be careful to keep the same proportions for each character throughout your manga.*

Here are some tips for drawing well-proportioned bodies.

The head, foot, and forearm are usually all the same length.

The height of the hand corresponds to the height of the face, from the base of the chin to the edge of the forehead.

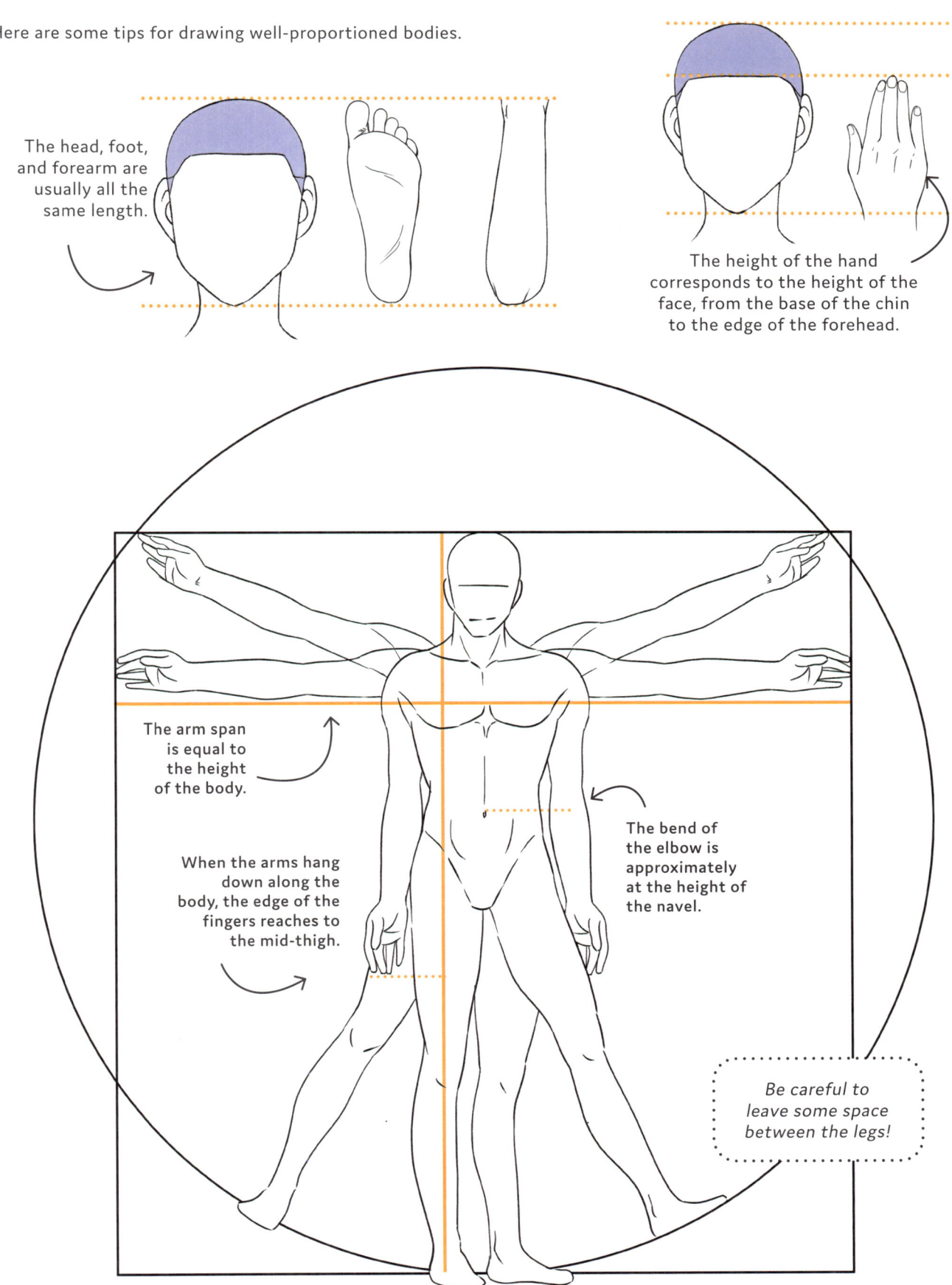

The arm span is equal to the height of the body.

When the arms hang down along the body, the edge of the fingers reaches to the mid-thigh.

The bend of the elbow is approximately at the height of the navel.

Be careful to leave some space between the legs!

Not all characters are the same height, and that's a good thing! Here are some examples of different head-to-body proportions that you might encounter in manga.

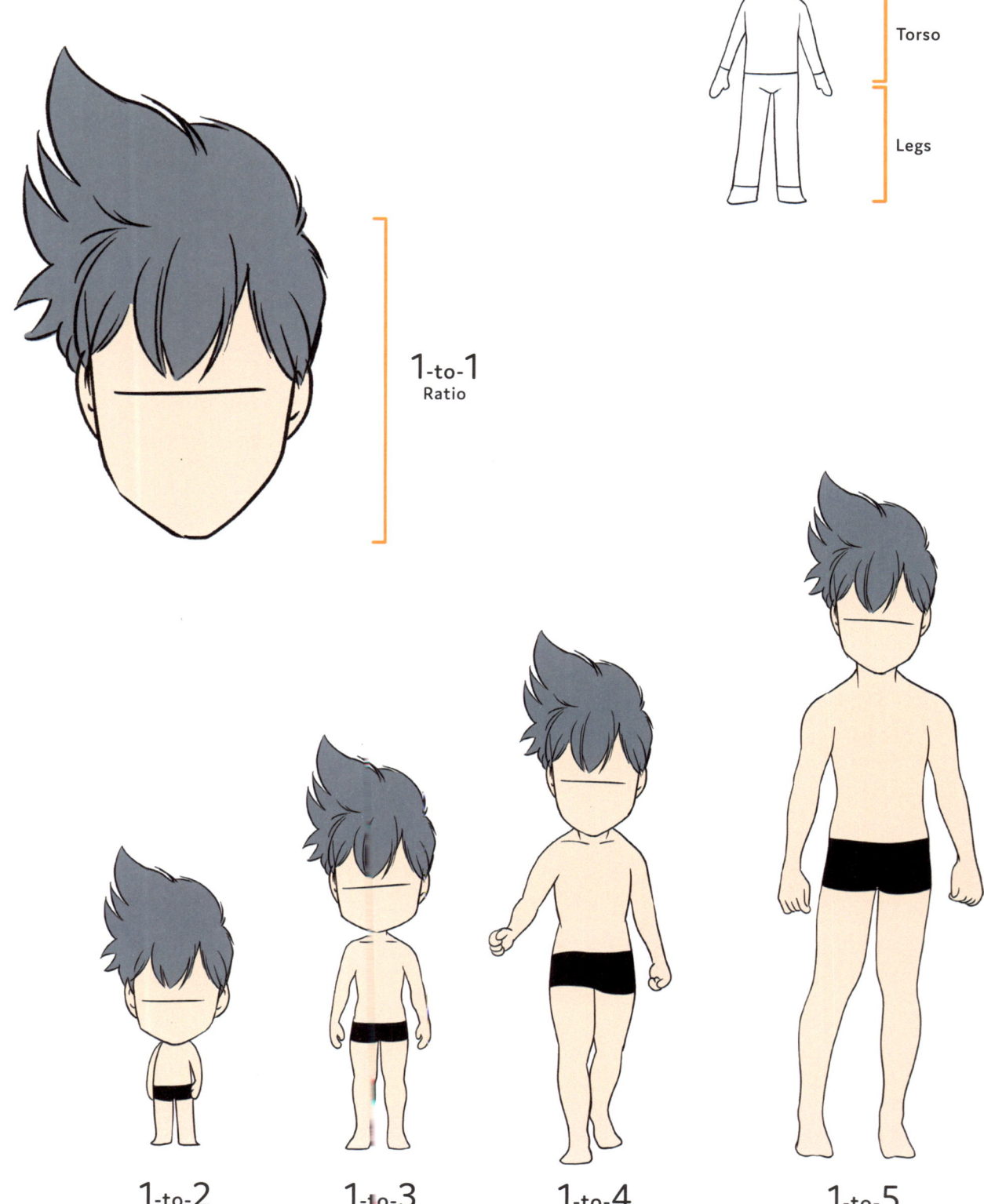

Head

Torso

Legs

1-to-1
Ratio

1-to-2
Ratio

1-to-3
Ratio

1-to-4
Ratio

1-to-5
Ratio

The smaller the head-to-body ratio (in other words, the larger the body gets in proportion to the head), the longer the legs.

1-to-6
Ratio

1-to-7
Ratio

1-to-8
Ratio

1-to-9
Ratio

DRAWING CHARACTERS WITH VARIED PHYSIQUES

People often start by drawing very beautiful characters with perfect physiques, but it is important to vary the body shapes in order to differentiate your characters and make them believable and relatable.

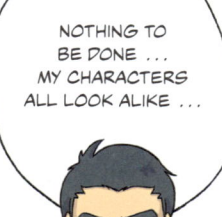

NOTHING TO BE DONE ... MY CHARACTERS ALL LOOK ALIKE ...

To allow your readers to recognize each character at first glance, you can draw them with different head-to-body ratios, but that will not always be enough for people to tell them apart.

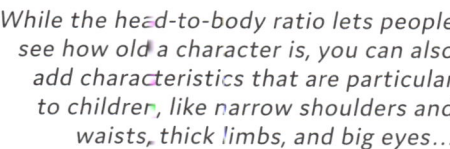

While the head-to-body ratio lets people see how old a character is, you can also add characteristics that are particular to children, like narrow shoulders and waists, thick limbs, and big eyes…

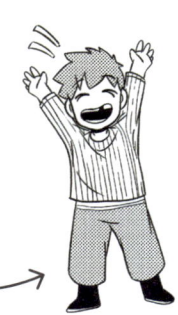
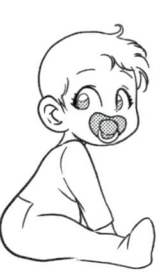

Older people, on the other hand, have longer faces. Their skin sags, giving way to wrinkles.

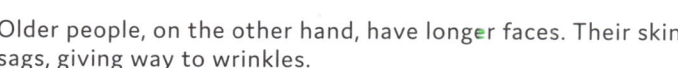

Underweight, or "skeletal," characters tend to share certain characteristics, such as more visible bones (as the term "skeletal" indicates) and more pronounced joints.

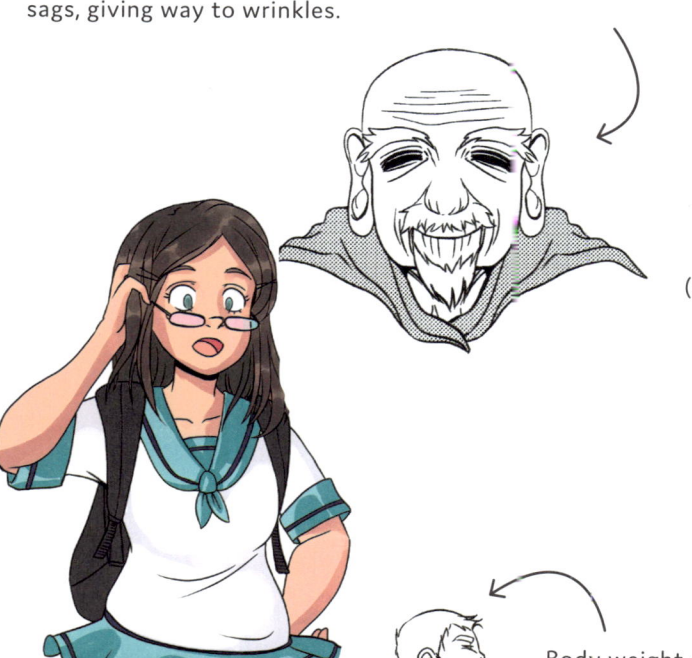

Body weight can be an interesting parameter to change to create different body shapes.

A plumper character will have certain enlarged areas: the stomach, thighs, arms, chin, buttocks, etc.

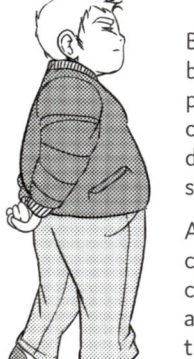

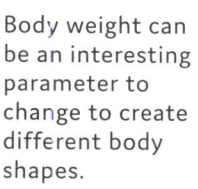

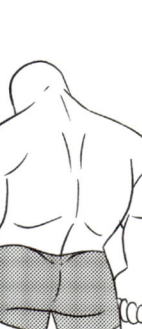

Some characters are very athletic and thus very muscled. To draw them, you have to have a good knowledge of the muscles of the human body and not be afraid to exaggerate them.

Not all characters hold themselves the same way. Their posture is an essential element of their representation.

Varying your characters' postures makes your scenes more realistic and can also, in some cases, convey the personality of the characters you draw.

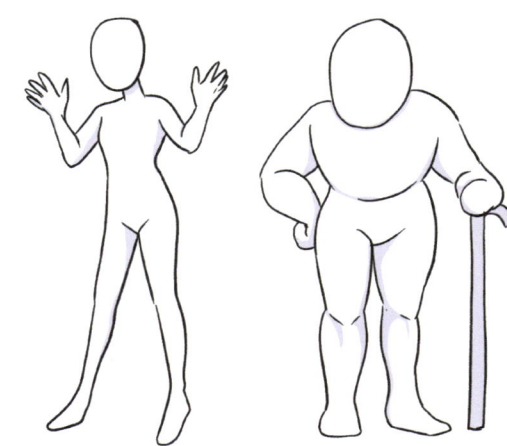

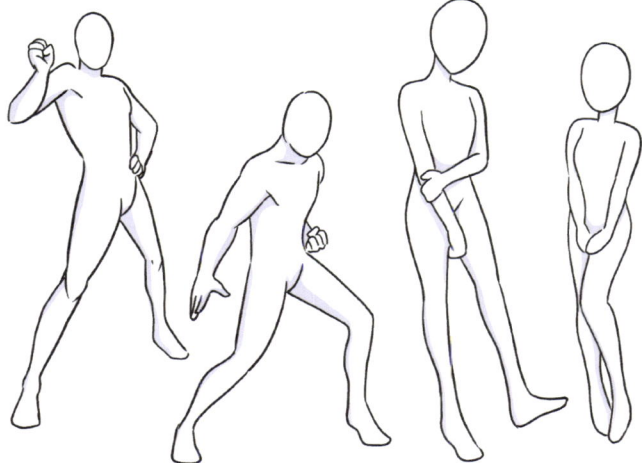

To draw different characters, you can modify several different parameters: the characters' **head-to-body ratio**, their **proportions**, their **body shapes**, and their **posture**.

All of these possible combinations take you further away from classic, canonical beauty and closer to reality.

As we saw for faces, geometric shapes can also serve as a basis for drawing bodies.

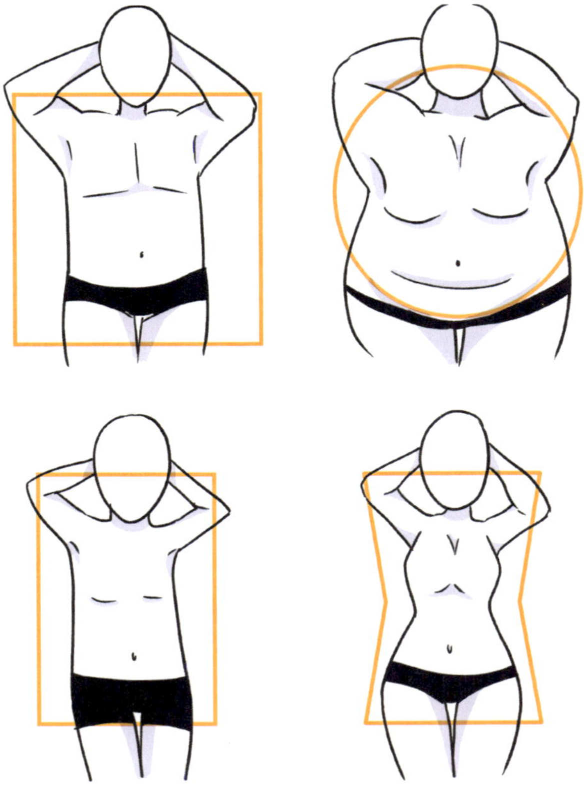

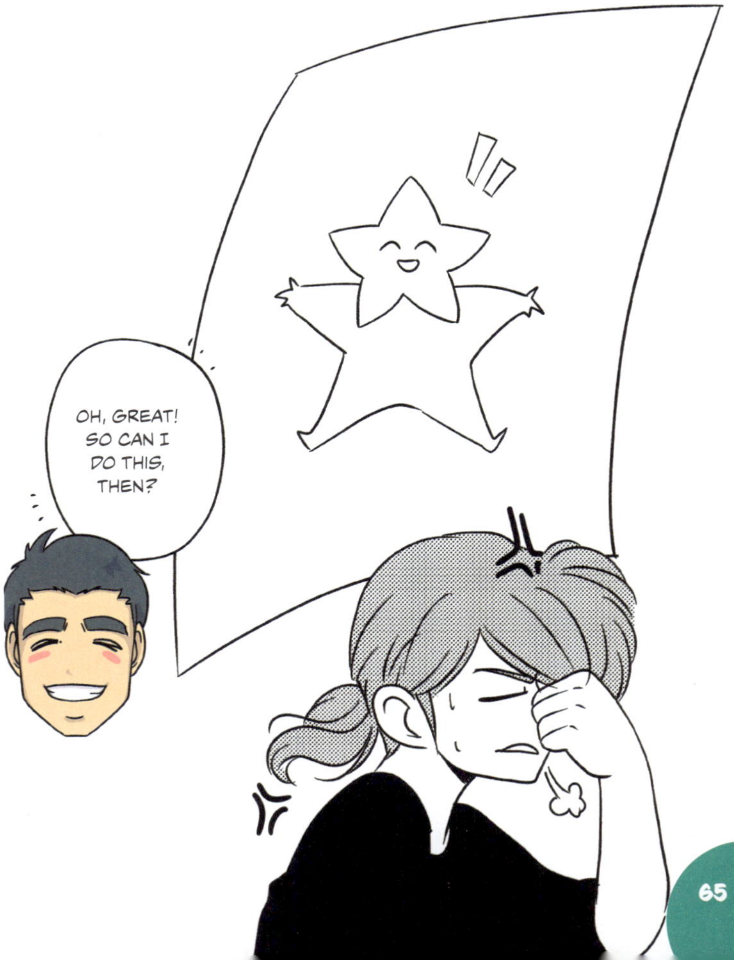

OH, GREAT! SO CAN I DO THIS, THEN?

SKELETON AND MUSCULATURE

While it is possible to simplify the human body by using geometric shapes, I nevertheless suggest that you study the elements it is made up of a little more closely.

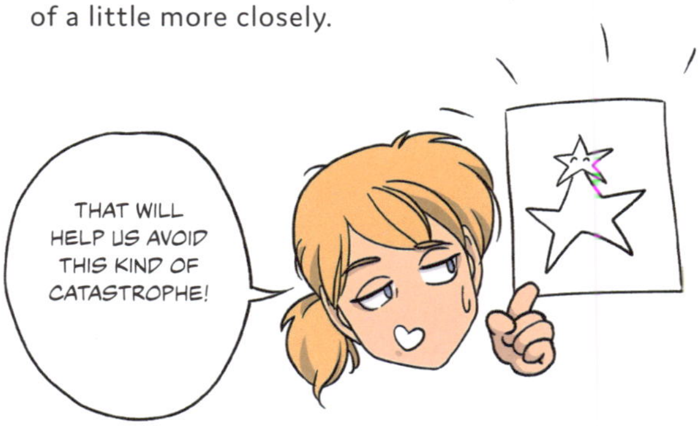

THAT WILL HELP US AVOID THIS KIND OF CATASTROPHE!

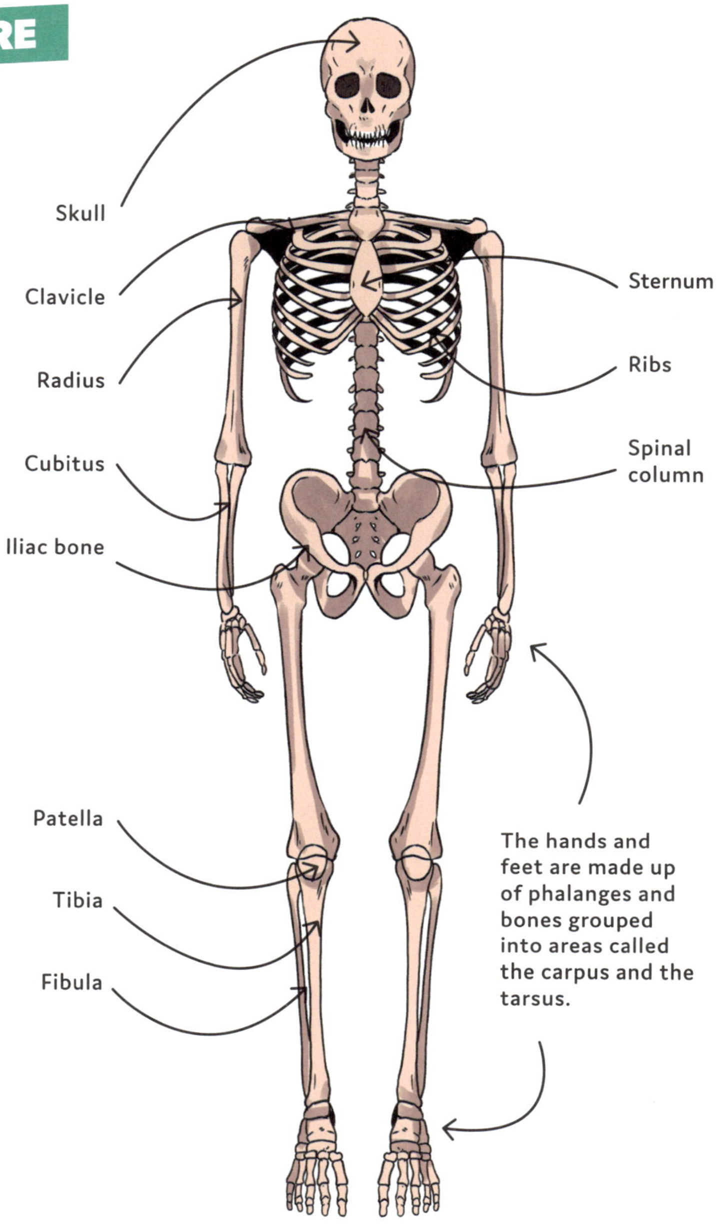

Scapula

Humerus

Coccyx

Femur

Skull

Clavicle

Radius

Cubitus

Iliac bone

Sternum

Ribs

Spinal column

Patella

Tibia

Fibula

The hands and feet are made up of phalanges and bones grouped into areas called the carpus and the tarsus.

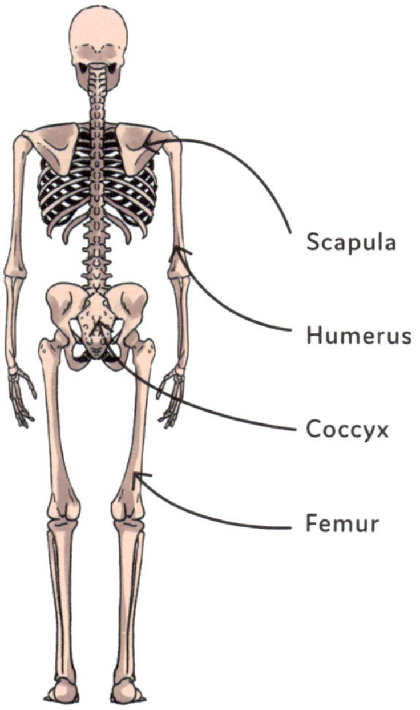

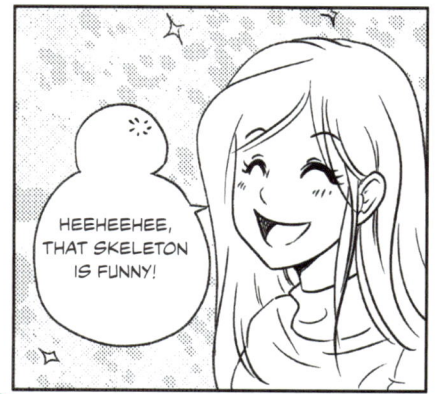

HEEHEEHEE, THAT SKELETON IS FUNNY!

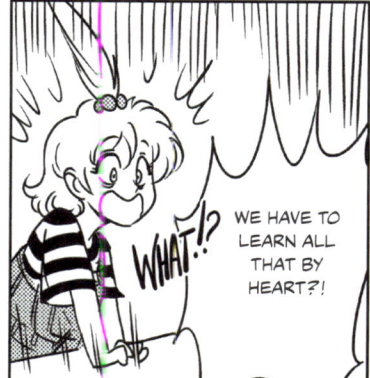

WHAT.!?

WE HAVE TO LEARN ALL THAT BY HEART?!

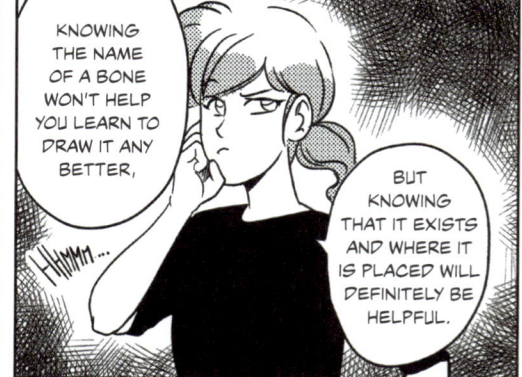

KNOWING THE NAME OF A BONE WON'T HELP YOU LEARN TO DRAW IT ANY BETTER,

HHMMM...

BUT KNOWING THAT IT EXISTS AND WHERE IT IS PLACED WILL DEFINITELY BE HELPFUL.

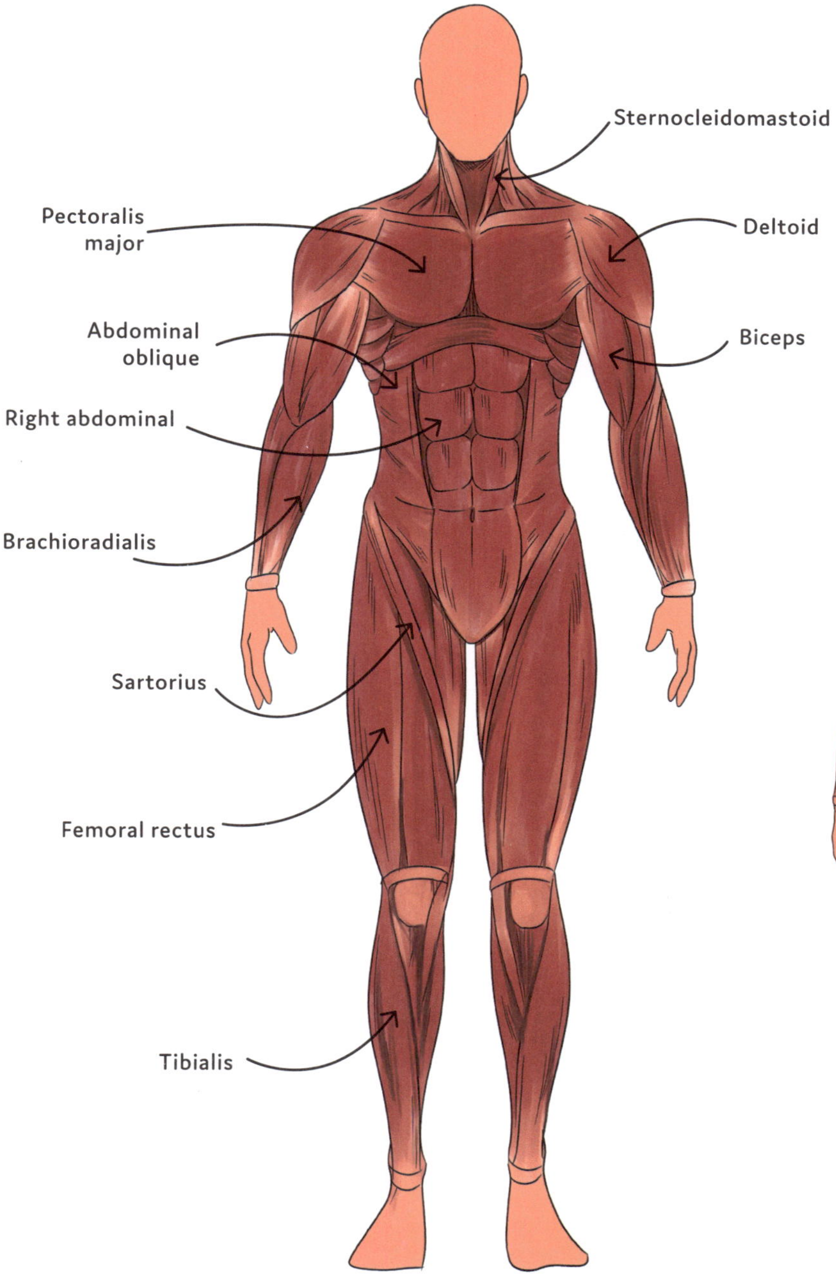

Sternocleidomastoid

Pectoralis
major

Deltoid

Abdominal
oblique

Biceps

Right abdominal

Brachioradialis

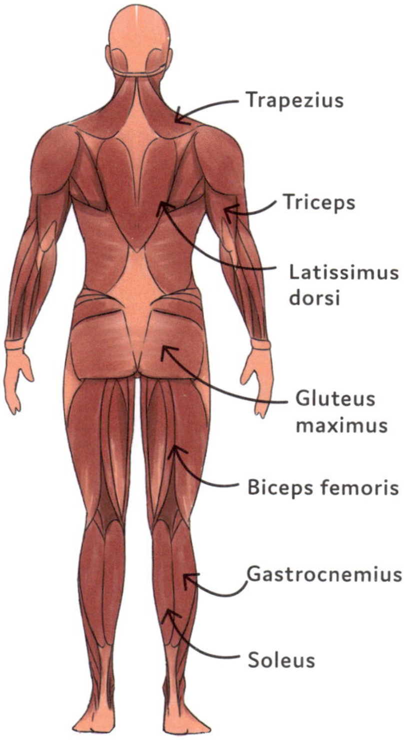

Trapezius

Sartorius

Triceps

Latissimus
dorsi

Femoral rectus

Gluteus
maximus

Biceps femoris

Gastrocnemius

Tibialis

Soleus

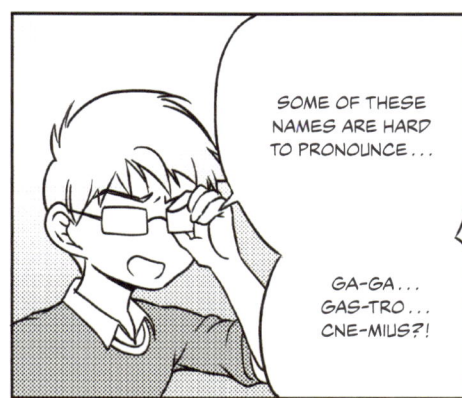

SOME OF THESE NAMES ARE HARD TO PRONOUNCE...

GA-GA... GAS-TRO... CNE-MIUS?!

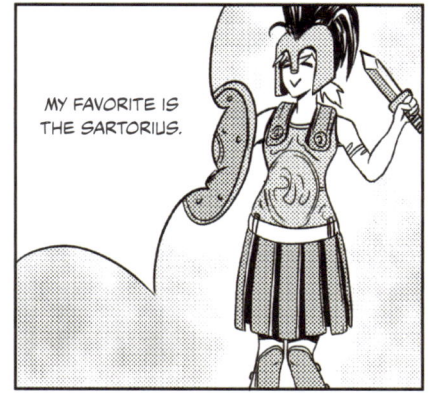

MY FAVORITE IS THE SARTORIUS.

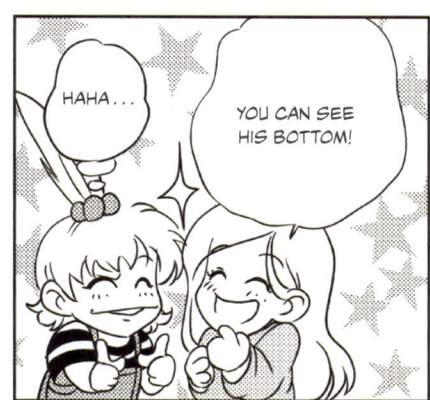

HAHA...

YOU CAN SEE HIS BOTTOM!

Let's take a somewhat closer look at the various parts of the body and what we need to remember about them in order to draw them.

THE TORSO

The prominent muscles of the neck (the sternocleidomastoids) come together at the sternum.

The pectorals are very pronounced in athletes, for example, and almost invisible in younger people who have not yet developed their muscles.

The sternum is connected to the shoulders by the clavicles, which are very easy to see under the skin.

There are six abdominals, which is easy to remember because of their nickname of "six pack."

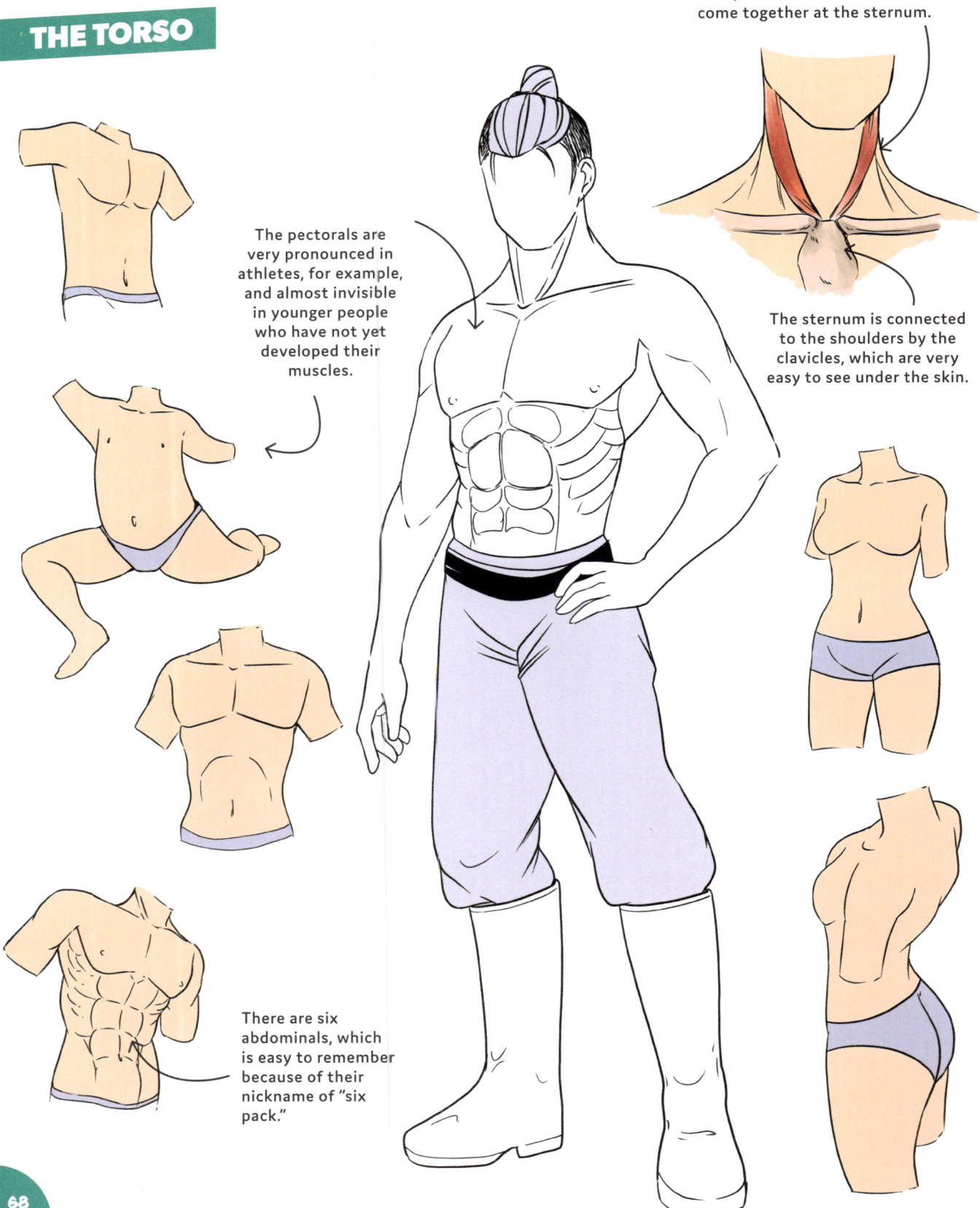

THE BACK

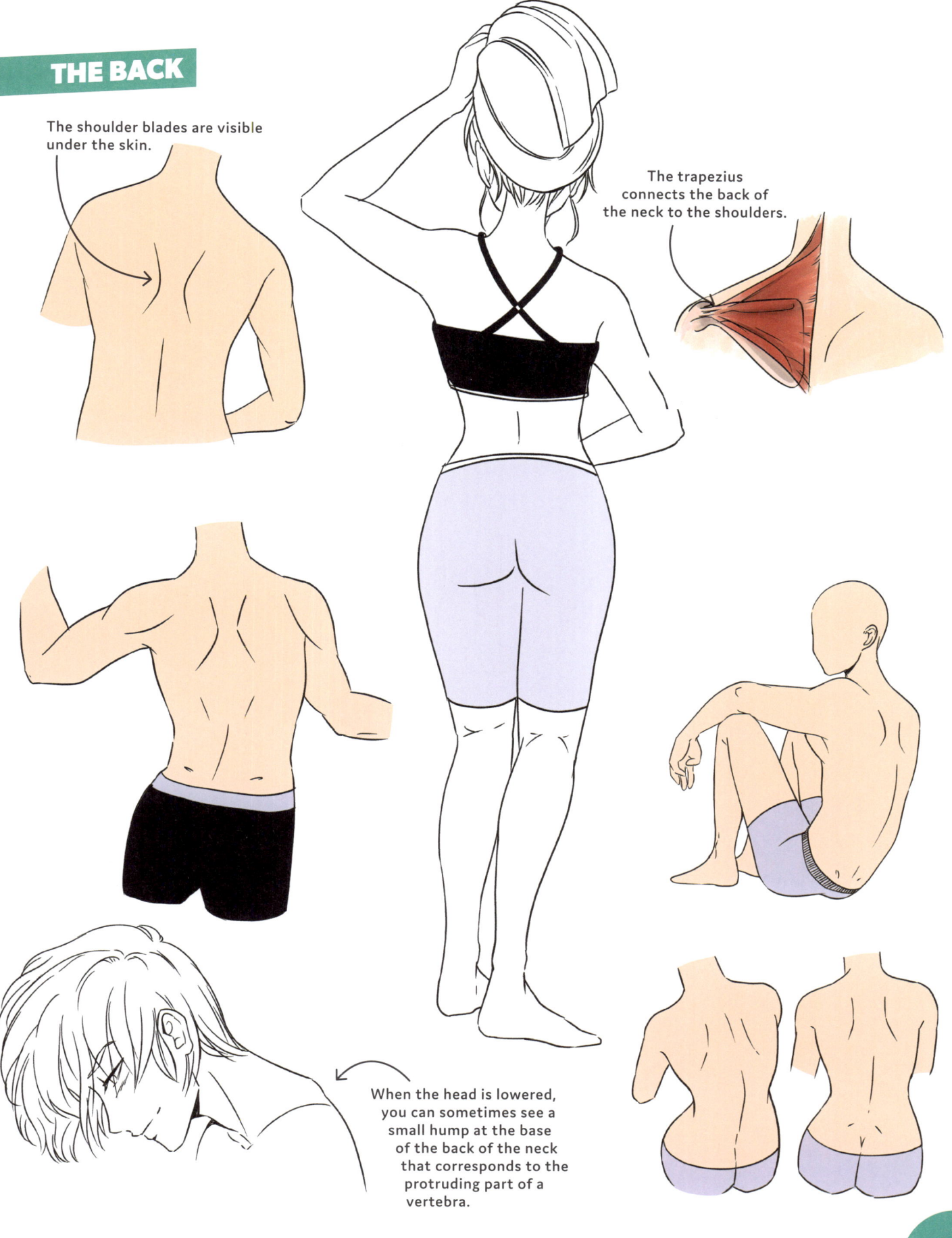

The shoulder blades are visible under the skin.

The trapezius connects the back of the neck to the shoulders.

When the head is lowered, you can sometimes see a small hump at the base of the back of the neck that corresponds to the protruding part of a vertebra.

THE LEGS

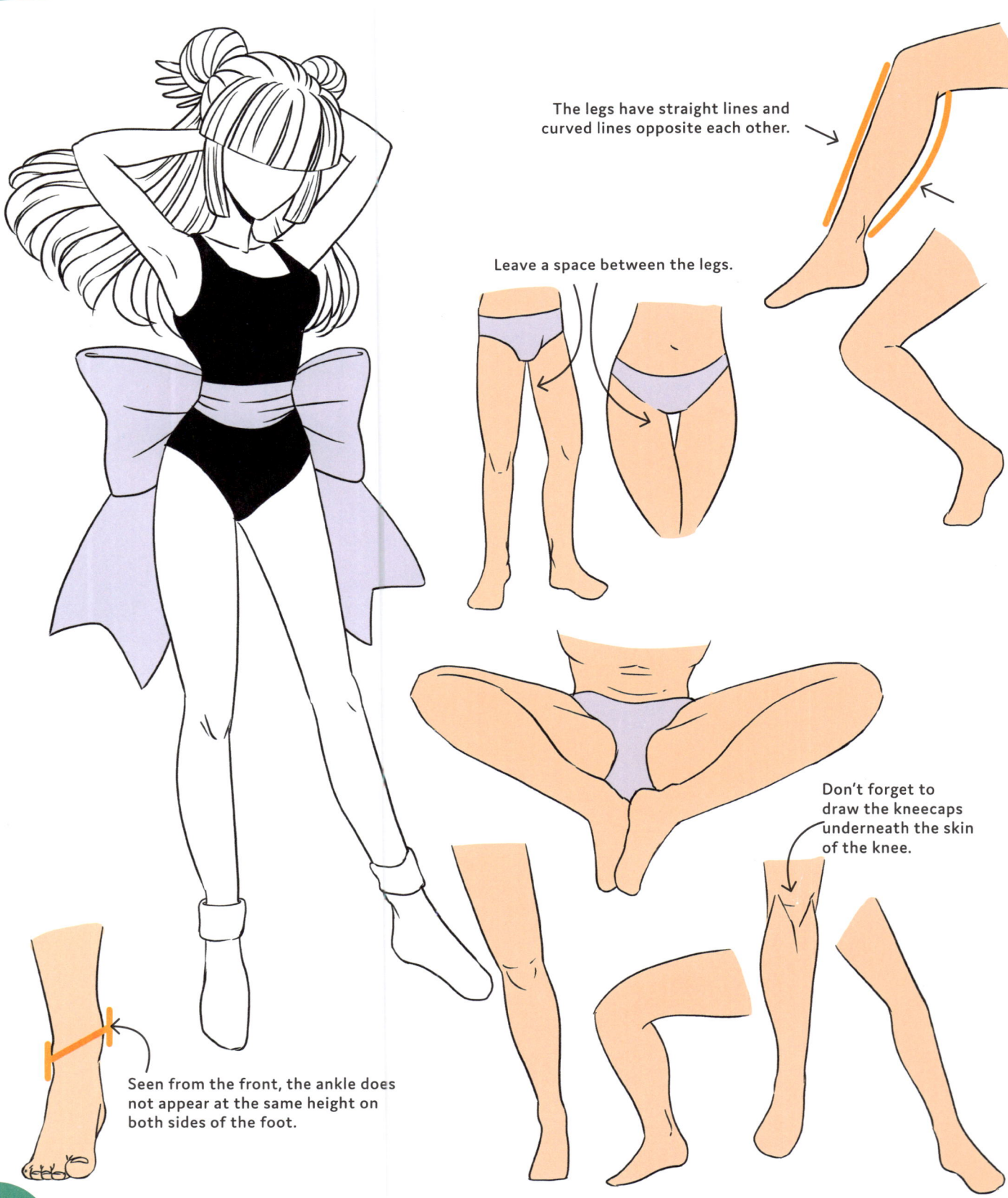

The legs have straight lines and curved lines opposite each other.

Leave a space between the legs.

Don't forget to draw the kneecaps underneath the skin of the knee.

Seen from the front, the ankle does not appear at the same height on both sides of the foot.

THE FEET

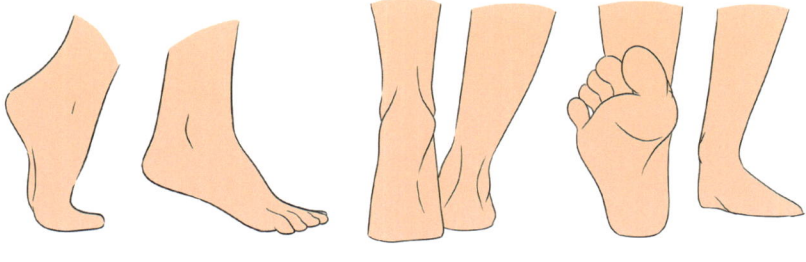

The foot can be broken up into several parts in order to draw it more easily.

We start with the bottom part, where we find the heel, the sole of the foot, and the part where the toes attach. Then we can add the toes. The big toe is the widest toe and has only two phalanges, while the other toes each have three.

The top of the foot is slightly rounded. It roughly follows the shape of a trapezoid to where it joins the ankle.

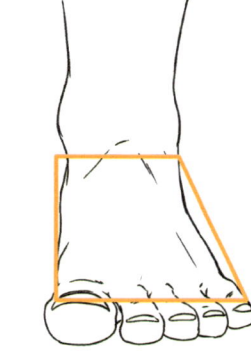

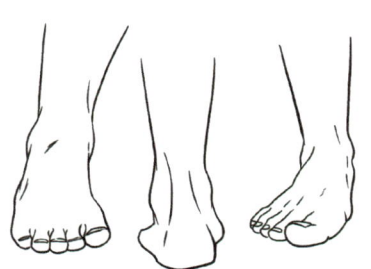

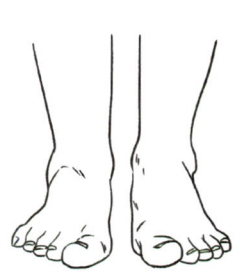

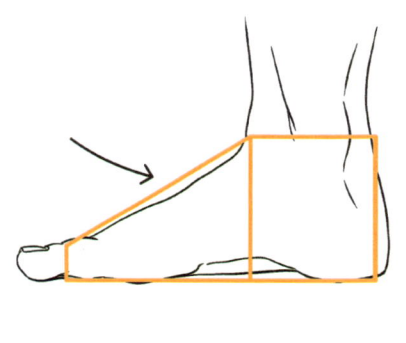

The foot and the knee are the same width.

The foot is wider than the ankle.

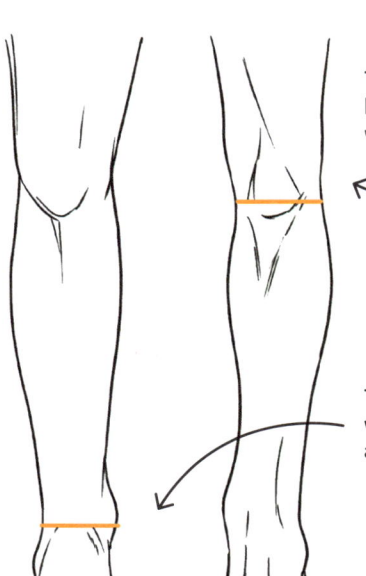

The toes fit into the arc of a circle that can be drawn above them in order to establish the length of each toe.

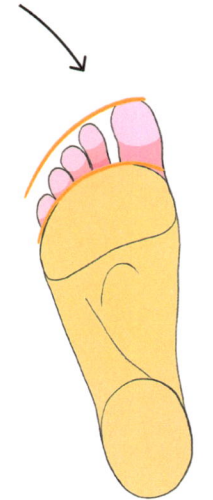

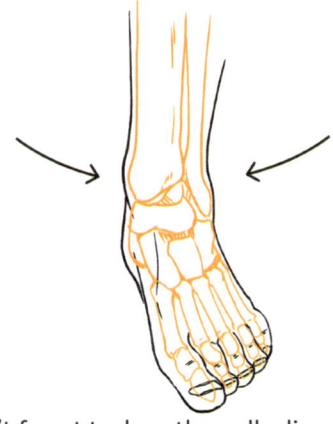

Don't forget to draw the malleoli, which are at the ends of the tibia and the fibula. These two bones are very prominent.

THE ARMS

The upper limbs are seen more often in manga than the lower limbs.

Observe carefully how they are articulated.

The deltoid covers the pectoralis major, which passes over the biceps.

The arm is seen either foreshortened or elongated, depending on the pose.

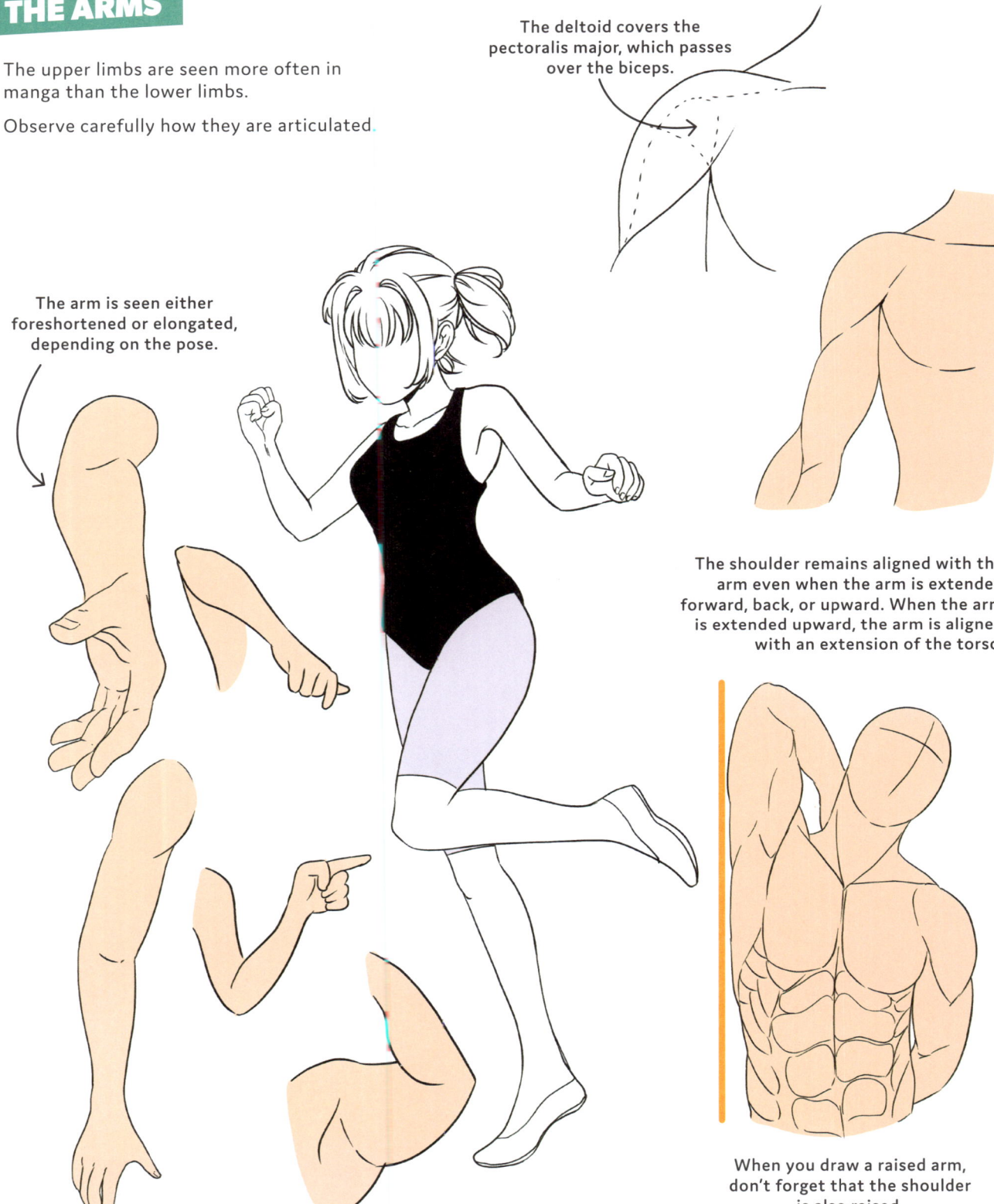

The shoulder remains aligned with the arm even when the arm is extended forward, back, or upward. When the arm is extended upward, the arm is aligned with an extension of the torso.

When you draw a raised arm, don't forget that the shoulder is also raised.

THE HANDS

The hand can be broken up into three parts: the palm, the thumb, and the four fingers, from the index finger to the pinky finger.

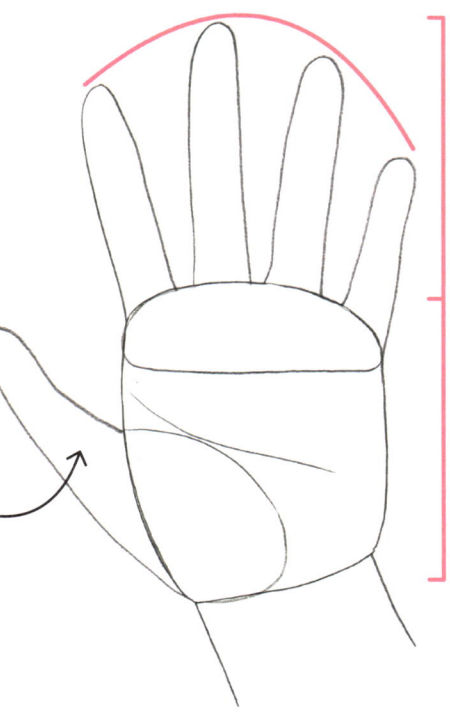

The height of the four fingers taken together is equal to the height of the palm. But the individual fingers are not all the same length. As with the toes, their length follows a curve.

The thumb is the widest finger; its attachment point is at the base of the palm, near the wrist.

The phalanges make it possible to bend the fingers. The thumb has two visible phalanges, while the other fingers each have three.

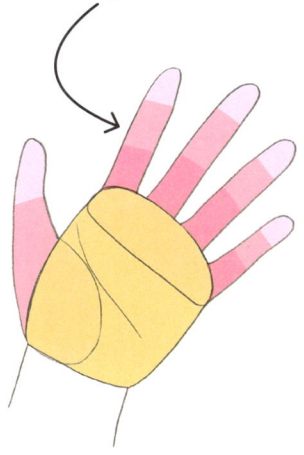

The nails make up half of the last phalanx.

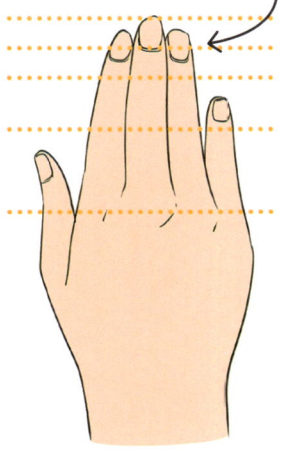

At rest, the fingers are slightly bent.

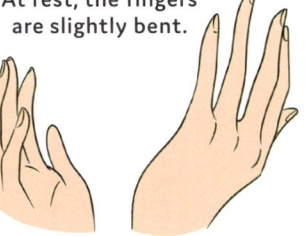

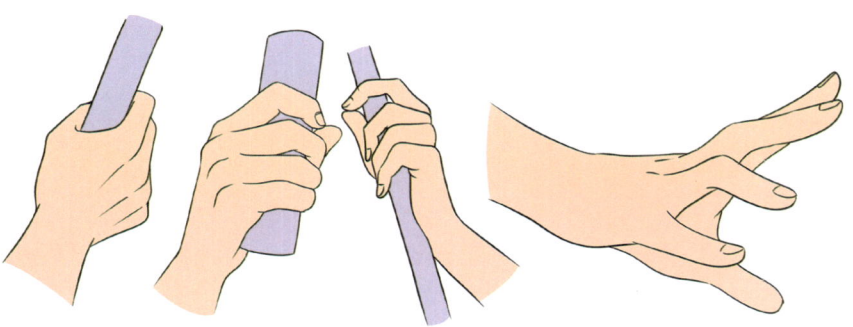

TIP

Whatever position the hand is in, always draw it in this order: first the palm, then the zones where the fingers are attached, and then the fingers themselves.

73

CHIBI CHARACTERS

Chibi are small, distorted characters that are super cute!

Their body can be equal to about one or two times their head height. They have simplified and exaggerated attributes, like caricatures, which makes them look childish and cute.

Their faces are often very expressive. Their hands are smaller and less detailed.

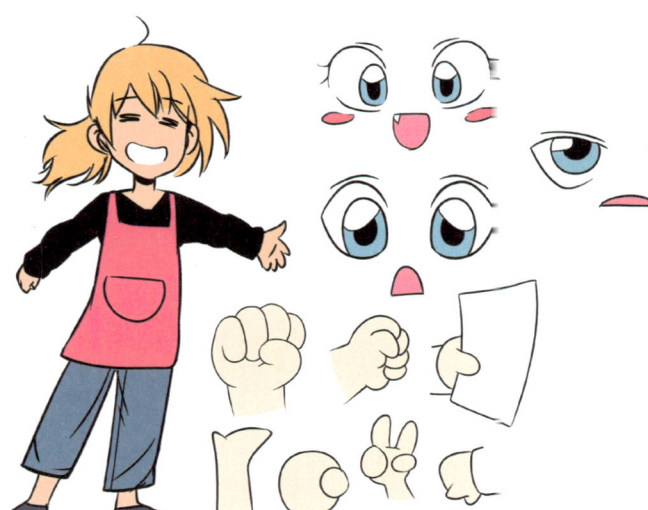

Sometimes, chibi features are used to make a character or a scene funny. In that case, most of the elements are exaggerated.

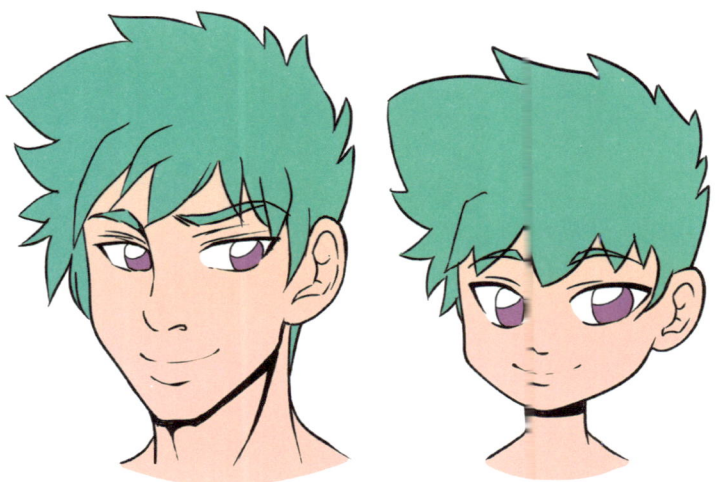

Sometimes, some of the principal or secondary characters are represented as chibi throughout the story. This graphic choice **accentuates the character's childlike or inferior status**.

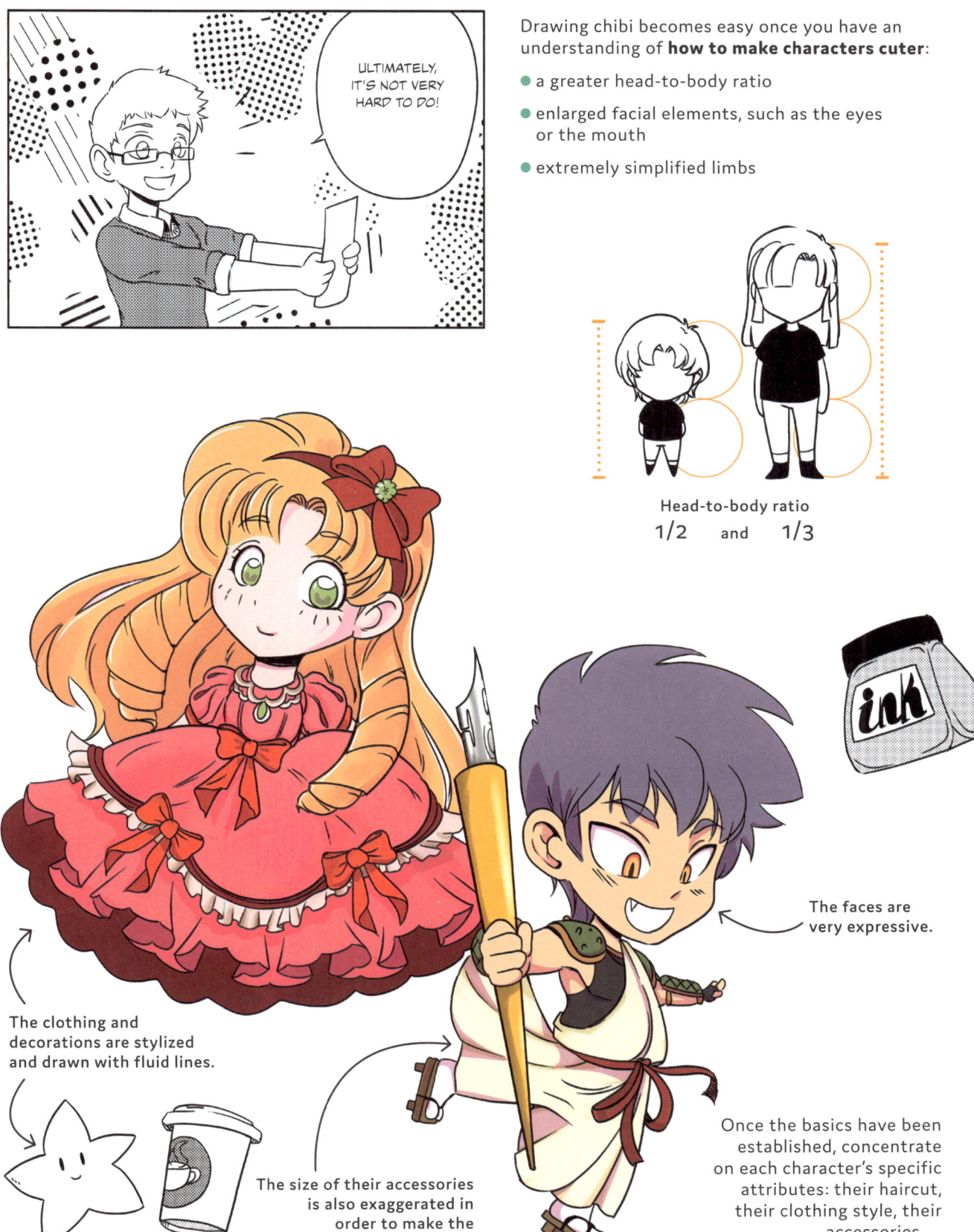

ULTIMATELY, IT'S NOT VERY HARD TO DO!

Drawing chibi becomes easy once you have an understanding of **how to make characters cuter**:

- a greater head-to-body ratio
- enlarged facial elements, such as the eyes or the mouth
- extremely simplified limbs

Head-to-body ratio
1/2   and   1/3

The clothing and decorations are stylized and drawn with fluid lines.

The size of their accessories is also exaggerated in order to make the characters stand out.

The faces are very expressive.

Once the basics have been established, concentrate on each character's specific attributes: their haircut, their clothing style, their accessories . . .

ANTHROPOMORPHS

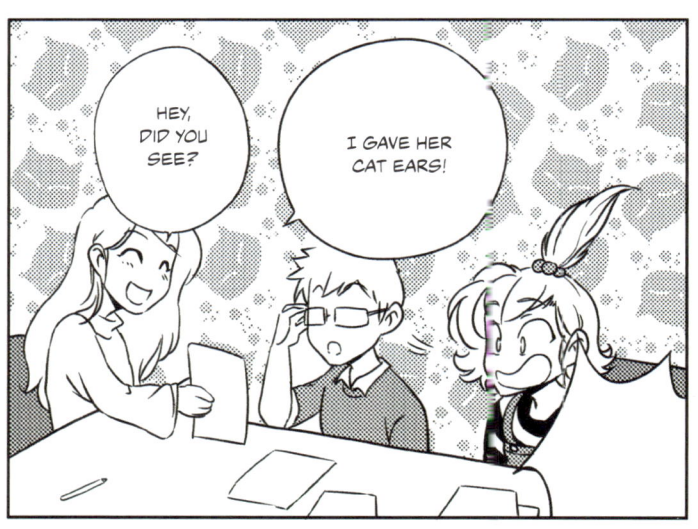

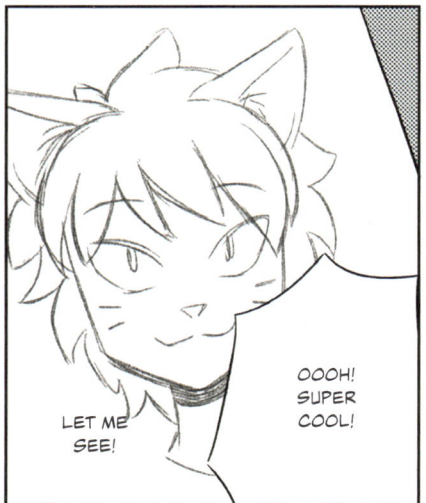

When you give a human form to an animal, an object, or a concept, we call it anthropomorphism.

You'll often find characters with animal features in manga. They're called **kemonomimis**.

The animal attributes can be subtle, like cat whiskers or cat ears; or, on the contrary, they can be an important part of how the character is represented.

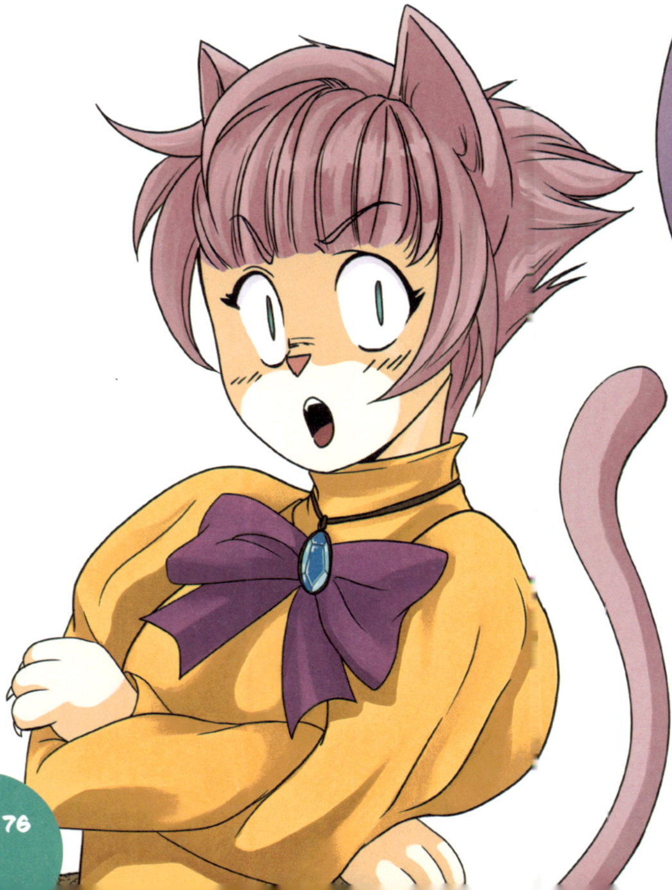

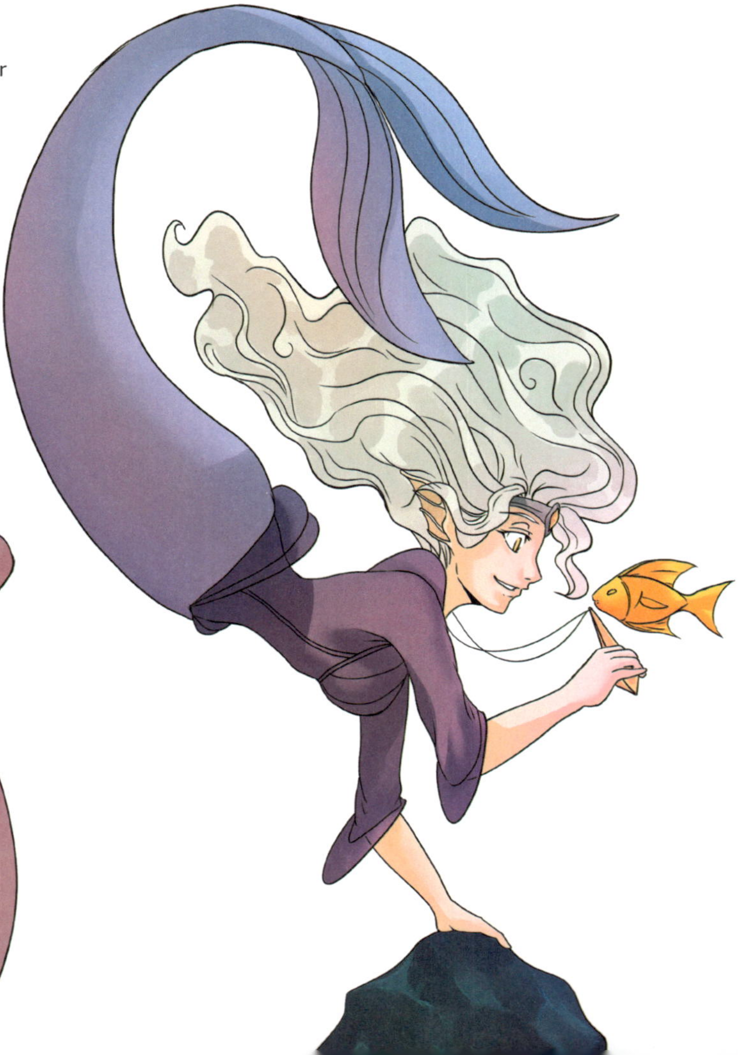

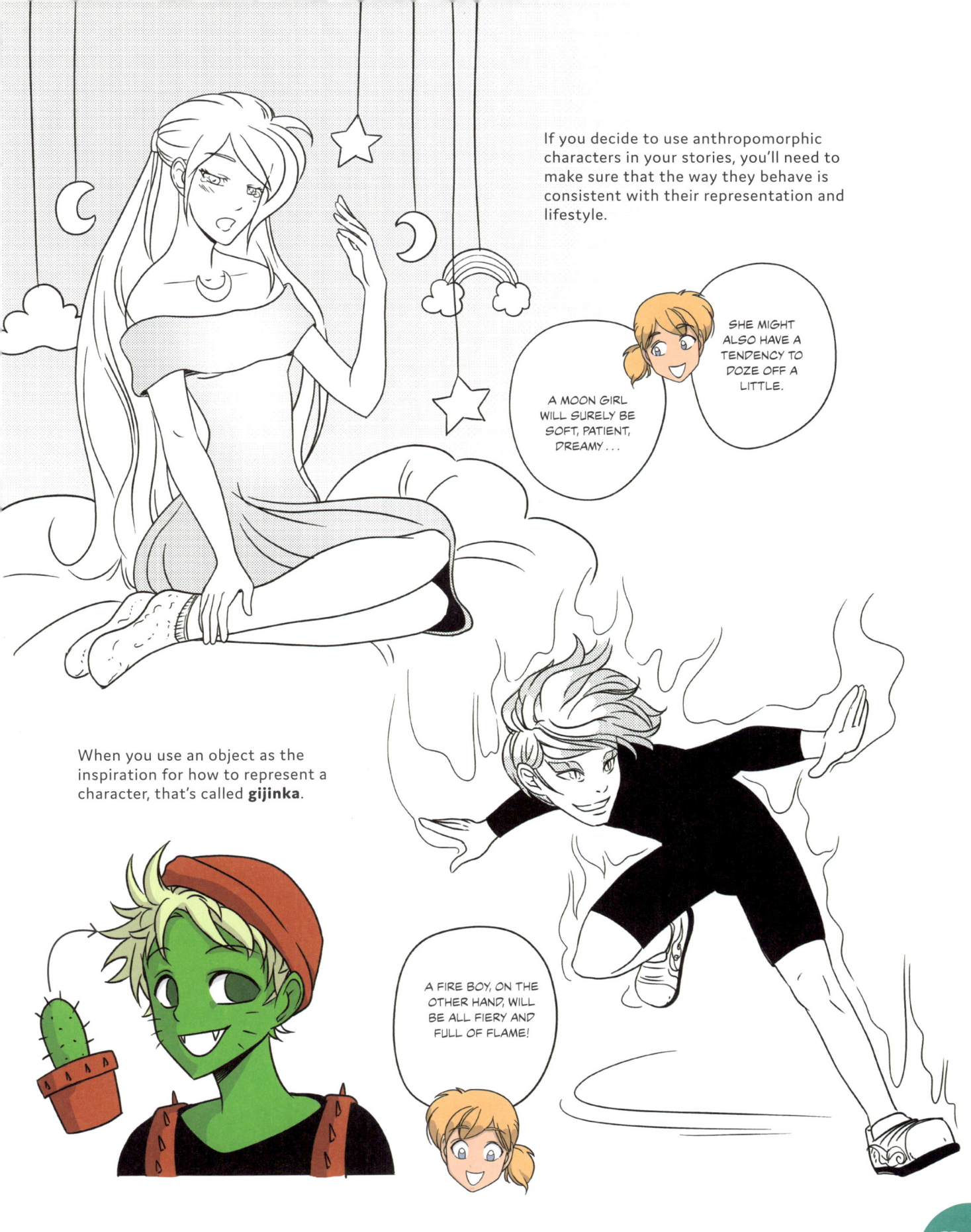

If you decide to use anthropomorphic characters in your stories, you'll need to make sure that the way they behave is consistent with their representation and lifestyle.

SHE MIGHT ALSO HAVE A TENDENCY TO DOZE OFF A LITTLE.

A MOON GIRL WILL SURELY BE SOFT, PATIENT, DREAMY . . .

When you use an object as the inspiration for how to represent a character, that's called **gijinka**.

A FIRE BOY, ON THE OTHER HAND, WILL BE ALL FIERY AND FULL OF FLAME!

Characters that are half-human and half-machine are called **mechas**. Their robotic attributes may be visible to a greater or lesser degree.

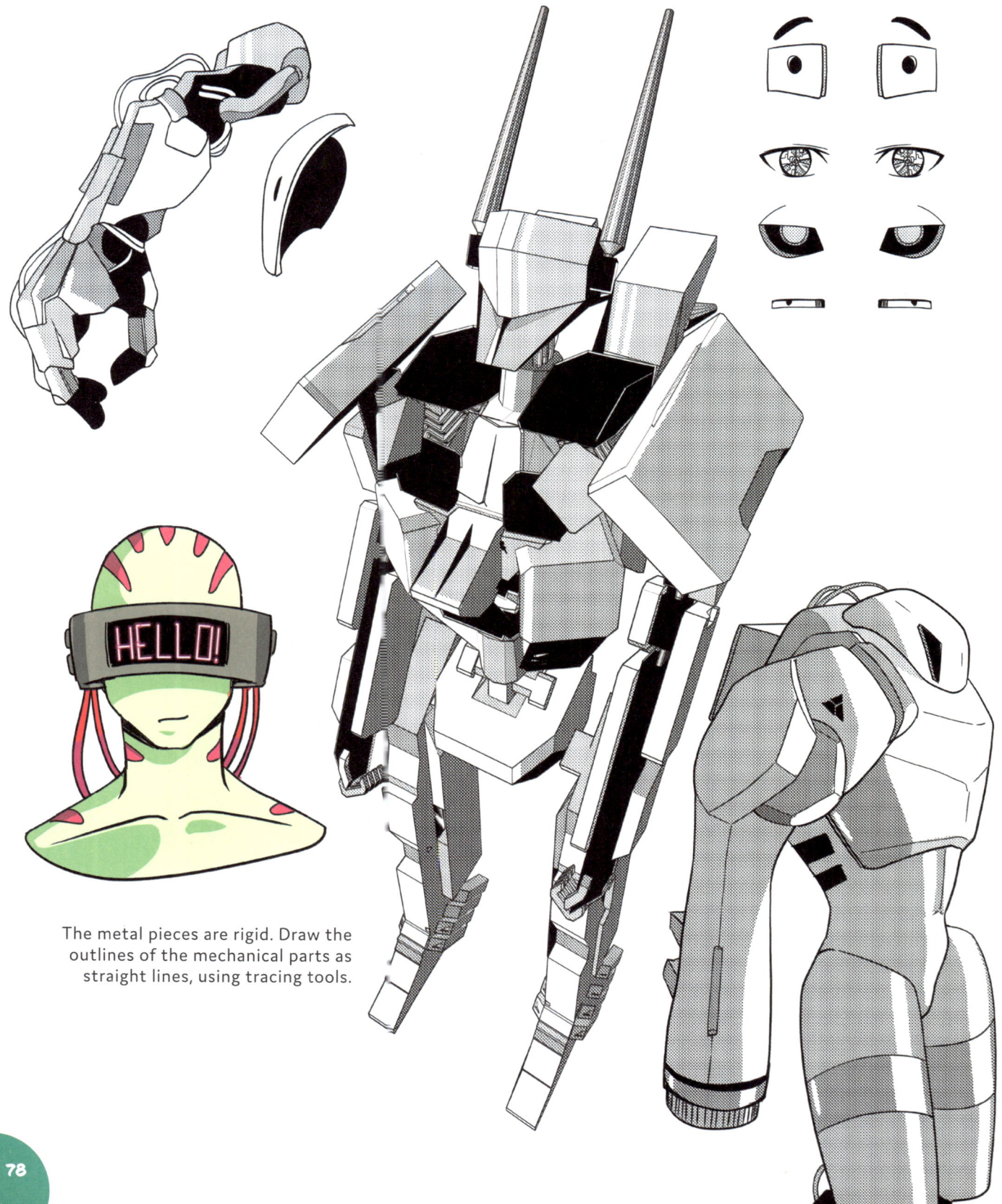

The metal pieces are rigid. Draw the outlines of the mechanical parts as straight lines, using tracing tools.

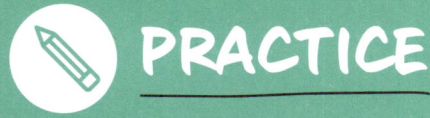 # PRACTICE

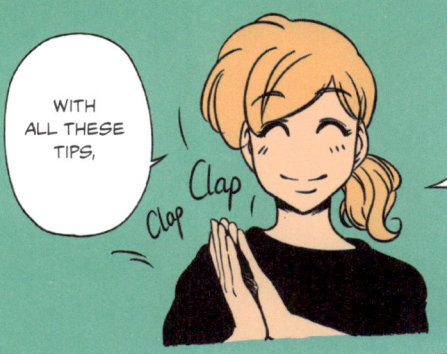

WITH ALL THESE TIPS,

Clap Clap

YOU WILL BE ABLE TO DRAW ALL OF THE CHARACTERS THAT YOU HAVE IN MIND.

Full-Length Characters

Draw the same character with different head-to-body ratios using the models on pages 62–63.

Draw several horizontal lines about an inch apart. This spacing corresponds to the head height of your future character.

Varied Physiques

Use the same guidelines as in the previous exercise. On the same page, draw several different characters with varied physiques: young, old, thin, round, muscled, short, tall...

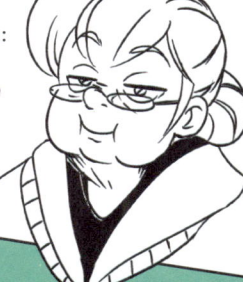

Chibi

Because the body of a chibi is about two or three times as tall as its head, draw two or three circles stacked vertically, then draw the different parts of the character, exaggerating the size and appearance of the elements of the face and body as much as possible.

Anthropomorphic Characters

Once you feel comfortable with the different shapes a body can have, you can give your character either animal or conceptual characteristics. Invent your own anthropomorphic characters.

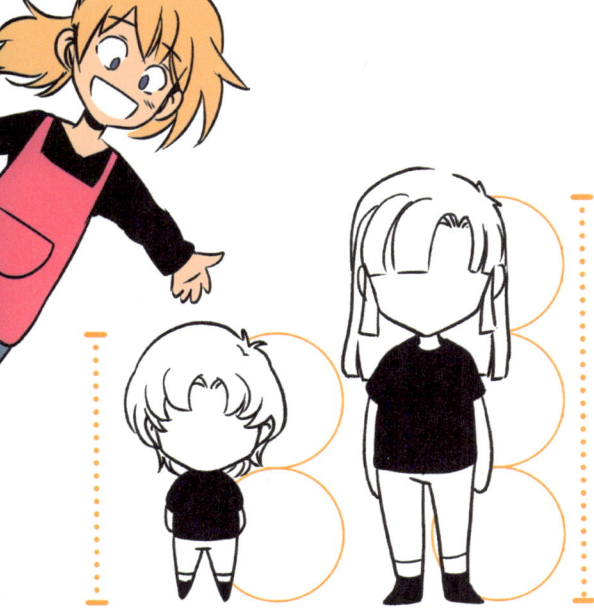

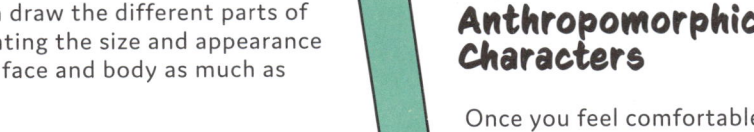

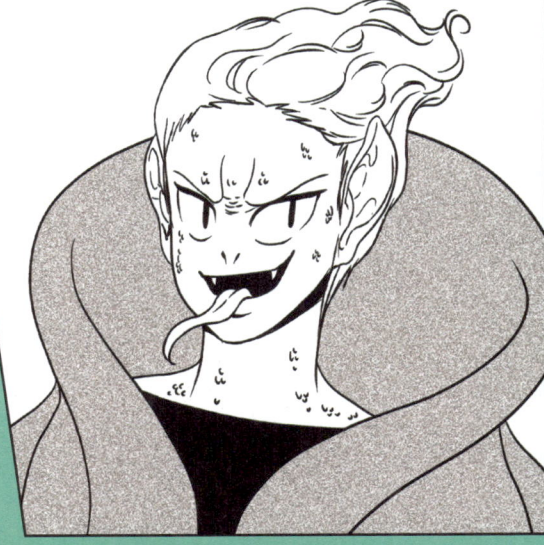

THE BODY IN MOTION

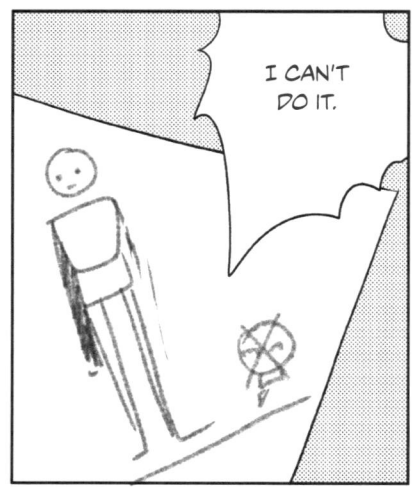

I CAN'T DO IT.

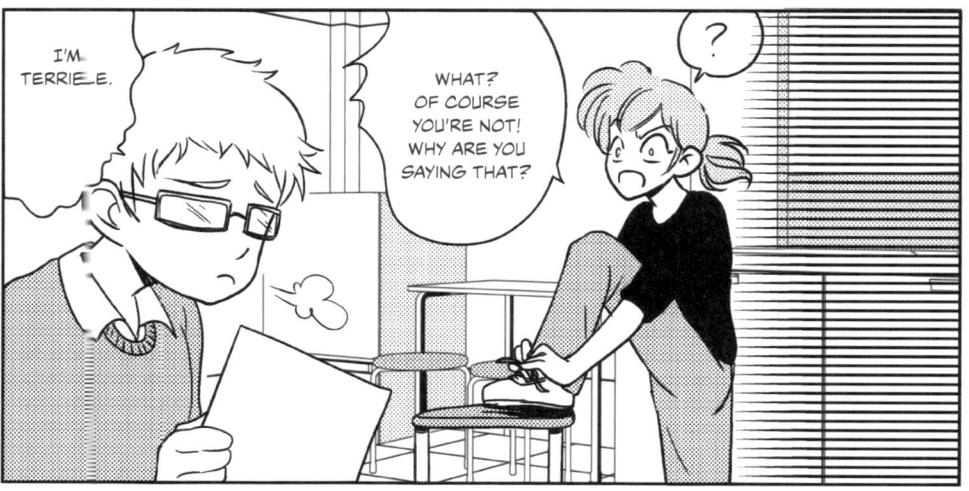

I'M TERRIBLE.

WHAT? OF COURSE YOU'RE NOT! WHY ARE YOU SAYING THAT?

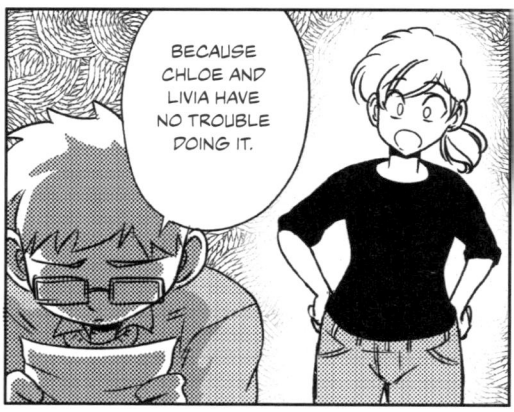

BECAUSE CHLOE AND LIVIA HAVE NO TROUBLE DOING IT.

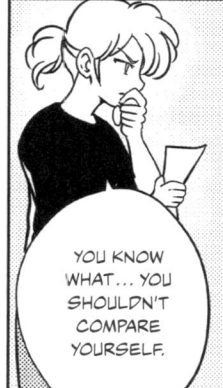

YOU KNOW WHAT... YOU SHOULDN'T COMPARE YOURSELF.

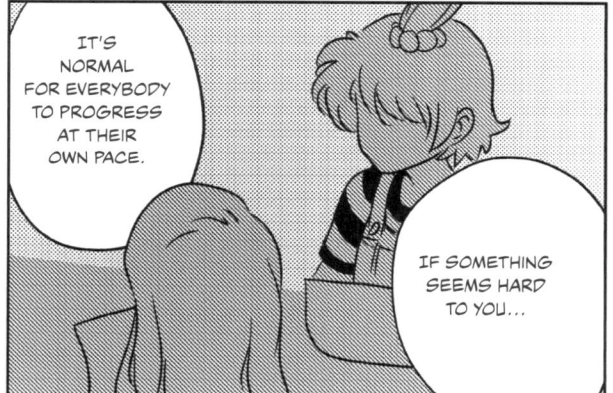

IT'S NORMAL FOR EVERYBODY TO PROGRESS AT THEIR OWN PACE.

IF SOMETHING SEEMS HARD TO YOU...

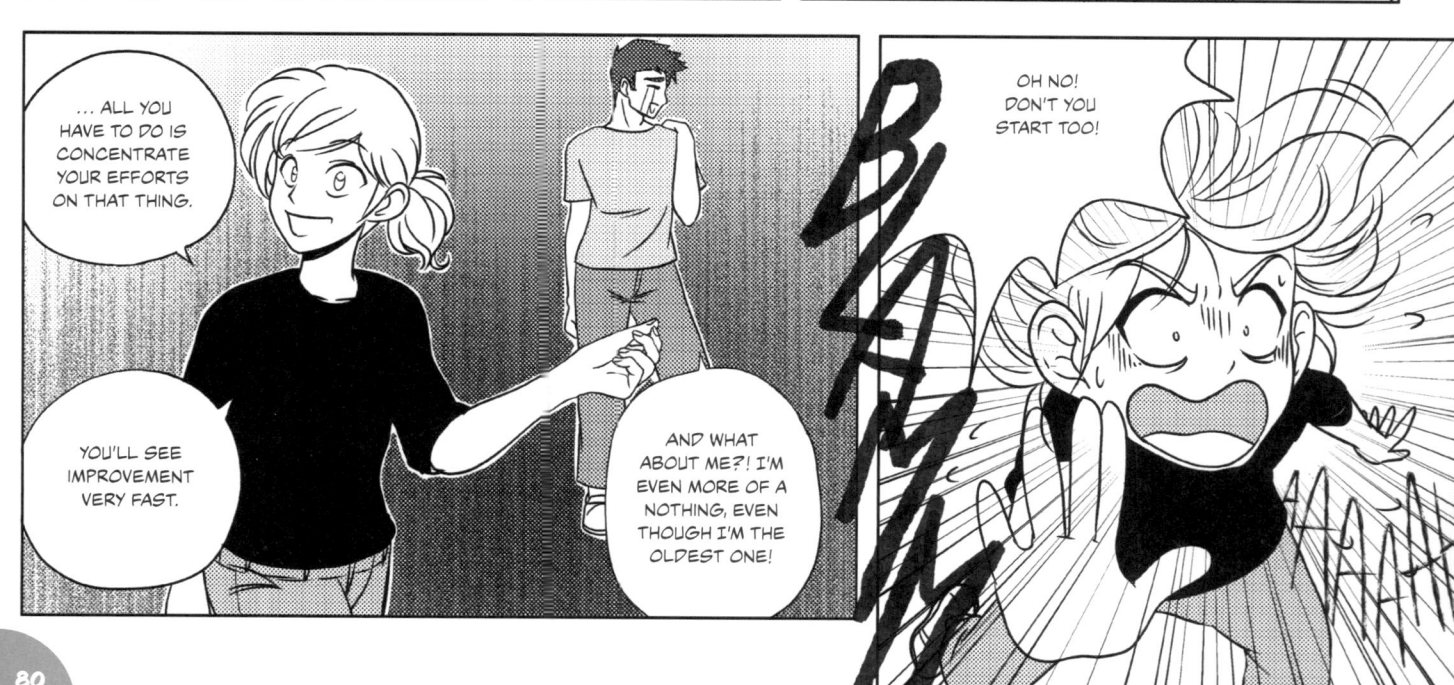

... ALL YOU HAVE TO DO IS CONCENTRATE YOUR EFFORTS ON THAT THING.

YOU'LL SEE IMPROVEMENT VERY FAST.

AND WHAT ABOUT ME?! I'M EVEN MORE OF A NOTHING, EVEN THOUGH I'M THE OLDEST ONE!

OH NO! DON'T YOU START TOO!

In order to bring your character to life, it is essential to draw the character in motion. But you also have to keep the character in balance.

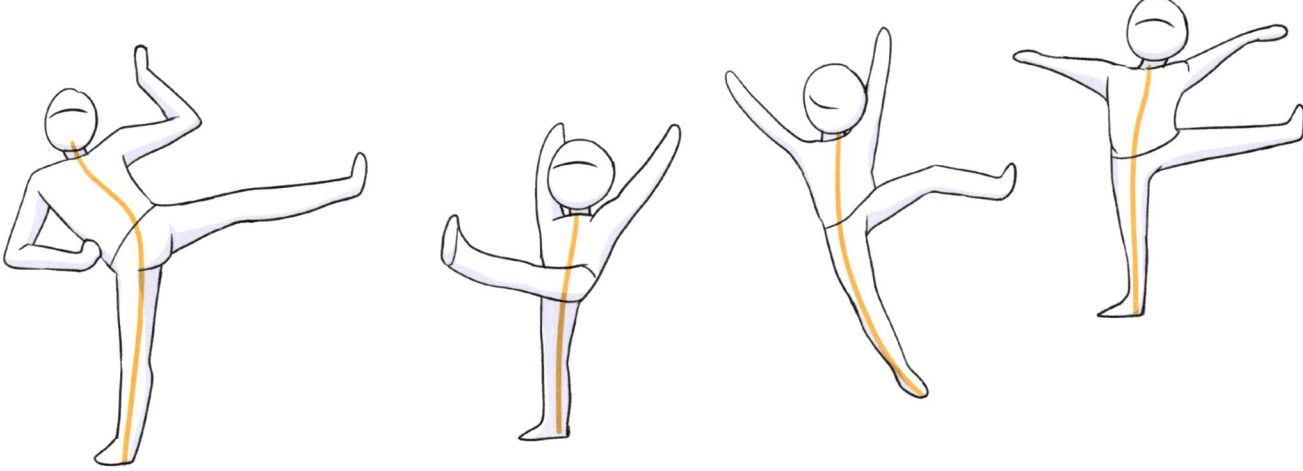

If we look at the characters in motion above, we can isolate their action lines, their **centers of gravity**, and **at least one limb that is ensuring that the character remains stable**.

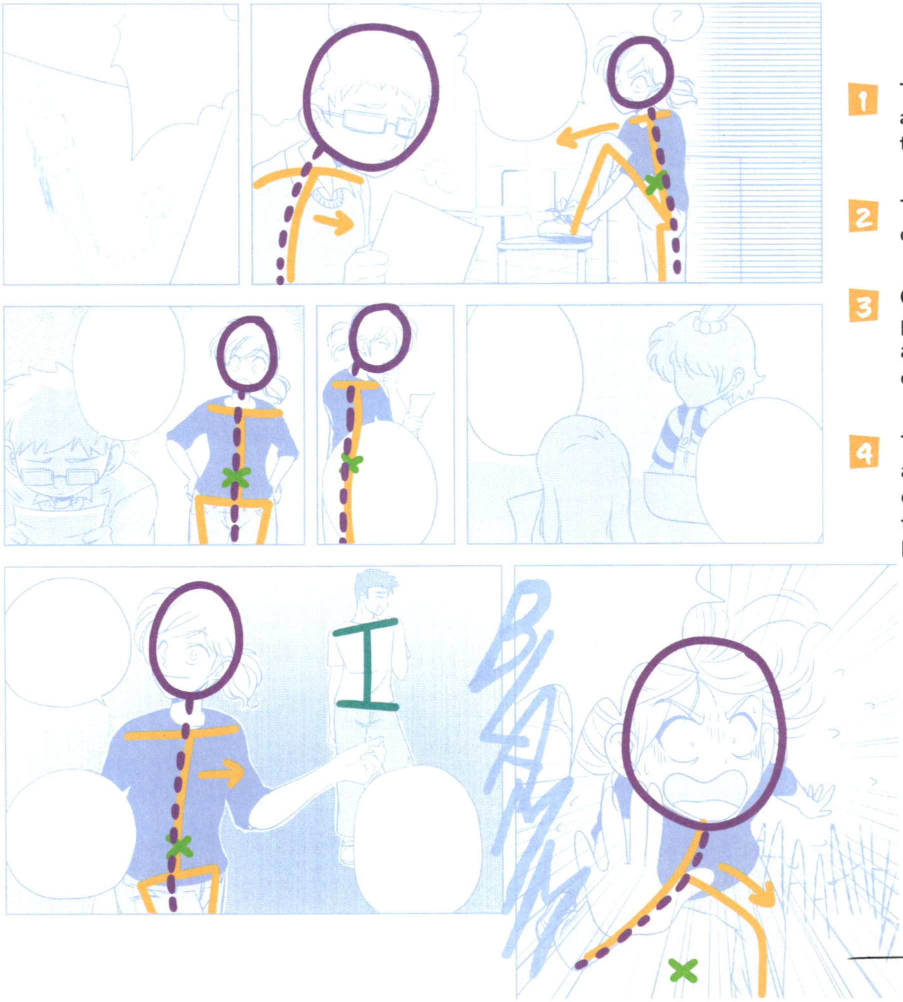

1. The head is placed within the axis of whatever is ensuring that the character remains stable.

2. The action lines give direction to the movement

3. **Contrapposto** is a relaxed pose in which the shoulders and the hips are aligned opposite each other.

4. The center of gravity is the point at which the body's masses balance each other. It changes according to the character's pose, and it is what keeps the character from falling.

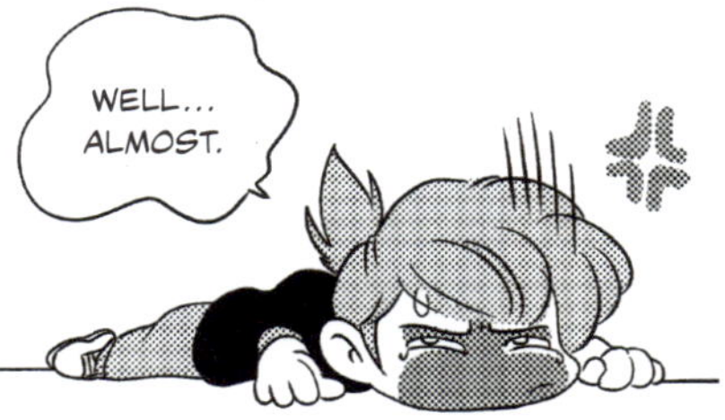

WELL... ALMOST.

WALKING

To maintain balance while walking, the limbs balance each other out on either side of the body. The left arm and the right foot go forward while the right arm and the left foot go back.

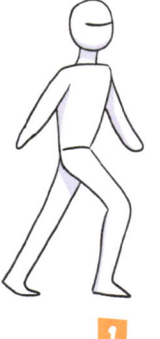 **1**
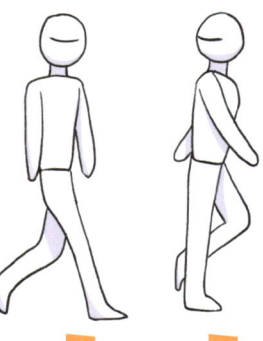 **2**
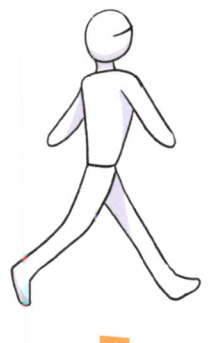 **3**
4

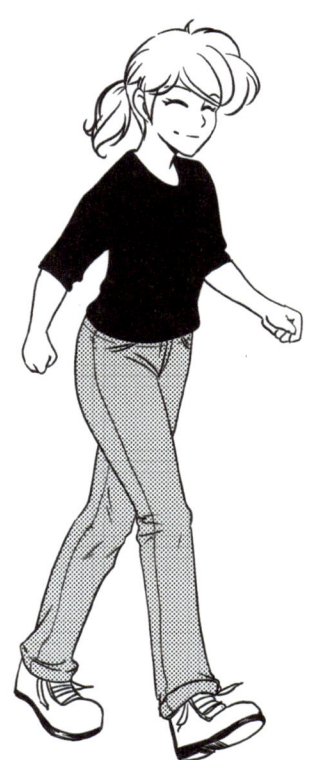

First, we put our heel on the ground, and then we finish the movement with our toes.

RUNNING

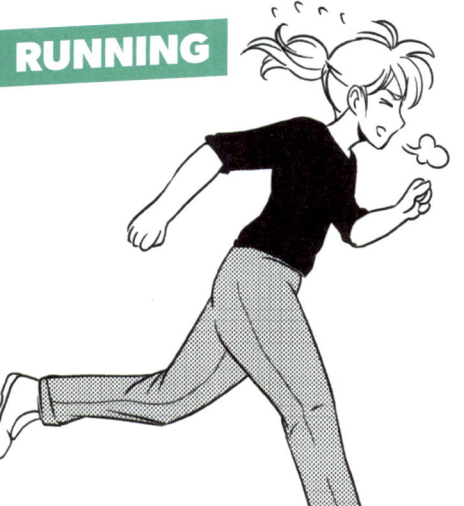

Running is similar to walking, except that we have a tendency to lean forward.

A character can run in different ways. Pay attention to the incline of the action line and to the character's balance!

First draw a little string figure and then add the details.

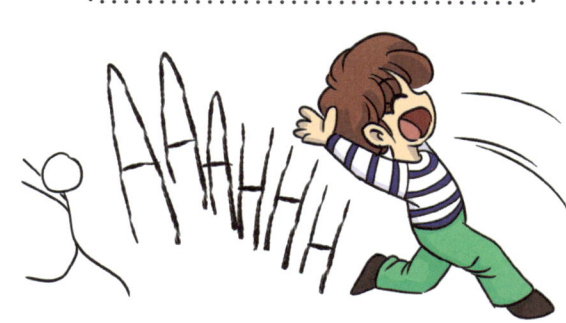

JUMPING

A jump is made up of several different actions:

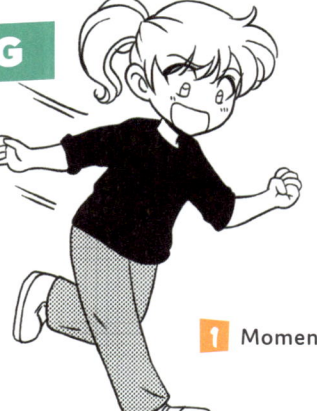

1 Momentum

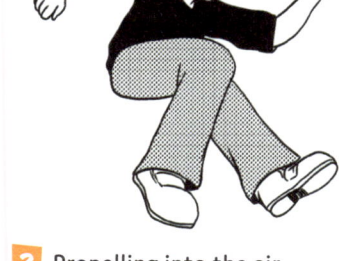

2 Propelling into the air

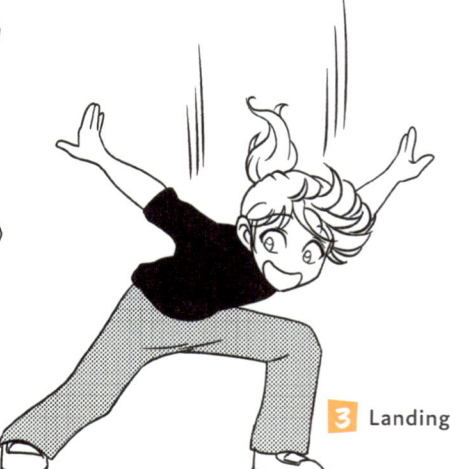

3 Landing

THE SEATED POSITION

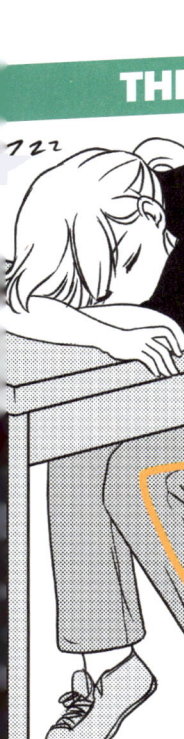

Carefully observe the action lines and the points of balance in this position for each character.

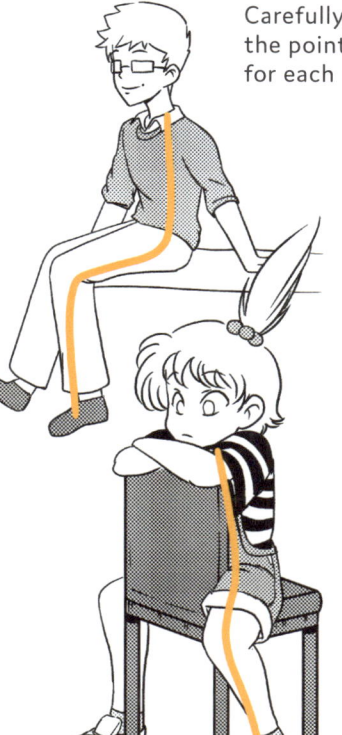

Certain postures can provide clues about the personality of the characters. This is body language.

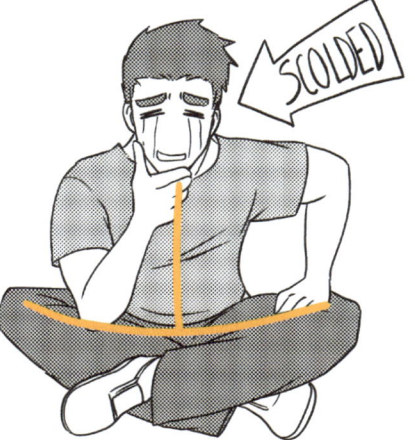

SCOLDED

PRACTICE

1 To draw characters in motion, I encourage you to start with string figures.

OK, BUT IT'S STILL KIND OF COMPLICATED TO DRAW CHARACTERS IN MOTION,

WITH ALL THE ELEMENTS THAT YOU HAVE TO INCLUDE.

THINK ABOUT BREAKING IT DOWN INTO SIMPLE SHAPES!

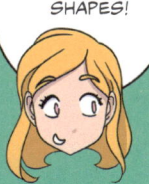

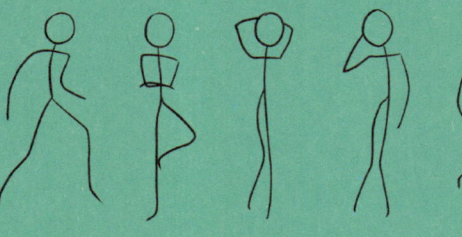

2 Practice drawing poses using these simple little forms

TIP

The first silhouettes you draw don't have to be very big, but don't be afraid to take up enough room on the page so that you can produce your final drawings.

CLOTHES

To dress our characters, we draw clothes or pieces of fabric by drawing their external outlines and their folds.

Fabric is usually flexible. Thus, it is constrained by several different forces: gravity, in other words its weight, which pulls it downward; elements that can hold it back or push it forward, like a part of the body or an object; and something that might set it in motion, like the wind.

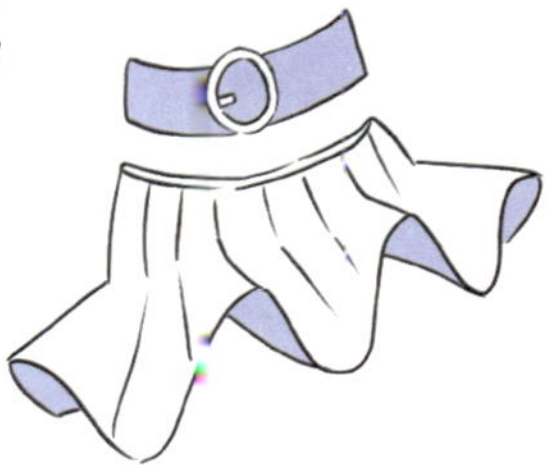

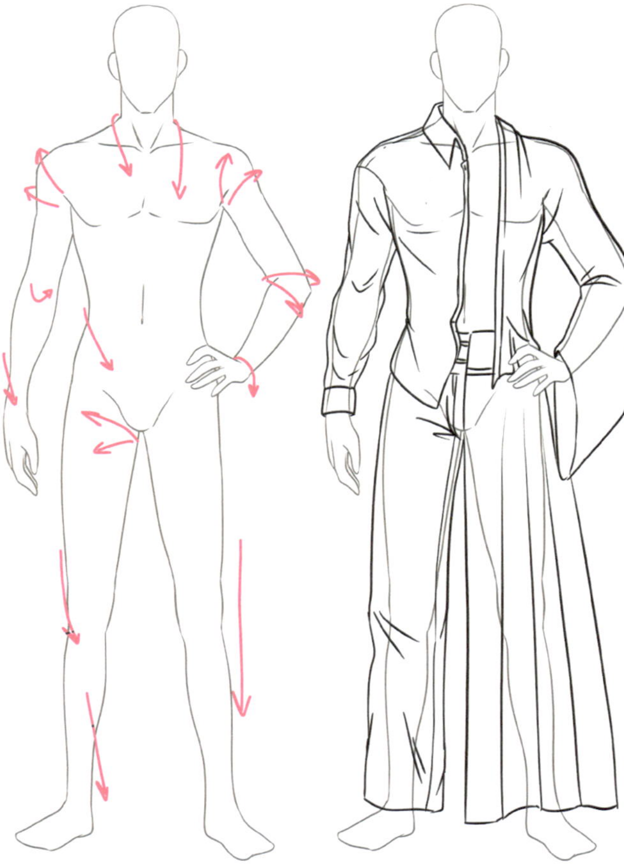

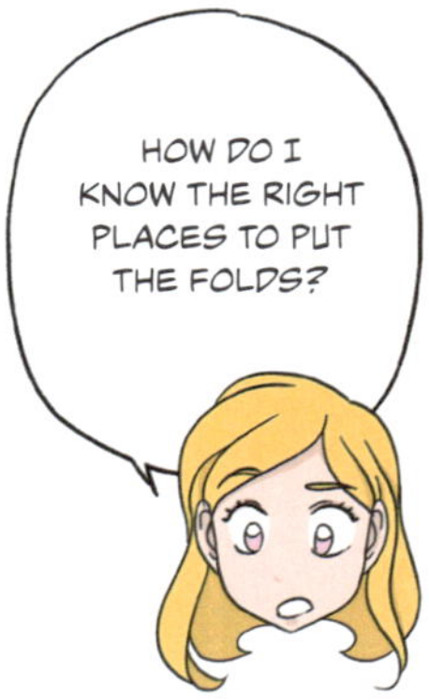

HOW DO I KNOW THE RIGHT PLACES TO PUT THE FOLDS?

A flexible fabric will mold itself to the shapes of the object or the character that we place it on.

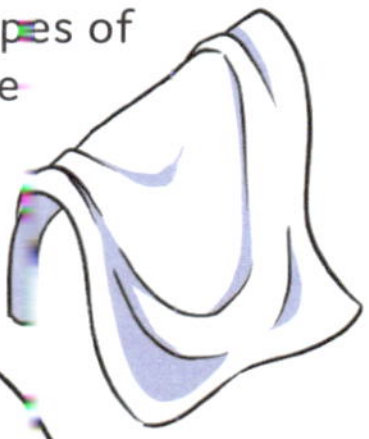

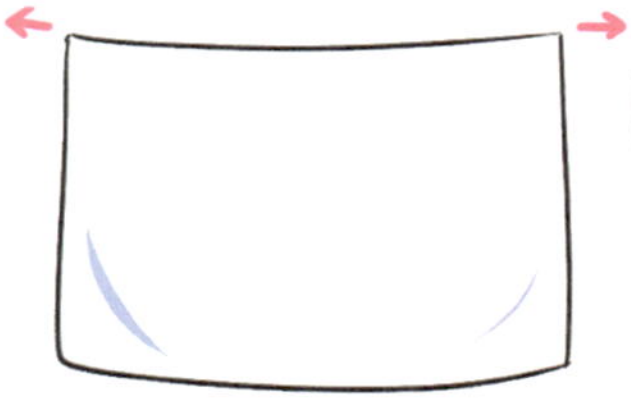

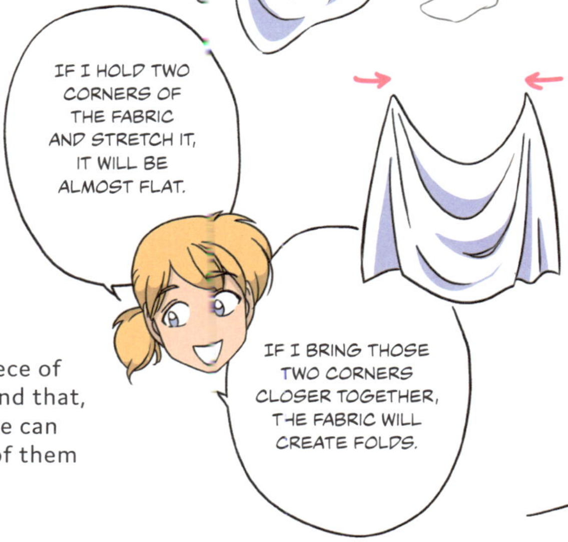

IF I HOLD TWO CORNERS OF THE FABRIC AND STRETCH IT, IT WILL BE ALMOST FLAT.

IF I BRING THOSE TWO CORNERS CLOSER TOGETHER, THE FABRIC WILL CREATE FOLDS.

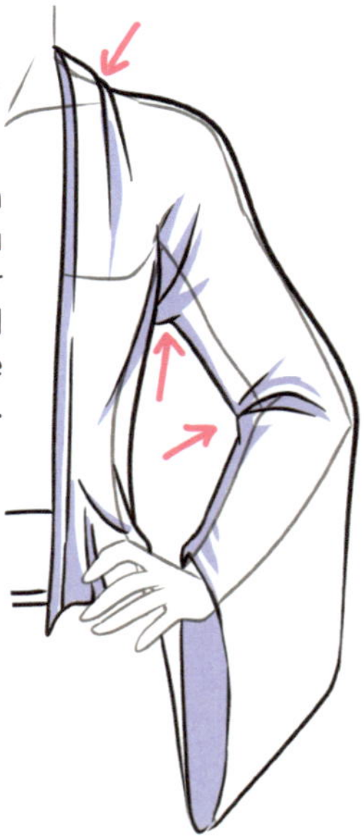

Don't forget that a piece of fabric has two sides and that, thanks to the folds, we can sometimes see both of them at the same time.

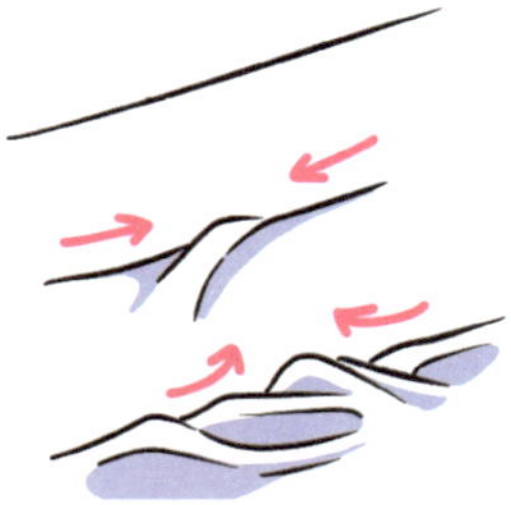

You can see this on a sleeve when you bend your arm, for example: folds will form on the inside of the elbow.

The straighter and thicker the lines you draw, the heavier and more rigid the fabric will appear.

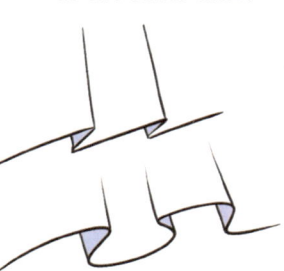

FABRIC FOLDS

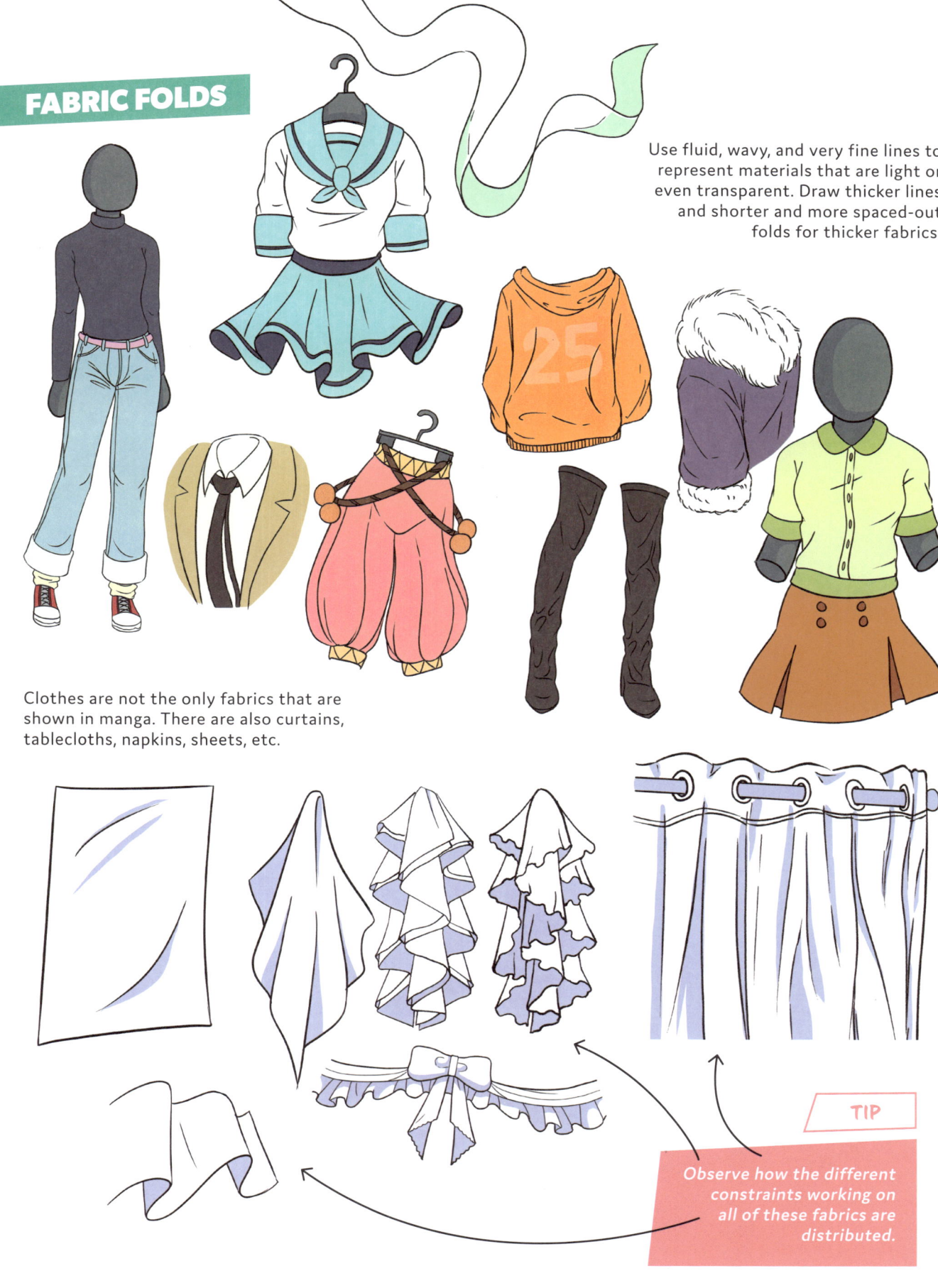

Use fluid, wavy, and very fine lines to represent materials that are light or even transparent. Draw thicker lines and shorter and more spaced-out folds for thicker fabrics.

Clothes are not the only fabrics that are shown in manga. There are also curtains, tablecloths, napkins, sheets, etc.

TIP

Observe how the different constraints working on all of these fabrics are distributed.

SHOES

Now that you have learned how to draw your characters' feet, you can have fun with giving them shoes.

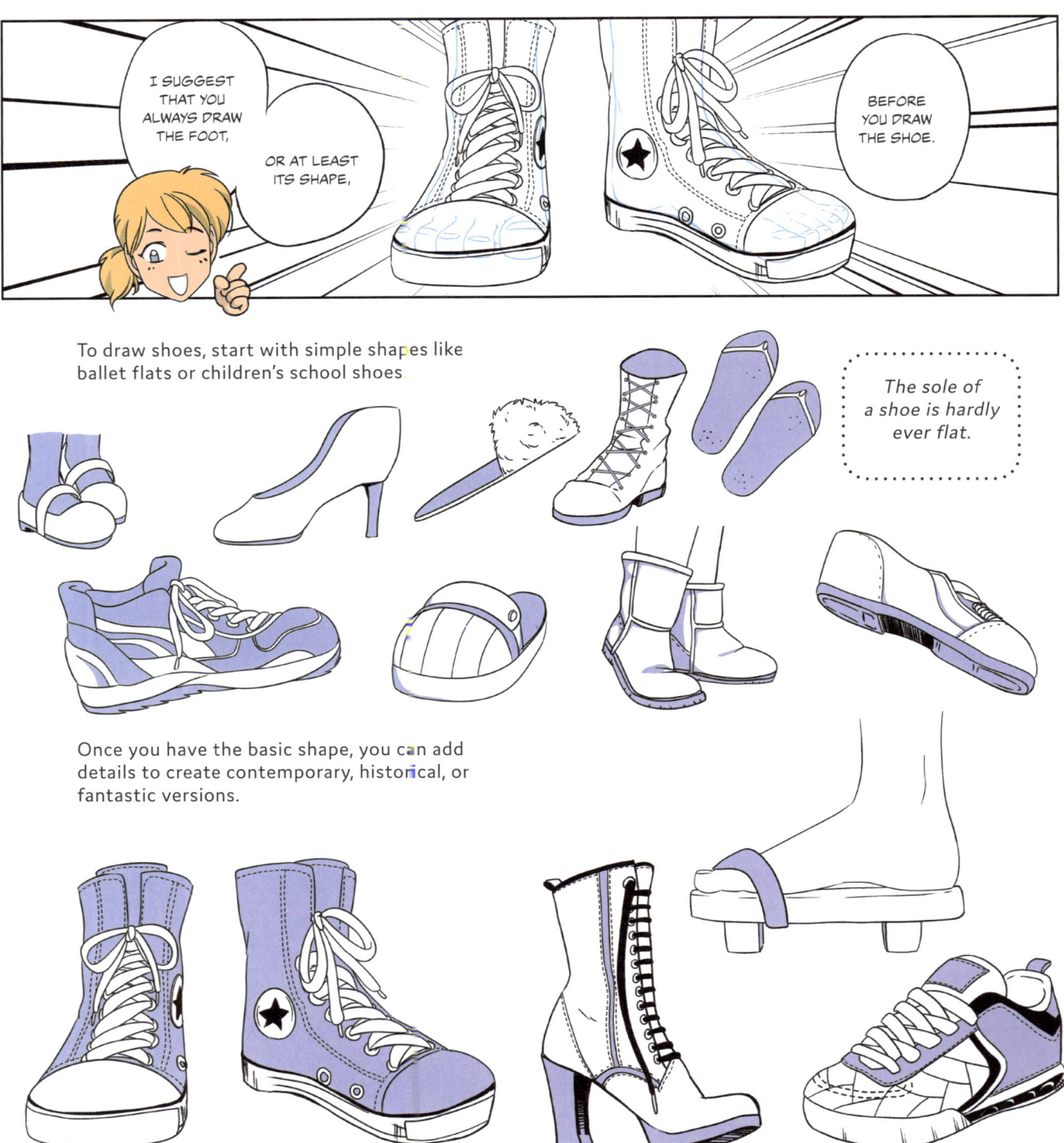

> I SUGGEST THAT YOU ALWAYS DRAW THE FOOT,
>
> OR AT LEAST ITS SHAPE,
>
> BEFORE YOU DRAW THE SHOE.

To draw shoes, start with simple shapes like ballet flats or children's school shoes.

The sole of a shoe is hardly ever flat.

Once you have the basic shape, you can add details to create contemporary, historical, or fantastic versions.

ACCESSORIES

Shoes are not the only accessories you will use to round out your characters' wardrobes. Whatever the object start by observing its shapes, then draw the initial shapes without pressing too hard on your pencil, and then finally add the details a little at a time.

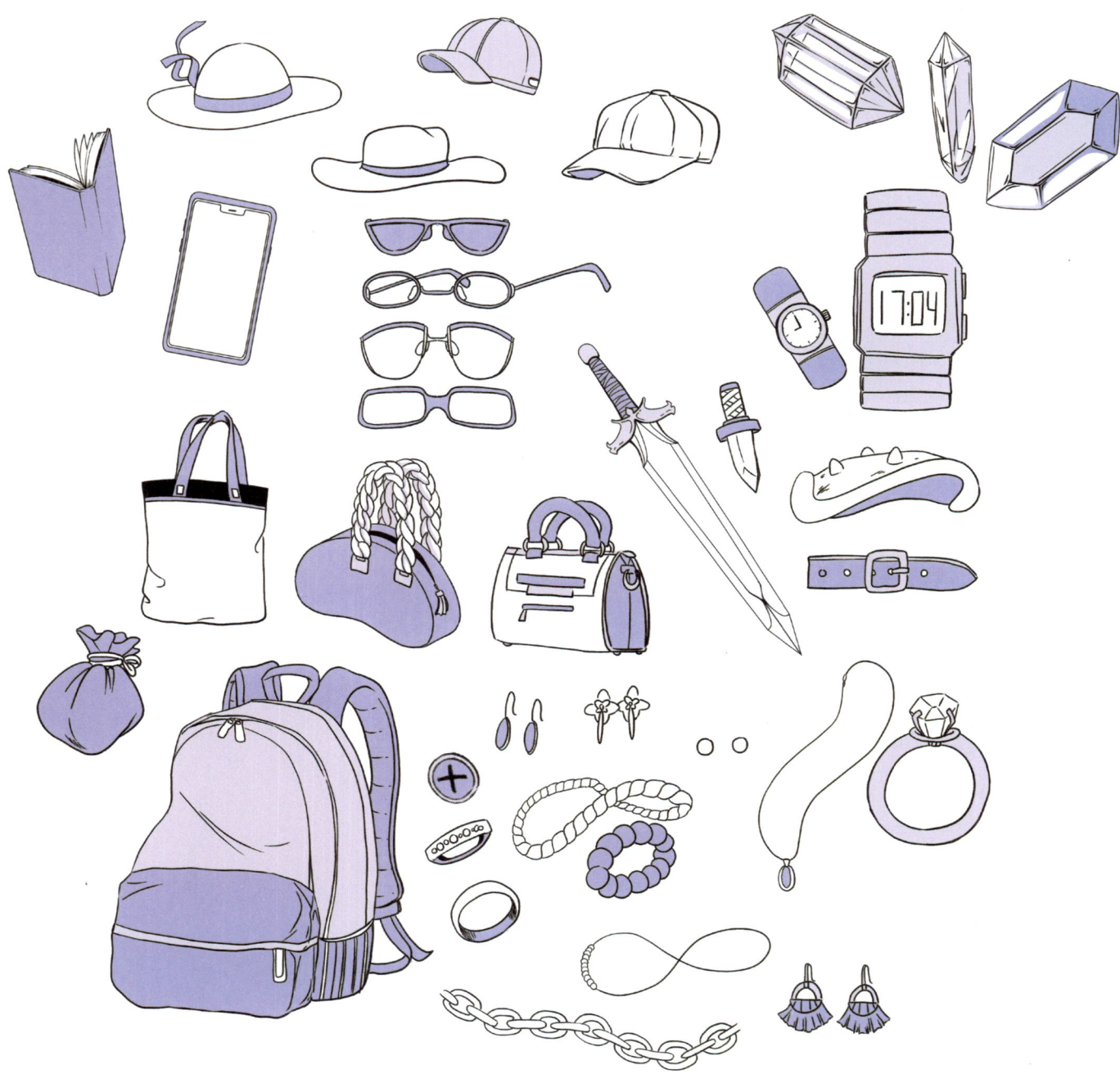

CREATING MANGA STORIES

DEFINING YOUR PROJECT

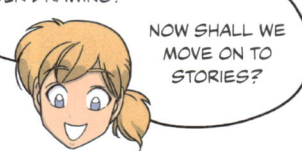

GOOD FOR YOU, YOU'VE MADE A LOT OF PROGRESS IN YOUR DRAWING!

NOW SHALL WE MOVE ON TO STORIES?

Not all stories are made to be told in the manga format. When you start writing a manga, it is important to define what story you imagine telling and who it is addressed to right from the start, so that you can be sure not to make a mistake.

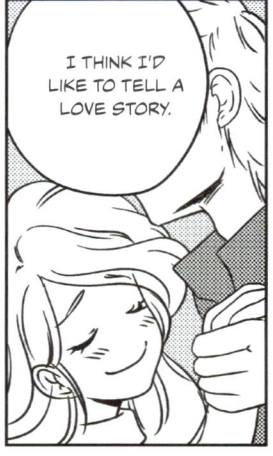

I THINK I'D LIKE TO TELL A LOVE STORY.

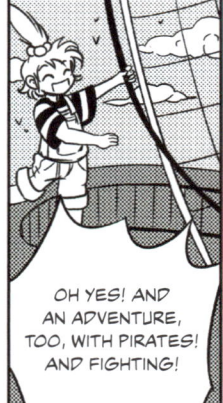

OH YES! AND AN ADVENTURE, TOO, WITH PIRATES! AND FIGHTING!

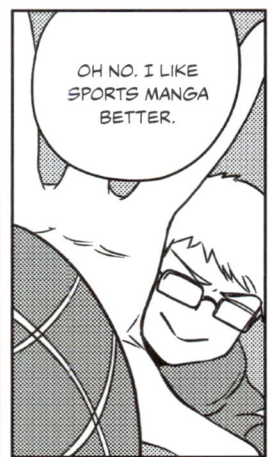

OH NO. I LIKE SPORTS MANGA BETTER.

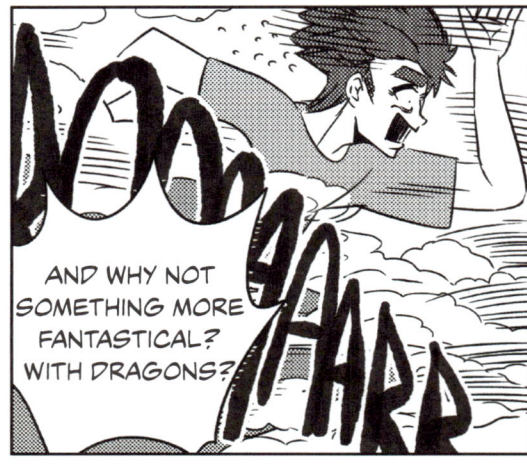

AND WHY NOT SOMETHING MORE FANTASTICAL? WITH DRAGONS?

AAAARR

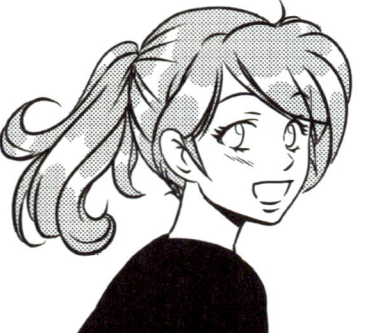

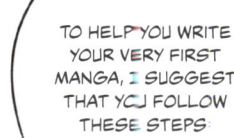

TO HELP YOU WRITE YOUR VERY FIRST MANGA, I SUGGEST THAT YOU FOLLOW THESE STEPS:

Whether your goal is to have fun, express yourself, practice, or even to become the greatest mangaka of all time, you will need a plan in order to finish your project.

1. Learn about the different genres of manga.
2. Create unique characters.
3. Find and organize your ideas.
4. Choose a theme.
5. Choose the style and tone of your story.
6. Create a storyline.
7. Develop the story and put it in order.
8. Choose the dialogues.
9. Put together the **story board**.
10. Draw the boards.

If you're just at the beginning of your adventure, keep it simple! Start with short stories, then add more difficulty a little bit at a time by making your projects longer and longer.

THE DIFFERENT MANGA GENRES

A story is not told the same way in a novel, in a film, and in a manga.
You will not necessarily be showing the same things on paper that you do on the screen.

In Japan, the narrative genres are categorized according to the theme they deal with and the readership that is being targeted:

Shonen

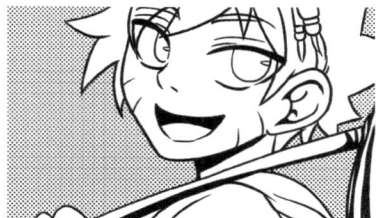

Audience:
10-to-16-year-old boys

Recurring themes:
friendship,
self-confidence,
motivation, pushing
yourself to excel.

Les **protagonistes** majoritairement masculins cherchent à devenir les plus forts ou à atteindre un objectif.

Shojo

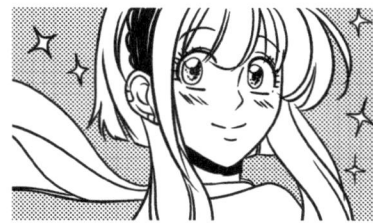

Audience:
10-to-16-year-old girls

Recurring themes:
first love, friendship,
hobbies, school,
magic, sorcery.

The main characters, who are often female, experience storylines full of strong emotions.

Seinen

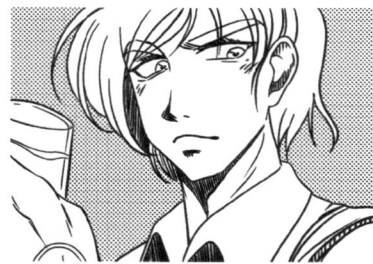

Audience:
men 16 years old
and up

Recurring themes:
police investigations,
politics, technology,
science, psychology,
sexuality.

Seinen include more complex plots, higher stakes, and more "adult" scenes than shonen do.

Josei

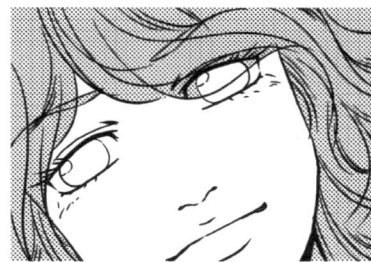

Audience:
women 16 years old
and up

Recurring themes:
career, love, sexuality,
"slice of life."

Josei include more complex plots and the scenes are more "adult" than in shojo.

Kodomo

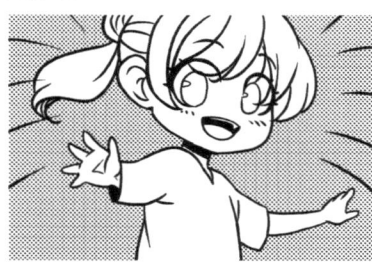

Audience:
6-to-11-year-old kids

Recurring themes:
friendship, the quest
for identity.

The childish characters in this genre are discovering the world that surrounds them. They are often accompanied by animals or **kawaii**, fantastic creatures.

There are subgenres and derivative genres like isekai, for example, which presents characters crossing a dimension to discover a parallel universe in which they will have to face new challenges in order to survive.

While respecting the genres that are appropriate to your age, I encourage you to read both "girl" and "boy" manga genres equally. Even though each story is unique in its conception, we can find common values that run through them all, such as self-confidence, friendship, and courage.

SHONEN

Shonen is the most popular genre among readers, and its composition is pretty simple. It generally features an ordinary, awkward, young male hero who has an encounter or makes a discovery that will change his life from one day to the next.

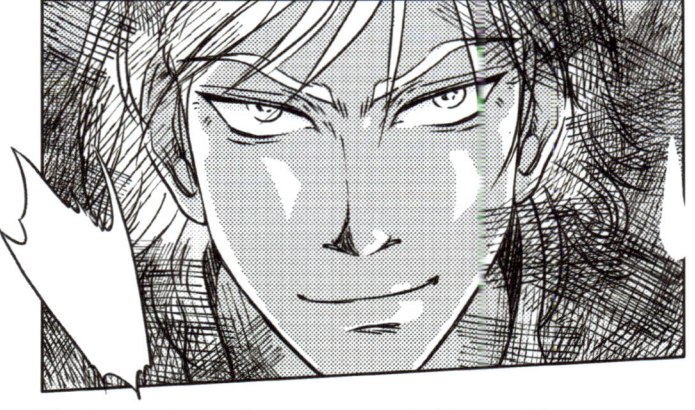

The hero, who is often accompanied by a guide, a master, and/or traveling companions, then uses his powers in a new universe in order to succeed in a quest or win a competition. During the course of his adventures, he learns to master his potential powers and takes advantage of every new confrontation to become stronger. Because his goal is often to become the best!

> When the hero has an epic adventure, we call it a **nekketsu** shonen.

> The **gakuen** shonen, on the other hand, takes place in a school setting and makes it possible to deal with more down-to-earth themes, such as friendship, bullying, and academic failure…

> Sports are the main theme of some **supokon** shonen.

The dynamic inking, very often done with a G pen, uses strong differences in line thickness.

The action is presented in dynamic panels.

The hero tries to become a better version of himself.

Sound effects, speed lines, and emphasis lines are increased in order to make everything more dynamic.

Shonen characters often take part in fights. It can be useful to draw them with lots of muscles for more credibility.

Screens are either not used at all or used very sparingly in order to leave more room for inking techniques.

IT'S JUST BETWEEN YOU AND ME NOW...

Relationships—whether romantic, friendly, professional, or even familial—are at the heart of shojo manga.

Some shojo address contemporary themes like bullying and harassment, gender equality, racism, homophobia, and ecology.

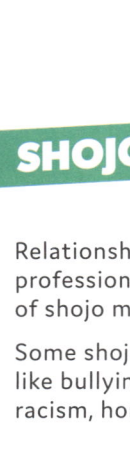

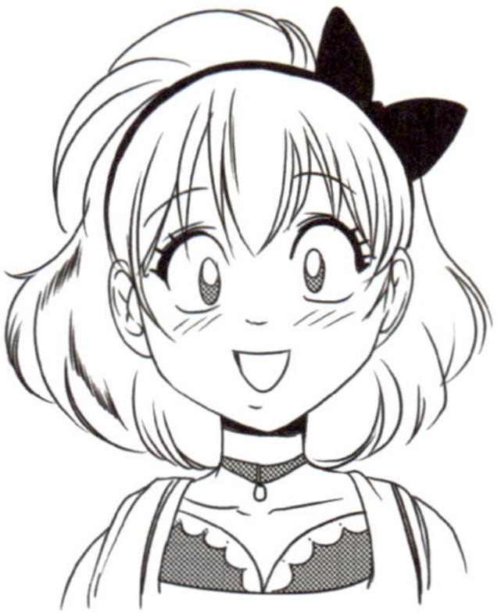

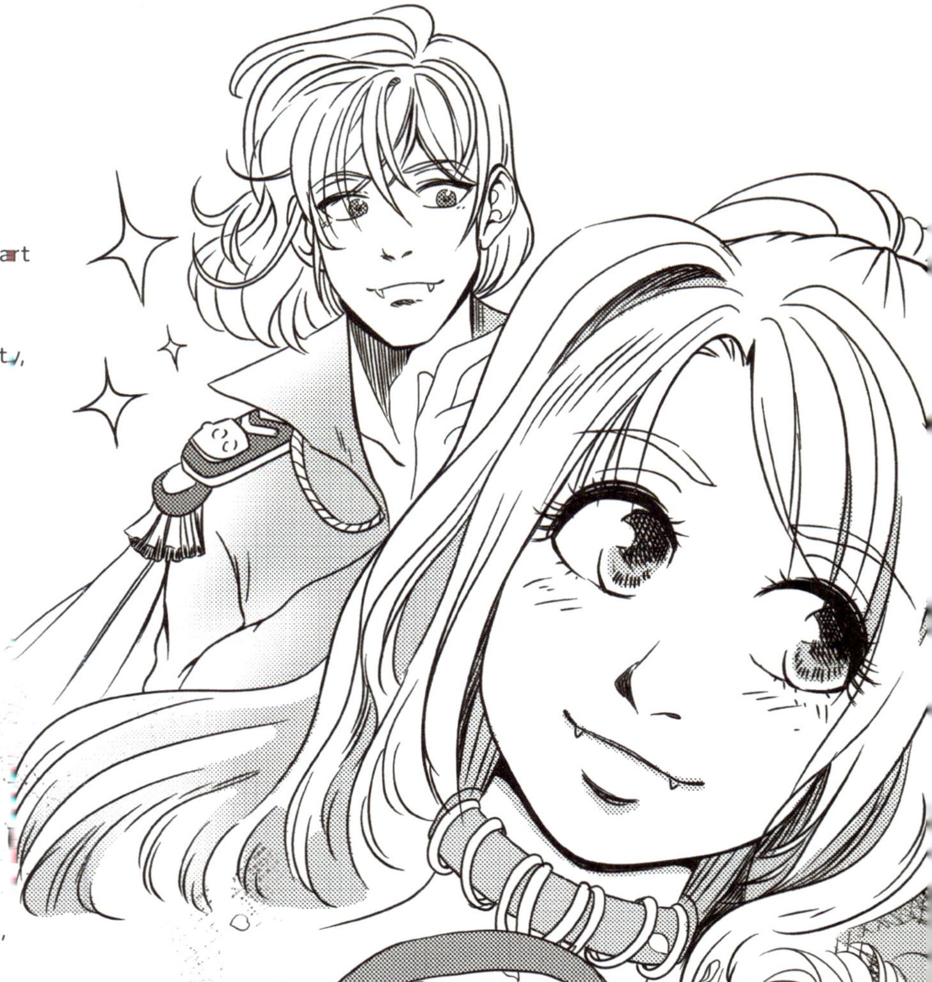

Sometimes, you can also find action scenes, magic, and sorcery in shojo.

When action and fighting techniques are featured in shonen manga, they focus on the **protagonist's** emotions during the final due .

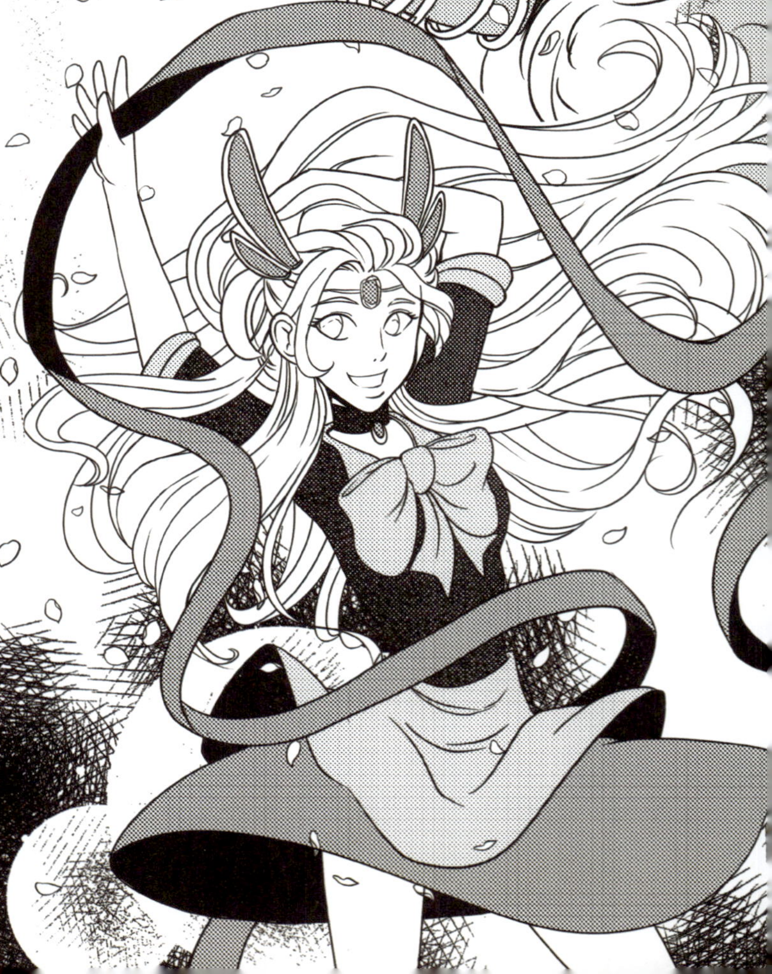

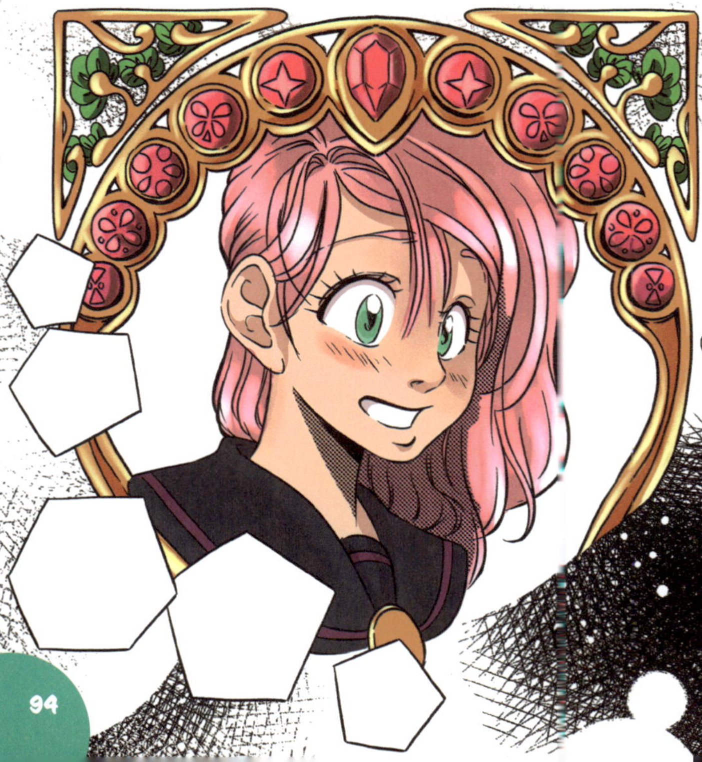

Screens are heavily used in shojo manga to bring more nuance into the representation of emotions.

The ink lines are often fine, fluid, and rounded. A Maru pen can be used to draw shojo manga.

The presence of visual gags lightens up scenes that would otherwise be too serious.

The main character is often a young girl.

Removing the borders of the panels allows the reader to become more intimate with the characters.

The characters are often slender, with a great deal of attention to detail in the faces.

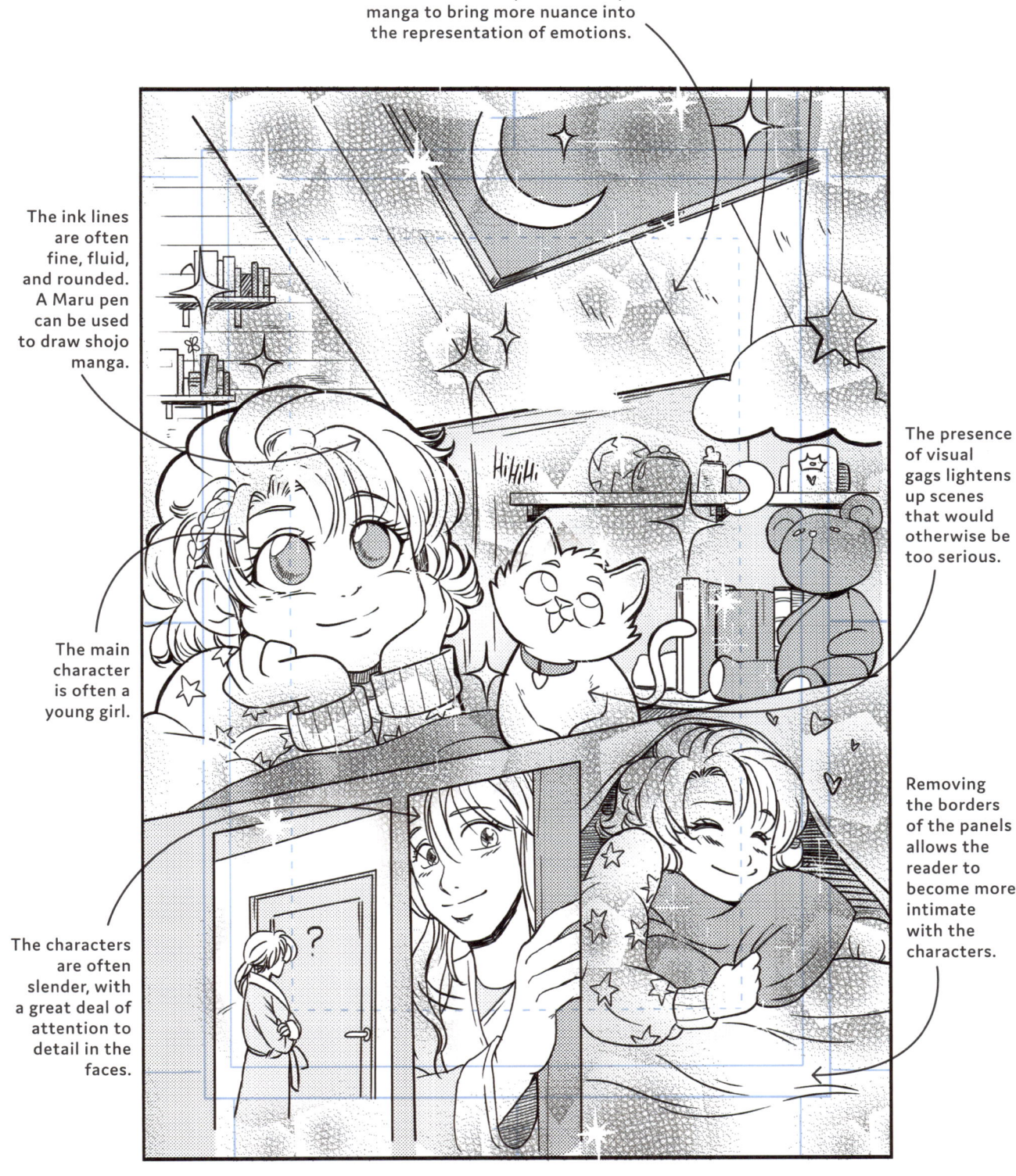

The board is divided up in such a way as to match the emotions. The panels are large and there are fewer of them, leaving enough room to show the emotions.

STANDARD CHARACTER TYPES

Here is a little overview of the main standard character types that can be found in manga.

The Shonen Hero

An often-awkward young man with a monotonous life who has an unexpected encounter that leads to adventures, accompanied by supporting characters.

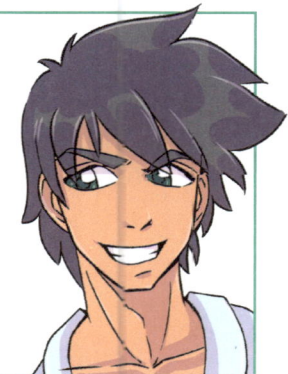

The Shonen Heroine

A brave, determined young woman who is usually searching for a loved one or trying to restore balance or take revenge.

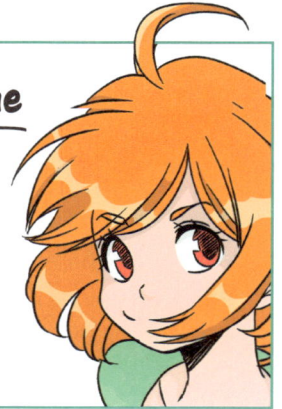

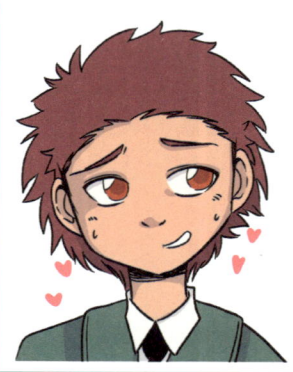

The Shojo Hero

A shy, sentimental young man who has to learn how to go outside his comfort zone in order to achieve his goals.

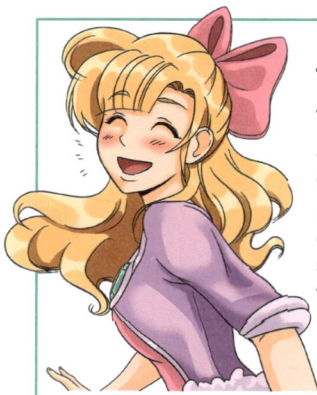

The Shojo Heroine

A young woman with natural charm and who is often positive but also naive and awkward. She is sensitive, shy, and in search of love or friendship.

All the heroes and heroines share the fact that they possess particular assets that make them unique. They are fighting to defend moral values that are precious to them, even if they sometimes remain naive, overgrown children.

The Best Friend and Confidant

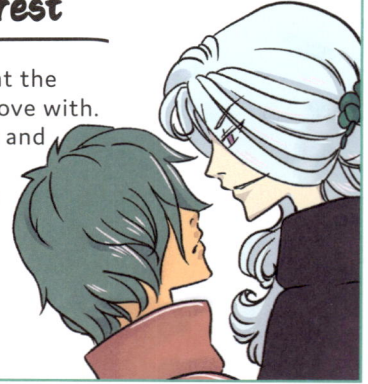

Their role as supporting characters is essential to the story. Often the same age as the main character, they provide support to the hero or heroine and use their skills in their service. They provide key information to the readers and act as a link between the different characters.

The Love Interest

This is the person that the hero or heroine is in love with. Their character traits and their almost-perfect physique impress the protagonist to the point of paralyzing them.

The Character in Distress or Disappeared Character

This is a mysterious character whom we are never able to see. But this character is what makes the hero's or heroine's quest possible in some stories.

The Sage

Sometimes old, sometimes young, the sage is a character who guides the heroes toward their successes. This character often has the solution to the problem but is not in a position to carry out the plan themselves because of their advanced age. The sage accompanies the heroes in their discovery, acceptance, and development of their powers.

Parents

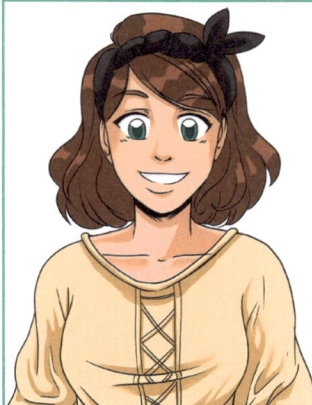

Parents are very much absent from manga stories. If they are involved in the plot, it is usually to represent an opposition or an obstacle to the progress of the main characters.

Rivals

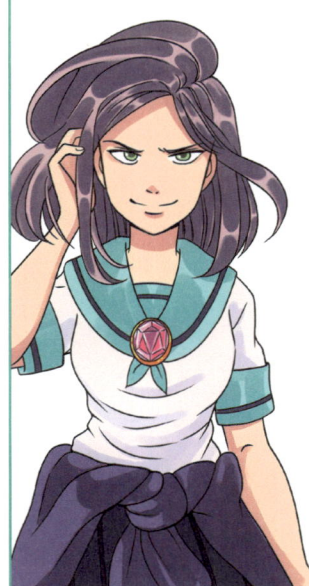

More beautiful, stronger, and/or smarter than the heroes, the rivals compete with them because they are aiming for the same goals. Sometimes they pretend to be allies and do not reveal their desires until later, in betrayal scenes that are as memorable as they are unexpected. And finally, they can sometimes change sides, rallying to the hero's or heroine's cause to confront greater obstacles.

Nemeses

These are the "bad guys" of the story, the ones who want the heroes to fail or who have opposite goals. Often depicted as physically or morally monstrous, they are always powerful and sometimes invincible. Manipulative, hiding in the shadows, tormented, present against their will… they always keep the heroes from moving forward at a certain point. These nemeses become more and more powerful over the course of the story and allow the **protagonists** to keep evolving to improve themselves.

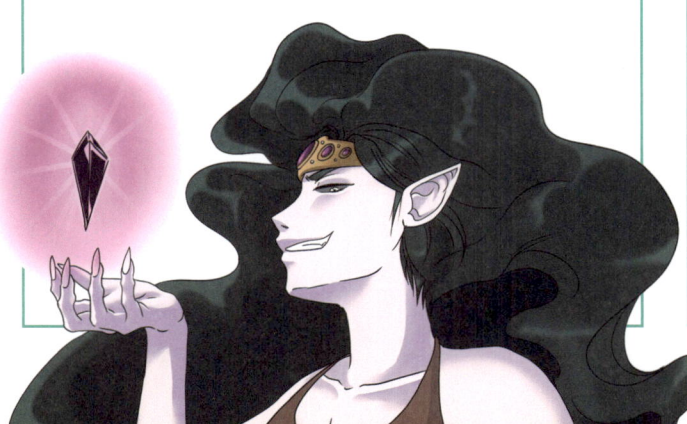

The Faithful Companion

This is often either a small animal or a monster. It accompanies the hero or heroine but takes on a different role than the best friend. The faithful companion may or may not be able to speak, but it always provides the hero or heroine with unwavering support.

CREATING ORIGINAL CHARACTERS

In manga, you have to tell the story from the point of view of the most interesting character. This means that you have to choose the **protagonist** very carefully.

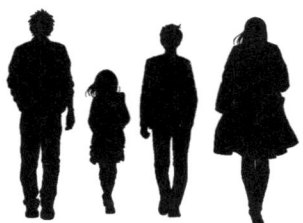

A successful character needs to make an impression. If the main character disappears behind the other characters, then that means that character is not really the hero or heroine of your story. If the main character is successful, we can recognize them just from their silhouette! This is the essence of character design.

Before starting to draw your characters, it's interesting to define their life story and their personality, and to equip them (or not) for everything that awaits them in your story.

Their personality leads them to make choices that are then expressed through the personal physical characteristics that define them: a hairstyle, a particular style of dressing, a set of gestures, a quirk, and even their body language.

The characters that you are going to create **will evolve between the beginning and end of your manga**. Ideally, they will progress, push themselves, and become a better version of themselves.

> *If a character is too powerful from the beginning, they will have a hard time finding their place in the story, which is trying to show an evolution.*

Every character reacts differently to the same obstacle.

Contradictory personality traits are interesting for developing a character.

Create believable characters that your readers will be able to identify with. If you give your readers the chance to feel the same emotions as your character, all throughout the story, you have succeeded!

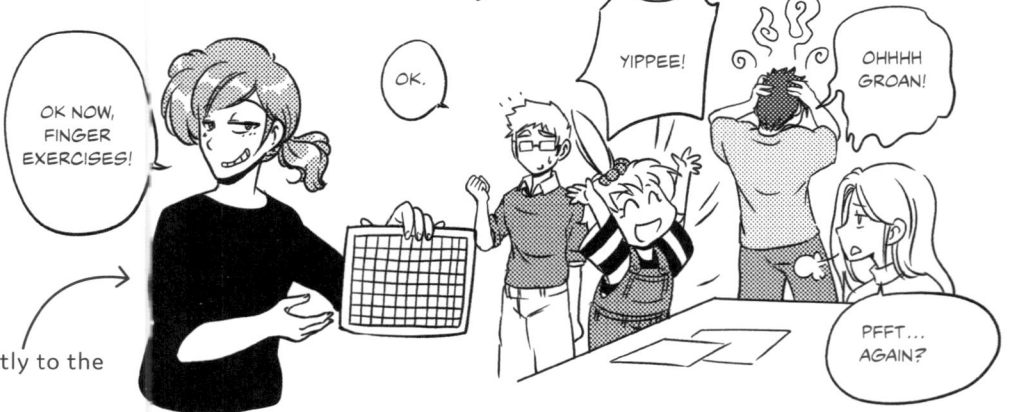

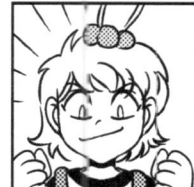

A girl who loves to fight.

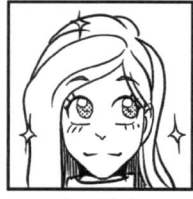

A girl with her head in the clouds, but very talented.

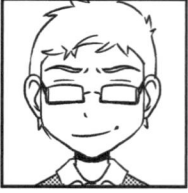

A shy boy, but very brave

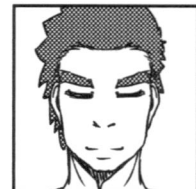

A muscular adult who would rather draw than play sports.

> *Your characters' faults will make them more human and relatable.*

FINDING THE RIGHT NAMES

Finding the right names for your characters is another important step. Each character's first name must be consistent with their background, their universe, and their personality.

Remember that the first name has to be a reflection of your character and must be appropriate for their universe. If your story takes place in Japan, it is very likely that you will come across heroes with Japanese names, unless your **protagonist** is a foreigner who has just moved there.

If your story takes place in an imaginary universe, you can invent new country names, city names, and also character names. **In that case, paying attention to sounds is the key to choosing your names well.** Some sounds have softer connotations than others.

A strong and charismatic character cannot have an overly sweet first name without losing credibility.

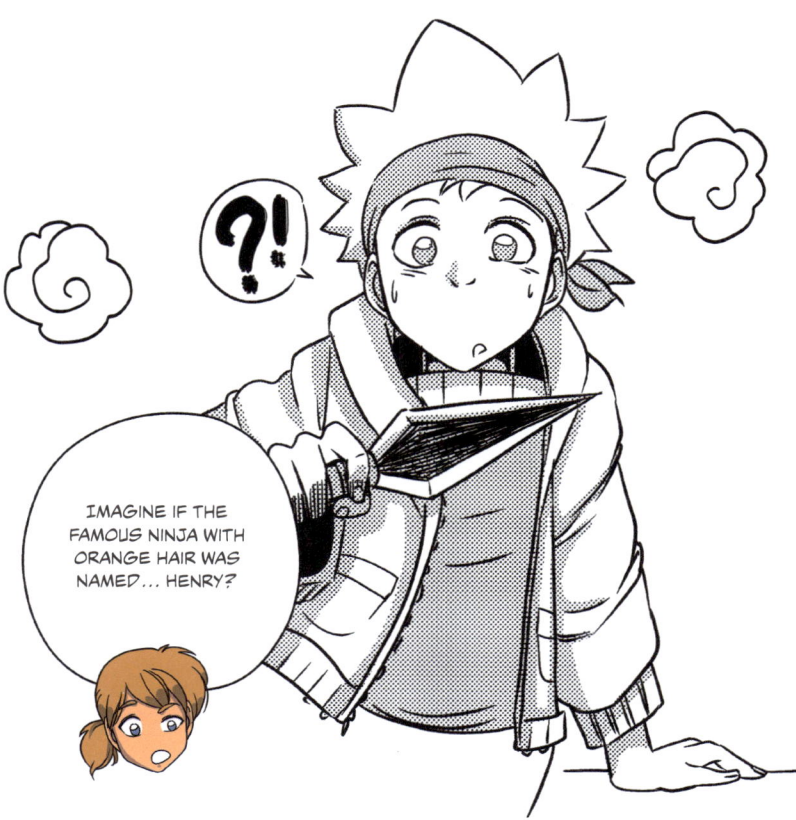

IMAGINE IF THE FAMOUS NINJA WITH ORANGE HAIR WAS NAMED... HENRY?

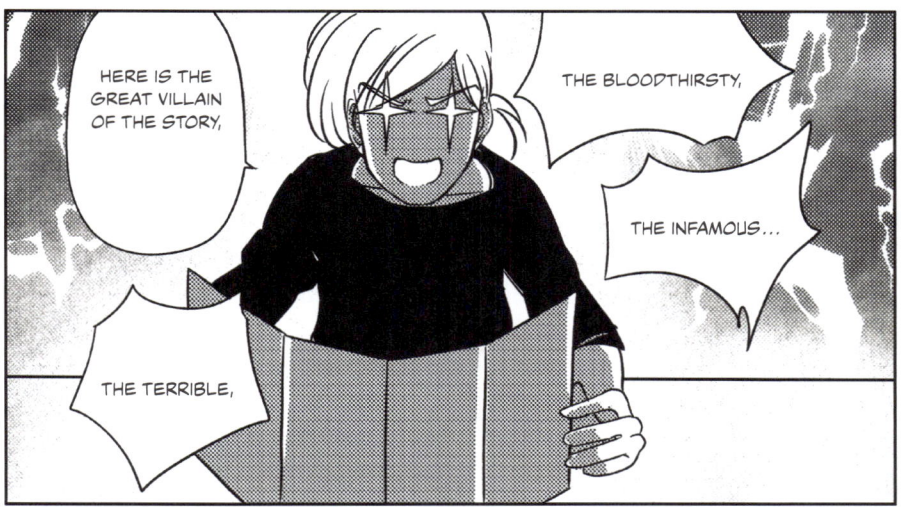

HERE IS THE GREAT VILLAIN OF THE STORY,

THE TERRIBLE,

THE BLOODTHIRSTY,

THE INFAMOUS...

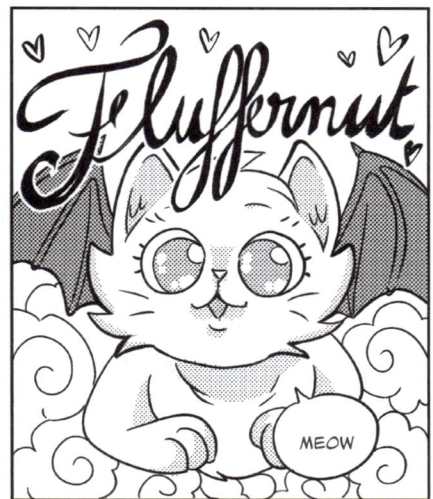

Fluffernut

MEOW

For rivals, think in terms of sounds with "K" or "CR" like Kraken, Arka, Arkenia, Tra, Dor, or Thork. For the heroes and heroines, think in terms of the sounds N and L.

The first names of the students that you are following along with in this book—Chloe, Alexis, Livia, and Rowan—were not chosen until the end of writing the book.

CHOOSING THE PERSONALITY AND PHYSIQUE

A character's personality and physique often go hand in hand.

A character with unusual physical traits may, in some cases, have low self-esteem, or, just the opposite, might take advantage of their difference to become an **iconic character**. In manga, everything is allowed, so you might as well let your mind go wild! Take advantage of the character creation stage to play with their various attributes: amplify them, exaggerate them, multiply them… in order to make an impression.

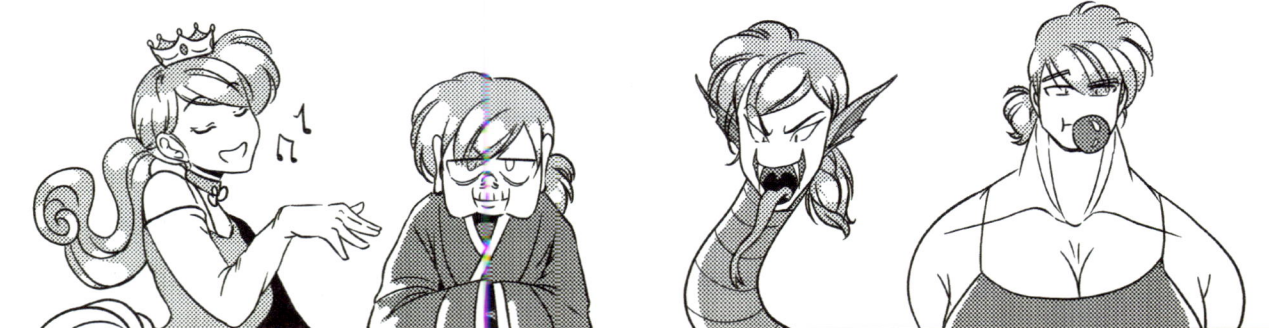

Your characters' physical attributes will give your readers some clues.

Heroes

Eyes wide open, extroverted, smiling.

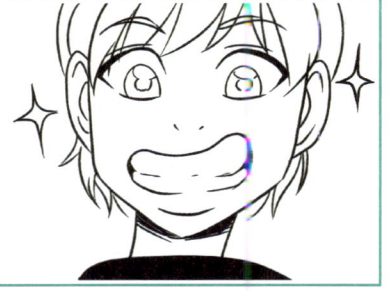

Bad Guys

Squinty eyes, narrow features, thin or nonexistent eyebrows.

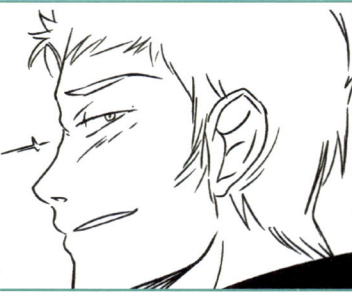

Friends

Round eyes, soft features.

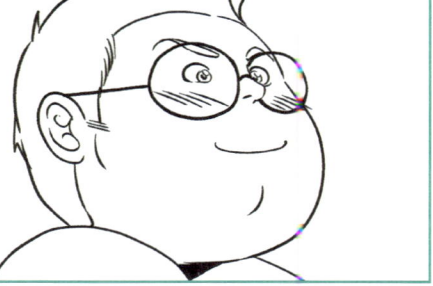

Shy Characters

Bangs or glasses to hide behind, understated expressions.

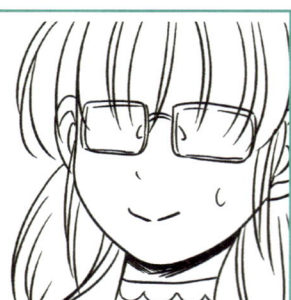

Strong Characters

Imposing muscles, well-defined features.

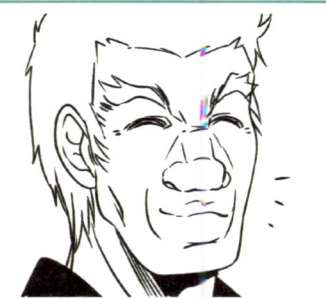

TIP

Your characters will not all be paragons of beauty, and that is a good thing, because characters who look different from each other make it easier to read the story.

Some physical characteristics are innate and genetic, such as the color of a character's skin, eyes, hair, or beauty marks and moles.

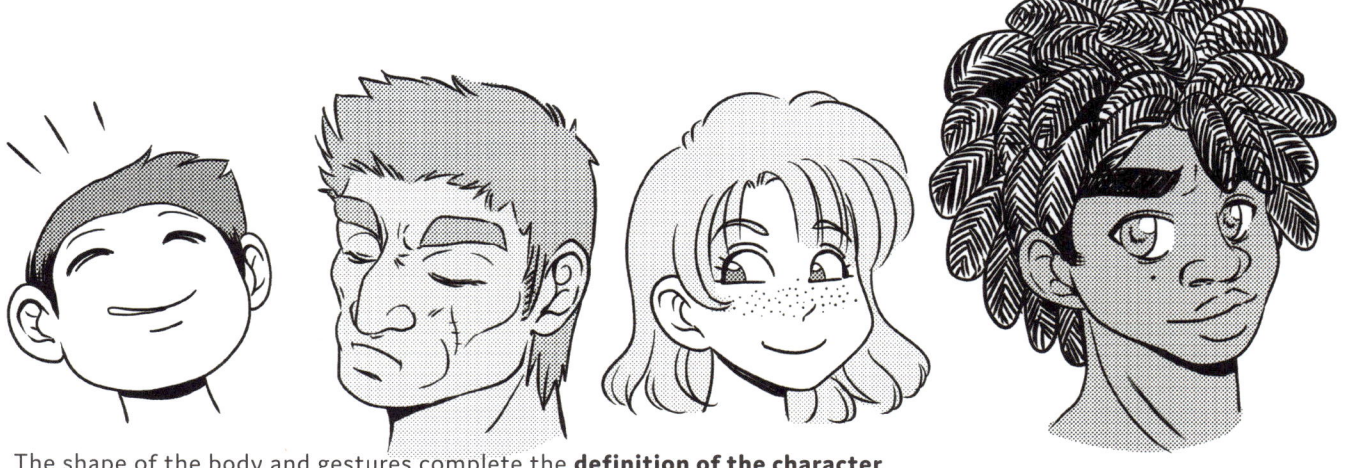

The shape of the body and gestures complete the **definition of the character**.

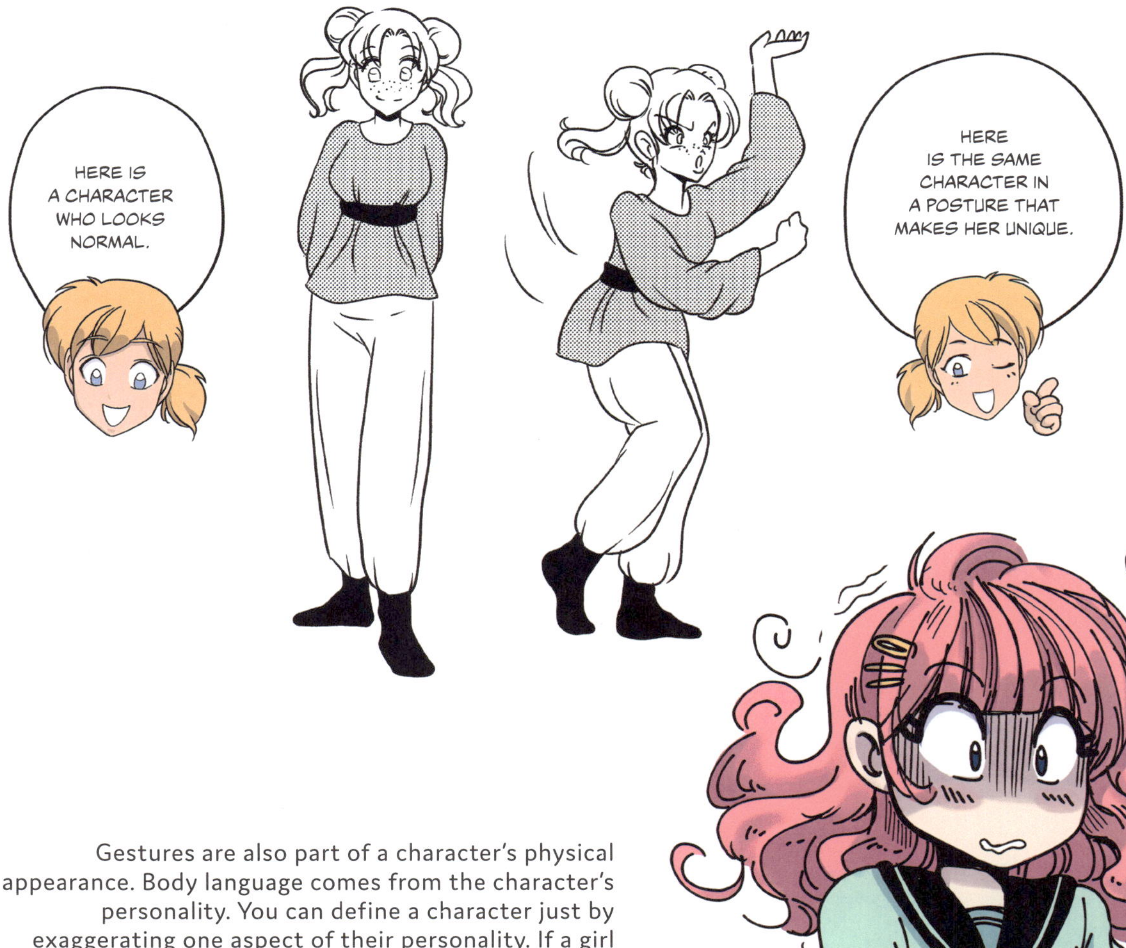

HERE IS A CHARACTER WHO LOOKS NORMAL.

HERE IS THE SAME CHARACTER IN A POSTURE THAT MAKES HER UNIQUE.

Gestures are also part of a character's physical appearance. Body language comes from the character's personality. You can define a character just by exaggerating one aspect of their personality. If a girl tends to be fearful, for example, you can use that character trait to make her distinctive.

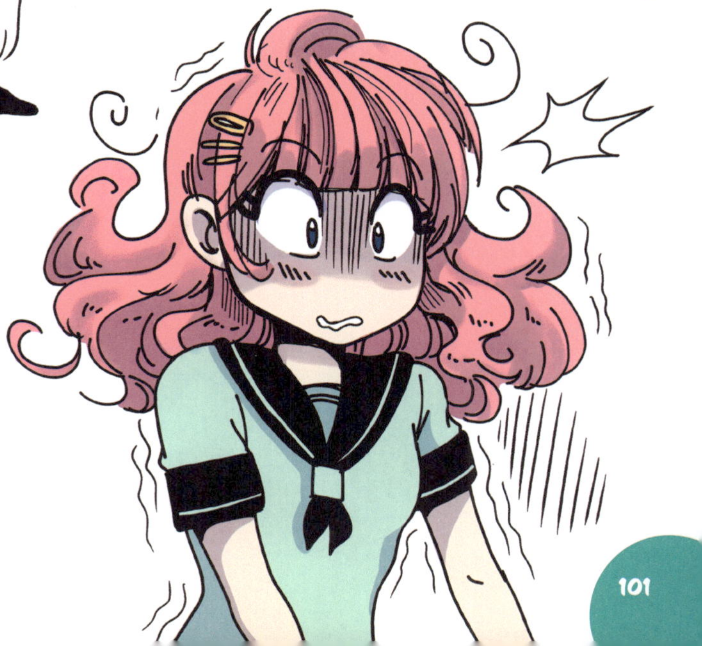

ATTRIBUTES

Scars, tattoos, accessories, etc., all help us to know more about a character. These attributes are a result of a character's personality and physique coming together.

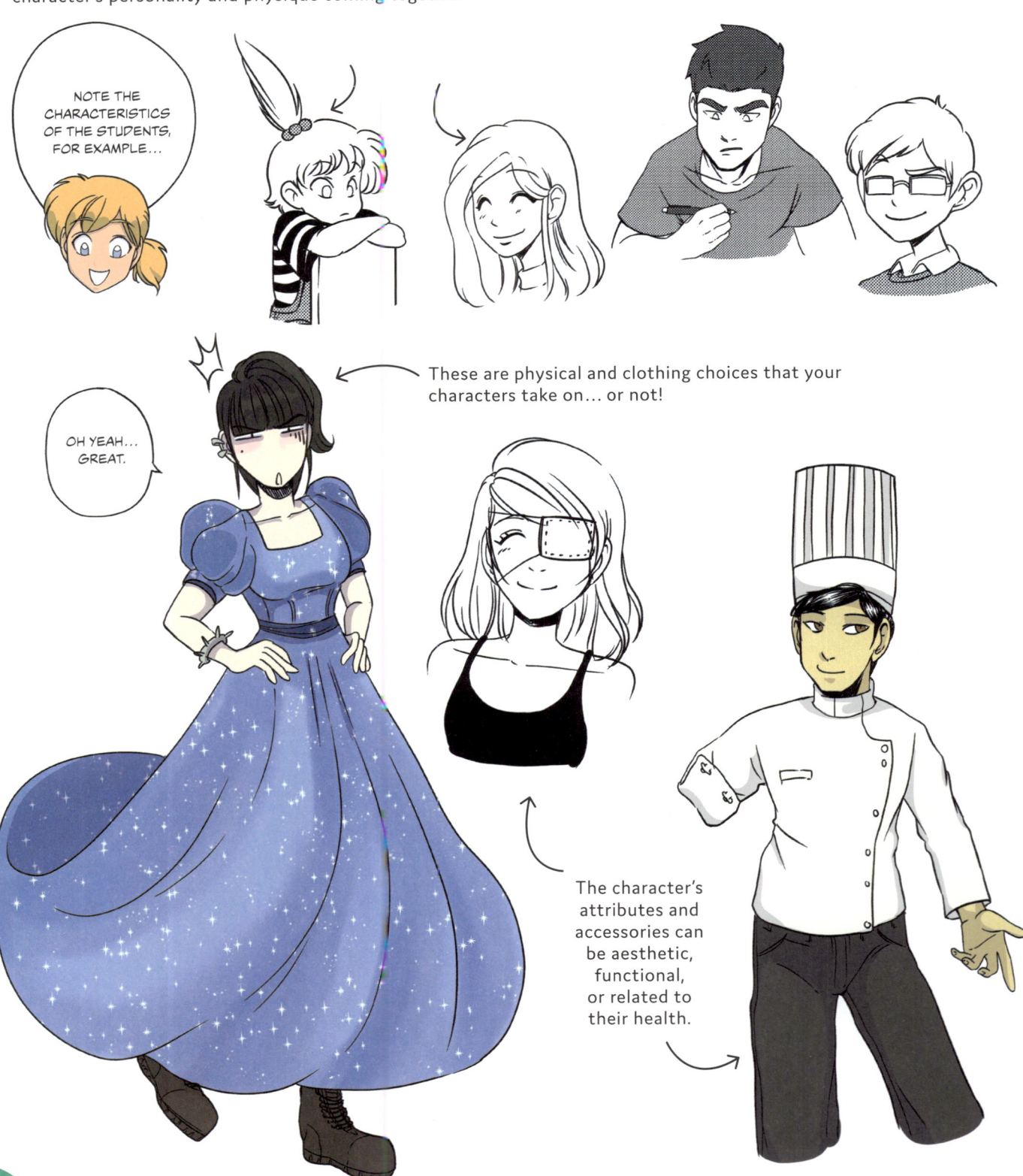

NOTE THE CHARACTERISTICS OF THE STUDENTS, FOR EXAMPLE...

These are physical and clothing choices that your characters take on... or not!

OH YEAH... GREAT.

The character's attributes and accessories can be aesthetic, functional, or related to their health.

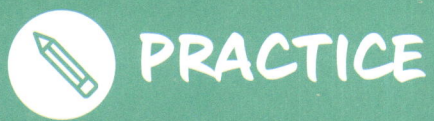

Creating a Character Design

Now it's time to imagine and design your first characters. Here is a template to help you clarify your ideas and sketch them out. Make a sheet for each of them, as in this example.

NAME: EVA

FRONT VIEW

DRAW YOUR CHARACTER IN FULL ACCORDING TO THEIR HEAD/BODY RATIO.

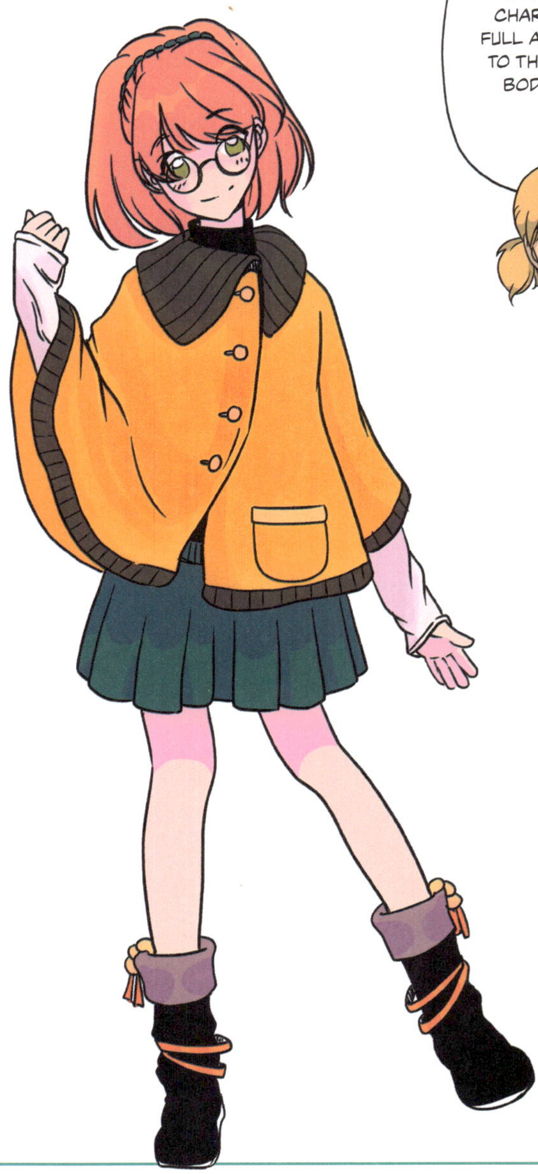

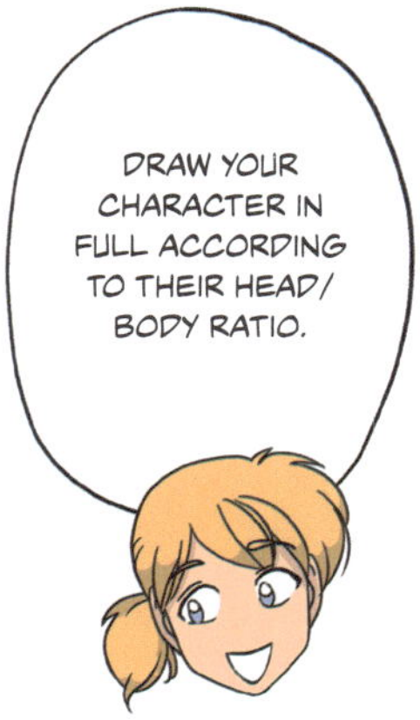

WRITE DOWN WHAT DEFINES YOUR CHARACTER.

IN PROFILE

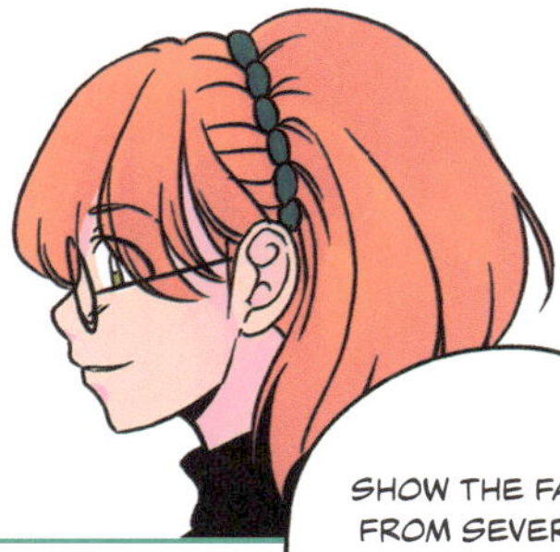

SHOW THE FACE FROM SEVERAL DIFFERENT ANGLES.

THREE-QUARTER VIEW

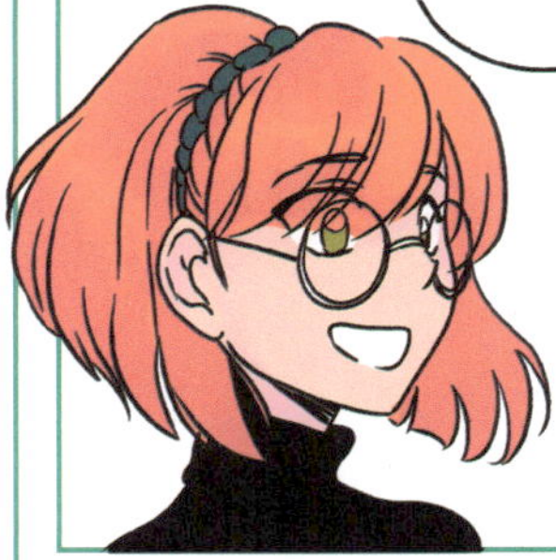

NOTES

IMAGINING STORIES FOR YOUR MANGA

CHOOSING A THEME AND FINDING AN IDEA

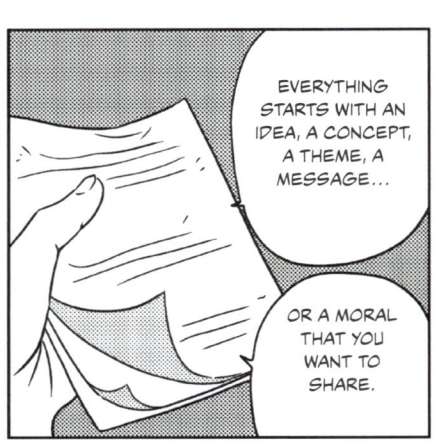

EVERYTHING STARTS WITH AN IDEA, A CONCEPT, A THEME, A MESSAGE...

OR A MORAL THAT YOU WANT TO SHARE.

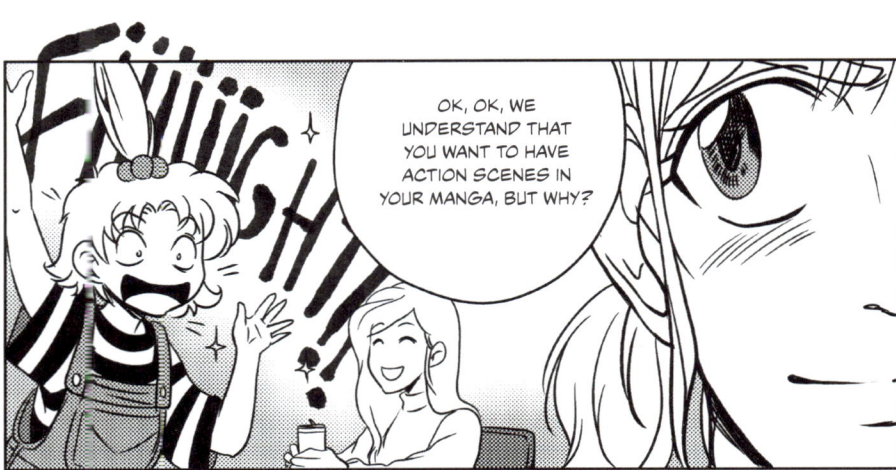

OK, OK, WE UNDERSTAND THAT YOU WANT TO HAVE ACTION SCENES IN YOUR MANGA, BUT WHY?

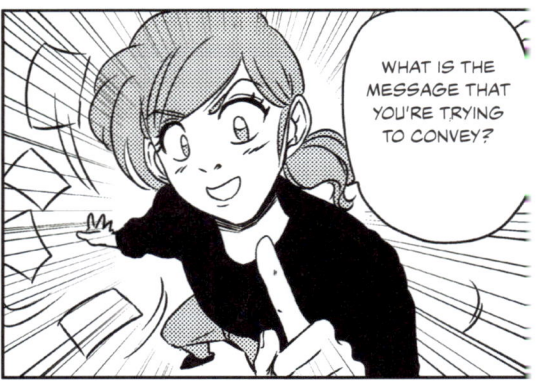

WHAT IS THE MESSAGE THAT YOU'RE TRYING TO CONVEY?

DO YOU WANT TO SHOW HOW YOUR HERO IS GOING TO OVERCOME OBSTACLES THANKS TO THEIR COMPETITIVE SPIRIT? OR IS YOUR MESSAGE MORE COMPLEX, FOR INSTANCE: VIOLENCE IS MAYBE NOT THE SOLUTION FOR ACHIEVING YOUR GOALS?

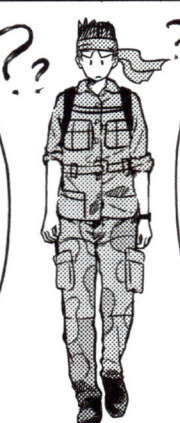

BY MAKING YOUR HERO TAKE PART IN A FIGHT, YOU WILL THEN HAVE THEM REALIZE THAT THIS IS NOT THE RIGHT WAY TO RESOLVE THEIR ISSUE, AND AS A RESULT, THAT IS ALSO THE MESSAGE THAT YOU WILL BE SENDING TO YOUR READERS.

You can have dozens of good ideas that come from asking yourself as many questions as possible about your characters' motivations. Choose the best ones and the ones that open up the most possibilities for highlighting the theme of your manga.

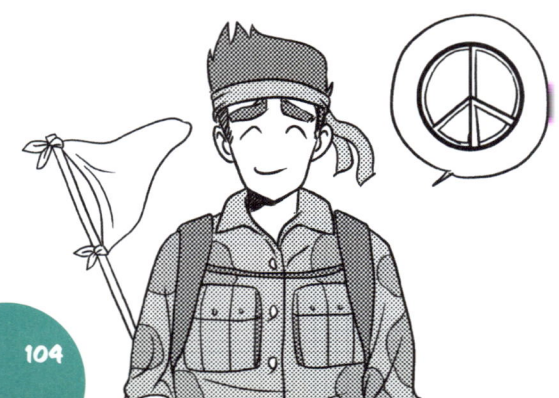

The **theme** is the heart of the work, the central subject of your story. The **idea** is the medium that you will use to present your theme in an original and interesting way.

You can be either "for" or "against" the theme that you address. It is up to you to get your message across using the different characters.

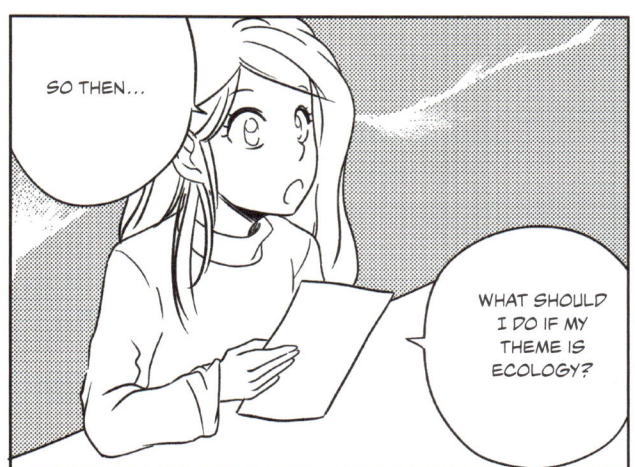

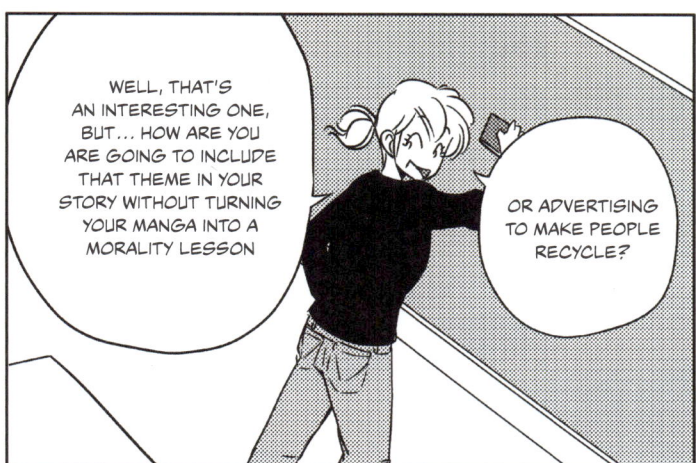

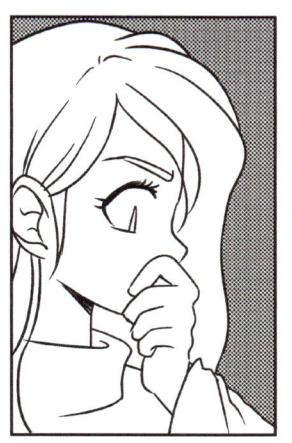

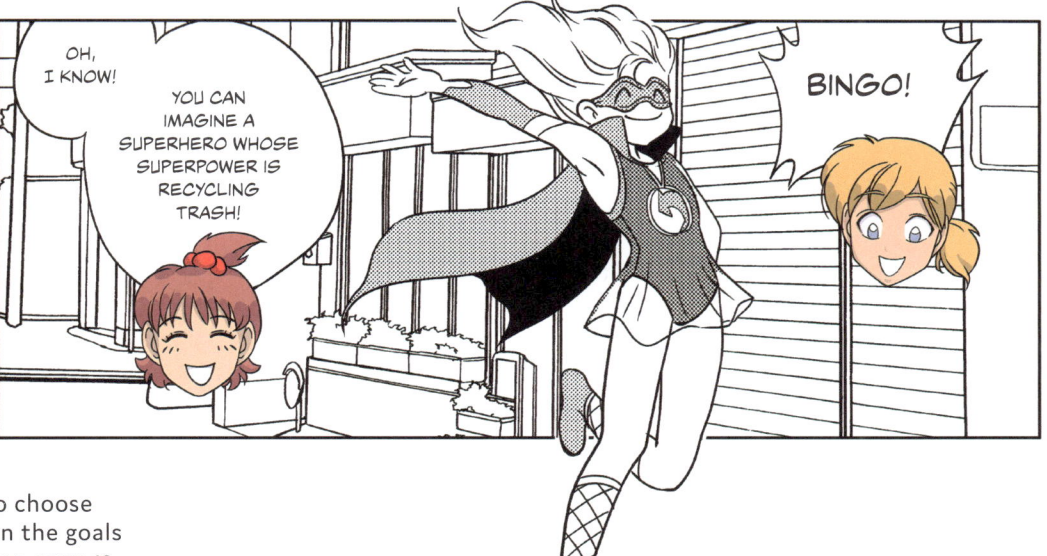

In any case, I invite you to choose simple, clear themes. As in the goals that you set for yourself on page 12, write something as clear as possible.

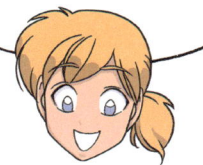

Avoid choosing themes that are too vague, like:
- War
- Racism
- Love

Make these themes more specific, for instance:
- Flourishing in spite of an atmosphere of conflict.
- Finding one's place in a hostile environment.
- Being anxious about a first declaration of love.

For every theme, find an idea that will make your story unique:
- A pacifist character in the middle of a conflict between humans and anthropomorphs.
- A stranded explorer on a planet in a faraway galaxy.
- A robot developing feelings for a human.

CHOOSING THE STYLE AND TONE

Once you have found your theme and your idea, it is time to define the style and tone that are appropriate for your manga.

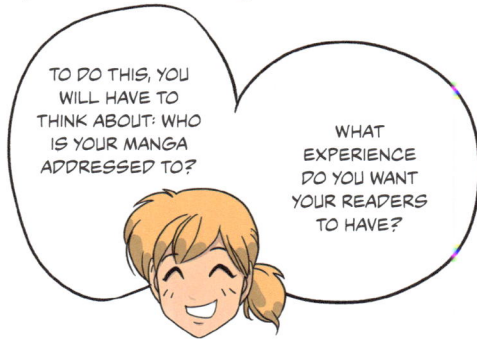

TO DO THIS, YOU WILL HAVE TO THINK ABOUT: WHO IS YOUR MANGA ADDRESSED TO?

WHAT EXPERIENCE DO YOU WANT YOUR READERS TO HAVE?

The **graphic style** helps to convey the theme and the message that you want your reader to understand. It can be very refined, stylized, or, on the other hand, very detailed.

Shojo

Shonen

Kodomo

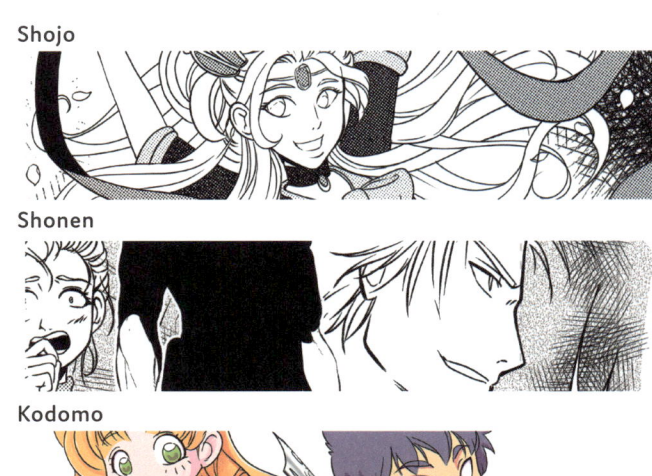

A manga is never 100% serious, cheesy, funny, dramatic, or dynamic all the time. On the other hand, you do have to maintain a constant tone in order to tell your story.

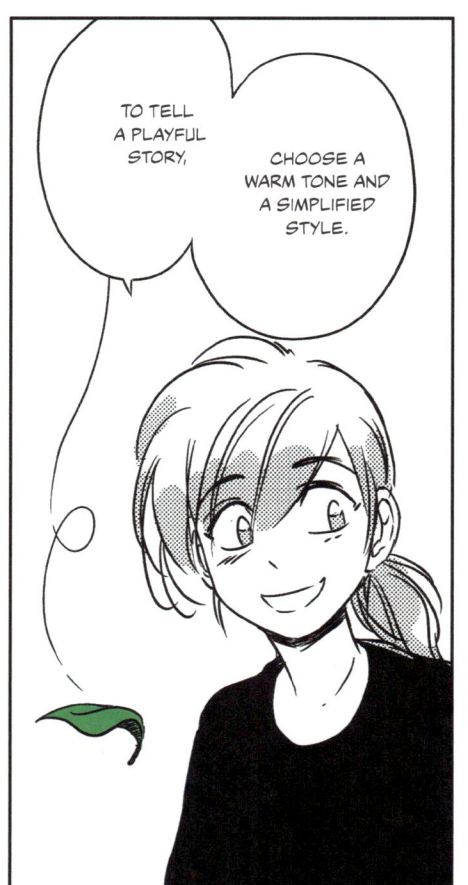

TO TELL A PLAYFUL STORY,

CHOOSE A WARM TONE AND A SIMPLIFIED STYLE.

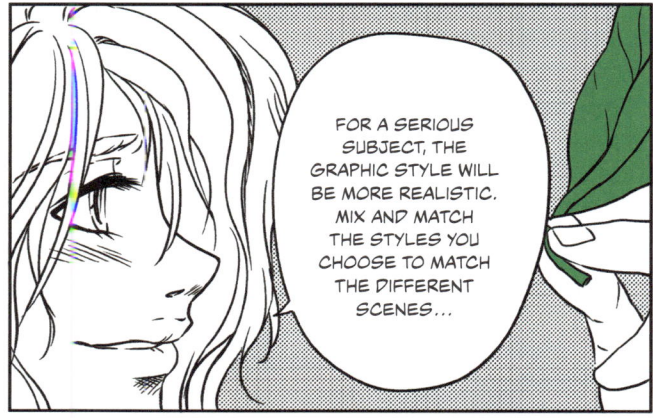

FOR A SERIOUS SUBJECT, THE GRAPHIC STYLE WILL BE MORE REALISTIC. MIX AND MATCH THE STYLES YOU CHOOSE TO MATCH THE DIFFERENT SCENES...

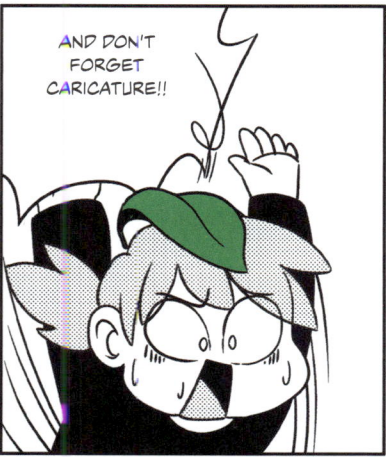

AND DON'T FORGET CARICATURE!!

It will be easier for you if you write a manga that reflects your own personality. Write what sounds like you before having fun with varying your styles.

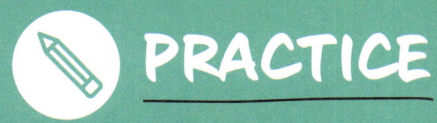

Starting a Project Handbook

A project handbook is a collection of all the ideas that you might have when you are writing a story. It often takes the form of a (paper or digital) folder and contains all sorts of documents: drawings, text, inspirations, plans, character info sheets, research…

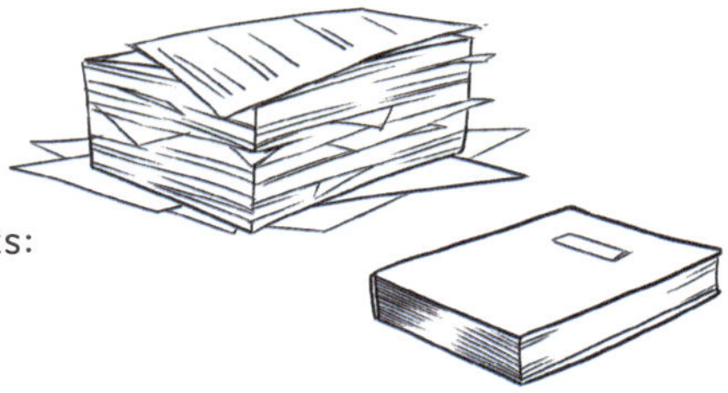

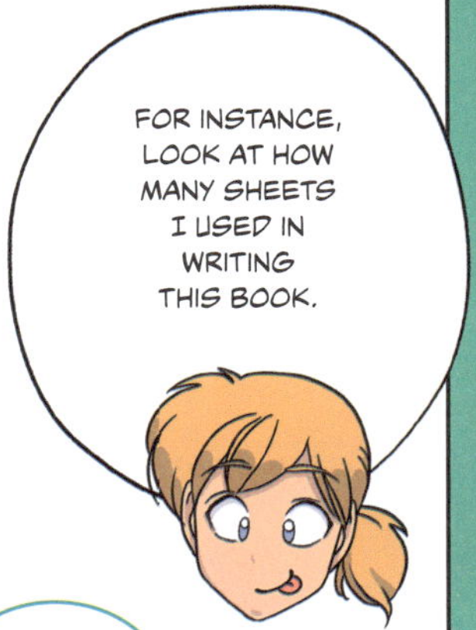

FOR INSTANCE, LOOK AT HOW MANY SHEETS I USED IN WRITING THIS BOOK.

Before you jump into writing your first storyline, I invite you to start your project handbook and include the following elements in it:
- A theme that is important to you.
- An idea that will make your manga original and interesting to read.
- The tone and style that best suit your work.

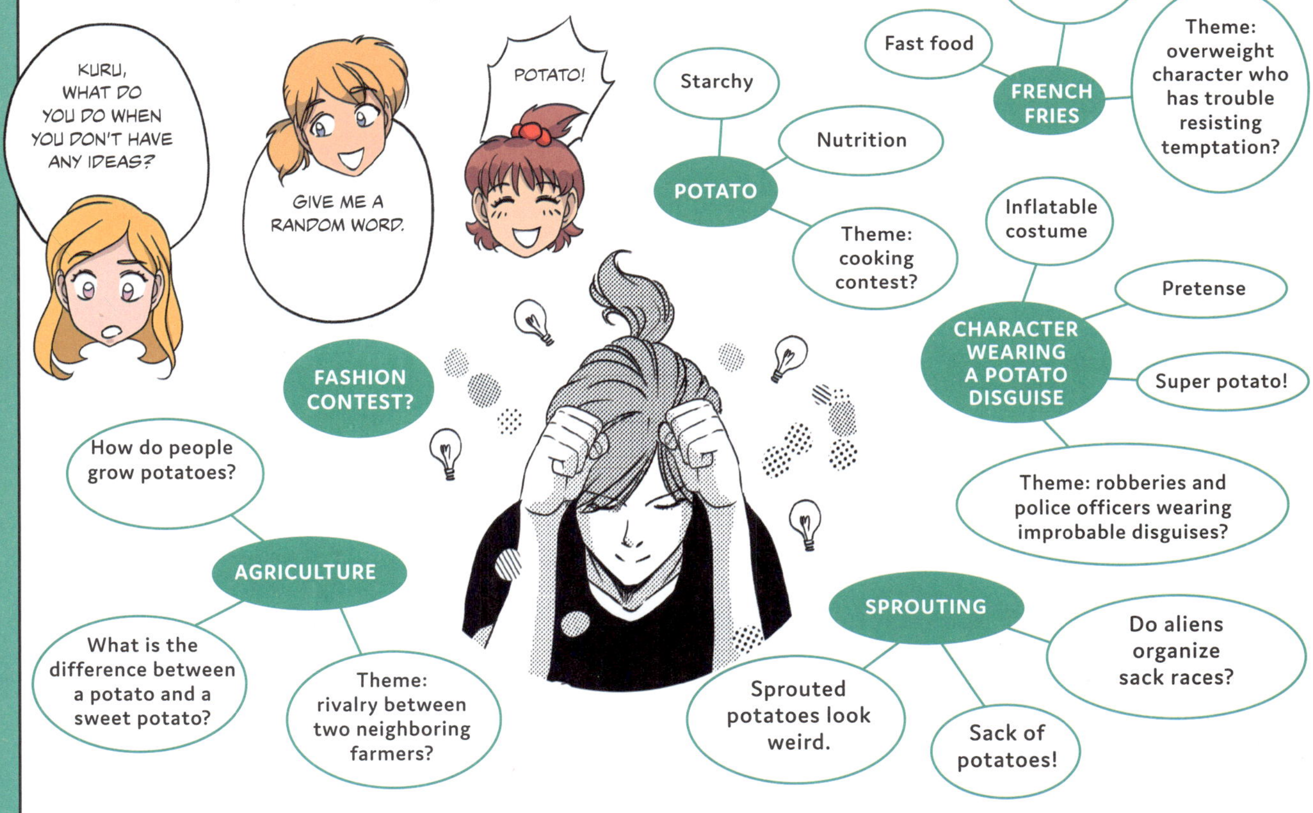

KURU, WHAT DO YOU DO WHEN YOU DON'T HAVE ANY IDEAS?

GIVE ME A RANDOM WORD.

POTATO!

Hard to stay on a diet

Fast food

Starchy

Nutrition

FRENCH FRIES

Theme: overweight character who has trouble resisting temptation?

POTATO

Theme: cooking contest?

Inflatable costume

Pretense

CHARACTER WEARING A POTATO DISGUISE

Super potato!

FASHION CONTEST?

How do people grow potatoes?

Theme: robberies and police officers wearing improbable disguises?

AGRICULTURE

SPROUTING

Do aliens organize sack races?

What is the difference between a potato and a sweet potato?

Theme: rivalry between two neighboring farmers?

Sprouted potatoes look weird.

Sack of potatoes!

*This technique of associating different ideas is called **brainstorming**.*

When we let our imagination run wild, we can turn up all kinds of ideas. It is up to you to figure out which one might be the most interesting to use.

To find more, there's nothing like inspiring resources. Read manga, listen to music, watch TV series and movies, look at masterpieces of art, follow your favorite artists on social networks. Sometimes, it doesn't take very much for something to click and unlock your story.

WRITING THE STORYLINE

Every story has already been told. If you set out to write an original, extraordinary, captivating story, you will soon realize that it sounds like something that already exists. This is normal, and it is reassuring for your readers to find established patterns in your stories.

There are several ways of writing a storyline and you can get inspiration from them to find the one that works best for you.

Some authors rely on the characters to write the story. They confront them with complex situations and then imagine how they will find solutions and thus progress in their adventure.

The adventures are the consequences of the characters' choices.

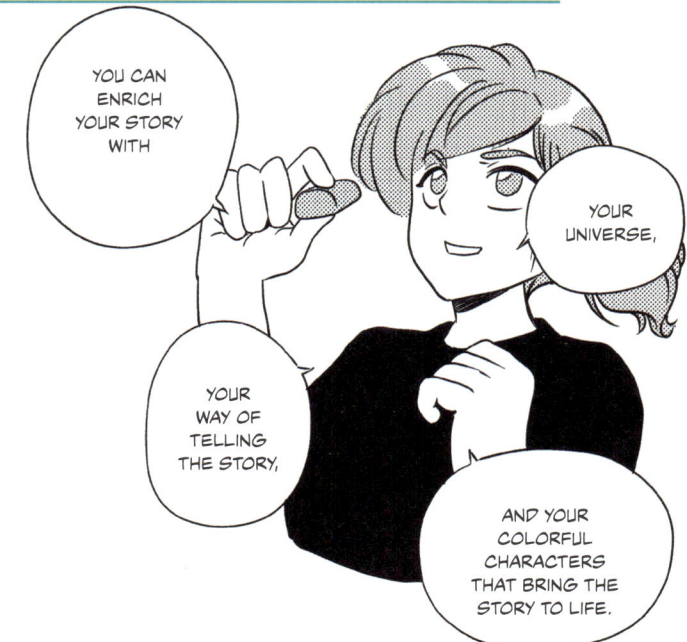

YOU CAN ENRICH YOUR STORY WITH

YOUR UNIVERSE,

YOUR WAY OF TELLING THE STORY,

AND YOUR COLORFUL CHARACTERS THAT BRING THE STORY TO LIFE.

Other writers prefer to start with a striking setting and then choose the **protagonists** later.

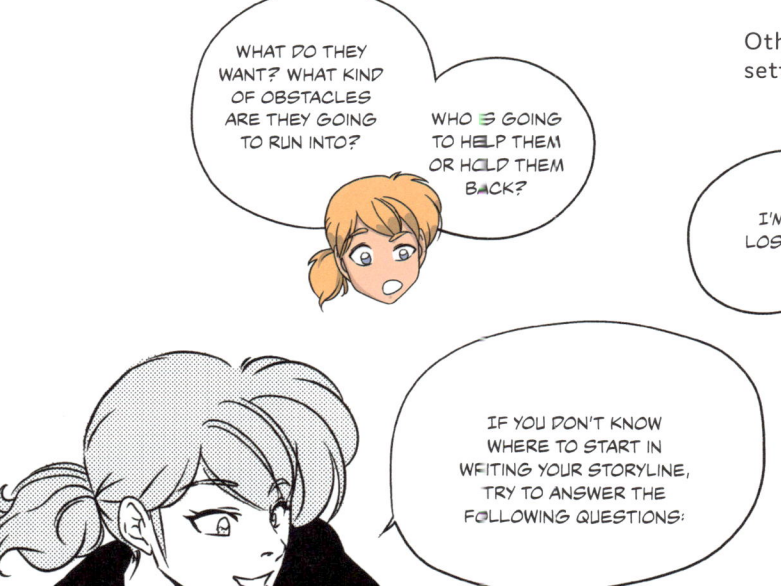

WHAT DO THEY WANT? WHAT KIND OF OBSTACLES ARE THEY GOING TO RUN INTO?

WHO IS GOING TO HELP THEM OR HOLD THEM BACK?

IF YOU DON'T KNOW WHERE TO START IN WRITING YOUR STORYLINE, TRY TO ANSWER THE FOLLOWING QUESTIONS:

I'M LOST!

If the ideas just aren't coming, start by setting the scene and then choosing where and how the story is going to take place.

Imagine your character in this universe and then send the character to complete a simple task like… asking somebody what time it is.

What's going to happen?

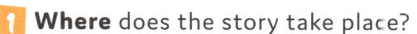

1. **Where** does the story take place?

2. **When** do the scenes happen?

3. **Who** is involved?

4. **What** is happening? **What's** it all about?

5. **How** are the protagonists going to achieve their goals?

6. **Why** are they doing all of this?
   Why is somebody trying to stop them?

THE NARRATIVE OUTLINE

All stories have a beginning, a middle, and an end.

A **narrative outline** is a skeleton to which we can add details and then flesh out our storyline.

This sequence is well-known to readers and can serve as a basis for writing your first storyline.

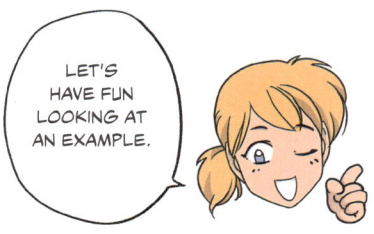

LET'S HAVE FUN LOOKING AT AN EXAMPLE.

In manga, everything has to be important to the story. Get rid of anything extraneous as quickly as possible.

If we look closely at these steps, we can see that box 4 could be eliminated and the story would remain comprehensible. In manga, there are frequently 4 steps, not 5, in the narrative outline.

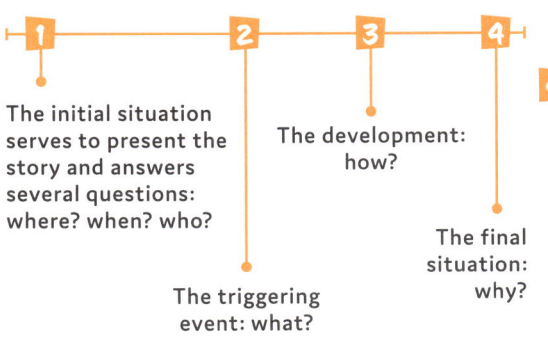

1 The initial situation serves to present the story and answers several questions: where? when? who?

2 The triggering event: what?

3 The development: how?

4 The final situation: why?

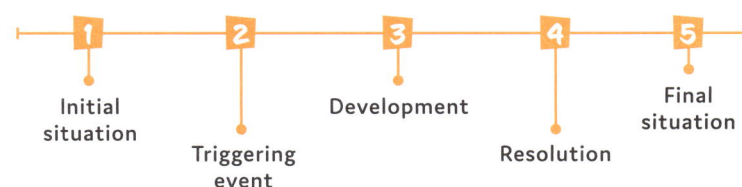

1 Initial situation
2 Triggering event
3 Development
4 Resolution
5 Final situation

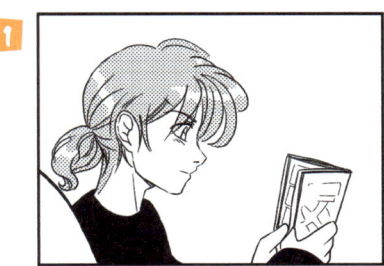

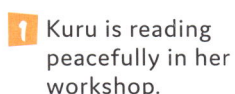

1 Kuru is reading peacefully in her workshop.

2 Some students arrive to learn how to draw manga.

3 Kuru shares her knowledge with them.

4 They make progress.

5 The students leave enriched and can now draw on their own.

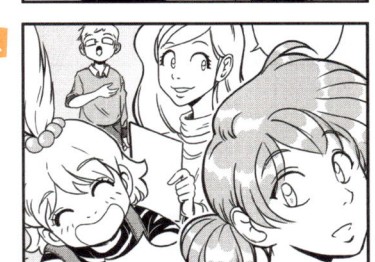

The development is the consequence of the triggering event. Each incident or twist calls for another one, while at the same time the tension is increased, until the **climax**.

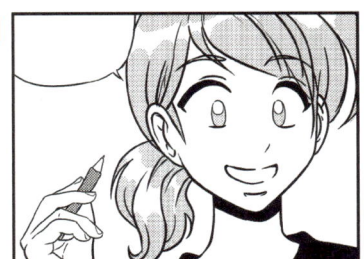

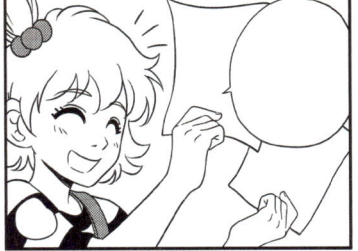

The climax is the most intense moment in the story. This is where we stop to leave our readers in suspense until the next chapter or the next volume of our manga.

The final situation brings us the answers that we have been waiting for so eagerly and brings about a new balance, from which the characters can start off again on new adventures.

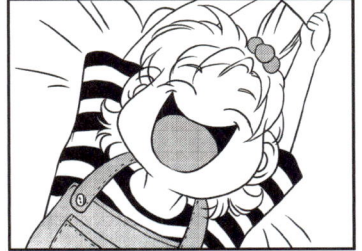

ESTABLISHED NARRATIVE OUTLINES

An established outline is a developed narrative outline that allows us to steer the events in the story toward a known resolution.

SO, IN OTHER WORDS, WE'RE JUST COPYING AN EXISTING STORY?

NO, BECAUSE THIS IS JUST A BASIC SKELETON THAT YOU'RE GOING TO USE TO DEVELOP YOUR OWN IDEAS.

Let's take the example of Romeo and Juliet, whose outline could be summarized as follows: **Two people, from opposing clans, fall in love and try to reconcile their two different worlds.**

COULDN'T THAT DESCRIPTION ALSO CORRESPOND TO THE STORY OF *POCAHONTAS?* OR *AVATAR?* ...

GREASE? WEST SIDE STORY? TWILIGHT? THE ROMANCE BETWEEN TAURIEL AND KILI IN *THE HOBBIT?* PRINCESS MONONOKE?

IF YOU LOOK CAREFULLY, YOU WILL EVEN FIND THAT PART OF THE FAMOUS ADVENTURES OF *ASTERIX* FOLLOWS THIS OUTLINE.

IT'S LIKE WHEN YOU DRAW A CHARACTER WHOSE SKELETON FOLLOWS A SET OF ESTABLISHED ANATOMICAL RULES. YOU'RE DOING THE SAME THING THAT MANY OTHER ARTISTS HAVE DONE, AND YET YOUR CHARACTERS WILL BE RADICALLY DIFFERENT.

Each of these stories has its own universe, characters, style, and adventures, but the skeleton remains the same.

Using identifiable skeletons for some or all of your story is reassuring to your readers because they can already anticipate the ending. A good writer will provide a universe, characters, and/or plot twists that will surprise their audience.

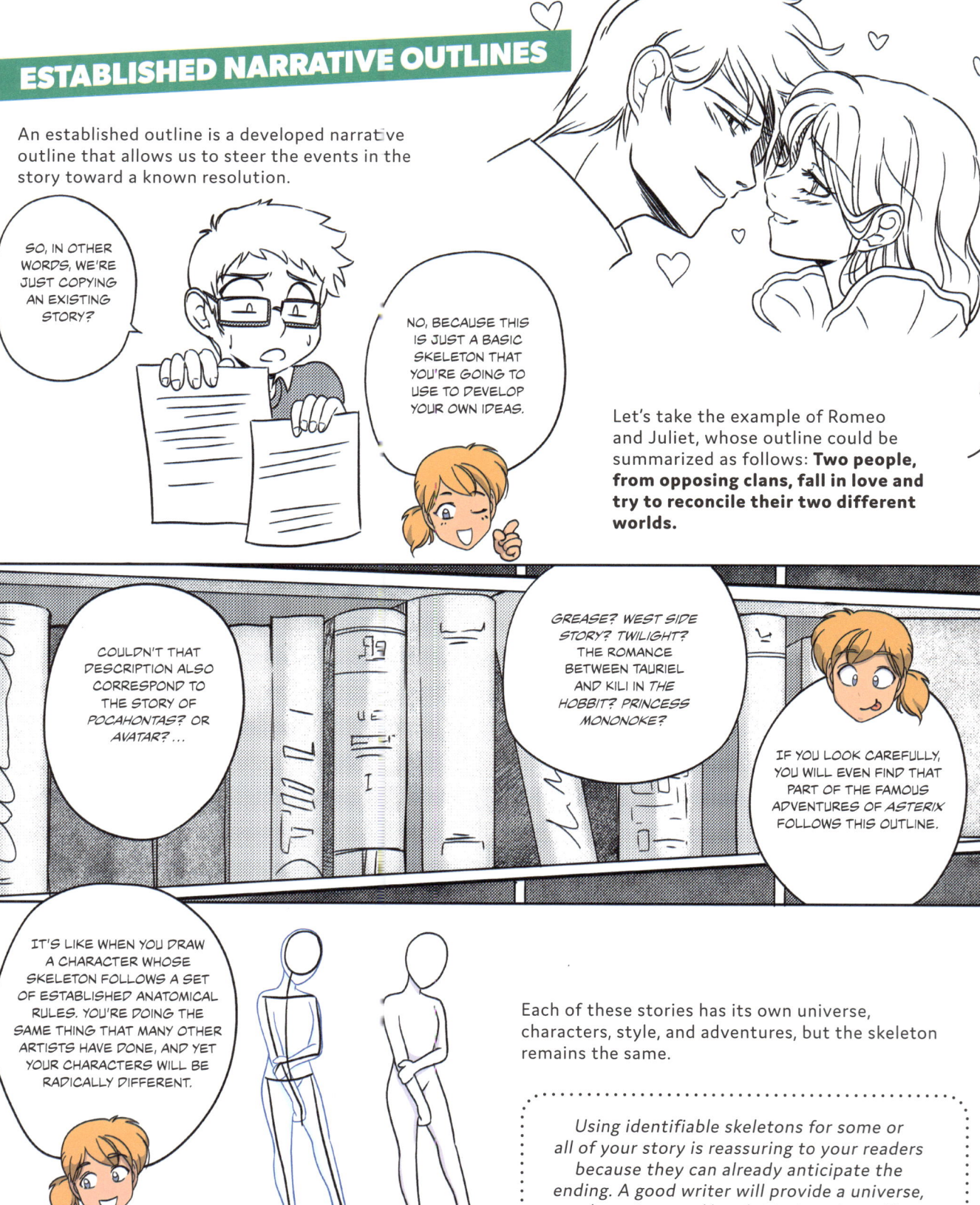

THE HERO'S JOURNEY

The difference between the famous French and Belgian *bandes dessinées* (illustrated comic novels like Asterix and Tintin) and manga stories is that in manga stories, **your characters will live out the story** that you have imagined for them and will grow over the course of the pages, with the goal of **becoming better versions of themselves**.

The **protagonist** starts out on an initial journey that will make him or her evolve through a series of very specific steps.

In his book *The Hero with a Thousand Faces*, Joseph Campbell presents the twelve stages of the hero's journey that you can see below:

1 The hero lives a peaceful life in their world of origin.

2 They respond to the call of adventure, which appears in the form of a challenge to be answered.

3 But they are afraid of the unknown.

4 With the support and encouragement of a mentor, they finally agree to respond to the challenge.

5 Once they have crossed the threshold of a new world, the hero cannot turn back.

6 They undergo trials, confront enemies, and surround themself with allies.

7 They reach the most dangerous point in their journey, where the object of their quest is located.

8 They face the formidable enemy: death.

9 They succeed in seizing the object that they covet.

10 The hero takes the road homeward, protecting their flanks.

11 They return to their world transformed.

12 They use the object they brought back with them to make their ordinary world better.

This narrative outline is particularly heavily represented in shonen manga, but it can also be found in film and literature.

TIP

Use these steps as inspiration for constructing the events and twists in your storyline.

DEVELOPING YOUR STORY

You have your ideas, your narrative outline, and an established outline to rely on for your first draft. Now it is time to develop the twists and turns of your story, and for this, it is useful to do some **research** into your universe.

This is particularly true if your stories take place in geographical areas or historical areas different from the ones that you live in.

Keep adding to your project handbook throughout the process of writing your storyline, putting in your ideas and the results of your research.

Every event in your story has at least **one cause and one consequence**.

Using the **deductive method** to write your storyline, we are going to choose a beginning scene and then imagine all of the possible consequences: what's going to happen next?

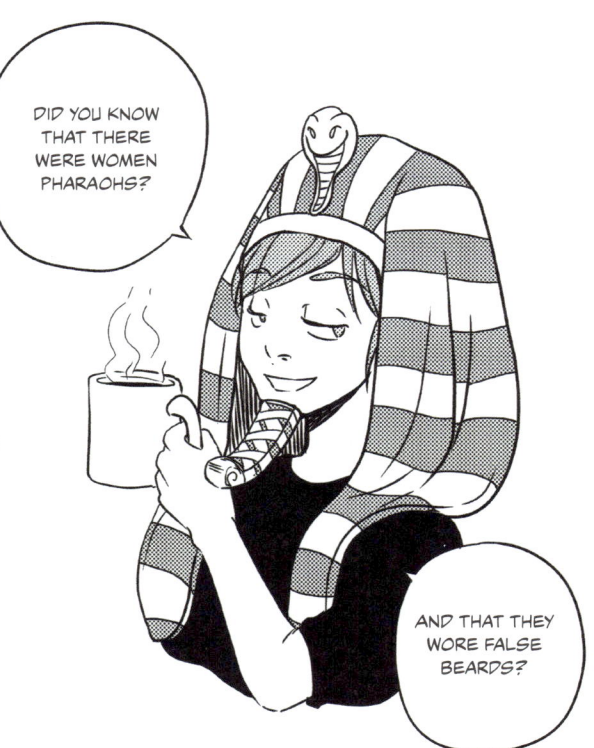

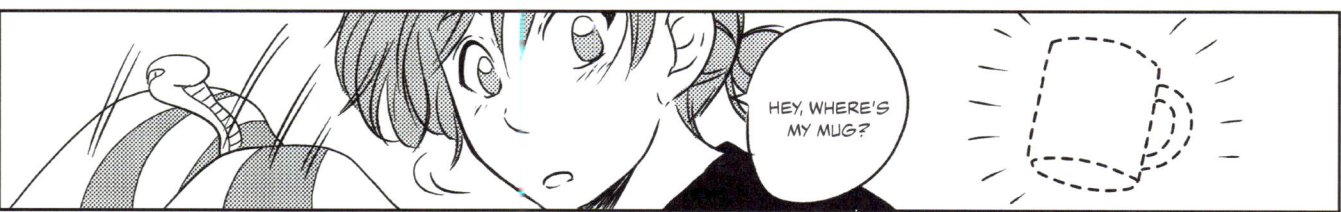

OPTION 1 | OPTION 2 | OPTION 3 | OPTION 4

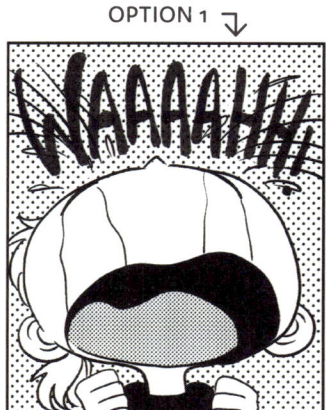

The reaction of a fussy, sensitive character could be interesting, but it doesn't really match the image we have established of the character so far.

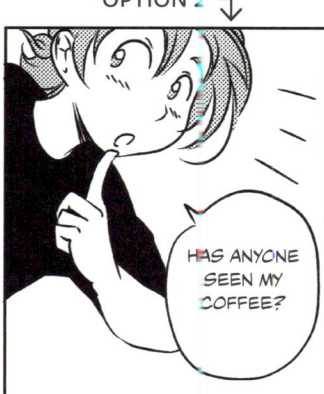

A very measured reaction is reassuring, but it is boring in terms of the story.

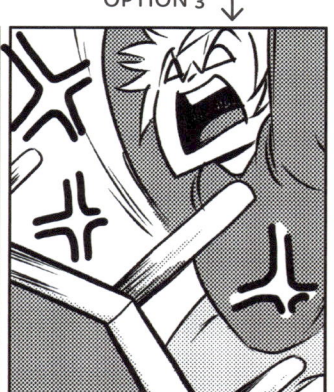

An exaggerated reaction transforms the scene into a gag. This can be interesting to the readers because the outsized reaction can continue to be deployed across several exchanges with the students.

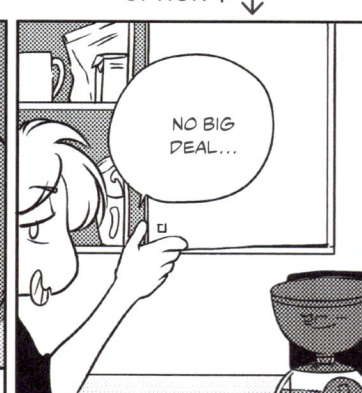

The character is presented as being shrewd and ready for anything. It will be interesting to develop this to see at what point they run out of resources.

It's up to you to choose the scene that offers the most possibilities for what comes next. You always want to leave a door open in the narration so that the **protagonist** can progress.

Another way to think about your storyline is to use the **inductive method**. You reimagine an initial scene and work backward through the clues to try to understand how and why we got to that place.

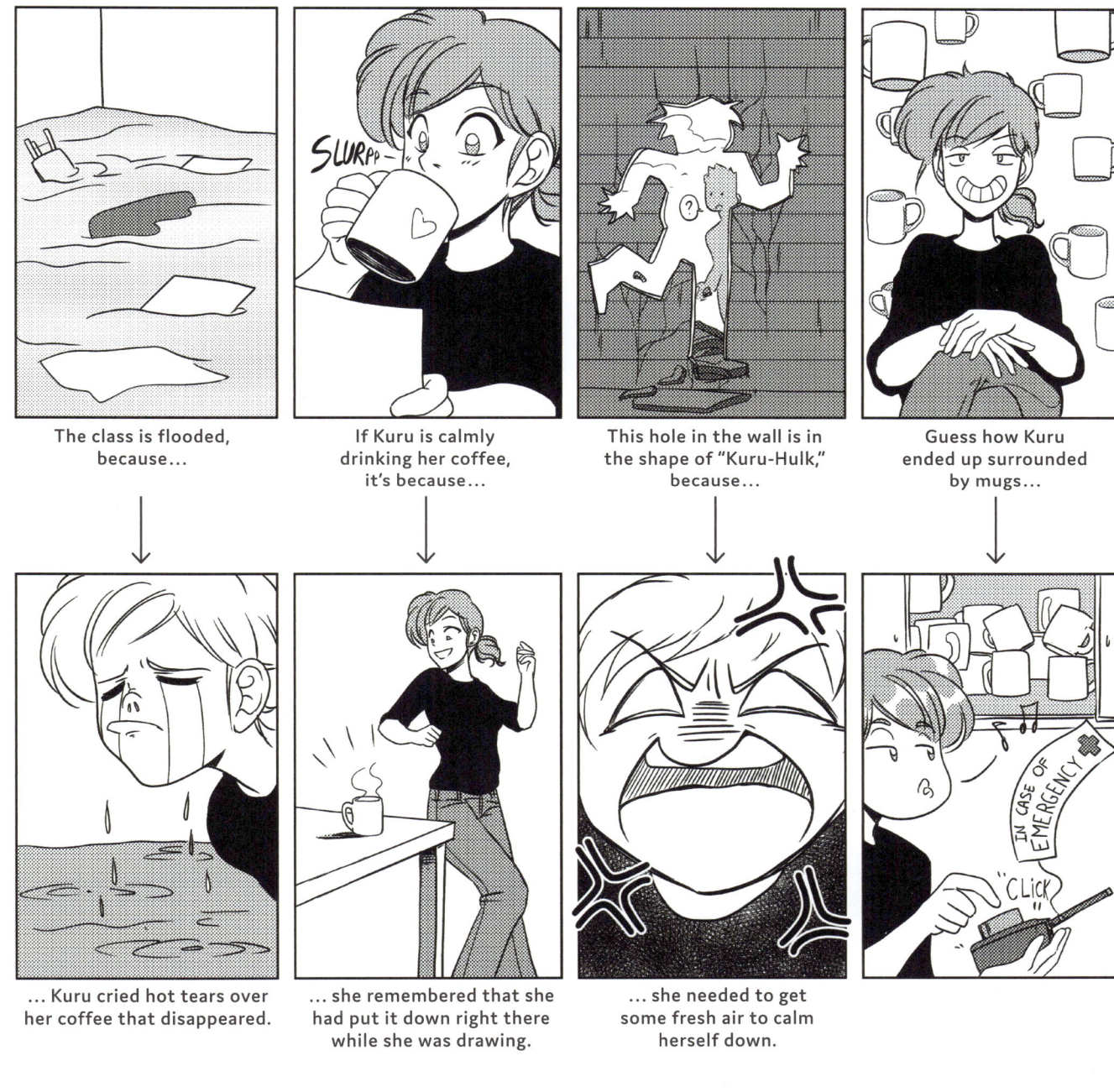

The class is flooded, because…

If Kuru is calmly drinking her coffee, it's because…

This hole in the wall is in the shape of "Kuru-Hulk," because…

Guess how Kuru ended up surrounded by mugs…

… Kuru cried hot tears over her coffee that disappeared.

… she remembered that she had put it down right there while she was drawing.

… she needed to get some fresh air to calm herself down.

Establish the timeline of your story a little bit at a time, taking into consideration your characters' personalities and the tone that you have chosen for your story.

A TIP

Put together a list of the adventures that you will then be able to write on a timeline.

SEQUENCING THE PLOT

Once you have established the timeline of the events in your story, you have a couple of different options:

- Telling everything in order.
- Creating a sequence for the plot and only showing a few excerpts in an order that will make the readers ask themselves questions.

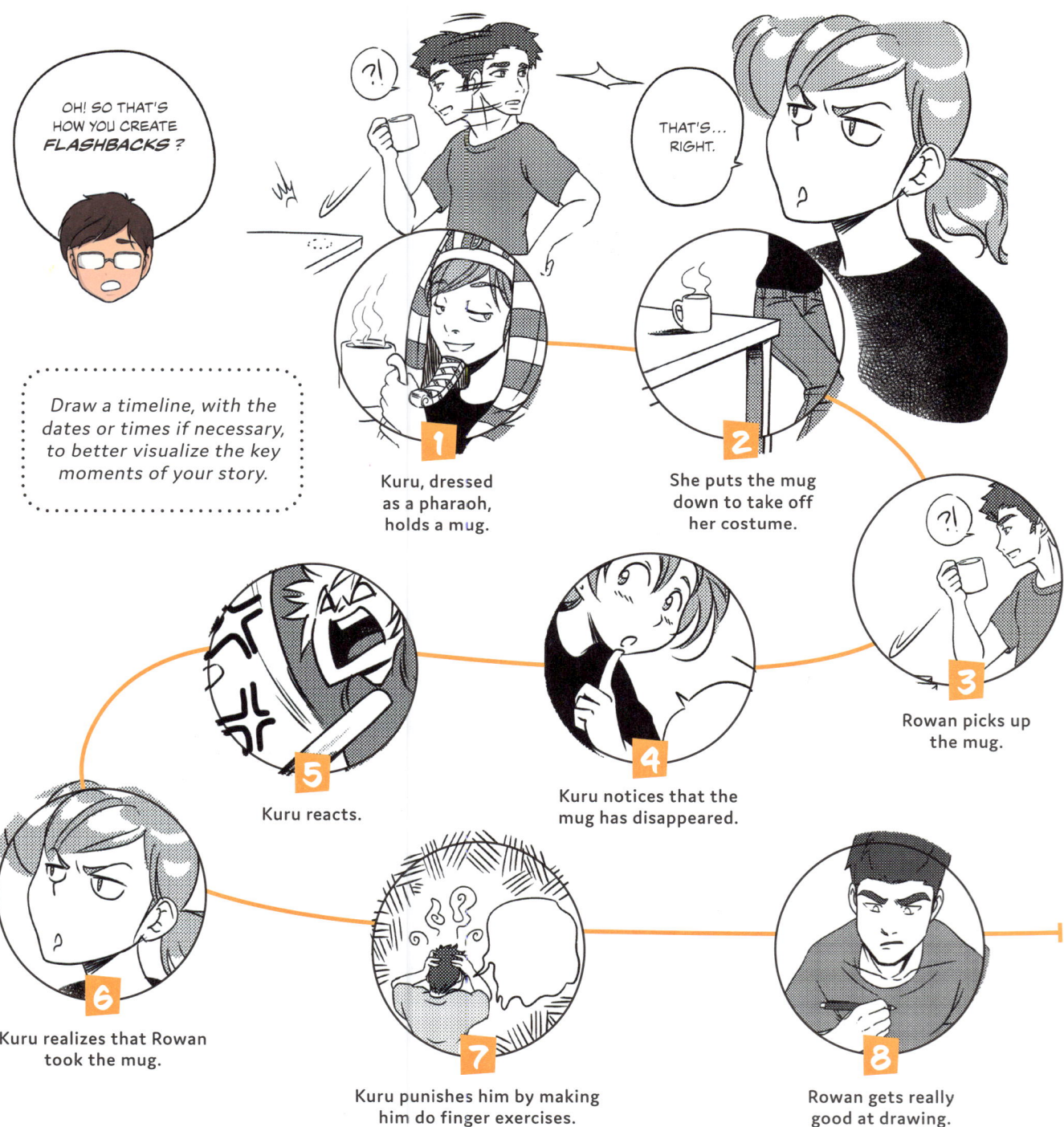

Draw a timeline, with the dates or times if necessary, to better visualize the key moments of your story.

1. Kuru, dressed as a pharaoh, holds a mug.

2. She puts the mug down to take off her costume.

3. Rowan picks up the mug.

4. Kuru notices that the mug has disappeared.

5. Kuru reacts.

6. Kuru realizes that Rowan took the mug.

7. Kuru punishes him by making him do finger exercises.

8. Rowan gets really good at drawing.

Choose **the beginning, the middle, and the end of your story,** which will not necessarily be in chronological order.

Kuru notices that the mug has disappeared. **4**

Kuru reacts. **5**

Kuru, dressed as a pharaoh, holds a mug. **1**

She puts down her mug to take off her costume. **2**

Rowan picks up the mug. **3**

Kuru realizes that Rowan took the mug. **6**

Kuru punishes him by making him do finger exercises. **7**

Rowan gets really good at drawing. **8**

8 Rowan gets really good at drawing.

1 Kuru dressed as a pharaoh, holds a mug.

2 She puts down her mug to take off her costume.

4 Kuru notices that the mug has disappeared.

3 Rowan picks up the mug.

6 Kuru realizes that Rowan took the mug.

5 Kuru reacts.

7 Kuru punishes him by making him do finger exercises.

PLEASE NOTE

If you decide to present the steps of the story out of order, be careful not to allow any continuity errors or inconsistencies to creep into your storyline.

Using the method above, **find the best sequence and determine the number of pages that your manga is going to have** before you develop your scenes and write your dialogues.

It is only once you have a well-defined number of pages that you will know whether you need to reduce or expand any given scene.

ALTERNATING MOMENTS OF TENSION AND MOMENTS OF CALM

Your story will have **moments of tension** (highlights in the action) and **moments of calm**. By alternating these throughout your story you will give it a rhythm and make it dynamic.

Here are three ways of showing Kuru reacting to the loss of her coffee.

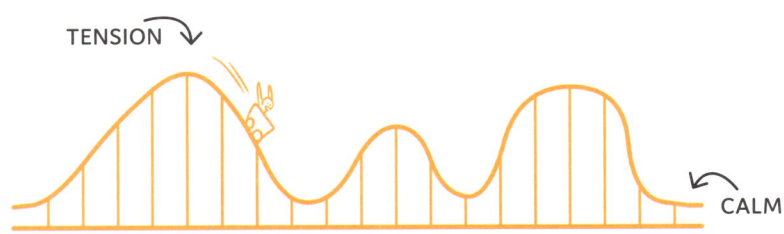

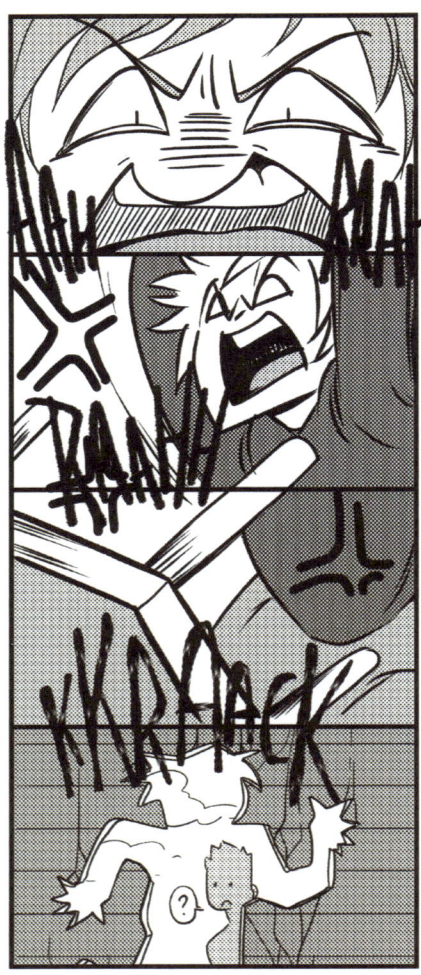

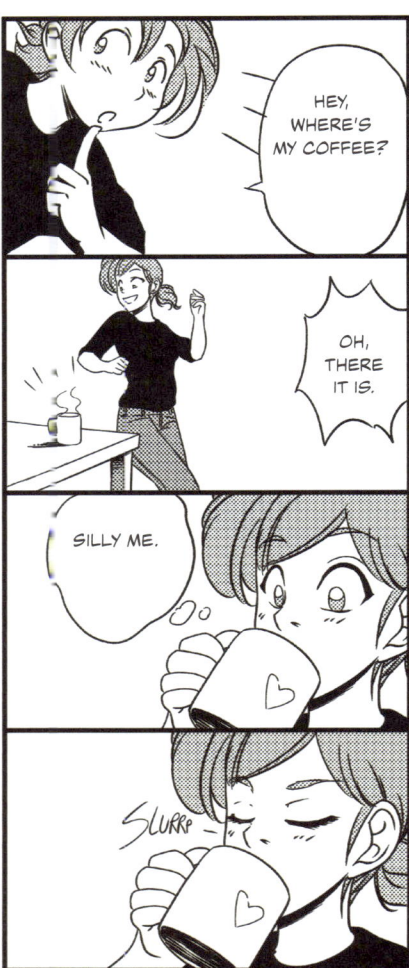

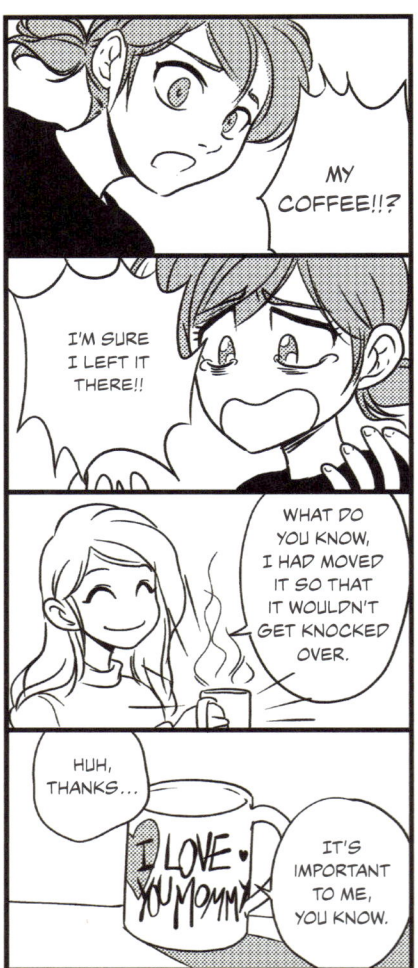

TIP

Give your readers a thrill by giving them action scenes along with scenes full of emotions.

YONKOMA

A yonkoma is a little story drawn in just four or eight panels. You have already seen this particular format on the preceding pages.

The tone is generally humorous because the short form lends itself to gags. All of the panels in a yonkoma are the same size, and you read them from top to bottom.

In a yonkoma, we find the four steps of the narrative outline.

> *Yonkoma appear as a bonus section at the end of manga or between the chapters, but they can also be used as a composition choice throughout the book.*

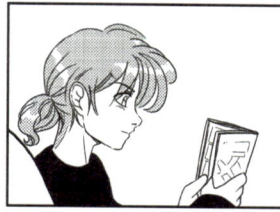

KI: initial situation

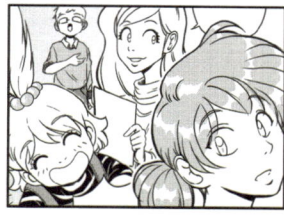

SHO: event

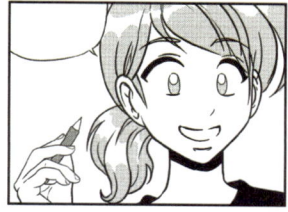

TEN: reversal

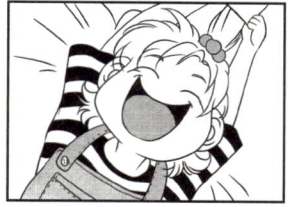

KETSU: final situation

PRACTICE

Creating a Yonkoma

Draw a column of four panels of the same size (6 x 8 cm), spaced the same distance apart (0.5 cm).

Choose a theme or a scene to represent, such as:

· A character with their head in the clouds walks down the street and trips.

· There is only one cookie left and two different characters are each trying to get it.

· Two characters mistakenly trade suitcases at the airport.

· A cat is sitting at a window, bored.

For example:

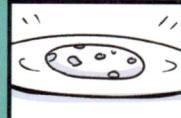

A cookie alone on a plate.

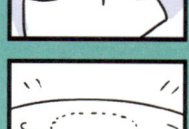

Two characters elbow each other to get the cookie.

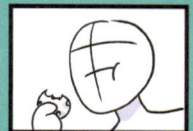

The cookie is gone.

A third person has eaten it.

Write a sentence to describe the contents of each panel, thinking in terms of the narrative outline, and then draw the contents of each panel.

To take this further, develop the sequence of four panels to make it into four pages.

DIALOGUES

Dialogues convey information to the readers that is essential for understanding the story.

In comic books and graphic novels, and especially in manga, **the dialogues and other text placed within the background serve as reinforcement** for the images shown in the panels.

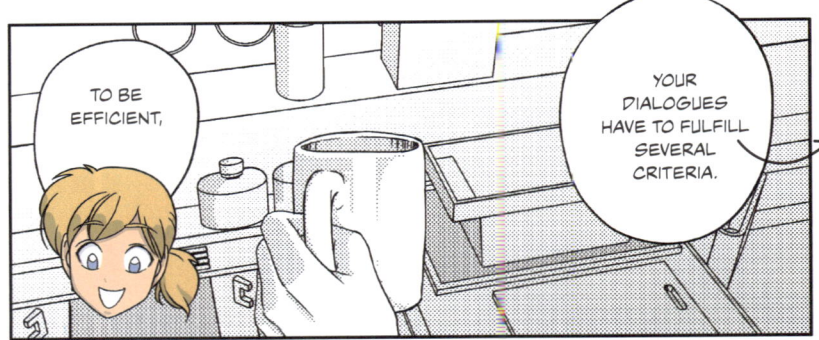

1 Be concise.

2 Convey the right information.

3 Be consistent with the character and the context.

4 Use the right vocabulary and tone.

Don't make your characters say something that we can already see in the pictures.

CHOOSING THE RIGHT DIALOGUE

The context will determine how your characters behave as well as the exchanges between them.

For every dialogue, we can work on the content—the **information to be conveyed**—as well as the form—**the level of the language, the tone, and the vocabulary.**

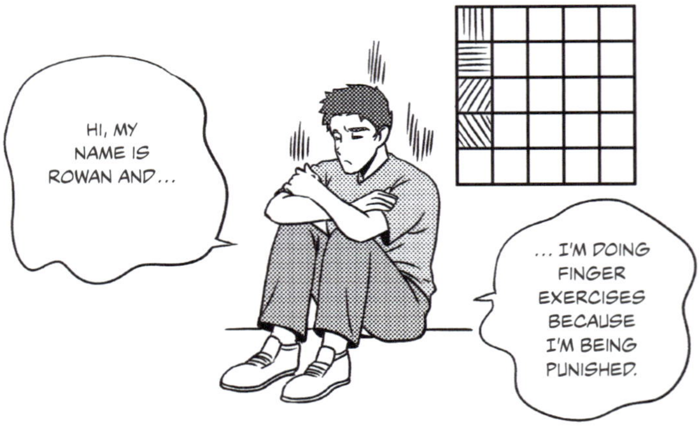

YOOHOO!! KURUUUU!!

HI, MY NAME IS ROWAN AND...

...I'M DOING FINGER EXERCISES BECAUSE I'M BEING PUNISHED.

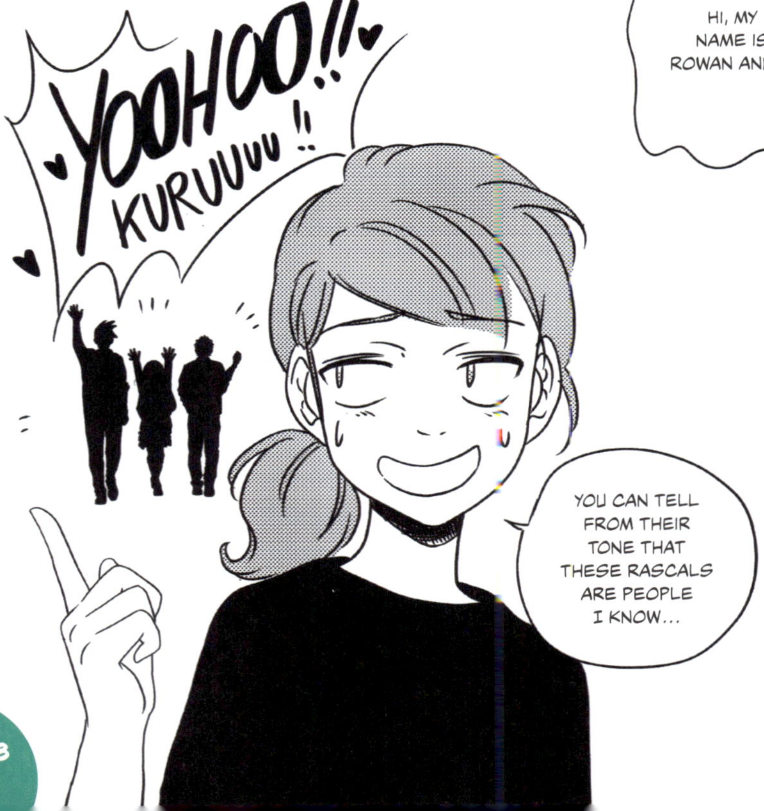

YOU CAN TELL FROM THEIR TONE THAT THESE RASCALS ARE PEOPLE I KNOW...

We don't talk the same way to ourselves, our family and loved ones, our friends, our colleagues, and strangers on the street.

Remember that in manga, there is no room for accidents or chance. Every picture and every word has to serve the story one way or another.

That means that a dialogue has to provide material to the readers: **information, clues, material for reflection, or revelations**.

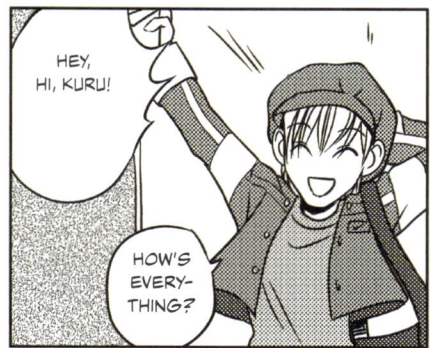
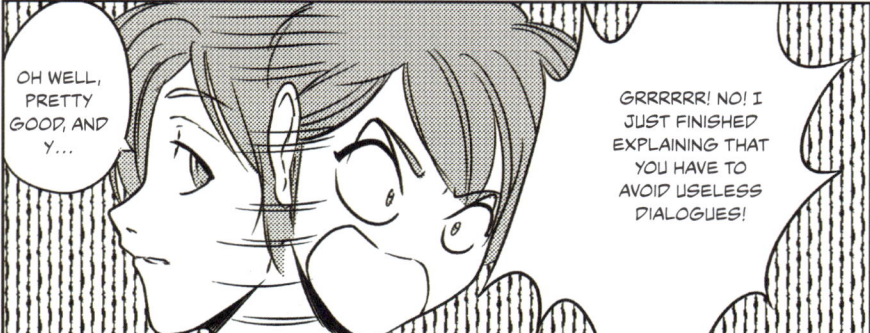

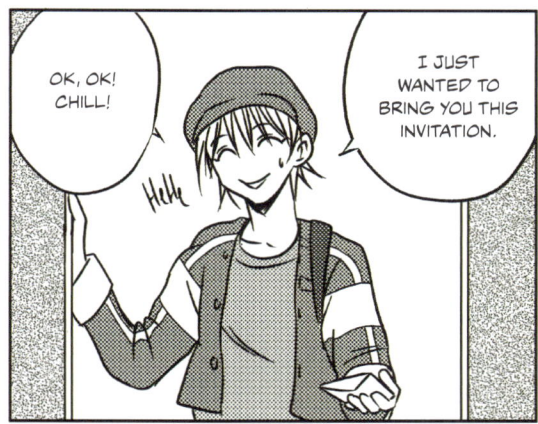

▲ This dialogue gives us new information and serves as an initiating element.

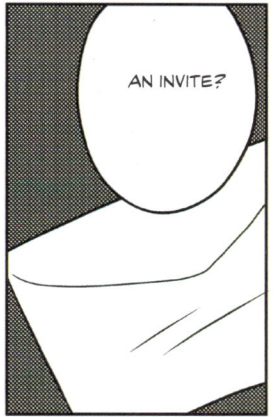

▲ The tone suggests that the two characters know each other well..

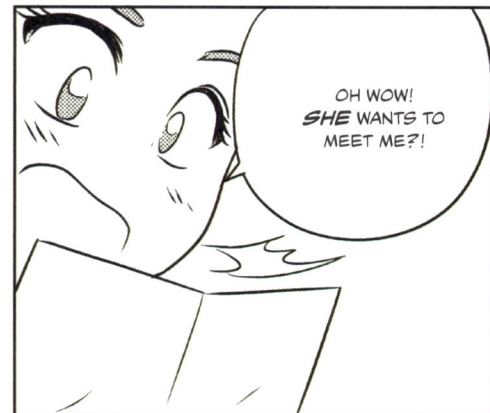

▲ Here, we are teased with some clues without being given any concrete information.

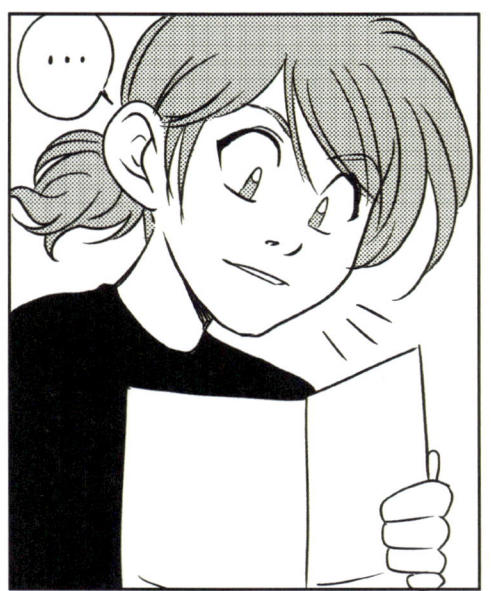

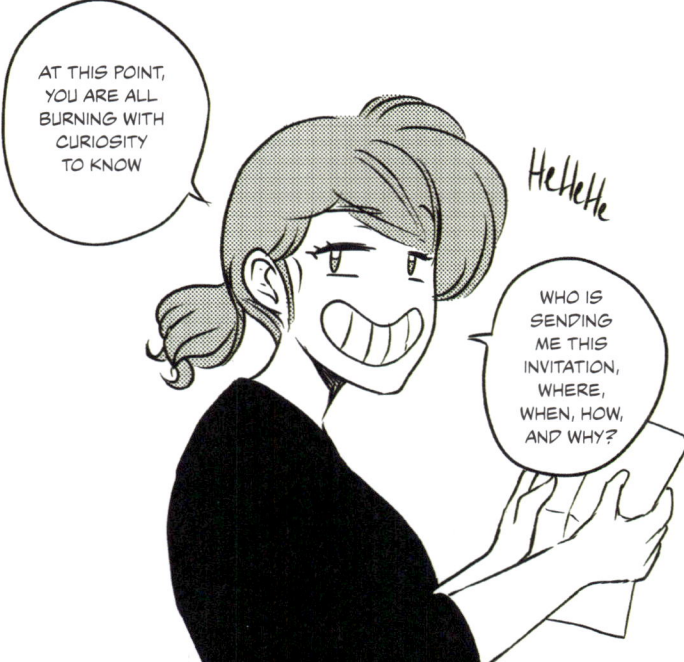

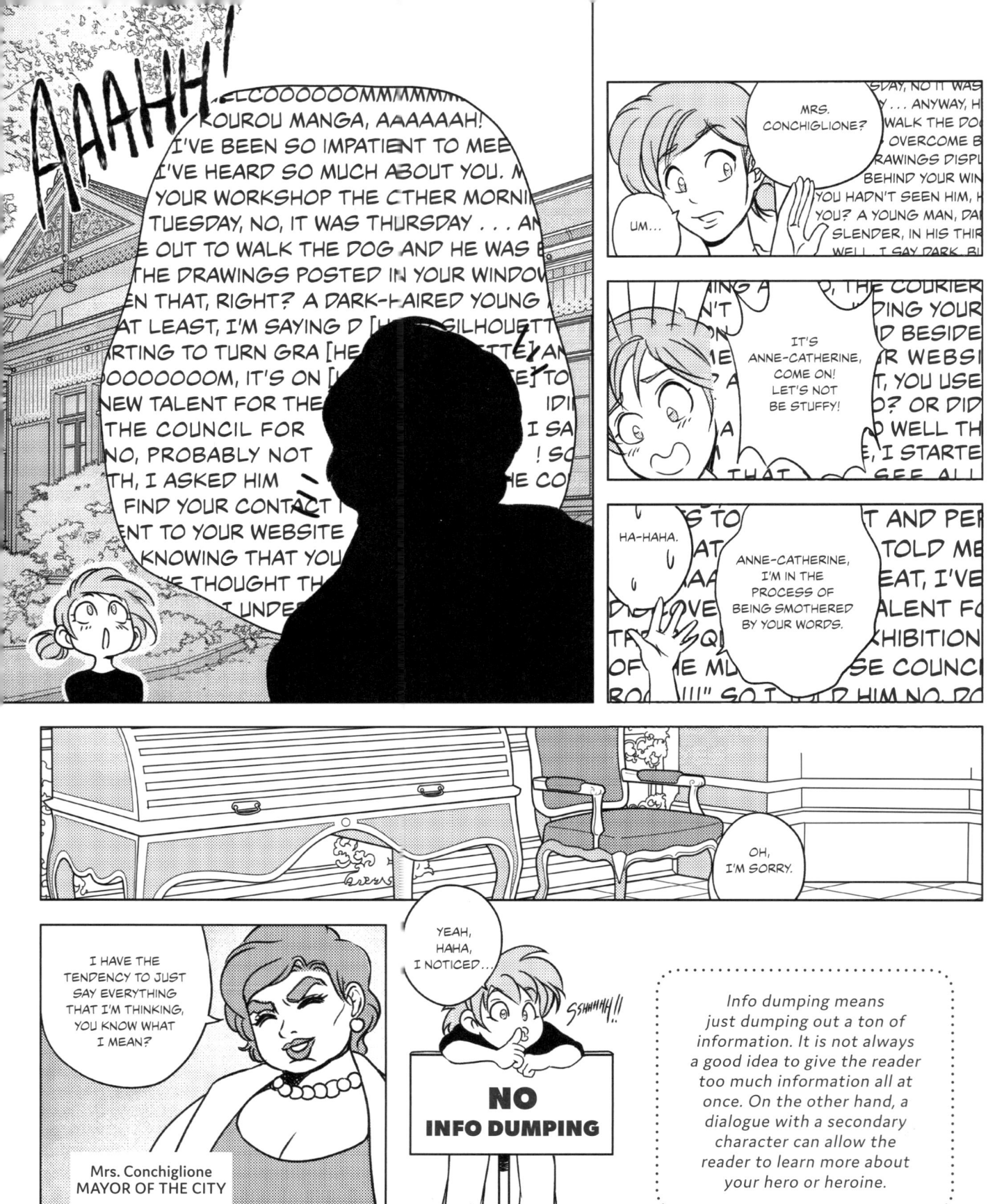

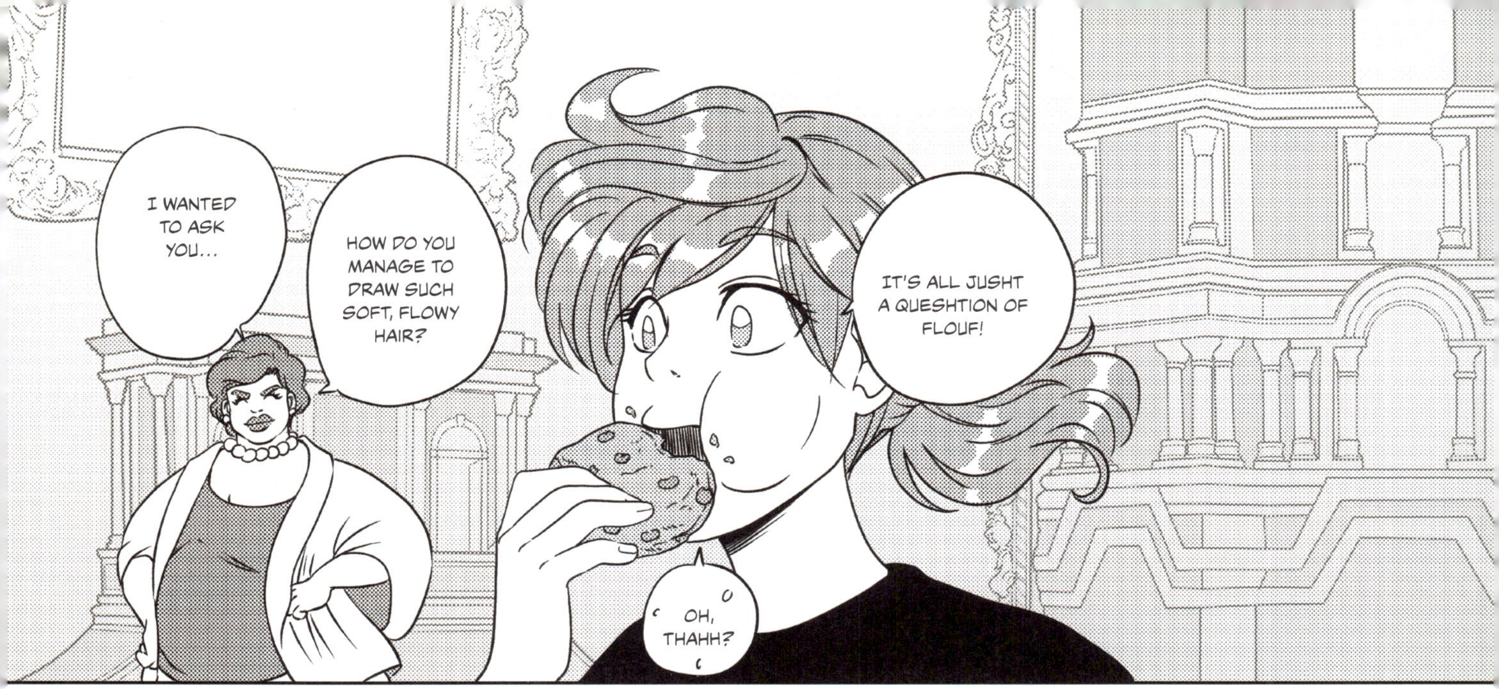

It's totally possible to invent words in manga, as long as they can be understood in the context and correspond to the vocabulary of the characters using them.

On the other hand, dialogues lose their flow as soon as the characters are given a vocabulary and a level of language that is not what we would expect from those characters:

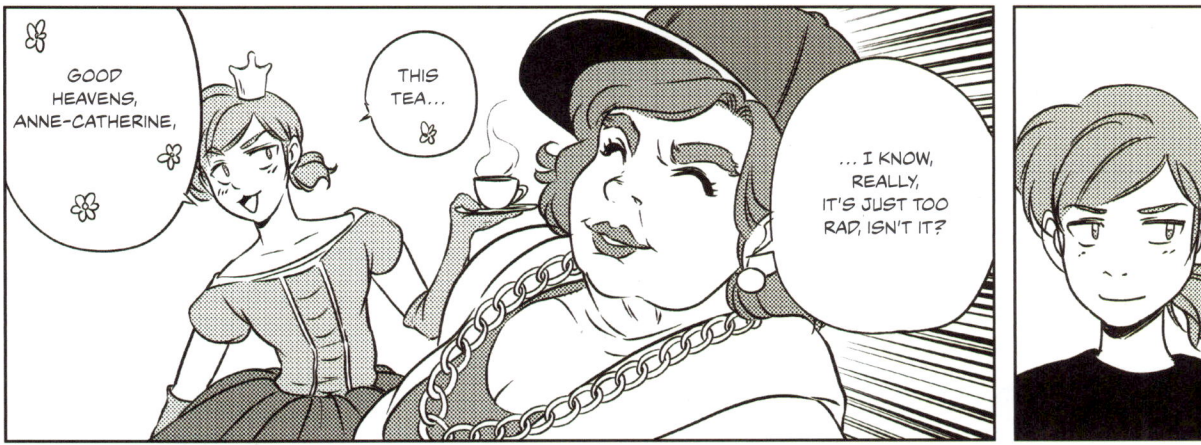

Vary the rhythm of the dialogues to avoid monotony. A long silence can be worth a thousand words!

In summary:
- Keep your dialogues as brief as possible.
- Don't be afraid to imagine voices in your head in order to let your character speak instead of yourself.
- Use a vocabulary, tone, and language level that are appropriate to the characters and the context.
- Invent words if it makes sense for the dialogue.
- Make the most of your text, and cut down on clutter, by including only the information that is needed to understand the story.

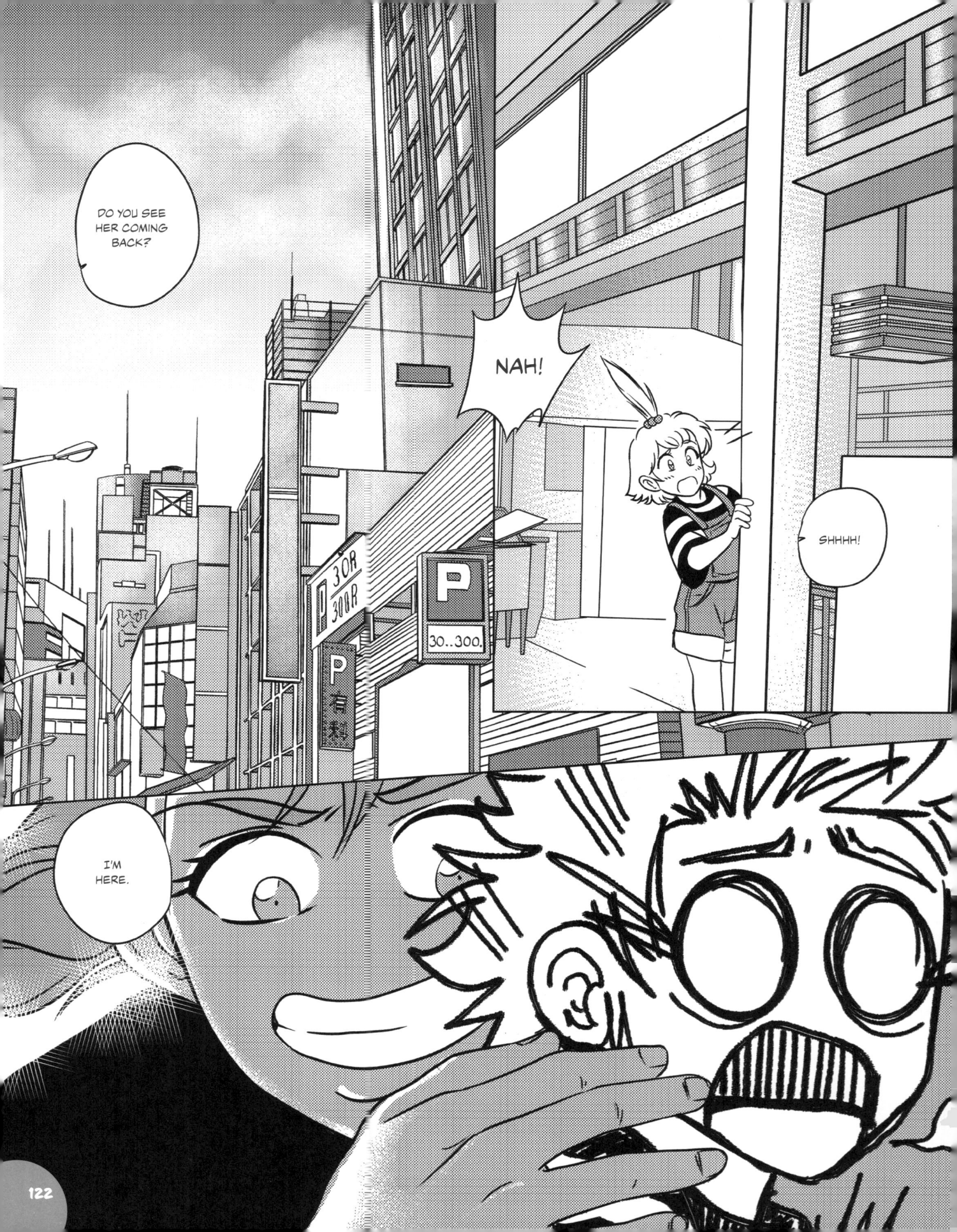

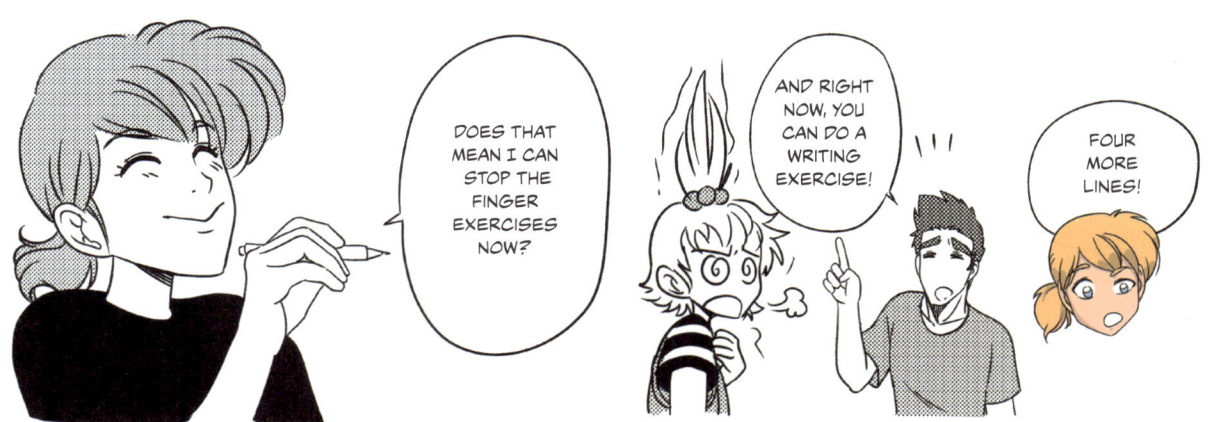

PRACTICE

Writing a Manga Storyline

Now that you have a clearer idea of how to put together a storyline, I invite you to start by writing short stories.

Find a theme or an idea, then summarize your story in a single sentence in which every word is important. This is what we call the **pitch**.

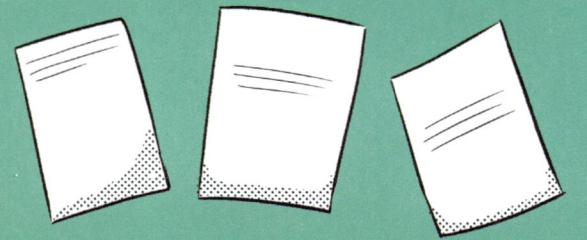

Answer the six key questions for the plot: **Where? When? Who? What? How? Why?**

Develop your story using the narrative outline or existing established outlines. Create a timeline, then determine the order of the sequences as you will present them.

Put together the casting for your manga by choosing interesting characters who fit your scenes, and give them lines that work for them.

TIP

You probably won't be able to write everything in one sitting. Feel free to take breaks!

THE STORYBOARD

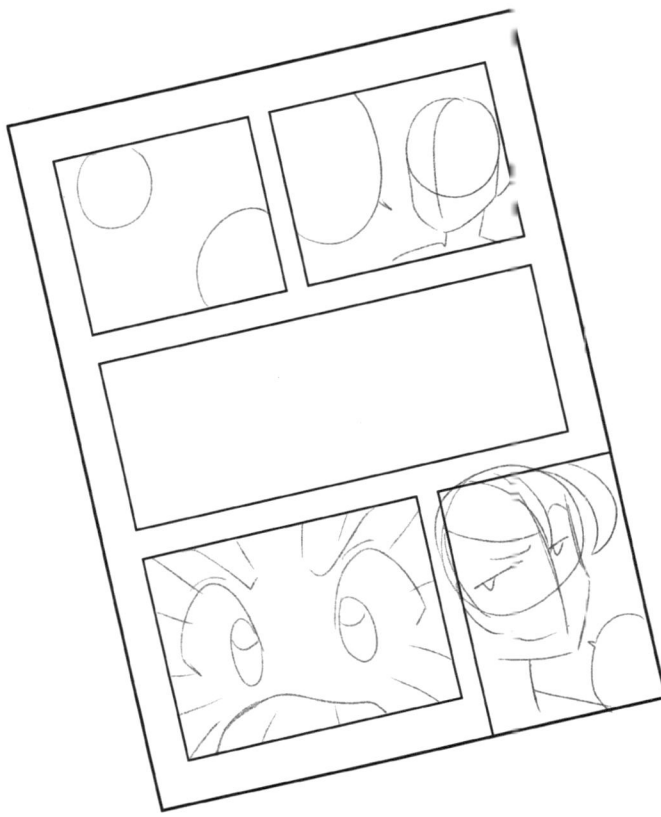

The **storyboard**, or **nemu**, is essential in manga. Do not neglect this step, in which you will draw a rough, brief, first version of your pages.

The storyboard step lets you transcribe the story that you have invented into images.

This step can be long and complicated for novices, because there is not just one way to make a good storyboard. Even the pros can make several different attempts before they start to draw their final boards.

The storyboard is to the final boards what the skeleton is to the characters. It needs to be well-structured so that you don't end up with a wobbly, incomprehensible story.

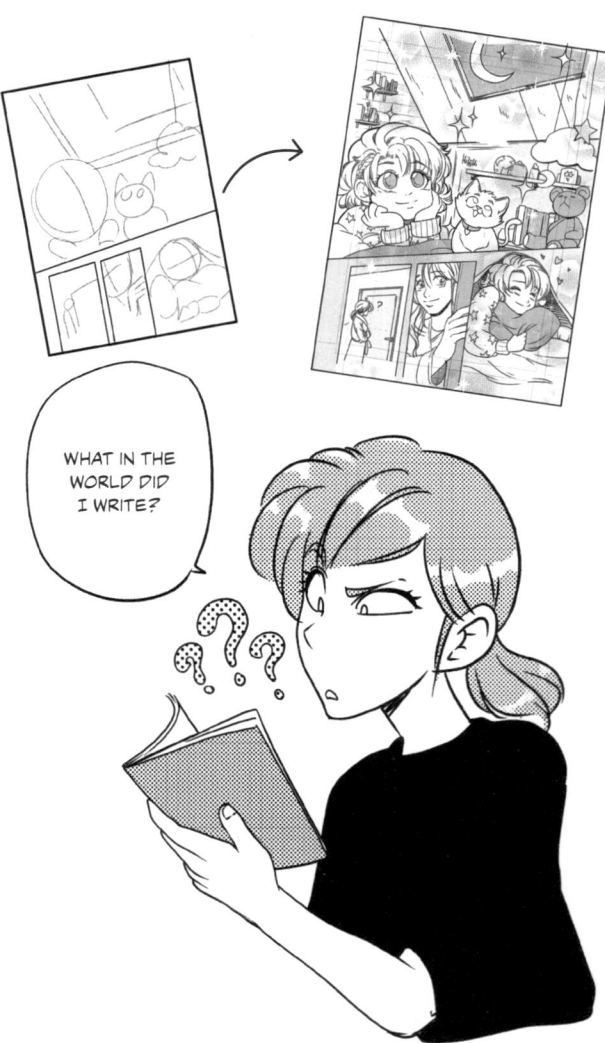

WHAT IN THE WORLD DID I WRITE?

Use this draft stage as a chance to experiment. You can try out your scenes and even change some of them.

At this stage, you don't have to know how to draw well. We learn by practicing! On the other hand, you do need to keep your writing legible and your drawings clear so that you will be able to read and recognize what you have put down.

Once the storyboard is done, there is no going back!

TRANSLATING YOUR TEXT INTO IMAGES

Your storyline is nicely written. You have found the right characters for your story, and now you need to make yourself into the camera operator to show what is happening in your story using **panels** and **sequences**.

At this stage, you can still change dialogues and scenes to make them livelier. Sequential art lets you tell a scene through a succession of key images, and it immerses the reader in the plot.

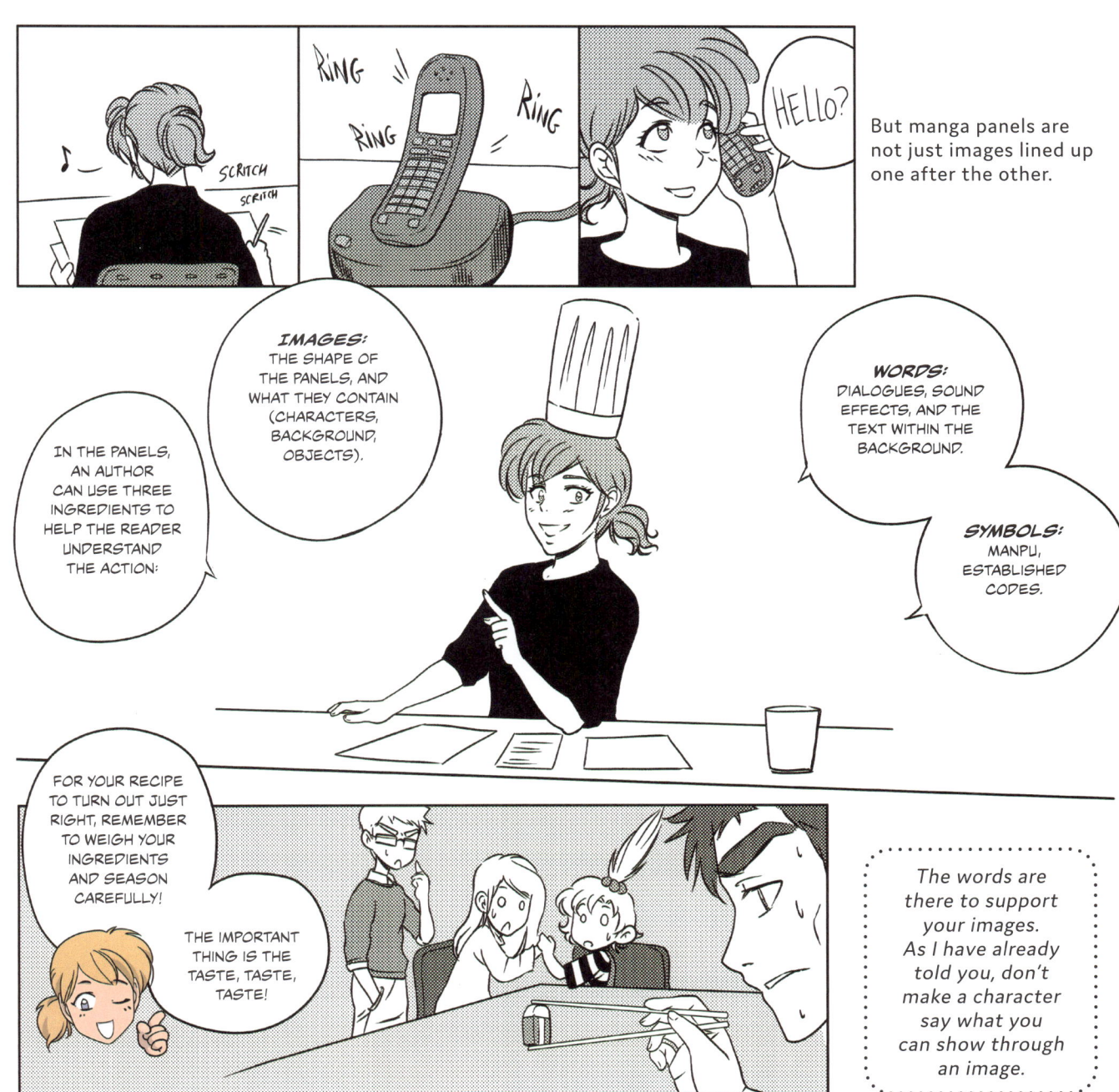

But manga panels are not just images lined up one after the other.

IMAGES: THE SHAPE OF THE PANELS, AND WHAT THEY CONTAIN (CHARACTERS, BACKGROUND, OBJECTS).

IN THE PANELS, AN AUTHOR CAN USE THREE INGREDIENTS TO HELP THE READER UNDERSTAND THE ACTION:

WORDS: DIALOGUES, SOUND EFFECTS, AND THE TEXT WITHIN THE BACKGROUND.

SYMBOLS: MANPU, ESTABLISHED CODES.

FOR YOUR RECIPE TO TURN OUT JUST RIGHT, REMEMBER TO WEIGH YOUR INGREDIENTS AND SEASON CAREFULLY!

THE IMPORTANT THING IS THE TASTE, TASTE, TASTE!

The words are there to support your images. As I have already told you, don't make a character say what you can show through an image.

125

PAGE COMPOSITION

The goal in **page composition** is to guide the reader in reading the story. Their eyes will scan the pages, following the **reading direction**, which you therefore have to define when you put together the storyboard.

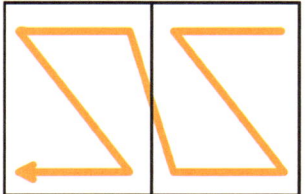

Manga are traditionally read from right to left, but you can, of course, choose to draw them in the Western reading direction, from left to right.

Every page is drawn on an individual sheet or file, in the board format that you've chosen. But when the reader is reading, they will always have two pages open in front of them.

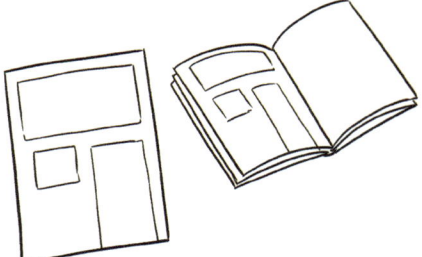

In other words, reading is done two pages at a time, and this is a key point to remember when you are building your storyboard. Picturing how the panels will be distributed on a board is called layout.

For a successful layout of your boards, you have to keep in mind the information that you want to convey and the tone of the story, and ensure that everything is legible without going outside the margins.

Let's take a look at what the blue guidelines on manga boards correspond to.

> *As of this point, mangaka have to be thinking about the bound version of their manga.*

Cutting line: this corresponds to the edge of the page when the manga is printed. Everything outside of this line is destined to disappear.

Bleed: zone outside the cutting line.

Safe zone: the safe zone, whose boundaries are indicated by dotted lines, is the area in which important text and information must be positioned. The borders of the panels are usually aligned on the edges of this zone.

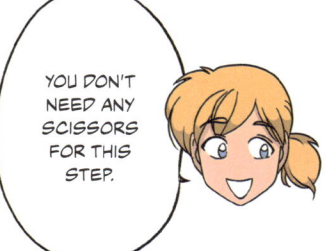

YOU DON'T NEED ANY SCISSORS FOR THIS STEP.

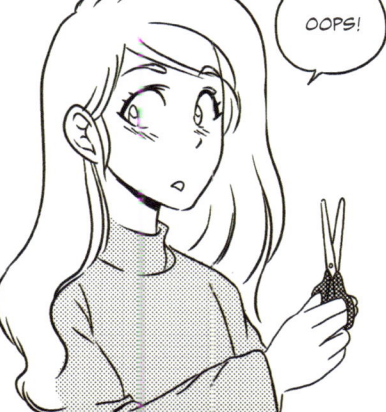

OOPS!

TIP

Think about the space that the binding of the book will take up, and leave an appropriate margin on the left or right side of each board, depending on which page you are working on.

Each double-page spread, whichever direction it is read in, has to give the readers information: a presentation, an explanation, and/or a revelation.

With all of these clues, your readers will be asking themselves questions that you will be answering in the pages that follow.

There are certain strategic locations that the reader's gaze will turn toward and that you need to know how to use well to best convey these clues.

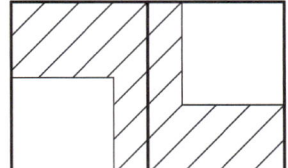
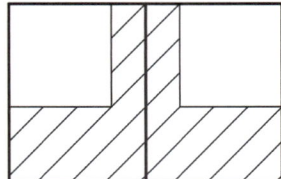

Strategic Positions

← Japanese reading direction

Final panel: this closes the scene or invites you to read the continuation on the next page. This panel allows you to create suspense by starting a sentence without finishing it, for example.

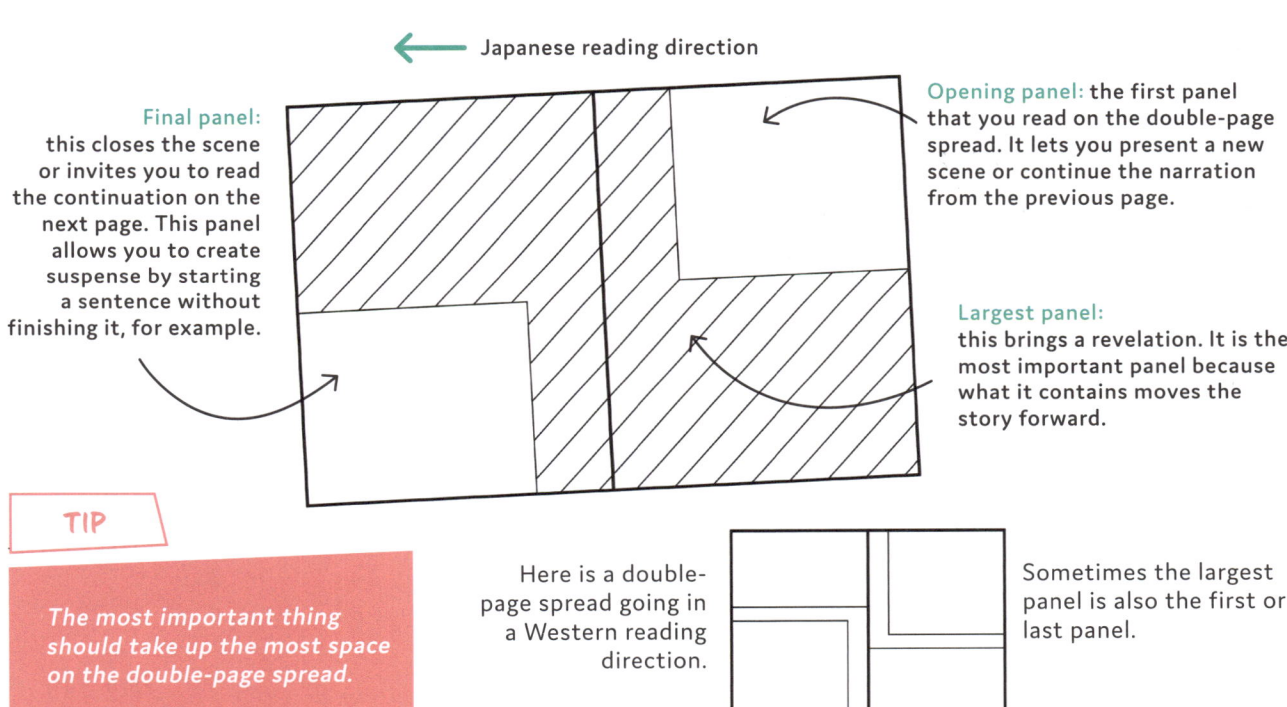

Opening panel: the first panel that you read on the double-page spread. It lets you present a new scene or continue the narration from the previous page.

Largest panel: this brings a revelation. It is the most important panel because what it contains moves the story forward.

TIP

The most important thing should take up the most space on the double-page spread.

Here is a double-page spread going in a Western reading direction.

Sometimes the largest panel is also the first or last panel.

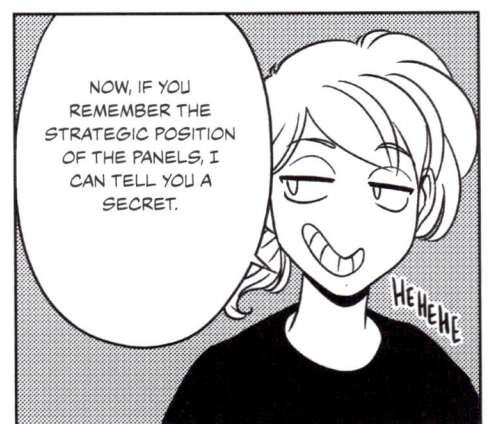

NOW, IF YOU REMEMBER THE STRATEGIC POSITION OF THE PANELS, I CAN TELL YOU A SECRET.

HEHEHE.

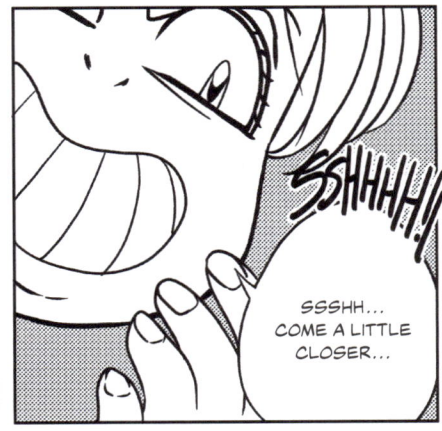

SSHHHH!!

SSSHH... COME A LITTLE CLOSER...

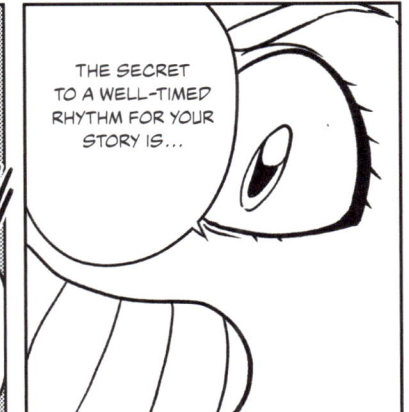

THE SECRET TO A WELL-TIMED RHYTHM FOR YOUR STORY IS...

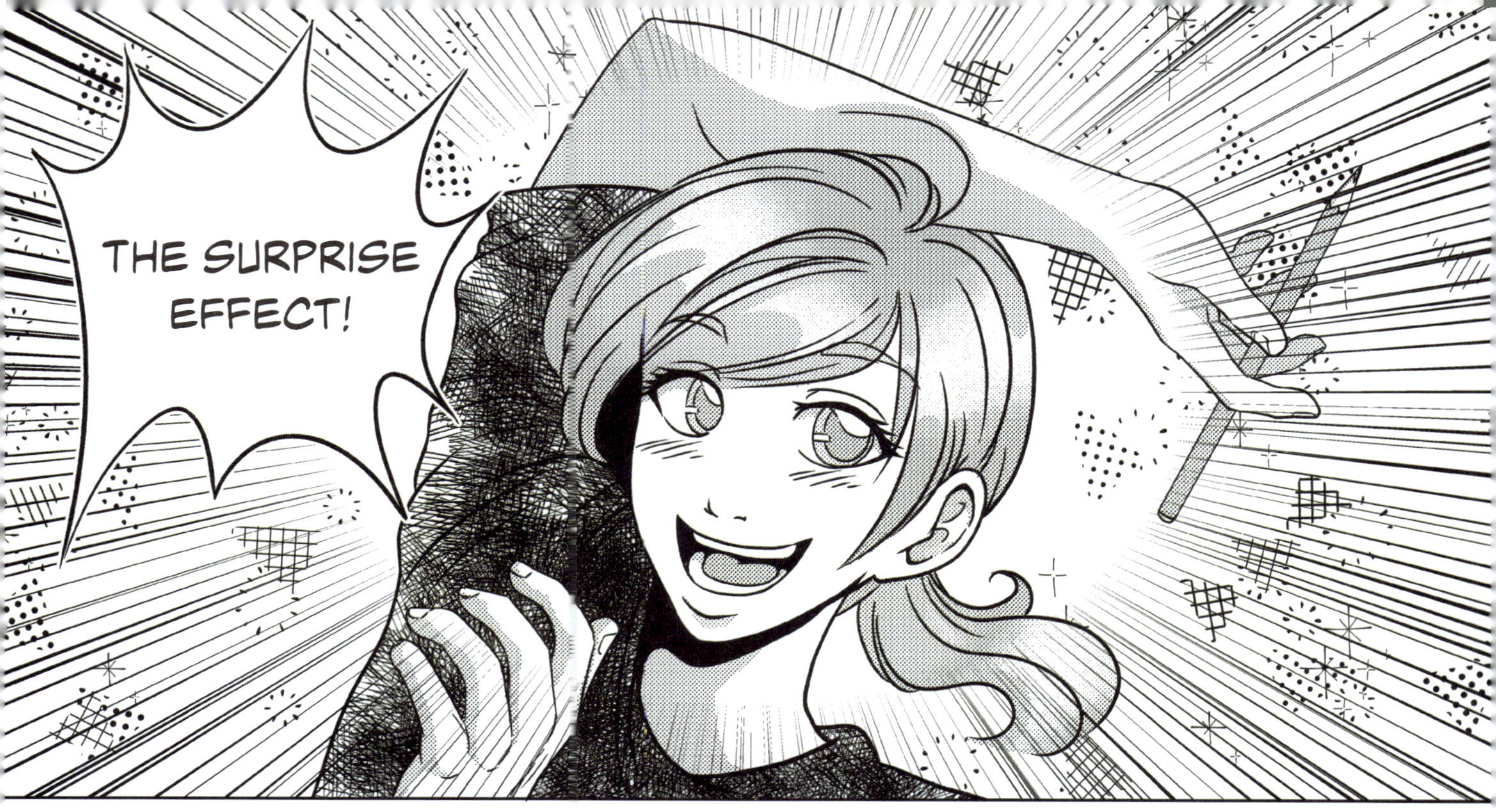

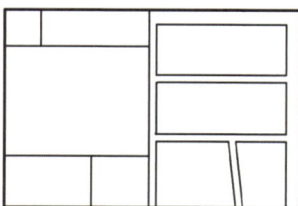

THE SURPRISE EFFECT!

The introductory panel on this double-page spread contains the revelation. Therefore, it has to be large enough to emphasize the information and highlight…the surprise effect.

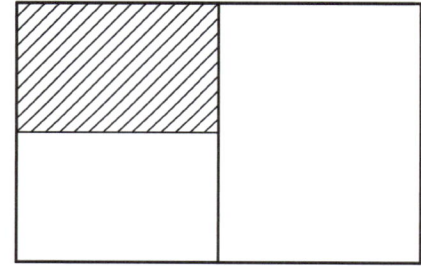

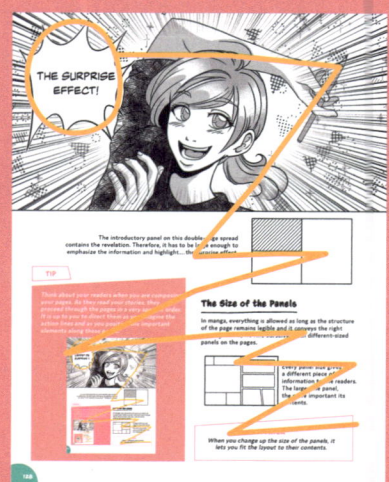

The Size of the Panels

In manga, everything is allowed as long as the structure of the page remains legible and it conveys the right message. Thus, we find ourselves with different-sized panels on the pages.

Every panel size gives a different piece of information to the readers. The larger the panel, the more important its contents.

The Shape of the Panels

The panels allow you to compartmentalize the information. They can have different shapes: square, rectangular, long, wide, diagonal.

Some panels will bleed off the end of the page. This technique involves removing part of the frame to open up a path toward the universe of the story.

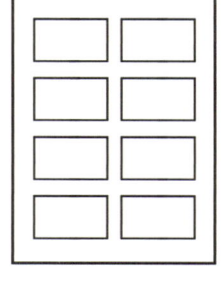

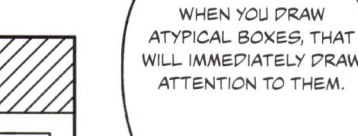

WHEN YOU DRAW ATYPICAL BOXES, THAT WILL IMMEDIATELY DRAW ATTENTION TO THEM.

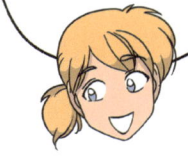

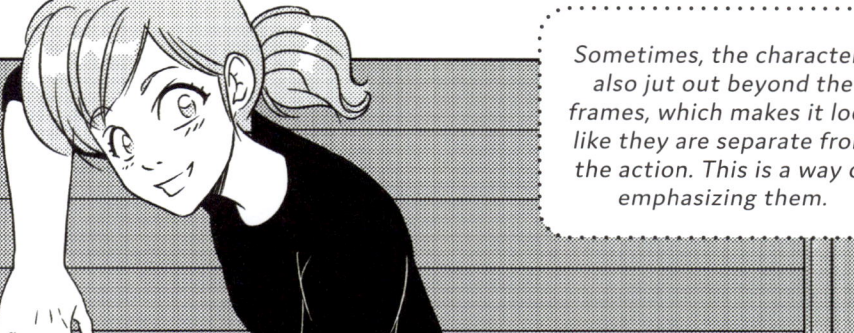

A panel is a little window into an imaginary world. If it doesn't have a definite limit indicated by its border, the reader crosses the frame and finds themself plunged right into the middle of the action.

Sometimes, the characters also jut out beyond the frames, which makes it look like they are separate from the action. This is a way of emphasizing them.

Double-Page Spreads

Sometimes, a piece of information, a revelation, or a scene is so important that the author decides to devote the space of **an entire double-page spread to one single panel**.

Double-page spreads like that are not just positioned randomly in the narration. They allow you to introduce a new character or a location with an incredible setting that the readers can immerse themselves in.

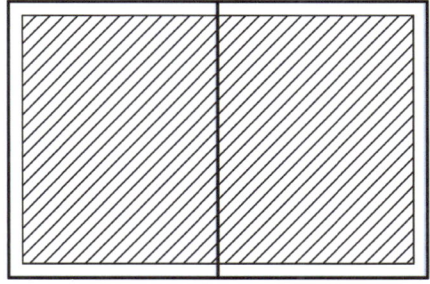

These double-page spreads can also serve as a culminating point for the narration. For an epic battle or a declaration of love, the double-page spread can show either the climax or the downfall of a scene.

In manga, nothing is left to chance! The position, the size, and the number of panels are all crucial for telling your story correctly.

THE CONTENTS OF THE PANELS

The composition of a panel serves to guide the reader's gaze toward the next panel, while at the same time giving the reader the information they need in order to understand the story.

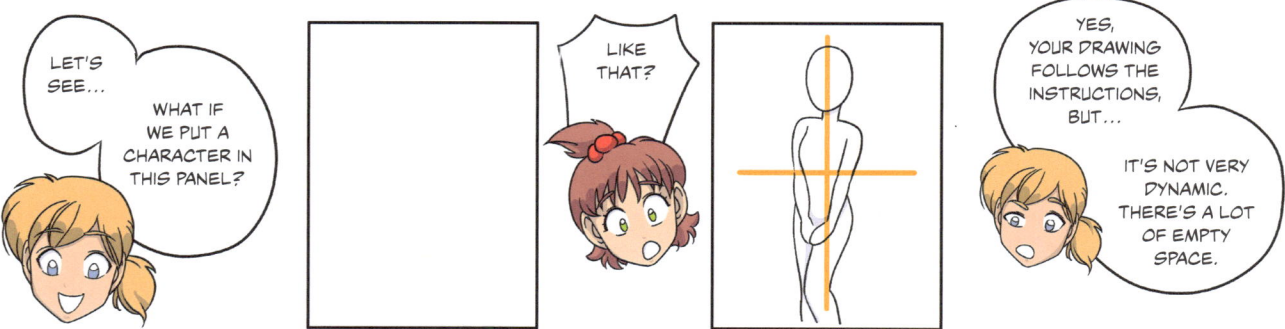

The **rule of thirds** tells us the key spots where the eye lands on an image. Let's try to position something at the intersections of the lines that divide the page in three, both horizontally and vertically.

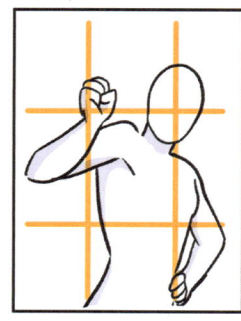
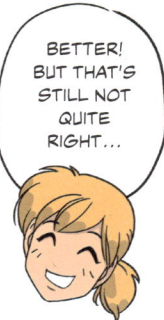
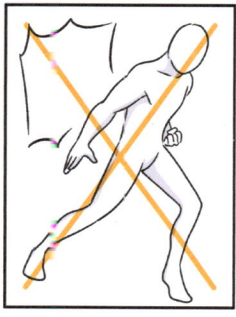
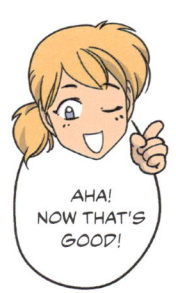
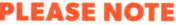

PLEASE NOTE
Remember to include speech bubbles and sound effects in your compositions!

As much as possible, avoid drawing characters who are standing up straight, facing front, right in the middle of the panel. Shift them to one side, make them move, change the angle we're seeing them at… I will come back to the question of composition on page 178.

Be careful not to guide your readers to the wrong next panel. Pay close attention to the direction of the action lines.

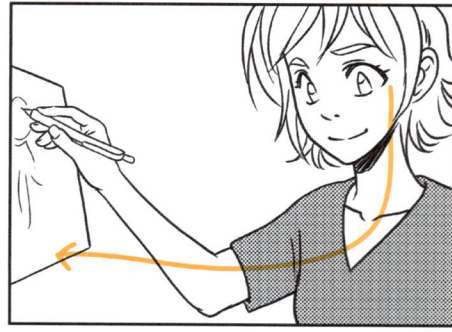

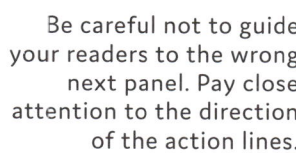

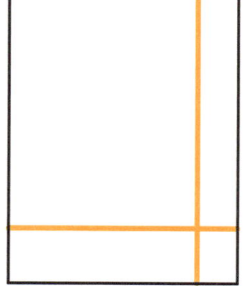
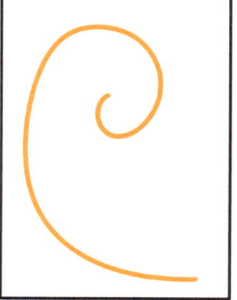
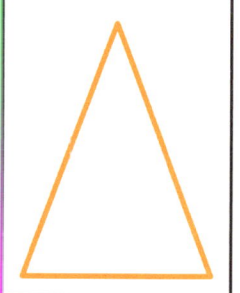

It's not necessary to show characters in every panel; in fact, it is better that you don't.

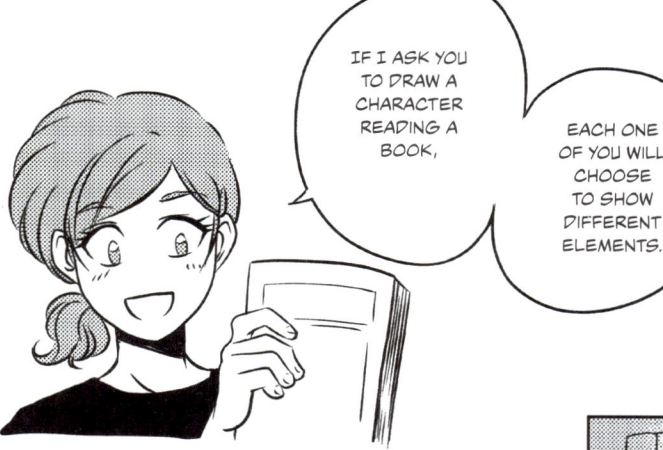

IF I ASK YOU TO DRAW A CHARACTER READING A BOOK,

EACH ONE OF YOU WILL CHOOSE TO SHOW DIFFERENT ELEMENTS.

TIP

If you want to go into this more deeply, I recommend Scott McCloud's books Understanding Comics: The Invisible Art and Making Comics.

What moment in the story are you going to show: what happened ahead of time, the beginning, the middle, the end, or what happened afterward? When the person sits down, opens the book, is reading, or puts the book down again? The finished book sitting on the bedside table?

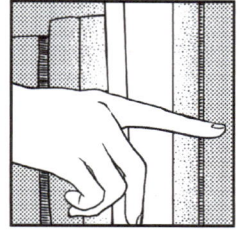
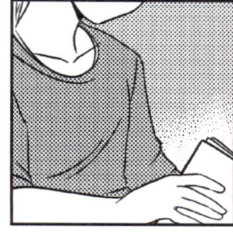
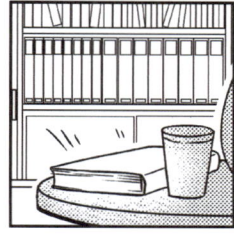

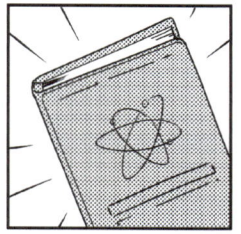
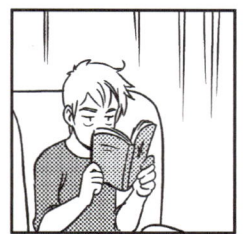
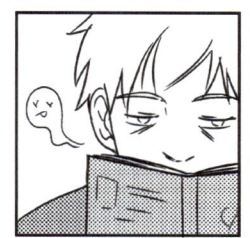

What elements are you going to draw? Just the book by itself? The cover? The inside? The character? The scenery?

What kind of distance and what kind of perspective best show the moment you have chosen? A view from farther away? Behind the window? A close-up of the cover of the book? A low-angle shot showing the character's face?

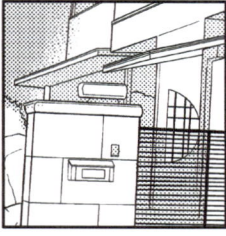
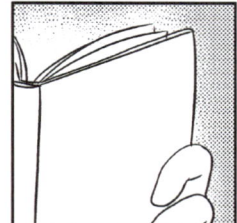
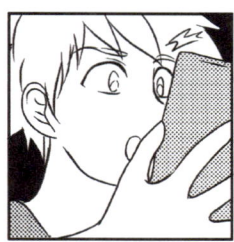

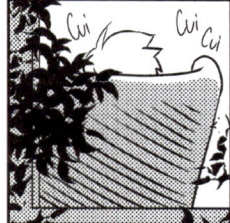
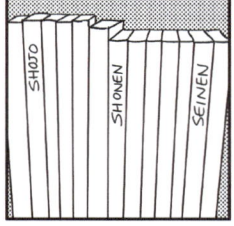
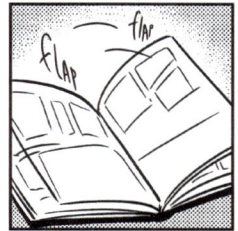

What dialogues, text, and sound effects will be useful for understanding the scene? A person who is reading by themselves doesn't speak, unless they're reading aloud. Does the text of the book need to be shown? Or do we need to include a sound effect so we can hear the sound of the page being turned?

What kind of intensity are you going to give to the scene? Is it a calm scene or a lively one?

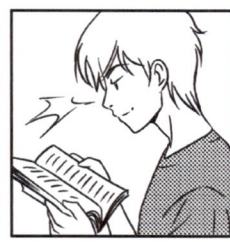
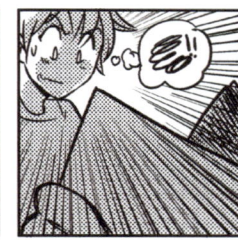
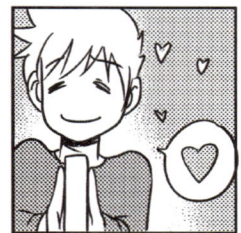

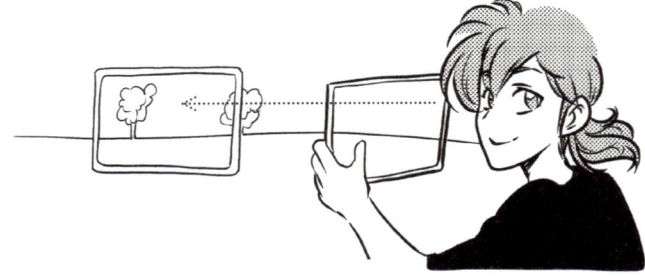

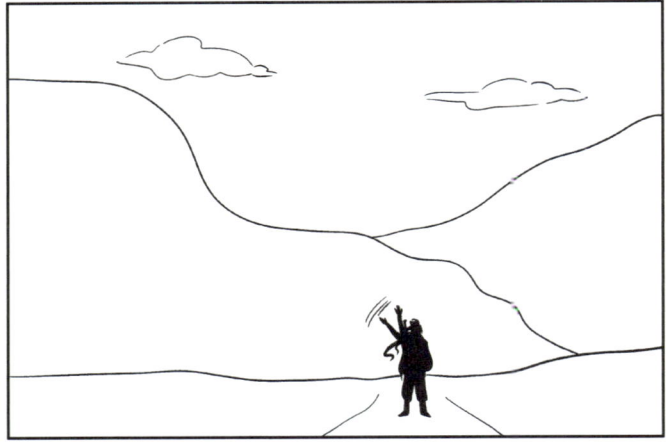

A panel is an opening into the universe of the story. This window can be closer to or further away from the subject we are looking at. This is called the **shot**.

The Different Shots

The Extreme Long Shot

This is a shot from a distance that allows us to have an overall view of a scene. It is generally used to present a location.

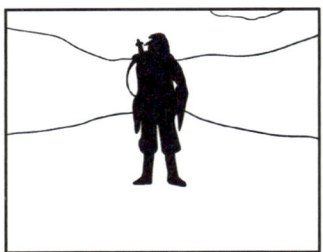

The Long Shot

Here we get a little closer to the subject or the action, but the background is still very much visible. The reader's attention is focused on an action.

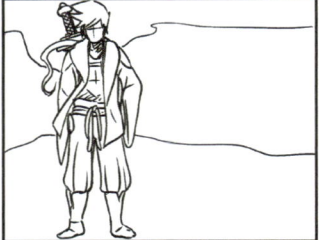

The Medium Long Shot

Here the character takes up the whole panel. This is a full-length shot that shows the entire character, from their feet upward. This shot shows us the character's posture and/or the action that is underway.

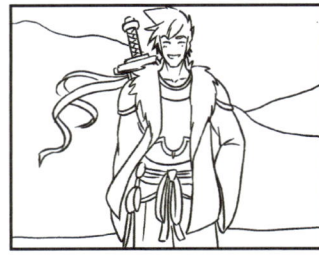

The Full Shot

Here the character is cut off at their knees. By getting closer to the character, we are entering into the action.

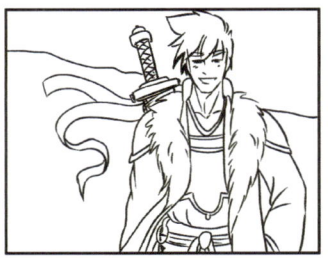

The Medium Shot

With this shot, we can still see the character's gestures. The details of their anatomy and of their attributes are becoming more and more visible.

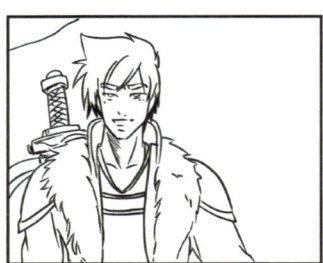

The Medium Close-Up Shot

Closer to the character, we are now in a position to hear what they might want to tell us.

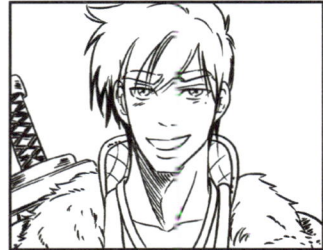

The Close-Up Shot

The close-up shot slides us into a position of intimacy with the subject. We use this shot to convey a character's emotions, for example.

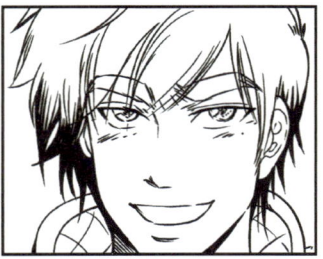

The Extreme Close-Up Shot

Here, the image is concentrated on a very close-up and very specific point. We can use this shot to highlight an object, a look, or a key piece of information.

*Watch out for **graphic overlaps** when you are drawing several different shots in the same panel. They will appear when the lines of the different shots cross or show as extensions of each other.*

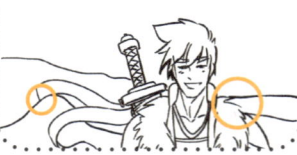

The Different Angles of View

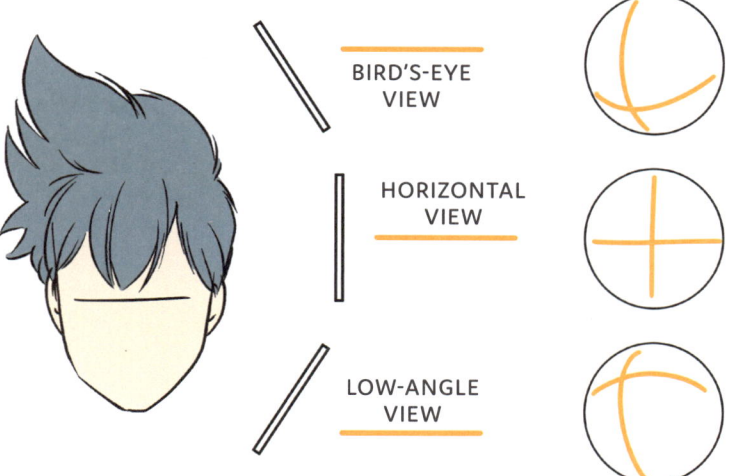

BIRD'S-EYE VIEW

HORIZONTAL VIEW

LOW-ANGLE VIEW

Once you have chosen what you are going to show and how far away the subject is going to be from the reader, you will need to define the height from which we are watching the scene. This is the perspective, or **angle of view**.

When you change the angle of view, you allow for a different reading of the same scene.

Low-Angle View

This angle allows us to see a scene, character, or object from below. This time, the character is higher up than we are, and thus in a position of power. Looking at the character this way also gives them a strong, superior, and impressive appearance.

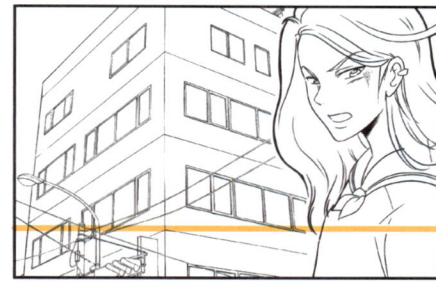

Horizontal View

This is the most common angle. The reader is placed at the same level as the scene or as the main character, in order to include them in the conversation, for instance.

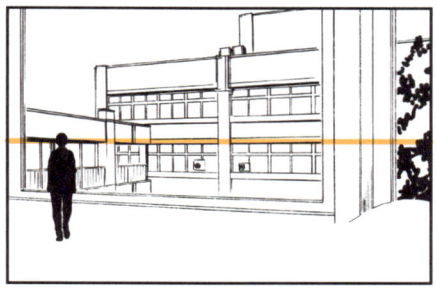

Bird's-Eye View

This angle is used to show a scene, a character, or an object viewed from above. By looking at it this way, we become larger than what we're looking at. This can be useful, for example, for showing a character who is having trouble.

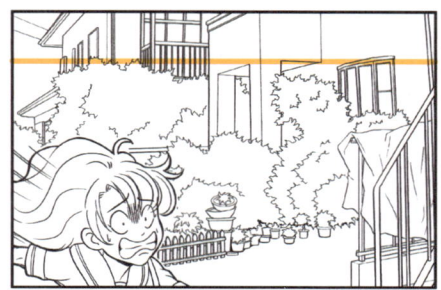

Oblique View

This is like looking at a scene while tilting your head. This angle adds some dynamism or creates a feeling of unease.

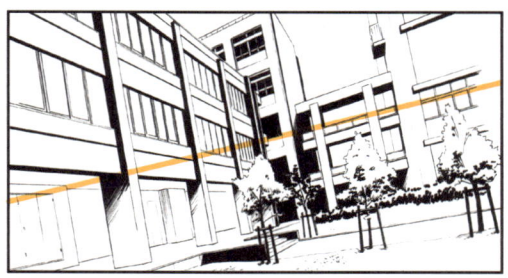

Subjective View

Sometimes, we might want to use this kind of angle in our manga. This is the case, for instance, when the reader takes the place of the subject and is looking at the scene in the character's place.

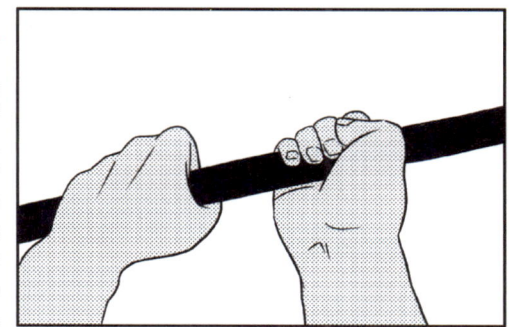

Shot and Reverse Shot

When we draw manga panels, we only show a part of the scene that is inside a frame delimited by the borders of the panels or by the physical limits of the paper pages.

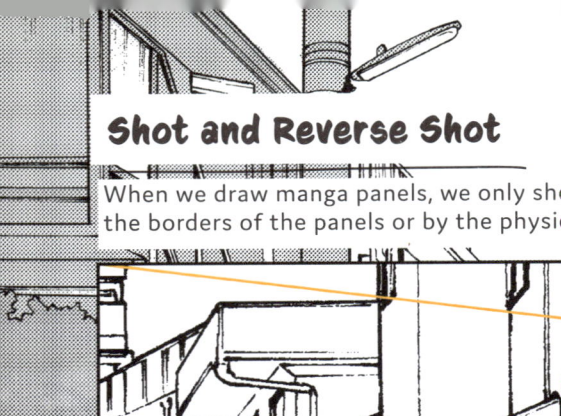
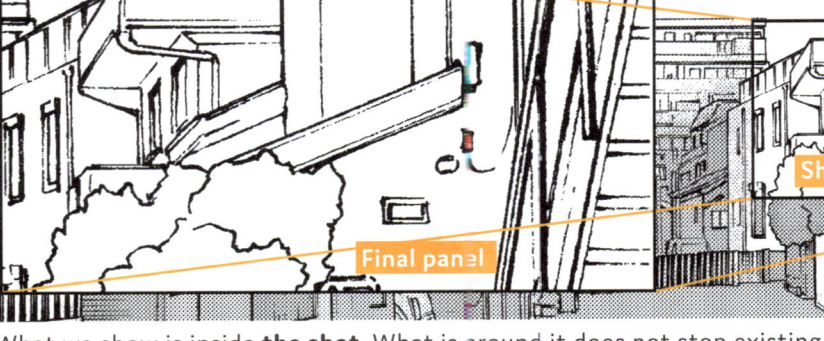

Offscreen

Shot

Final panel

What we show is inside **the shot**. What is around it does not stop existing, but we can't see it as long as it is **offscreen**.

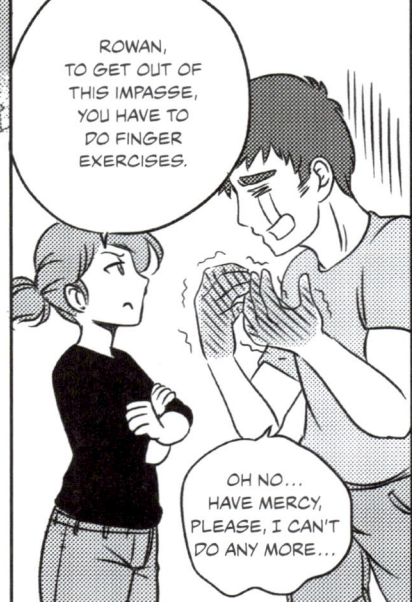

ROWAN, TO GET OUT OF THIS IMPASSE, YOU HAVE TO DO FINGER EXERCISES.

OH NO... HAVE MERCY, PLEASE, I CAN'T DO ANY MORE...

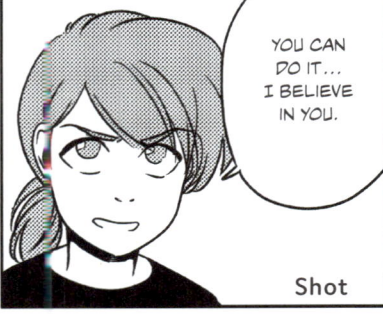

YOU CAN DO IT... I BELIEVE IN YOU.

Shot

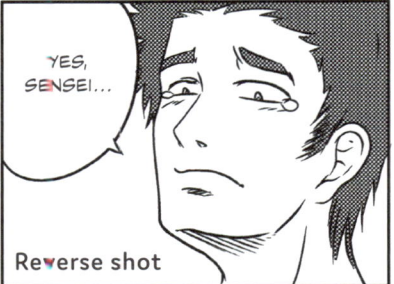

YES, SENSEI...

Reverse shot

To follow certain scenes and, in particular, conversations between characters, we alternate the view between the shot and the reverse shot, or in other words, a starting viewpoint and then its opposite within the same scene.

> *If the characters are facing each other, draw them in profile or in three-quarter profile within the panels.*

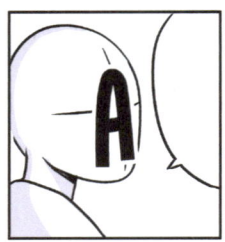
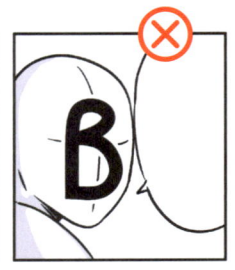

WATCH OUT FOR THESE MISTAKES!

Be careful to keep a consistent framing for the panels showing the shot and the reverse shot so as not to change the position of the characters in space. If they are facing each other, don't show them standing side by side.

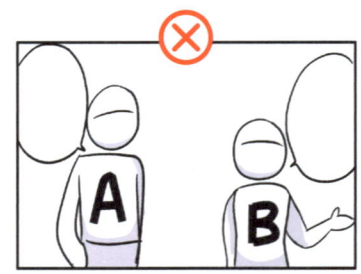

When we stage a conversation between two protagonists, the reader is positioned like a third person who is playing the role of the camera operator.

To keep the transitions between the panels consistent and avoid mistakes, imagine a line connecting your characters that the reader must never go beyond in order not to find themselves behind the scenes. This is the **180° line**.

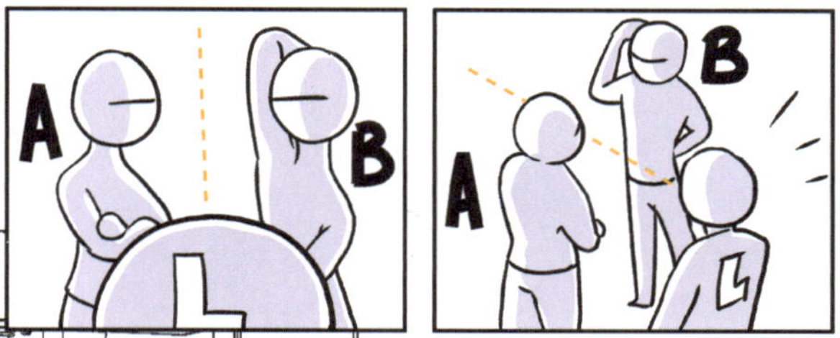

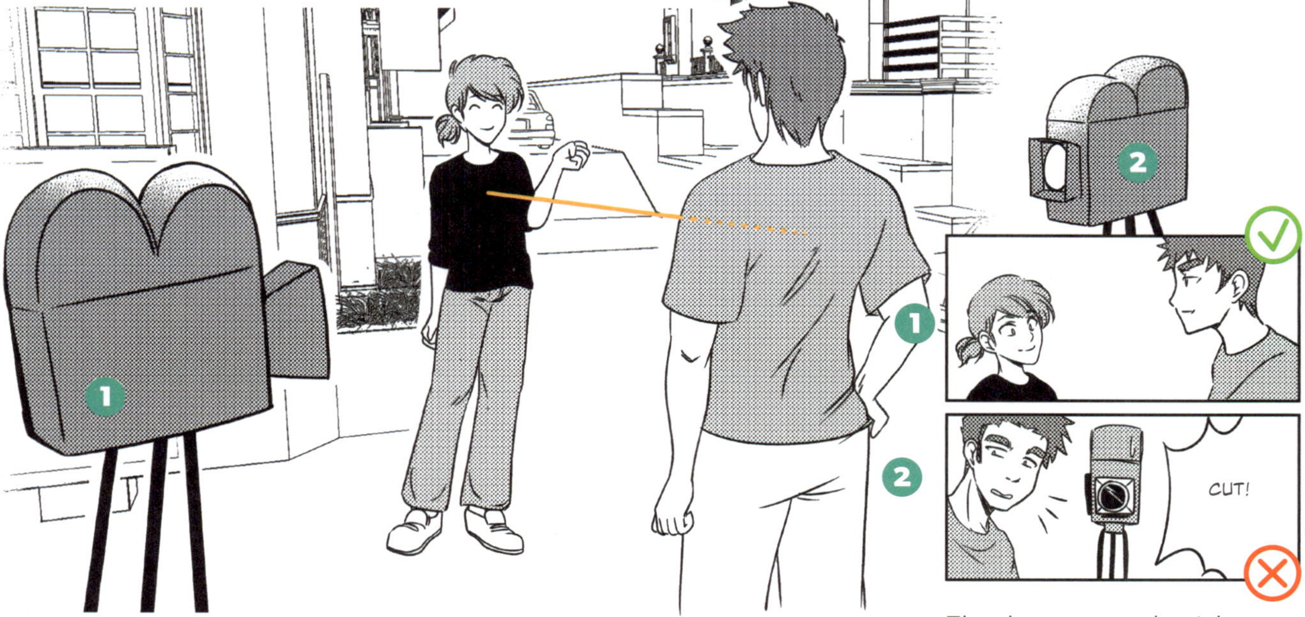

When you are drawing your storyboard, keep in mind the space that your characters will take up in the panels, but also the space required for the text: speech bubbles and sound effects.

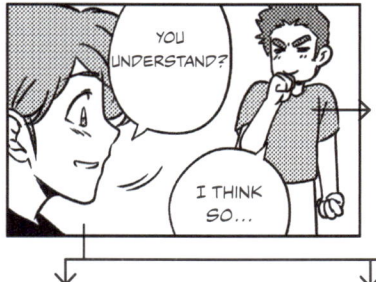

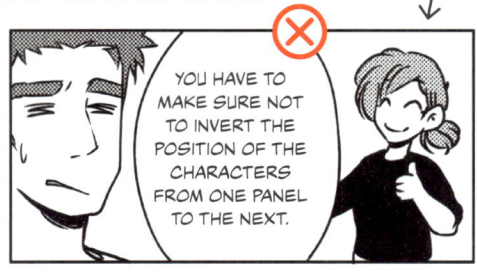

The character on the right has moved to the left so that he can be the first to speak in the dialogue, but this is not at all consistent in a scene where the two characters are not supposed to have moved.

There are other ways of placing the text in the right order while still respecting the 180° rule.

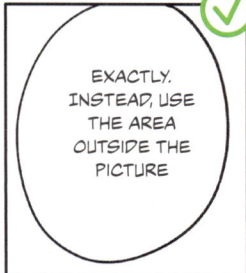

Offscreen

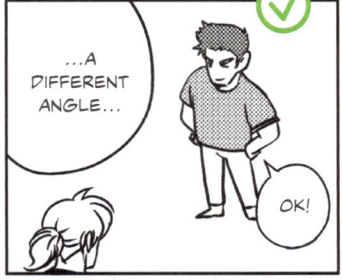

Bird's-eye view

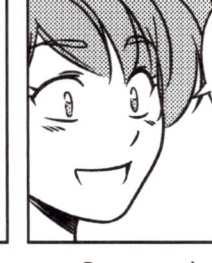

Reverse shot

CHOOSING THE RIGHT TRANSITIONS

The transitions between panels are just as important as their contents. In concrete terms, it is a question of choosing the contents of the following panels in such a way as to create different ways of sequencing.

The choice of transitions results in a different vision of the story.

LET'S LOOK AGAIN AT THE EXAMPLE OF OUR CHARACTER READING A BOOK (PAGE 131).

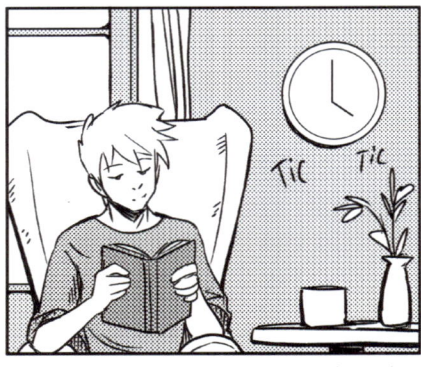 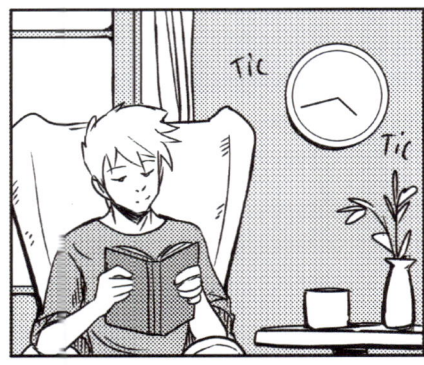 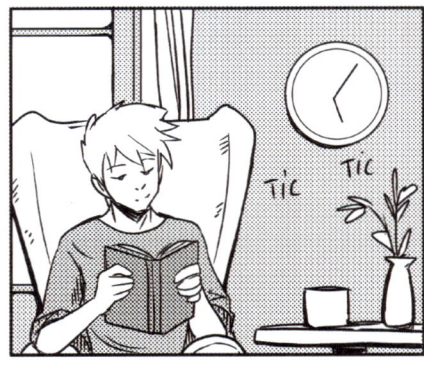

▲ The panels follow one after the other and are identical except for the clock, which lets us know that time is passing. The subject, the action, the angle of view, and the scene are all the same.

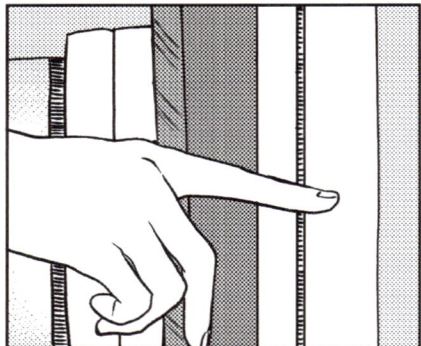 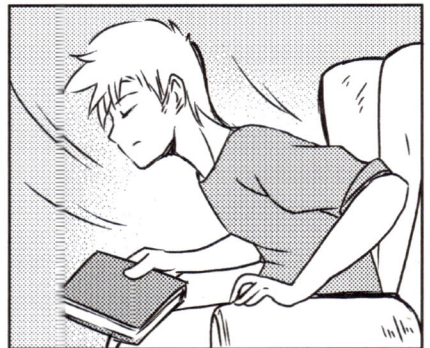 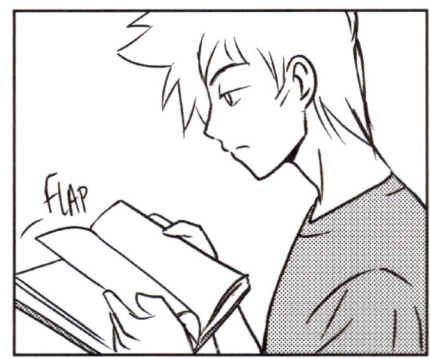

▲ The three panels show us a series of successive actions. These transitions give us extra information besides just that of time passing.

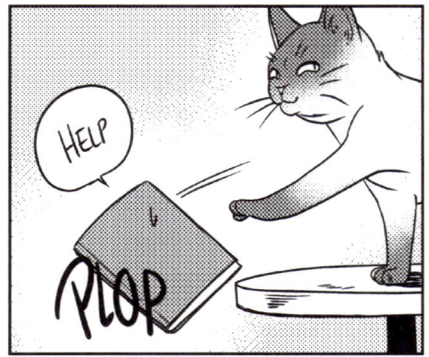 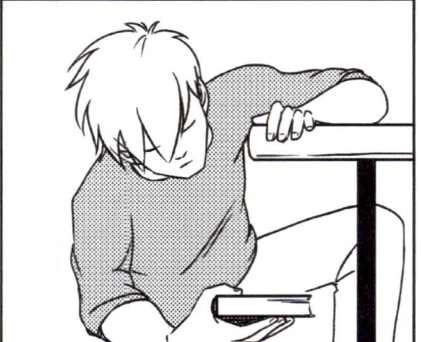 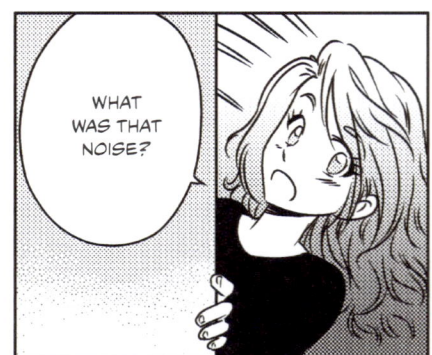

▲ Every panel presents a different subject: the cat, the reader, and the secondary character. With these transitions, we have an idea of the time passing, the subjects, and the action.

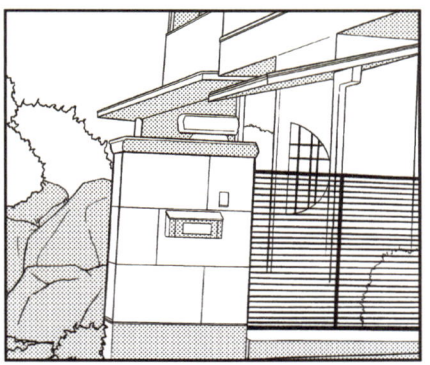 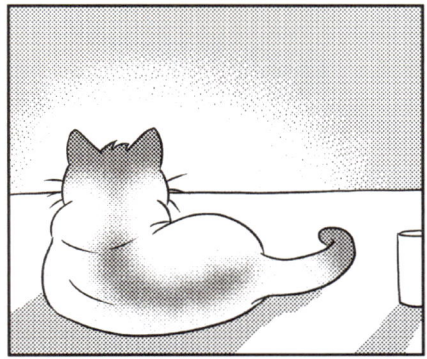 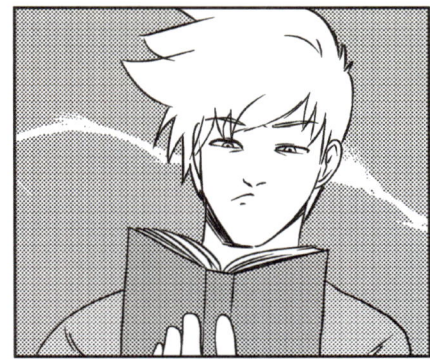

▲ The first two panels serve as an introduction to the subject that interests us in the final panel. Every transition takes us to a different scene and allows us to situate the subject and the action.

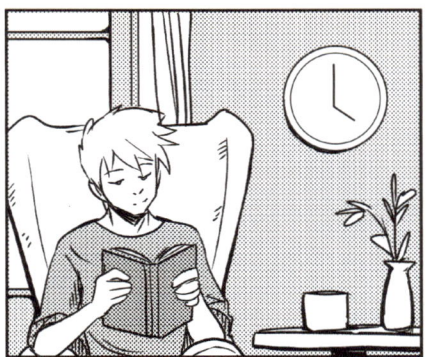 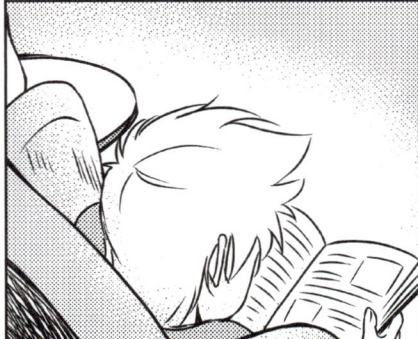 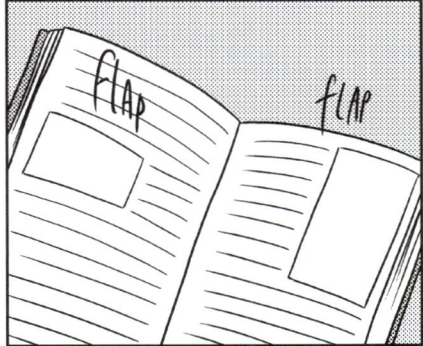

▲ The three panels have the same subject and the same action. The change in the viewing angle allows us to see the scene from all different sides. Thus, this scene must be very important.

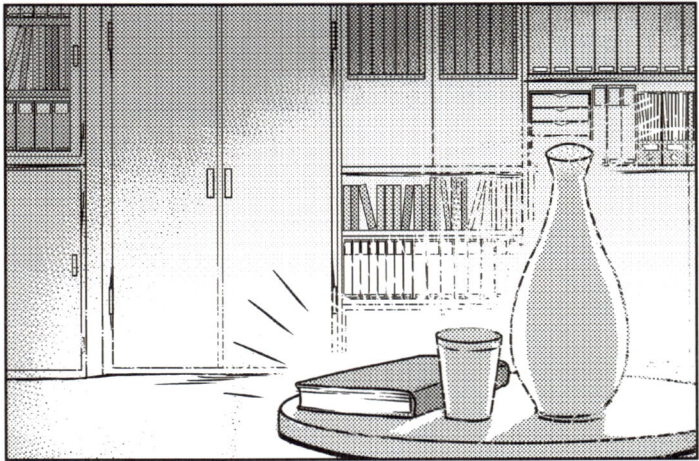

▲ Sometimes, a single panel is enough to let us understand that the action has taken place or will take place. The fact that the book is off the shelves lets us know that it's "in service."

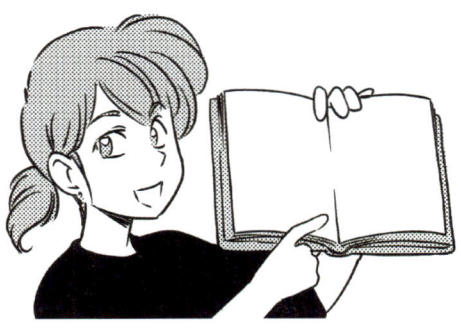

If the reading of the book has no effect on the story, then it is not necessary to show this scene in detail in your manga. However, if this is the starting point of an adventure, it becomes interesting to develop it, emphasizing the details.

THE PASSAGE OF TIME IN THE PANELS

Our gaze passes over the **gutters** without paying any attention to them, and yet they play an important role in page composition and in the representation of the passage of time.

The gutters are the spaces between the panels that result from cutting the board up into bands and then into vignettes.

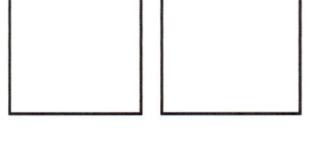

The horizontal gutters are larger than the vertical gutters. The sizes of the gutters stay the same from one page to the next.

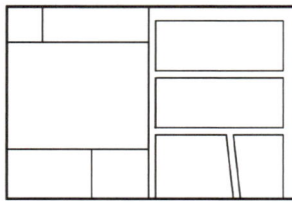

When the reader's gaze passes from one panel to the next, the presence of a space allows them the time for a brief pause, like a blink of the eyes. It is during this transition that we can make time move forward in the scene.

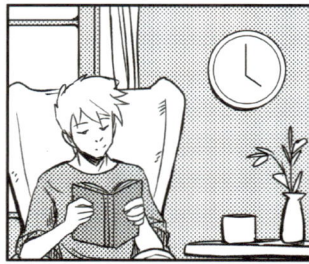 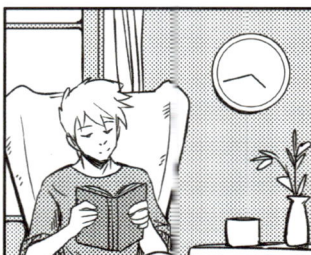 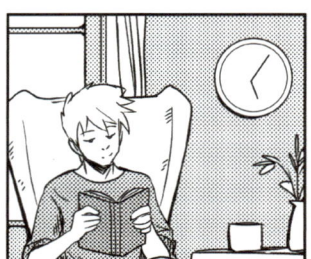

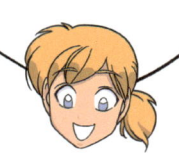

IF WE TAKE OUT THE SPACE OF THE GUTTERS BETWEEN THE PANELS, WE CAN SHOW SEVERAL SCENES AT THE SAME TIME.

The composition of the panel allows us to suggest that things are happening according to a particular timeline.

When we remove the borders of the panels, and thus also the gutters, the reader is immersed in the story and time slows down while they are moving through the panel. Time passes in between the panels, but also within them.

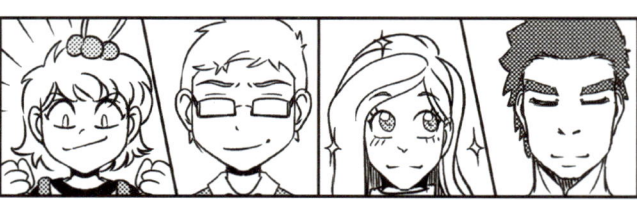

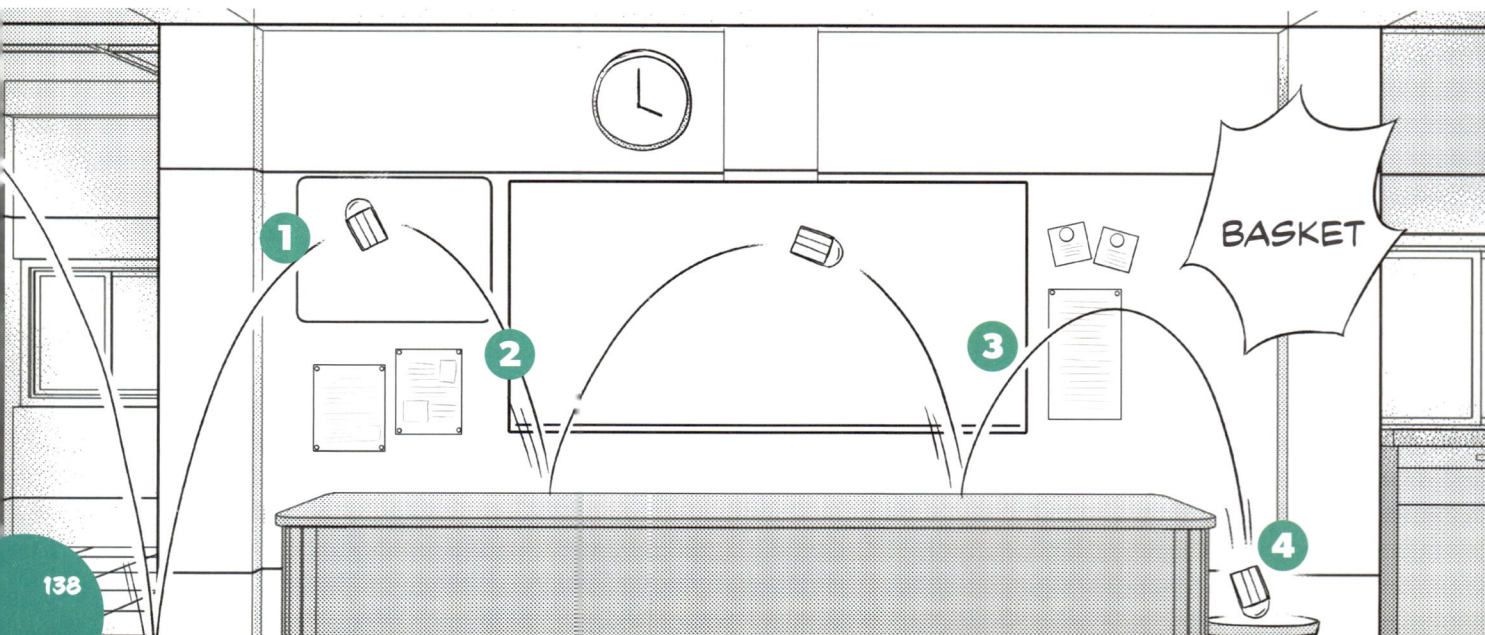

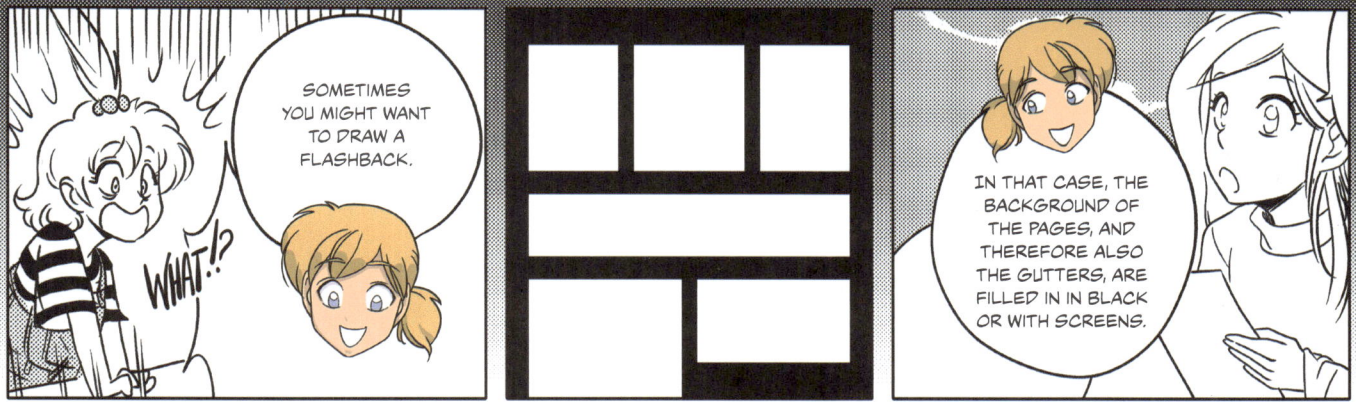

When we let a lot of time pass between the panels, we can call that an **ellipsis**.

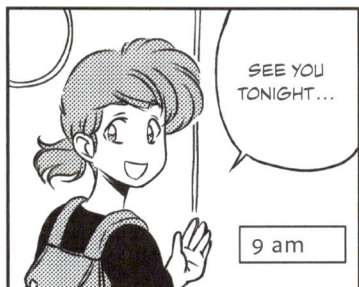

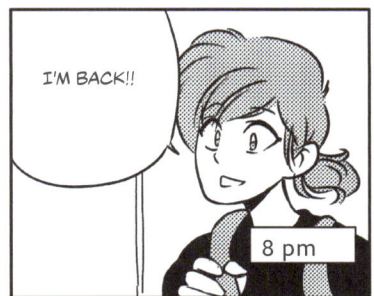

This is a way to make omissions and thus give the story a rhythm by leaving out the secondary scenes to concentrate on what's important. The reader only sees the information that is crucial and relevant to understanding the plot, but is still also able to use the context to reconstruct the scenes that are missing.

Ellipses are useful for **moving from one scene to another or one moment in the story to another**.

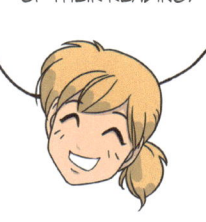

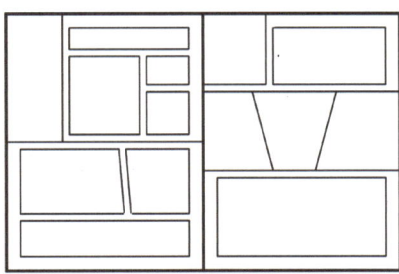

Fast

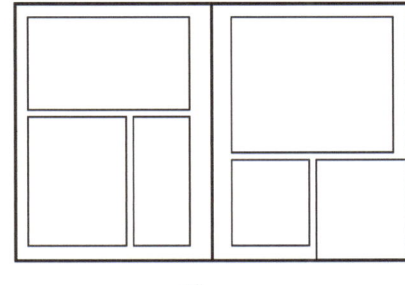

Slow

The more panels, and thus the more gutters, there are, the more the rhythm of reading speeds up.

And in the other direction, drawing large panels allows you to slow the action down.

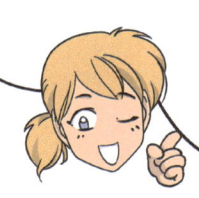

STAGINGS

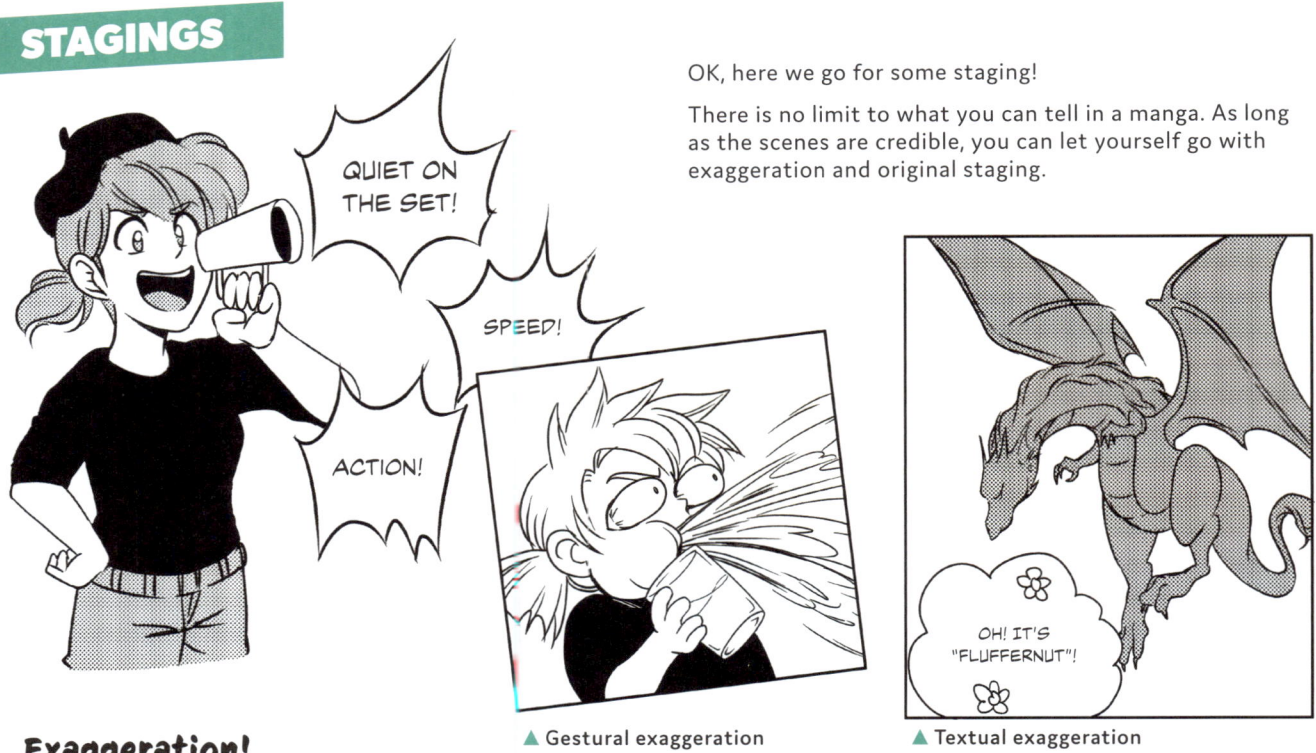

OK, here we go for some staging!

There is no limit to what you can tell in a manga. As long as the scenes are credible, you can let yourself go with exaggeration and original staging.

▲ Gestural exaggeration

▲ Textual exaggeration

Exaggeration!

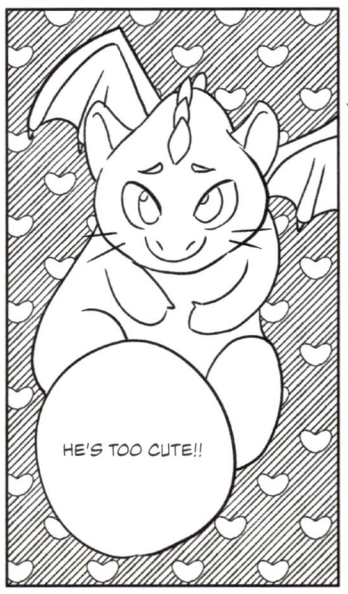

▲ Physical exaggeration

▲ Exaggeration of the viewing angle

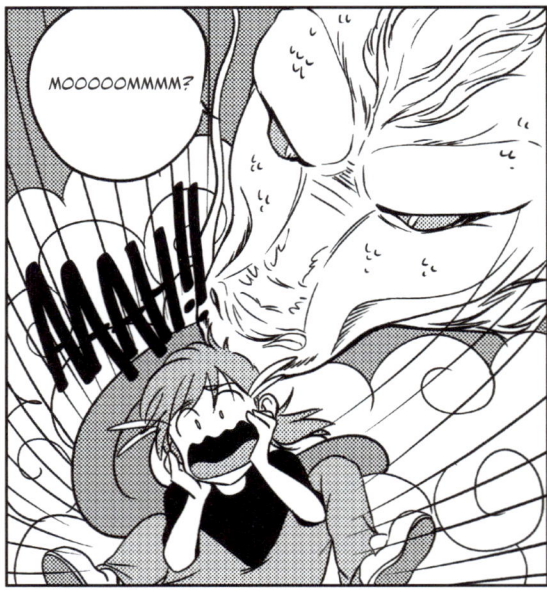

▲ Exaggeration of the intensity

As you can see above, you can integrate exaggeration into your pages in a variety of ways.

Be careful not to exaggerate everything because then you might make the exaggeration trivial. What makes the use of exaggeration interesting is when it is contrasted with a "normal" composition leading up to it.

Allegories

We often use objects or symbols to show emotions that we cannot entirely express just with the characters themselves. This is the principle of allegory.

Using symbols in your world gives you more room to tell your stories in an interesting way. These symbols can take the form of places, objects, animals, characters: a door opens on a meeting and slams shut when there is a breakup, a clock represents the passage of time, etc.

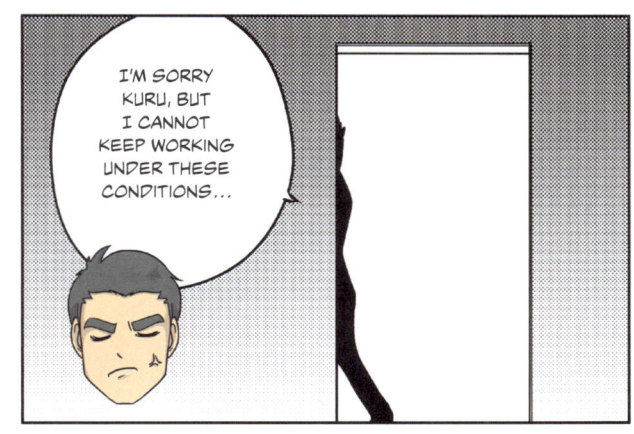

I'M SORRY KURU, BUT I CANNOT KEEP WORKING UNDER THESE CONDITIONS...

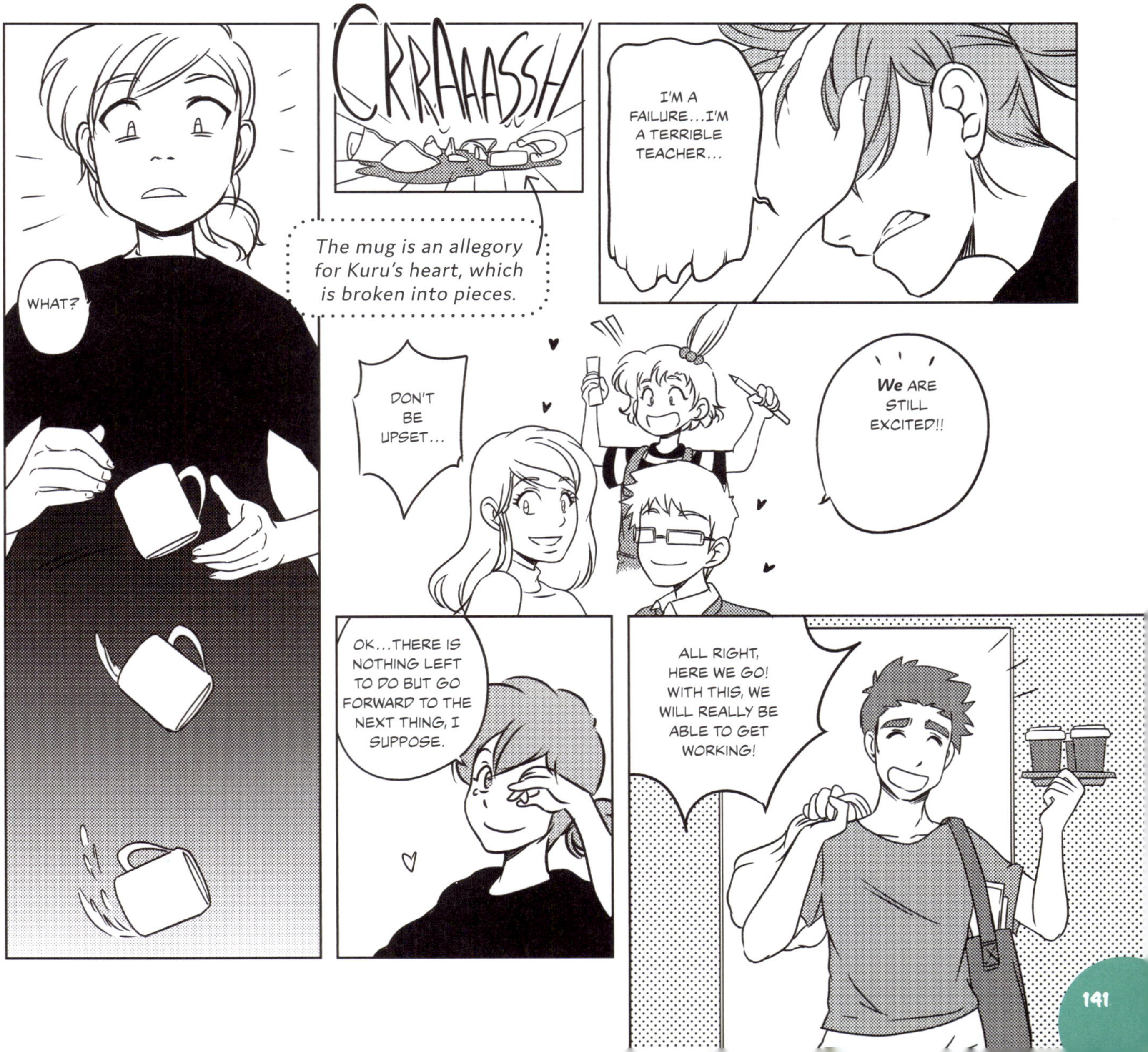

CRRAAASSH

WHAT?

The mug is an allegory for Kuru's heart, which is broken into pieces.

I'M A FAILURE...I'M A TERRIBLE TEACHER...

DON'T BE UPSET...

We ARE STILL EXCITED!!

OK...THERE IS NOTHING LEFT TO DO BUT GO FORWARD TO THE NEXT THING, I SUPPOSE.

ALL RIGHT, HERE WE GO! WITH THIS, WE WILL REALLY BE ABLE TO GET WORKING!

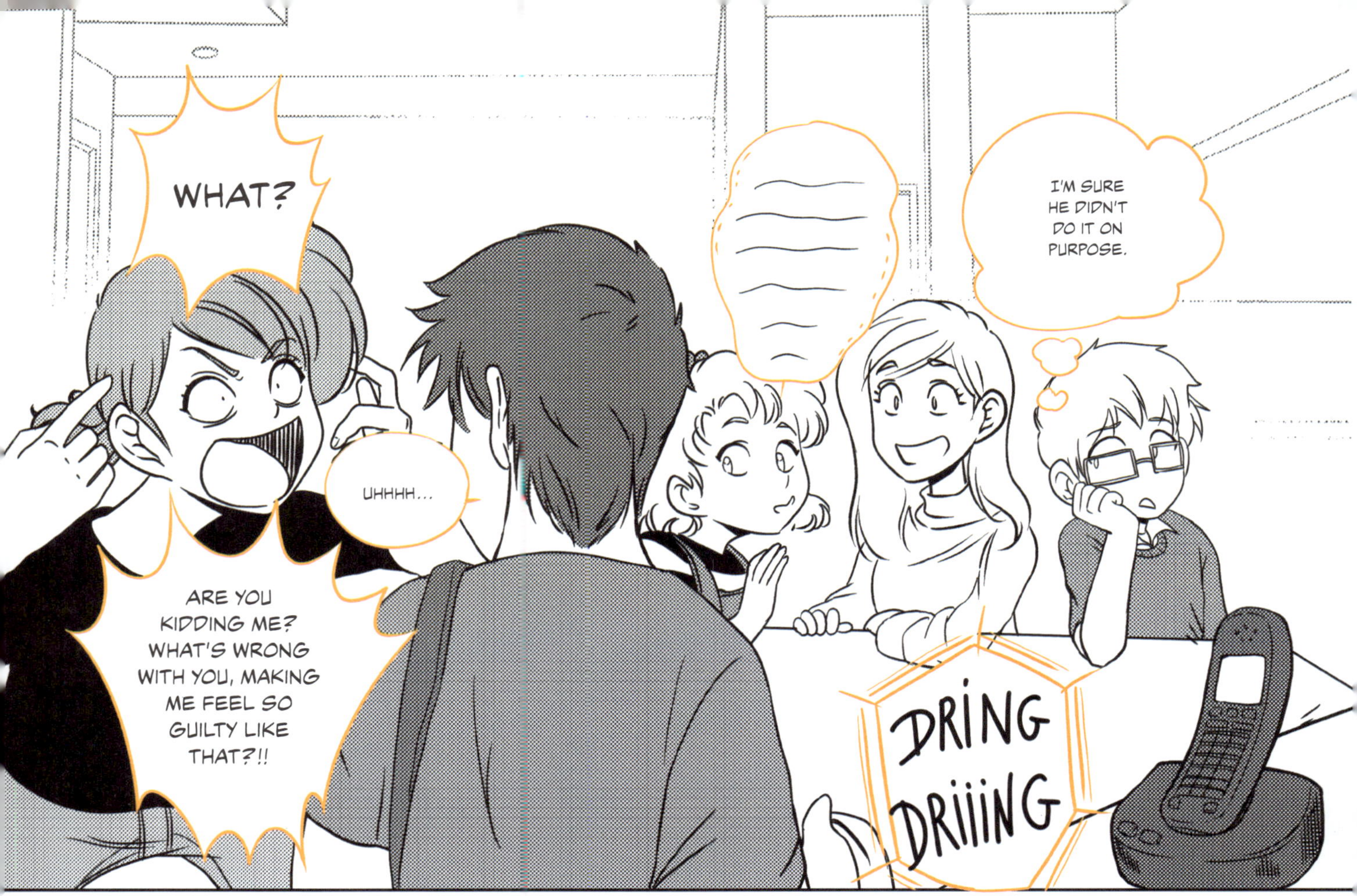

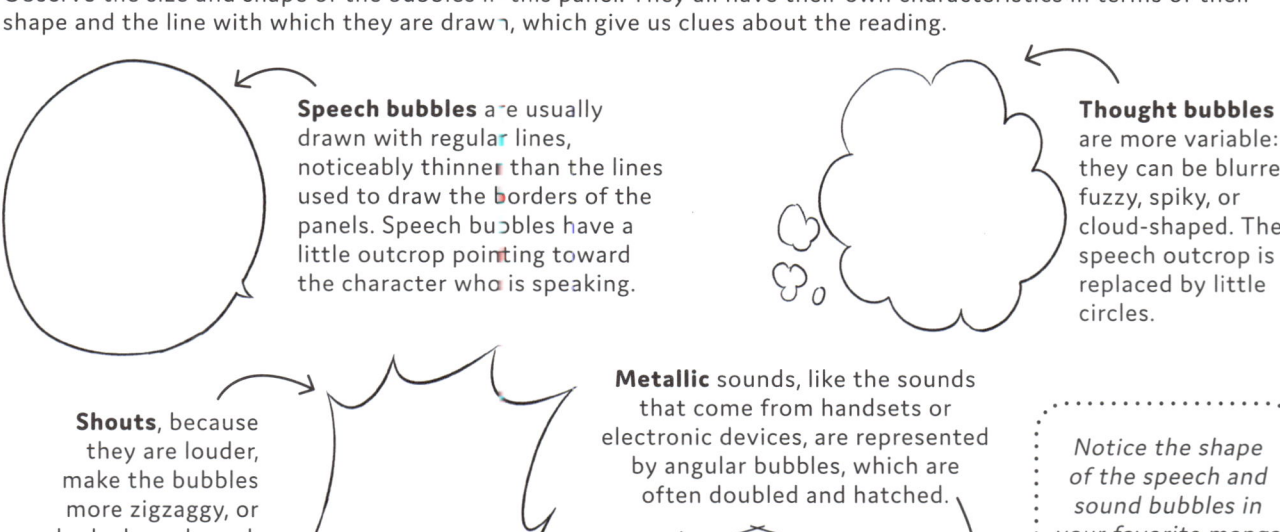

DRAWING SPEECH AND SOUND BUBBLES

Observe the size and shape of the bubbles in this panel. They all have their own characteristics in terms of their shape and the line with which they are drawn, which give us clues about the reading.

Speech bubbles are usually drawn with regular lines, noticeably thinner than the lines used to draw the borders of the panels. Speech bubbles have a little outcrop pointing toward the character who is speaking.

Thought bubbles are more variable: they can be blurred, fuzzy, spiky, or cloud-shaped. The speech outcrop is replaced by little circles.

Shouts, because they are louder, make the bubbles more zigzaggy, or hedgehog-shaped. The lines are heavier and more emphasized.

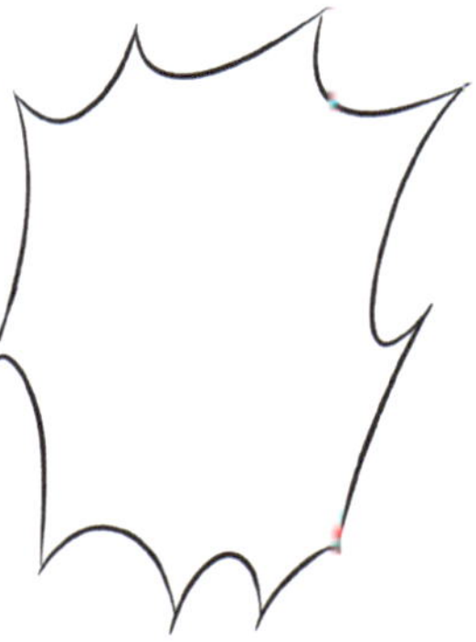

Metallic sounds, like the sounds that come from handsets or electronic devices, are represented by angular bubbles, which are often doubled and hatched.

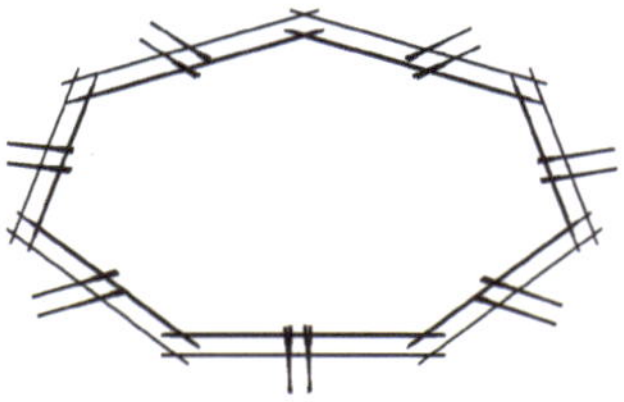

Notice the shape of the speech and sound bubbles in your favorite manga and have fun with copying them for practice.

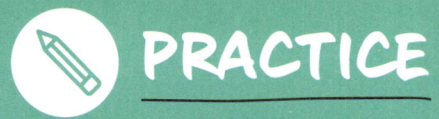

PRACTICE

All the conditions are now in place for you to be able to start putting into practice what we have looked at together, in your first storyboards.

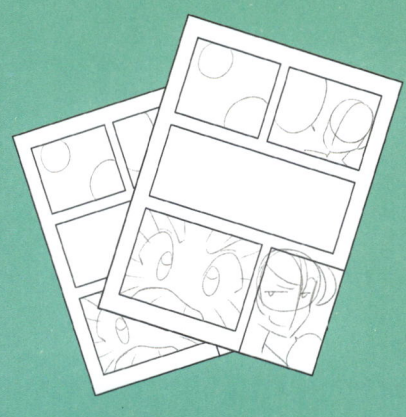

DON'T FORGET THE RECIPE FOR A GOOD STORYBOARD!

- *Compose your pages two at a time.*
- *Determine what the action lines will be to direct your reader's gaze.*
- *Use the right size, shape, and number of panels for what your story needs.*
- *Draw the important elements in strategic locations in the composition.*
- *Vary the framing to bring your sequences to life.*
- *Use a touch of exaggeration to season everything just right!*

Practice Creating a Storyboard

Go back to the character designs and the short stories that you imagined on page 117. Choose your favorite one and then create several different storyboards for the same story or scene:

- One in eight pages
- One in sixteen pages
- One in twenty-four pages
- One in thirty-two pages

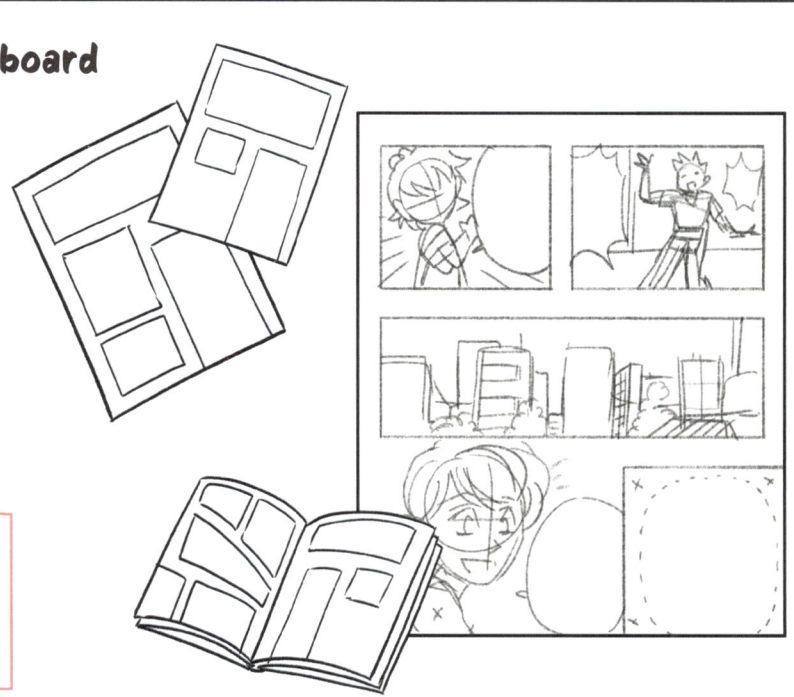

A TRICK

To get used to drawing on double-page spreads, create your storyboards in notebooks.

DRAWING THE BOARDS

When it's time to draw the final boards for your manga, you will start on a series of steps that takes you from your sketches to your final drawings.

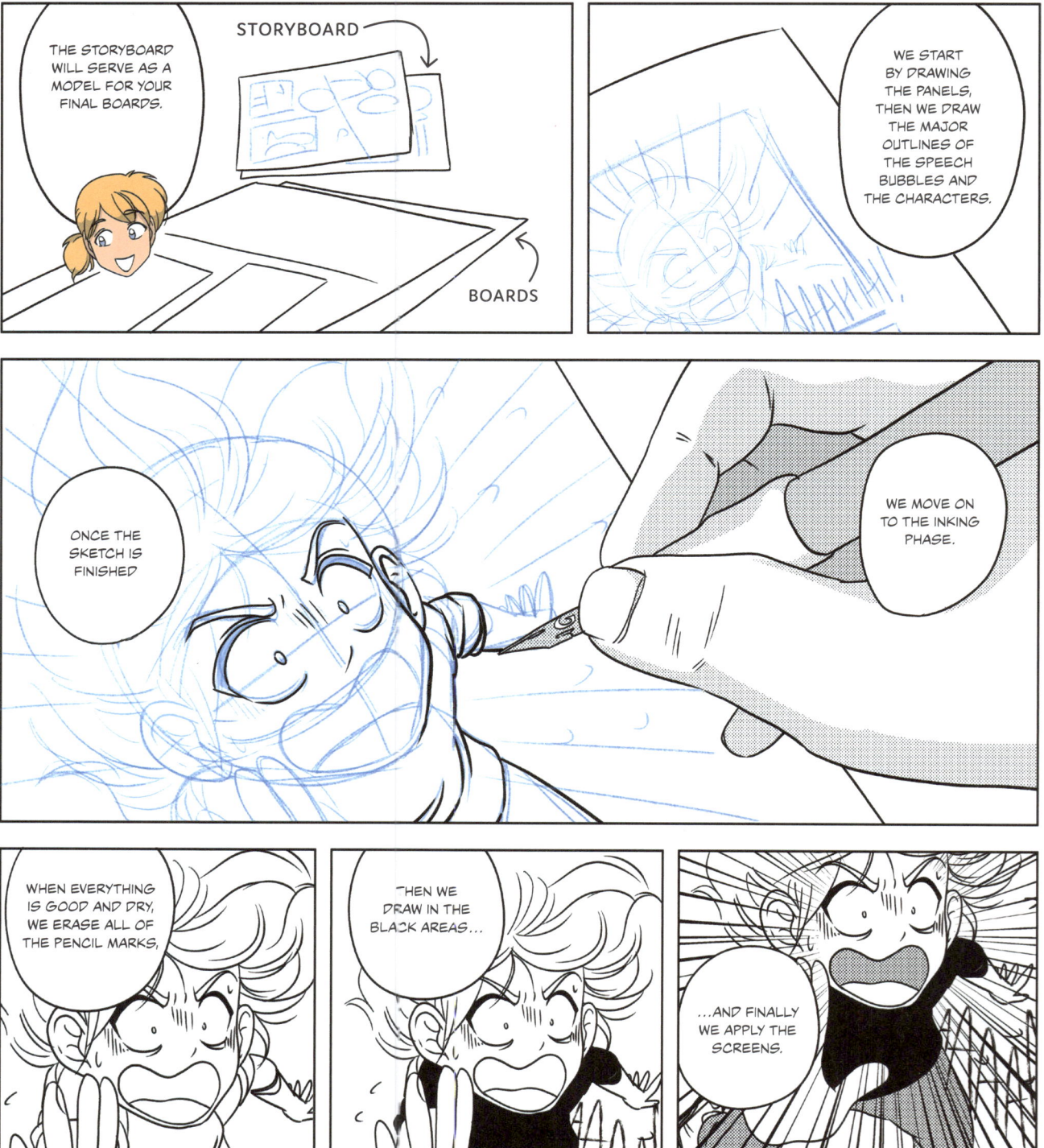

This final step can be done on paper or using a digital tool.

THE PENCIL SKETCH

There are several different ways to start sketching your boards, but I recommend that you follow this order:

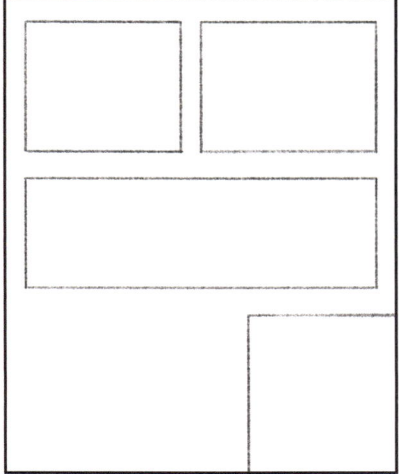

1 First draw the panels, as they will determine where your drawings and text should be positioned.

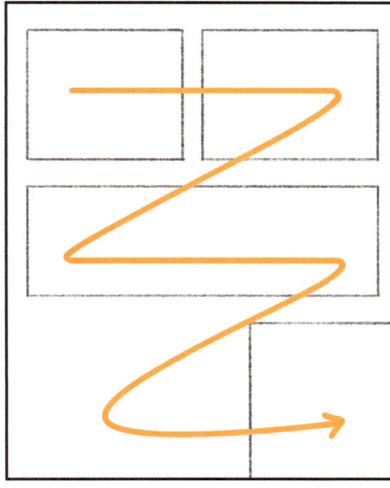

2 Check the placement of your action lines.

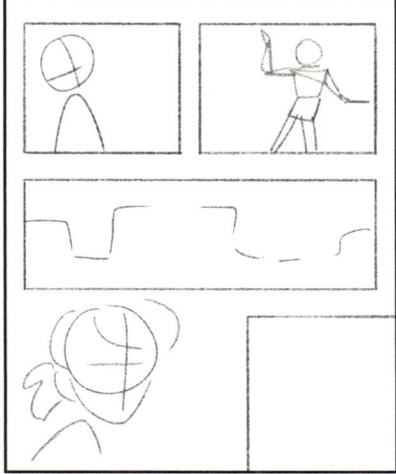

3 Position the most important shapes and construction lines for your characters.

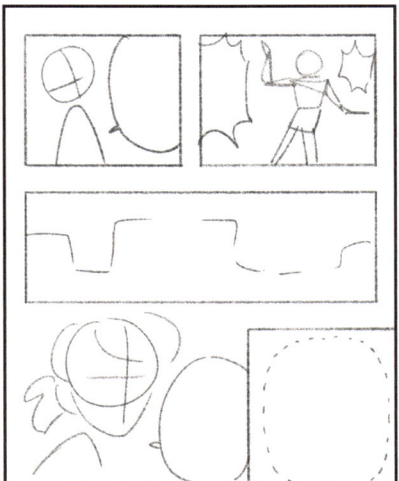

4 Draw the bubbles in the areas set aside for that effect.

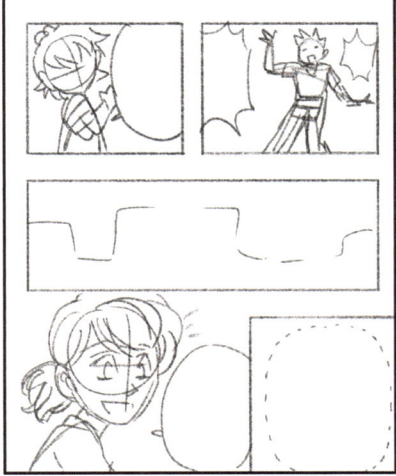

5 Add the details of your characters.

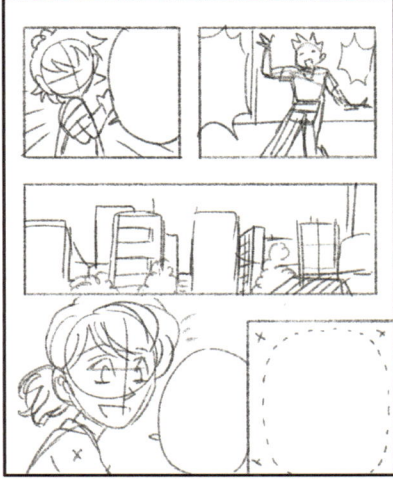

6 Finish up with the scenery and backgrounds.

> *Remember that all of the pencil lines you put on the page will end up disappearing after the inking phase. Think in terms of drawing light lines and don't fill in colored areas.*

INKING

Inking is the stage at which you go over your penciled drawing in black ink, using an inking tool (see materials on pages 22–23).

Every artist has their own methods and preferences for inking a drawing. You can use a variety of tools, alone or jointly, as you move through the pages: nibs, brushes, felt fineliners, ballpoint pens, digital tools…Likewise, an author can choose to change techniques even within the same board in order to get a particular effect.

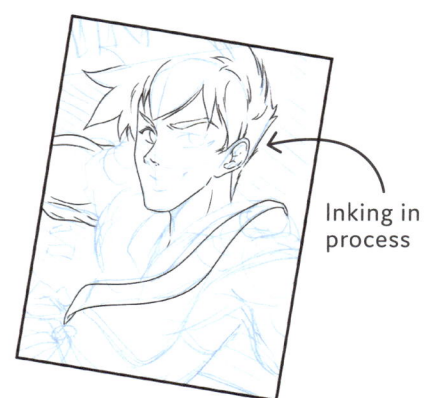
Inking in process

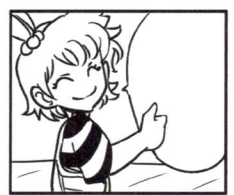
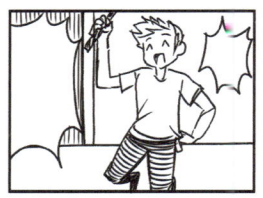
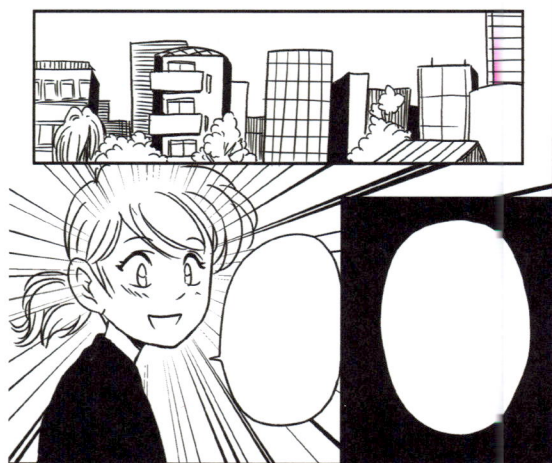

Pen nibs: The variations in line thickness that these give you are useful for giving shape and volume to your subjects.

Paintbrush: This allows you to fill in areas in black, but also to create more unstructured effects in the inked lines.

Felt fineliners: The regularity of the lines you can produce with these is very helpful for drawing the outlines of your panels, backgrounds, and speed lines.

Digital retouching: Digital tools can perfectly imitate the effects of traditional inking tools. We can use them to retouch or edit our boards on a computer.

Not all of the elements of a given board will be drawn at the same time.

Draw the borders of your panels, then go over all of the elements of the page in black, always going from the foreground to the background, ending with the finishing touches.

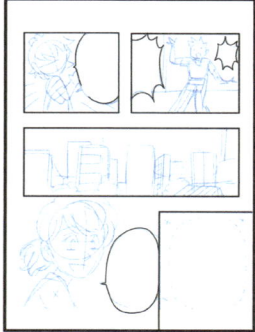
1 Panel borders and bubbles

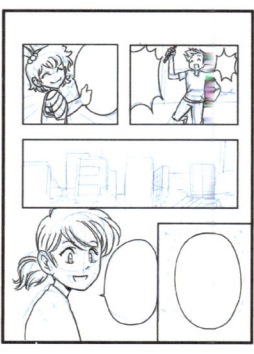
2 Characters in the foreground

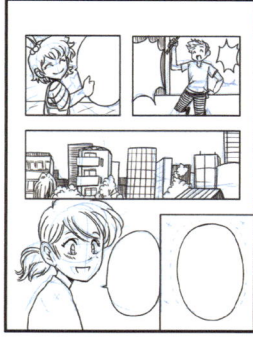
3 Background

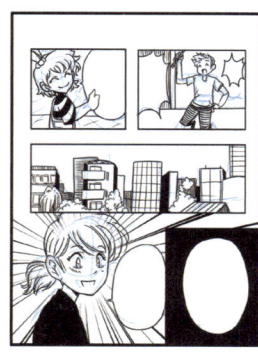
4 Finishing touches and filled-in areas in black

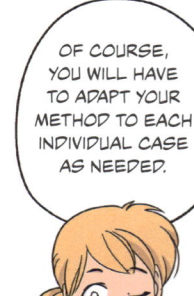
OF COURSE, YOU WILL HAVE TO ADAPT YOUR METHOD TO EACH INDIVIDUAL CASE AS NEEDED.

HOW DO YOU INK A DRAWING?

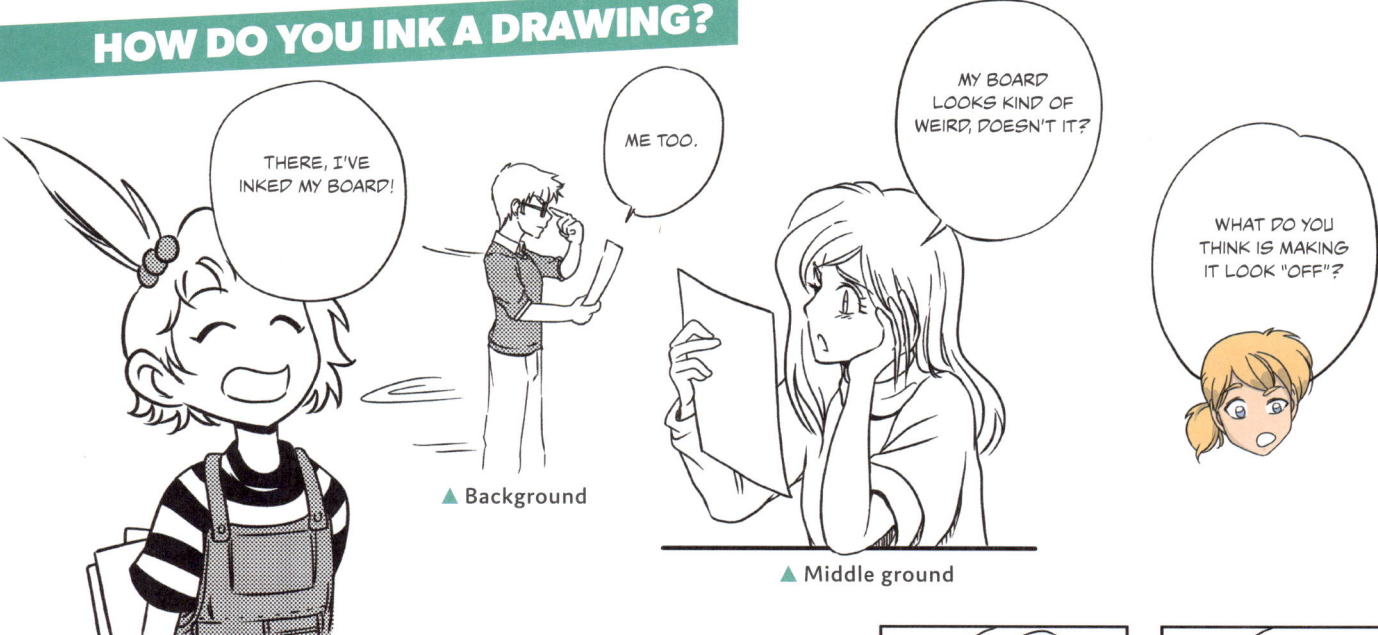

THERE, I'VE INKED MY BOARD!

ME TOO.

MY BOARD LOOKS KIND OF WEIRD, DOESN'T IT?

WHAT DO YOU THINK IS MAKING IT LOOK "OFF"?

▲ Foreground

▲ Background

▲ Middle ground

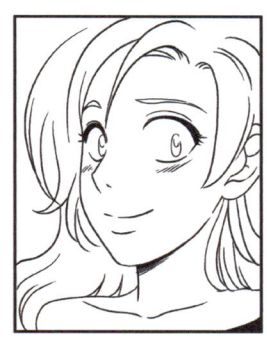

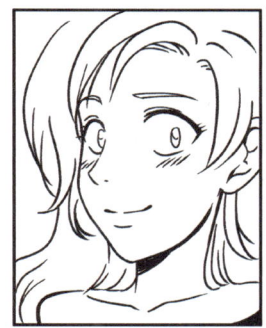

Chloé followed all the instructions carefully: First, she drew the panels…Then, she drew the foreground, and then the background—but she didn't vary the thickness of her lines.

The inking phase is not just a matter of going over all the lines in your drawing in black. You are going to have to vary the thickness and style of the lines, using your various inking tools.

Inking tends to "freeze" your drawings. Here are some tips for keeping your lines flexible and dynamic:

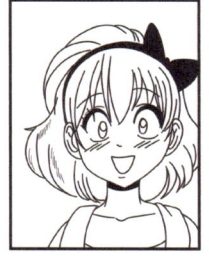

▲ Inking with a fineliner pen

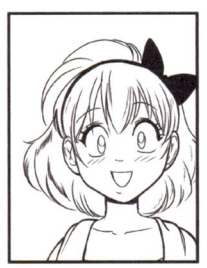

▲ Inking with a pen nib

- **Vary the thickness of your lines** to give your characters and objects some volume.

The outlines of heavy objects are thicker than the outlines of light objects. There can also be variations within the same object.

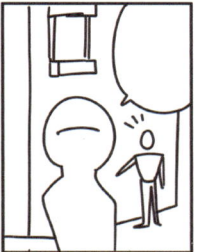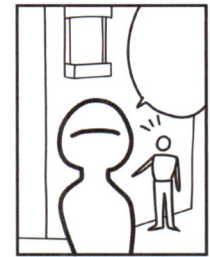

- Draw **lines of different thicknesses** for the elements **closer up and further away** in your image, from the thickest to the thinnest, respectively.

- **Take the light source into account** when you are doing your inking. The lines will be finer when they are well-lit, and thicker in shaded areas.

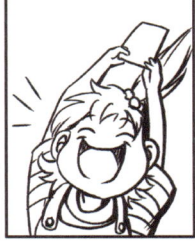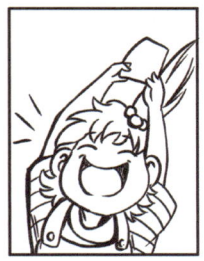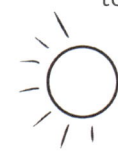

HOW DO YOU USE A MANGAKA PEN?

Pen nibs are the tool of choice for mangaka because they give you the ability to drastically vary the thickness of your lines.

It is important to learn how to hold your pen holder correctly and place the pen on the page in the right way to make the best use of the advantages it offers.

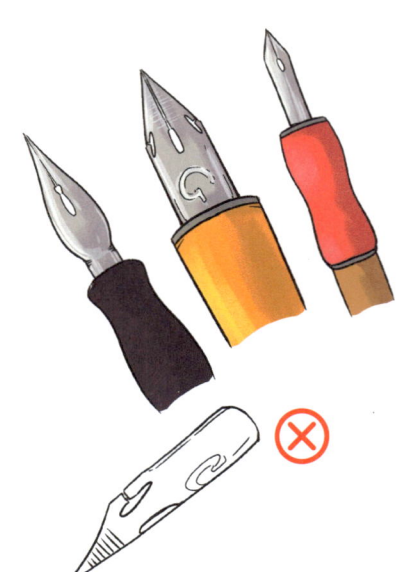

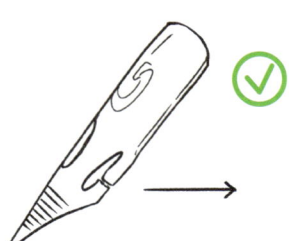

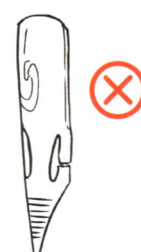

When you press on the page, the two metal blades of the nib will separate in order to deposit the ink there.

Before using a nib for the first time, you will need to prepare it by removing the rust-protection film. All you have to do is wipe it well with a dry cloth or a paper towel.

Your pencil sketch is clean and ready to be gone over in black, so we can start.

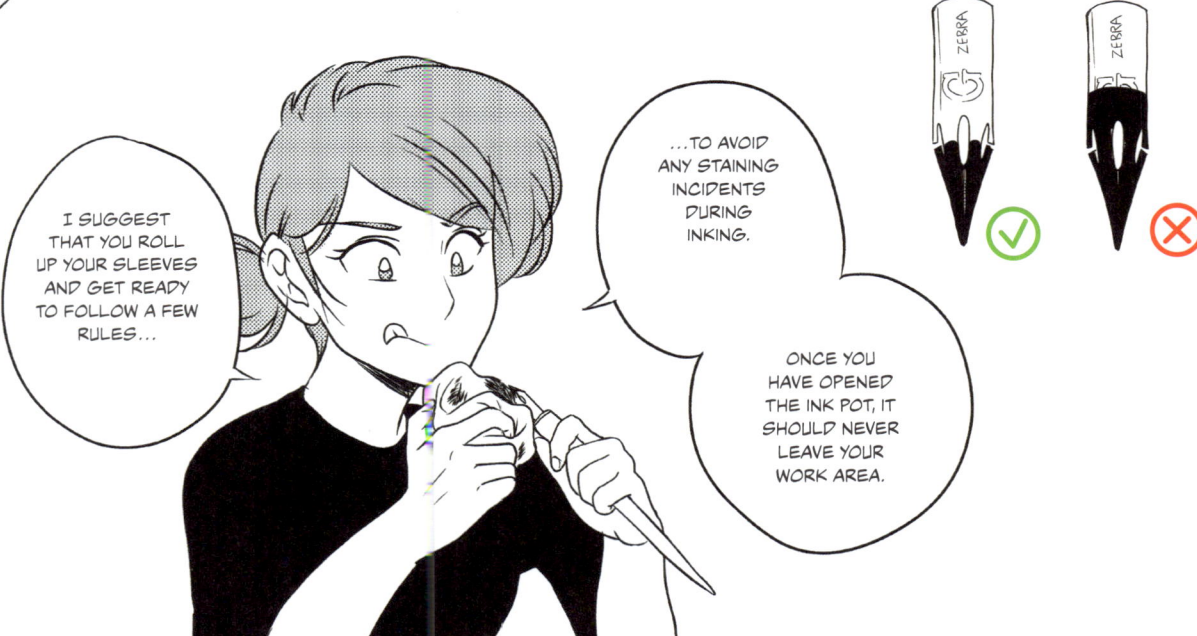

I SUGGEST THAT YOU ROLL UP YOUR SLEEVES AND GET READY TO FOLLOW A FEW RULES...

...TO AVOID ANY STAINING INCIDENTS DURING INKING.

ONCE YOU HAVE OPENED THE INK POT, IT SHOULD NEVER LEAVE YOUR WORK AREA.

Use a ruler with an anti-smudge edge to draw the borders of your panels with a pen nib.

Before we start, we sometimes use a kneaded eraser to lightly blur the pencil lines.

We draw the lines from front to back as if we were pulling the line toward us. The nib should be at a 45-degree angle to the page.

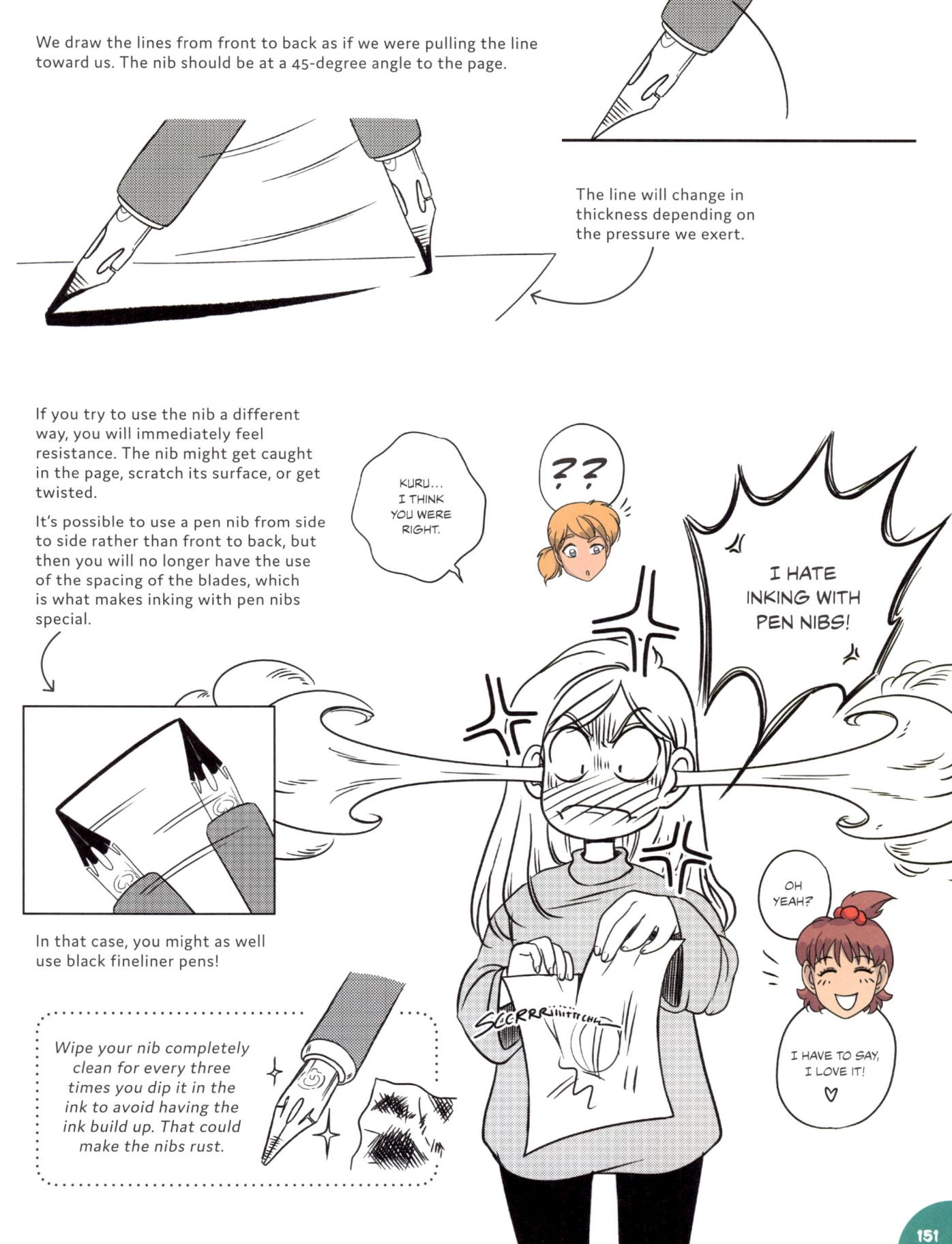

The line will change in thickness depending on the pressure we exert.

If you try to use the nib a different way, you will immediately feel resistance. The nib might get caught in the page, scratch its surface, or get twisted.

It's possible to use a pen nib from side to side rather than front to back, but then you will no longer have the use of the spacing of the blades, which is what makes inking with pen nibs special.

In that case, you might as well use black fineliner pens!

Wipe your nib completely clean for every three times you dip it in the ink to avoid having the ink build up. That could make the nibs rust.

KURU... I THINK YOU WERE RIGHT.

??

I HATE INKING WITH PEN NIBS!

OH YEAH?

SCCRRRjjjjtttchh

I HAVE TO SAY, I LOVE IT! ♥

Minimalist style

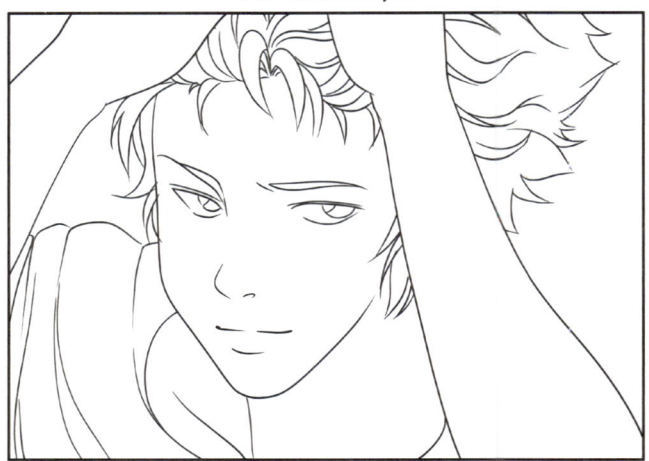

Rounded style

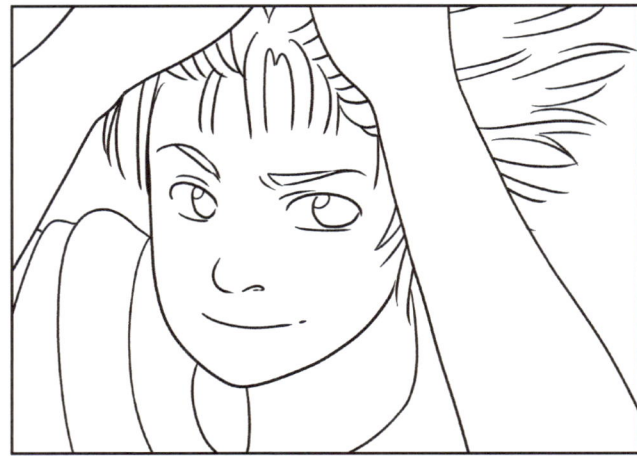

Emotional style

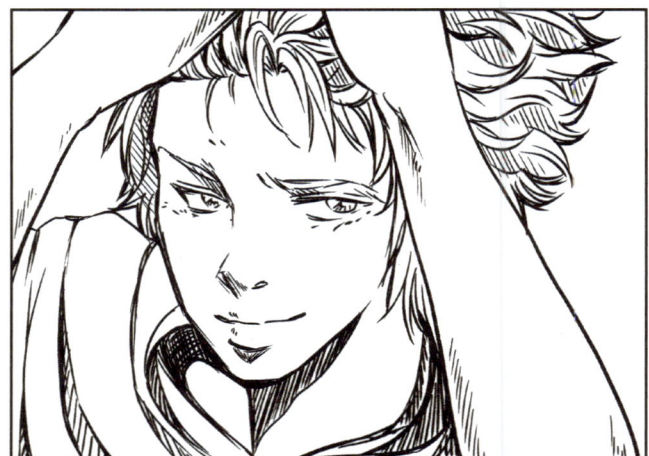

Realistic style

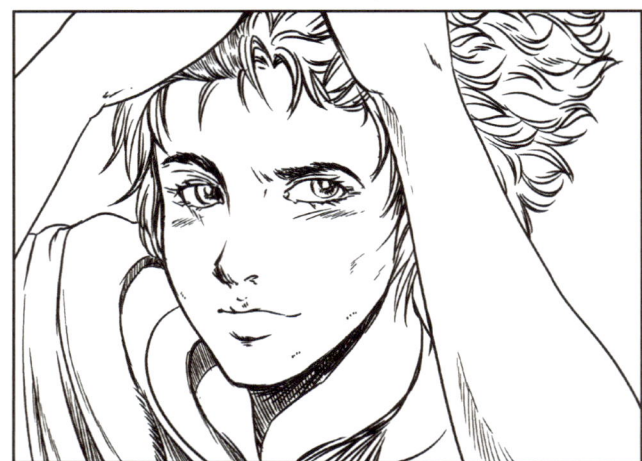

PRACTICE

Here are some ways to practice inking:

- *Practice on the same subject, using photocopies of your sketches to go over them in different ways.*
- *Try out different inking tools to see which one gives you the best results.*
- *Copy over the boards of some of your favorite authors. Carefully observe the style and thickness of their lines.*
- *Take a page from one of those authors and redraw it in your own style, from the pencil sketch to the inking stage.*

HOW DO I USE WHITE INK?

White ink can allow you to correct any inking mistakes, but it can also be used to create various **lighting or textural effects**.

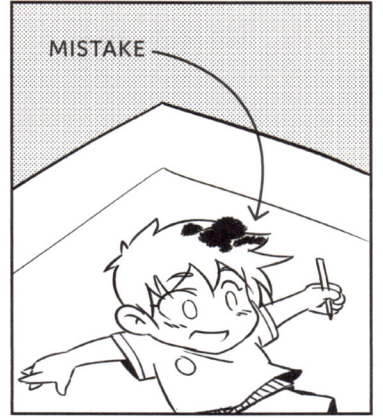

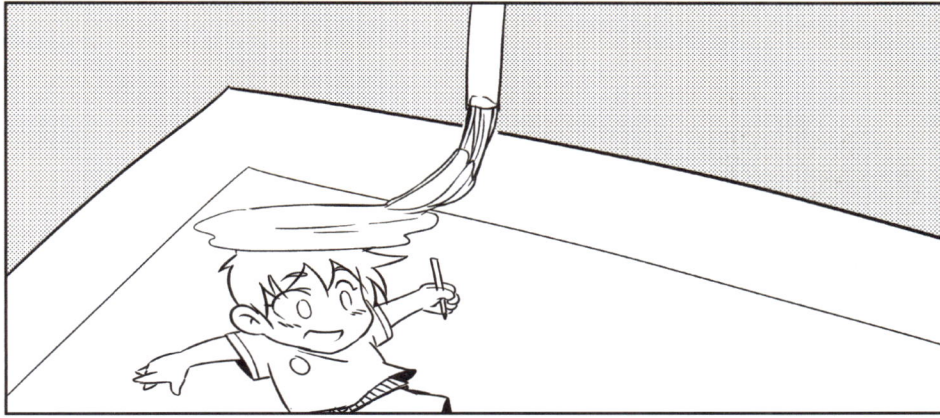

In a panel that you've already filled in with black, you can draw the outlines of a character using a pen nib with white ink. This gives you the effect of a negative.

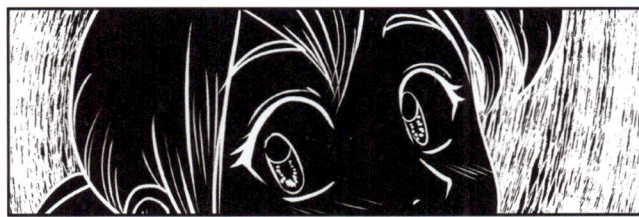

You can make splashes very quickly, either by blowing on the ink through a misting plate or a paintbrush, or by scratching at the bristles of a toothbrush soaked in ink. You can use splashes like this to draw starry skies, for example.

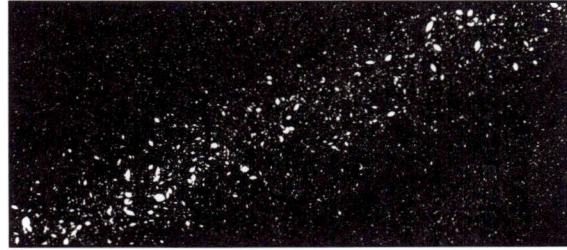

Don't be afraid to try out these techniques and think up new ones, using stencils, cotton pads, stamps, etc.

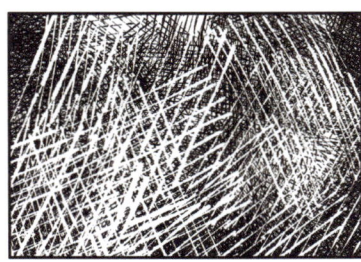

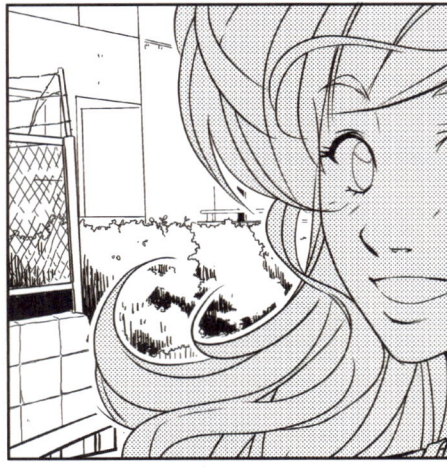

Because the ink has a covering texture, you can use it to go over the inking lines and create highlights or contours to separate the foreground from the scenery.

PERSPECTIVE

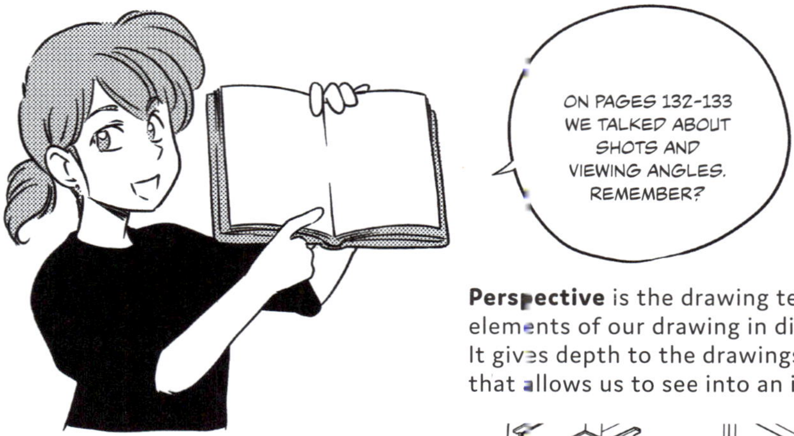

ON PAGES 132-133 WE TALKED ABOUT SHOTS AND VIEWING ANGLES. REMEMBER?

Perspective is the drawing technique that allows us to show the various elements of our drawing in different shots and from different viewing angles. It gives depth to the drawings, transforming the page or panel into a window that allows us to see into an imaginary world in three dimensions.

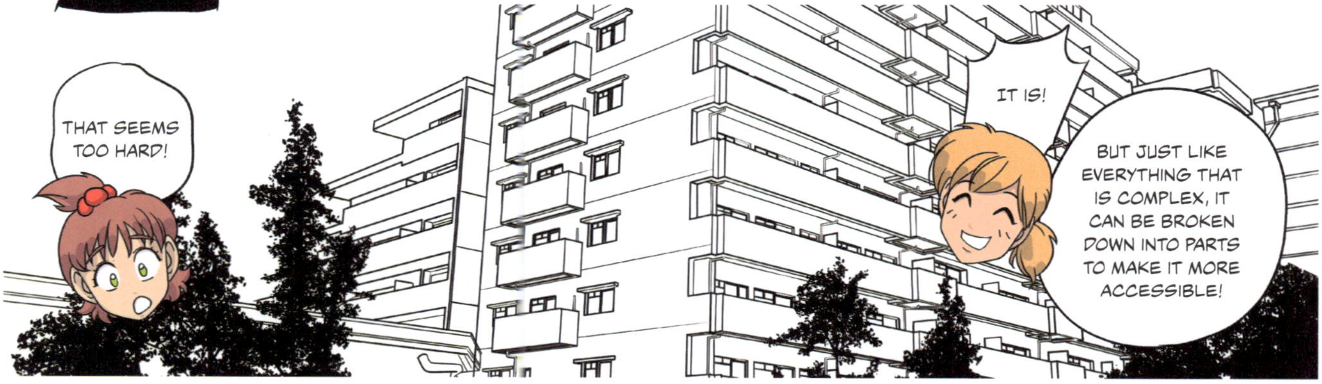

THAT SEEMS TOO HARD!

IT IS!

BUT JUST LIKE EVERYTHING THAT IS COMPLEX, IT CAN BE BROKEN DOWN INTO PARTS TO MAKE IT MORE ACCESSIBLE!

Let's create a drawing together using perspective.

Start by taking a sheet of paper and rotate it so you can draw in the landscape orientation.

Position your **horizon line**. This is a horizontal line that corresponds to the level of the spectator's eyes. It represents the line between the ground and the sky on the page.

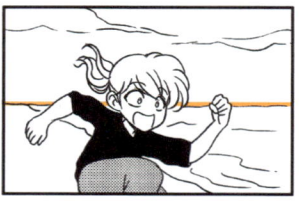

In a horizontal view, this line also corresponds to the level of the character's eyes.

To draw from a bird's-eye view, place the horizon line toward the top of the page. Move the line toward the bottom of the page to create a drawing from a low-angle view.

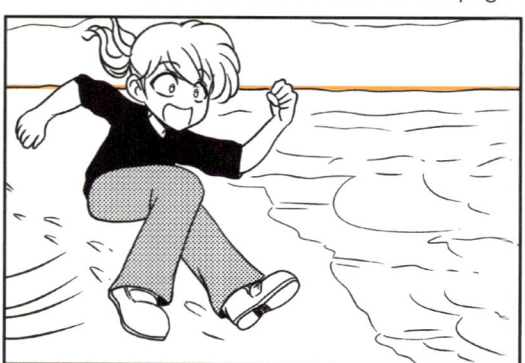

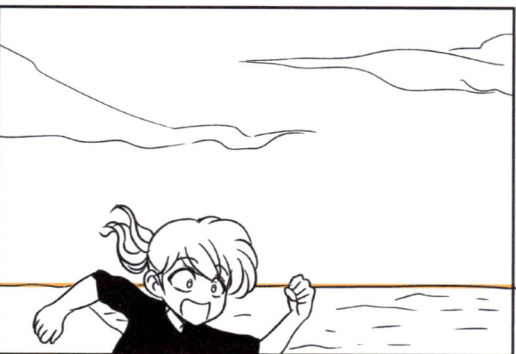

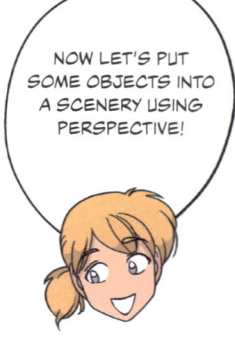

NOW LET'S PUT SOME OBJECTS INTO A SCENERY USING PERSPECTIVE!

ONE-POINT PERSPECTIVE

HERE IS A CUBE WITH ONE FACE POINTING TOWARD YOU.

In a horizontal view, the cube is centered on the horizon line.

This drawing is still a two-dimensional drawing because we can only see one face of the cube. In reality, the cube already has a volume and is pointing toward a vanishing point placed on the horizon line, exactly in the center of the face that we can see.

When we draw a **vanishing point** to one side of the cube, along the horizon line, and then **vanishing lines**, we can start to perceive its depth.

The vanishing lines connect the angles of the cube with the vanishing point.

We draw the outlines of the face of the cube that is directed away from us using the vanishing lines and a vertical line.

This cube is drawn from the cavalier perspective. This method does not use any vanishing points. The lines of the sides of the cube are parallel.

ONE-POINT PERSPECTIVE IS USED TO DRAW SIMPLE SCENERY AND BACKGROUNDS.

The vertical lines are perpendicular to the horizon line. The horizontal lines are parallel to the horizon line. The outlines of the faces that are pointed away from us are aligned along the vanishing lines.

To draw the cube from a bird's-eye view or a low-angle view, all you have to do is to position the visible face either below or above the horizon line.

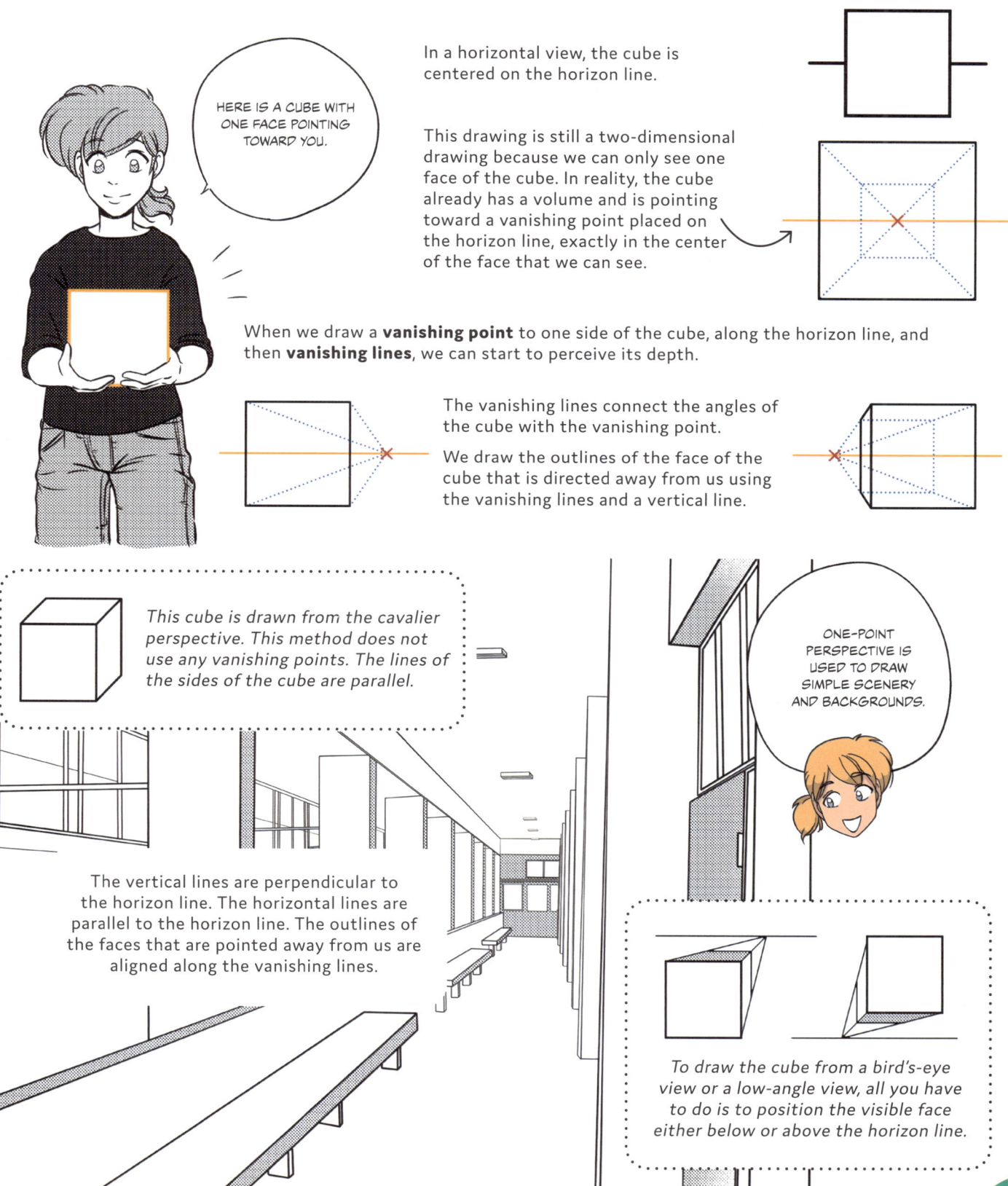

155

TWO-POINT PERSPECTIVE

In a horizontal view, each face of the cube is pointed toward a different vanishing point.

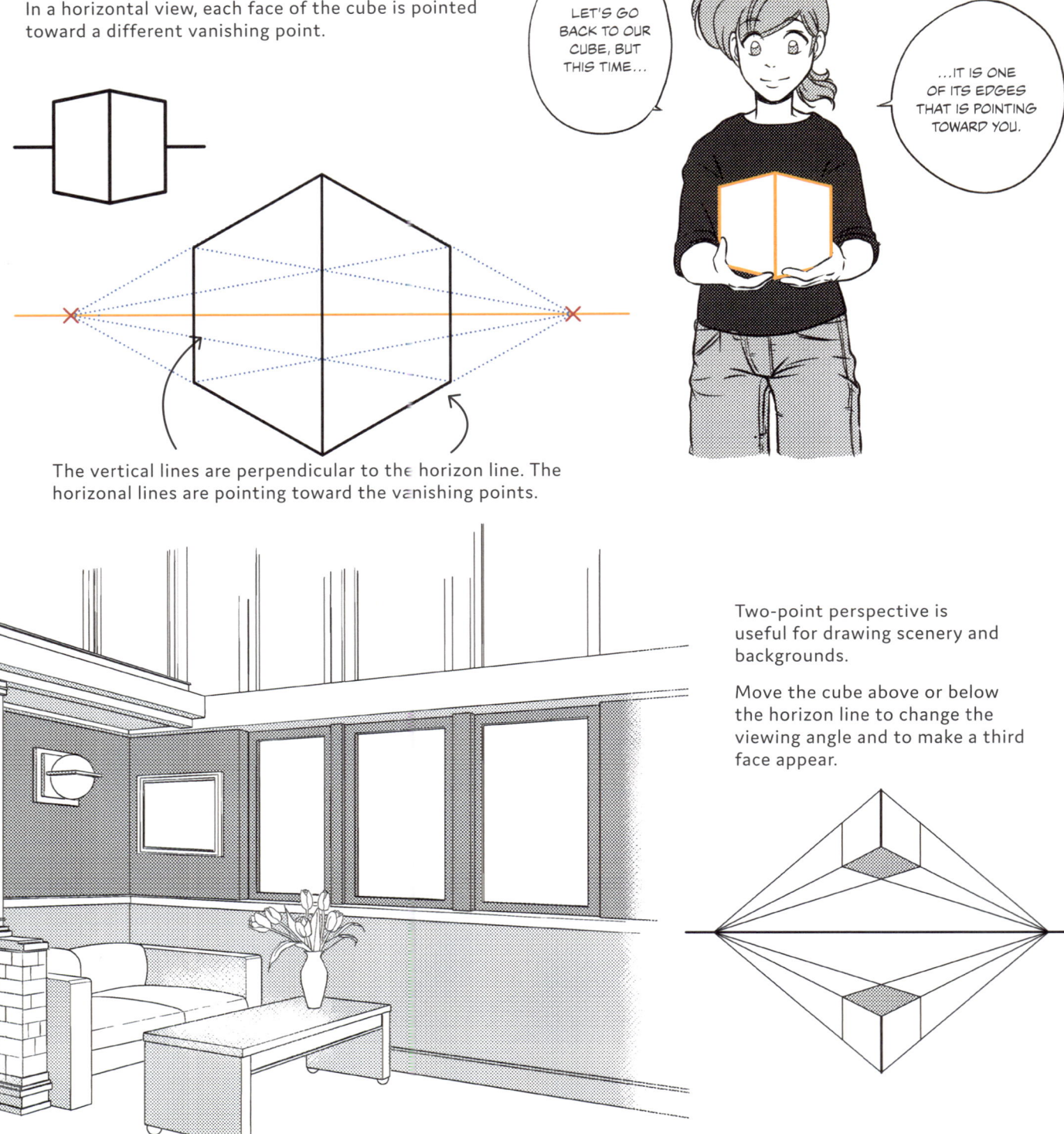

LET'S GO BACK TO OUR CUBE, BUT THIS TIME...

...IT IS ONE OF ITS EDGES THAT IS POINTING TOWARD YOU.

The vertical lines are perpendicular to the horizon line. The horizonal lines are pointing toward the vanishing points.

Two-point perspective is useful for drawing scenery and backgrounds.

Move the cube above or below the horizon line to change the viewing angle and to make a third face appear.

THREE-POINT PERSPECTIVE

NOW THE CUBE IS PRESENTING ONE OF ITS ANGLES IN YOUR DIRECTION.

Three of its faces are visible and drawn in the direction of two vanishing points placed on the horizon and a third one that is situated on a vertical axis.

Each edge of the cube is aligned on a different vanishing point.

Perspective allows us to see objects in three dimensions.

Face   Edge   Angle

By exaggerating the representation, we can deform an object or a character and make the scene more dynamic.

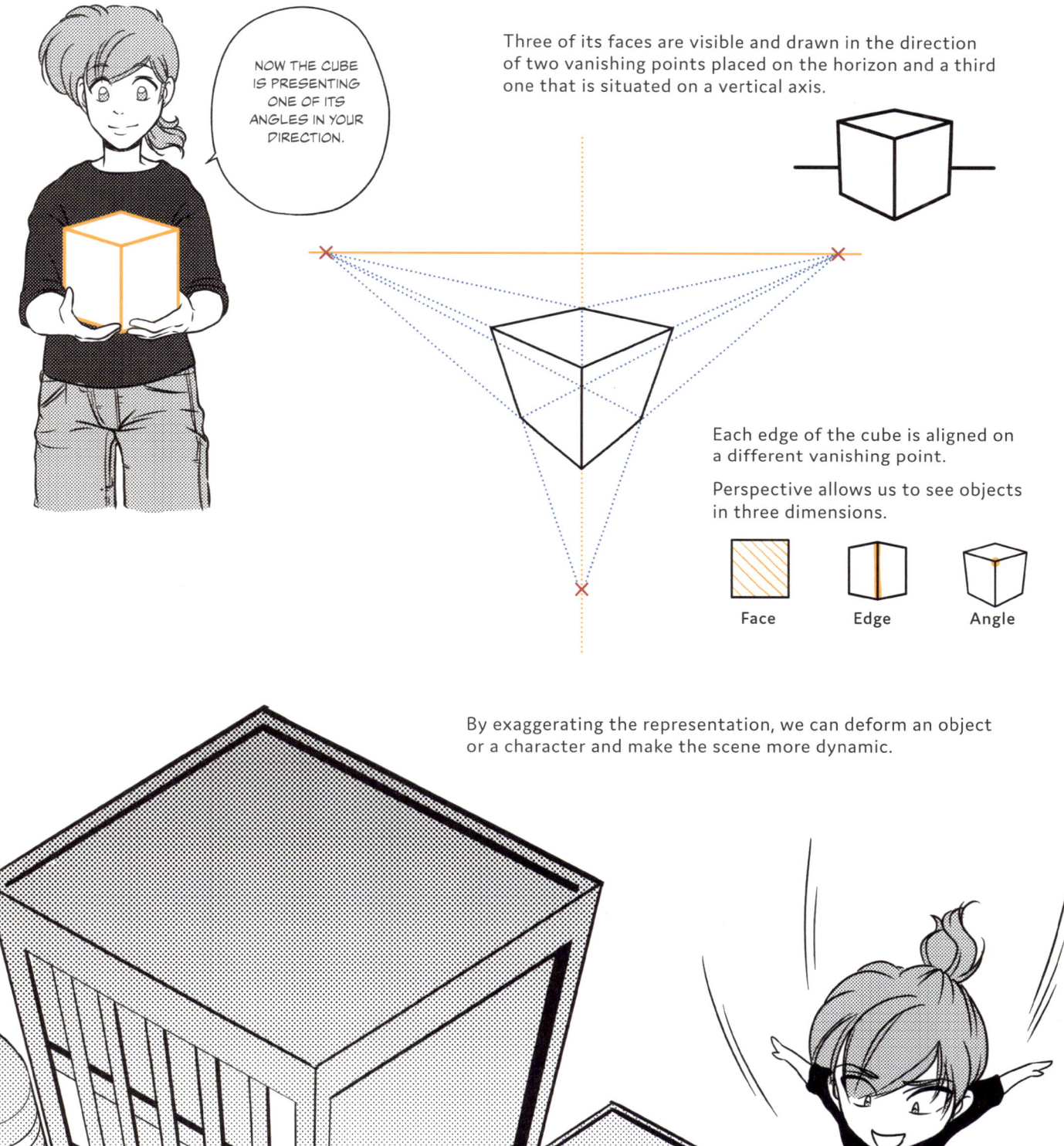

DRAWING SCENERY

To draw scenery, you first have to **determine the viewing angle** by positioning the horizon line, and then **choose the shot**.

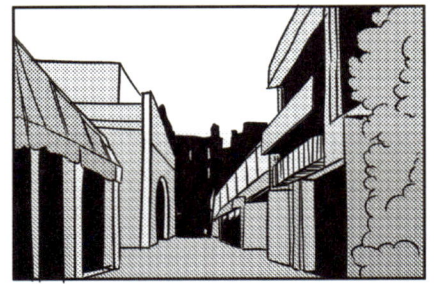 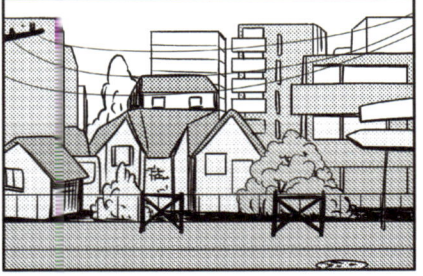 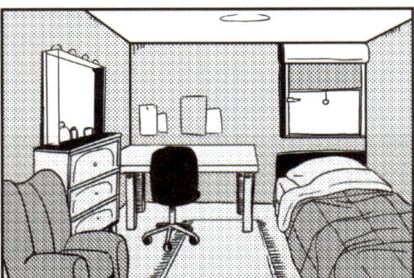

This interior setting has the particularity of showing both a floor and a ceiling. The horizon line continues to exist, but the wall of the room, as well as the furniture, keep the reader from seeing it.

Thanks to **perspective**, you can present a character in a multi-dimensional setting. The size of the character will determine how far away they are.

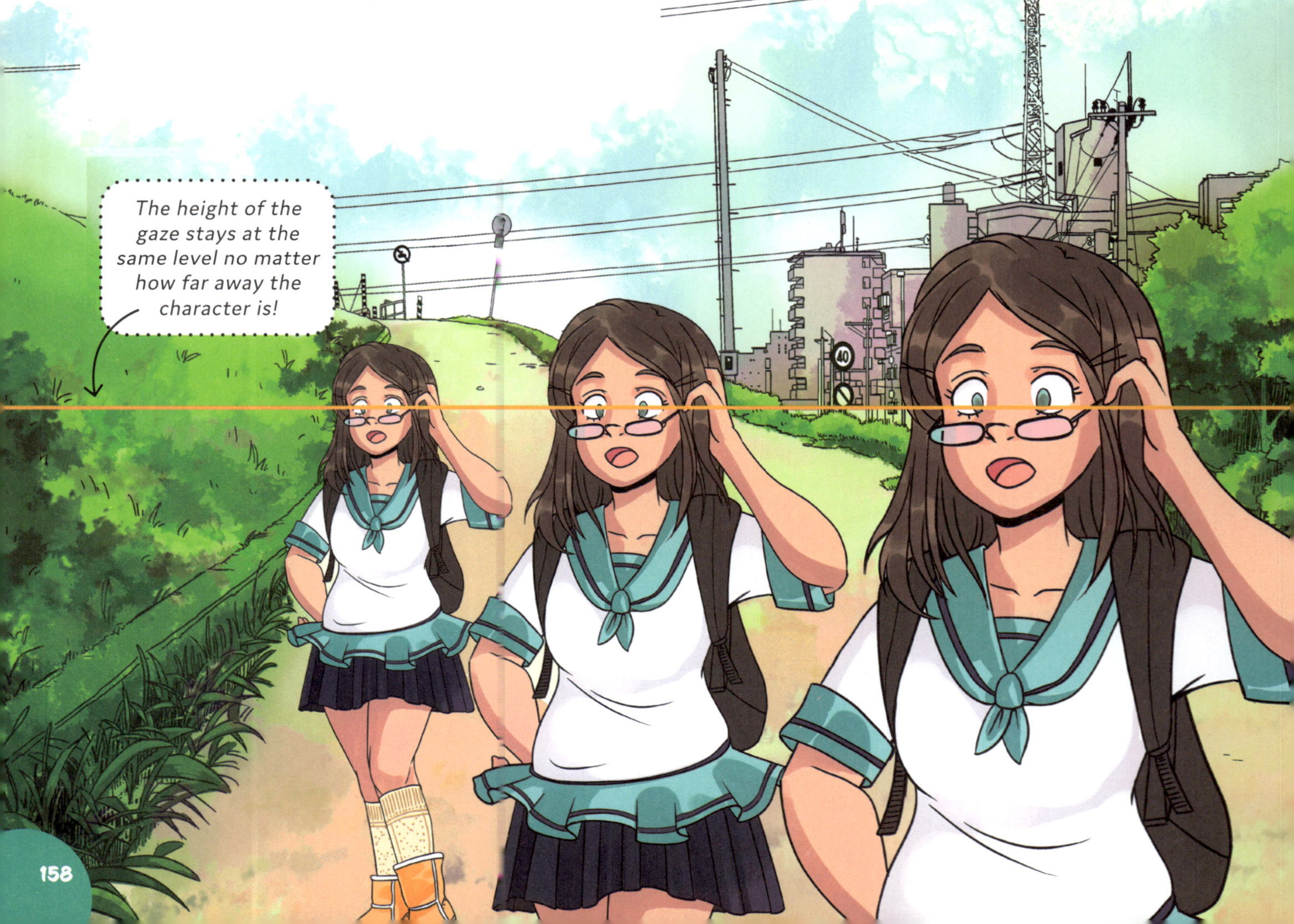

The height of the gaze stays at the same level no matter how far away the character is!

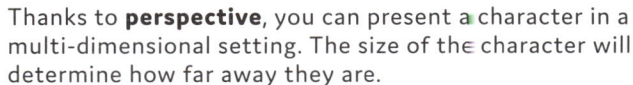

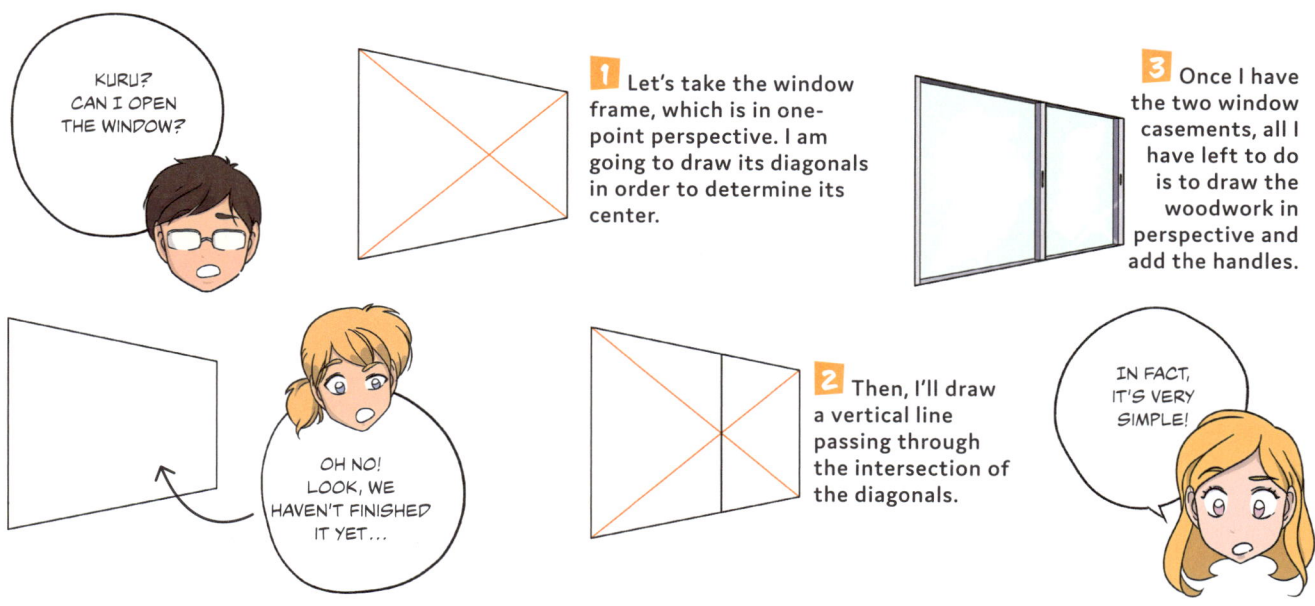

KURU?
CAN I OPEN
THE WINDOW?

1 Let's take the window frame, which is in one-point perspective. I am going to draw its diagonals in order to determine its center.

3 Once I have the two window casements, all I have left to do is to draw the woodwork in perspective and add the handles.

OH NO!
LOOK, WE
HAVEN'T FINISHED
IT YET...

2 Then, I'll draw a vertical line passing through the intersection of the diagonals.

IN FACT,
IT'S VERY
SIMPLE!

If you want to take it further, we can draw a tiled floor in perspective together.
Go through the steps with me!

1 Draw the horizon line and one vertical axis passing through the vanishing point. Place the first row of tiles by drawing a line parallel to the horizon line.

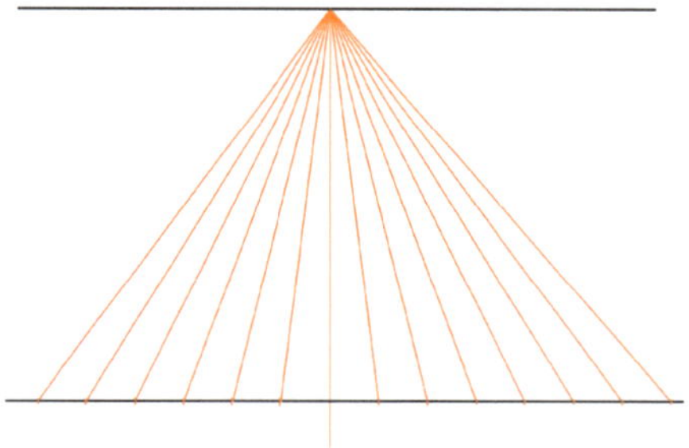

2 Determine the width of the tiles by placing equidistant marks along the horizontal line, then draw vanishing lines connecting each of the marks to the vanishing point.

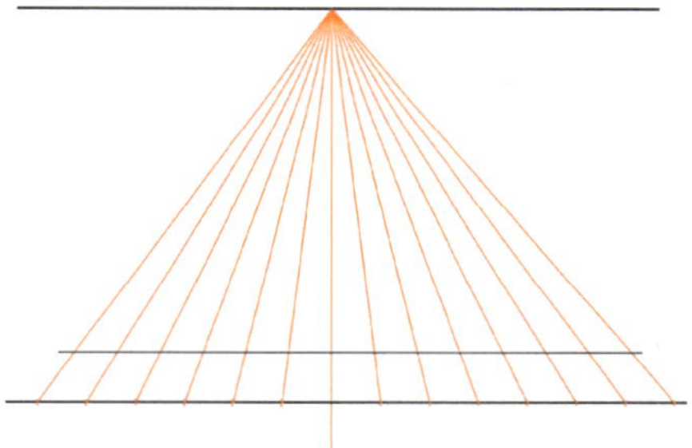

3 To choose the height of the tiles, position a mark along the vertical axis, then draw the horizontal line that passes through that point. Now we have our first row of tiles.

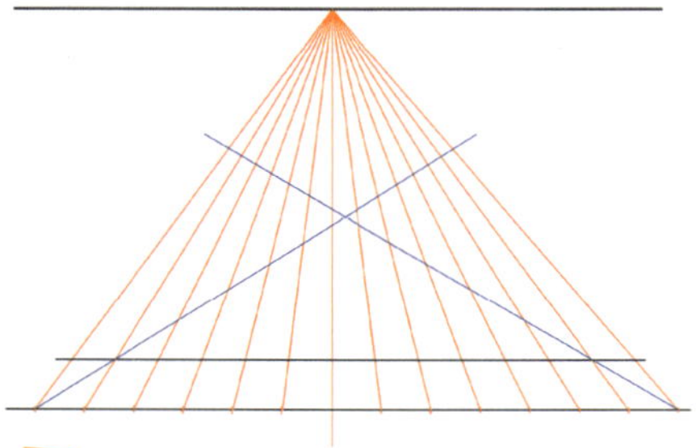

4 Draw the diagonals of the two tiles at the edges of the rows and extend them so that they intersect with the vanishing lines.

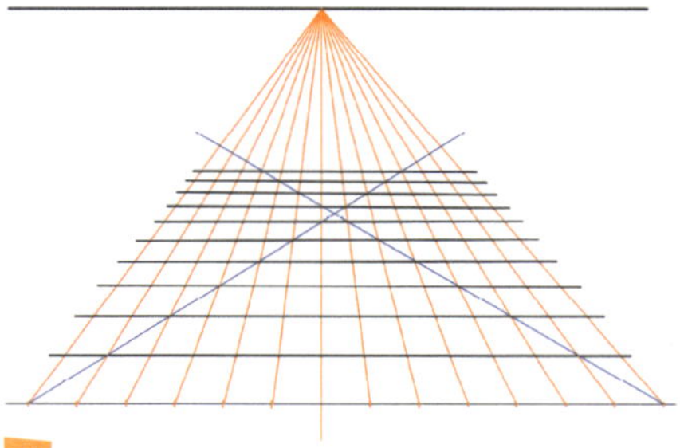

5 Now we can draw the next rows by connecting every intersection between the diagonals and the vanishing lines with horizontal lines.

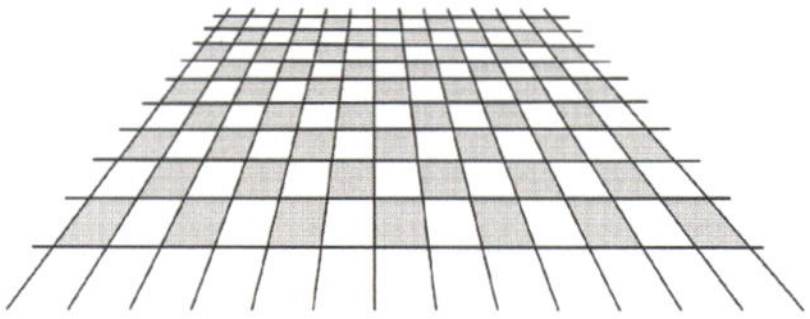

6 Here is the finished tiled floor!

159

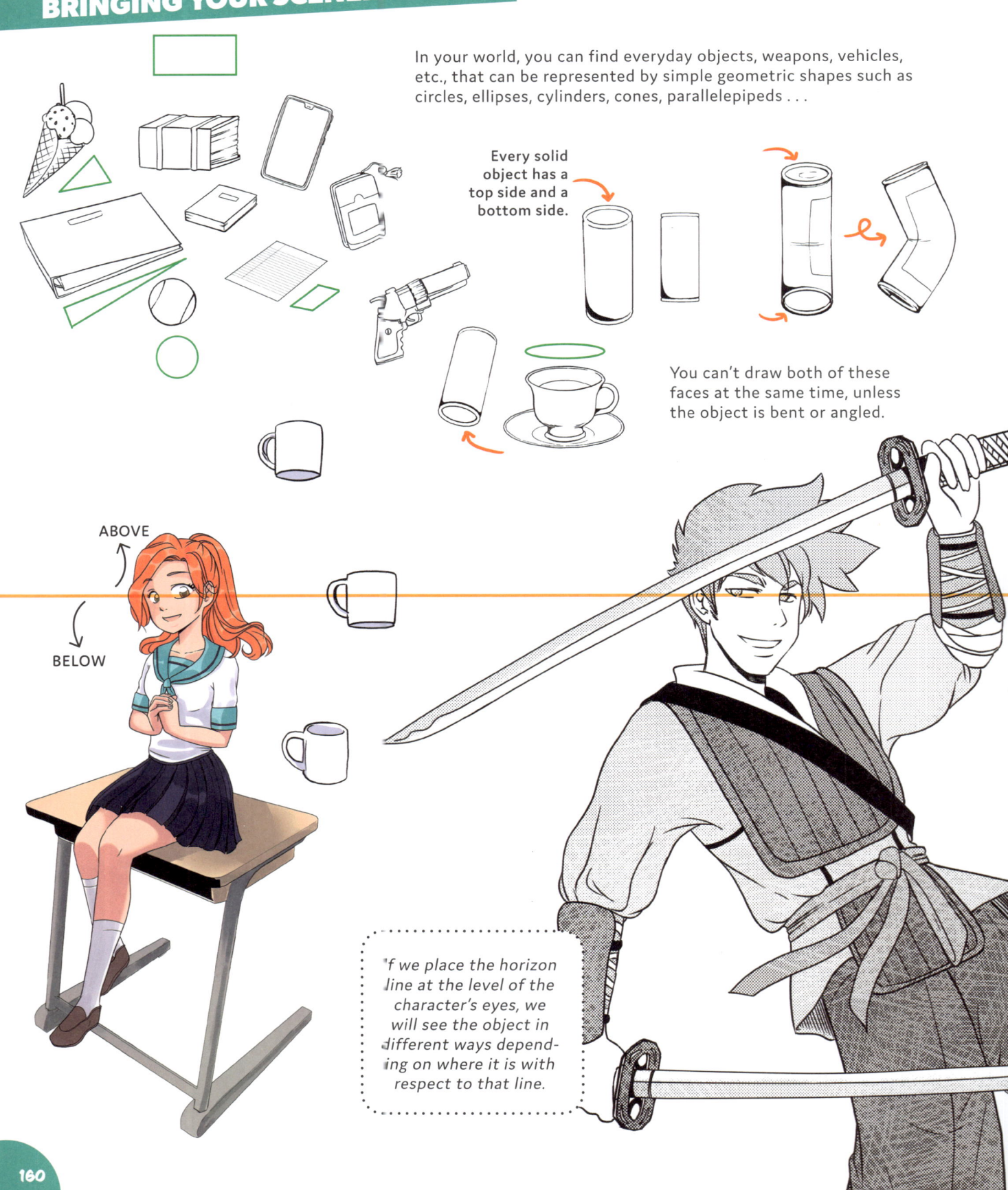

In your world, you can find everyday objects, weapons, vehicles, etc., that can be represented by simple geometric shapes such as circles, ellipses, cylinders, cones, parallelepipeds . . .

Every solid object has a top side and a bottom side.

You can't draw both of these faces at the same time, unless the object is bent or angled.

ABOVE

BELOW

If we place the horizon line at the level of the character's eyes, we will see the object in different ways depending on where it is with respect to that line.

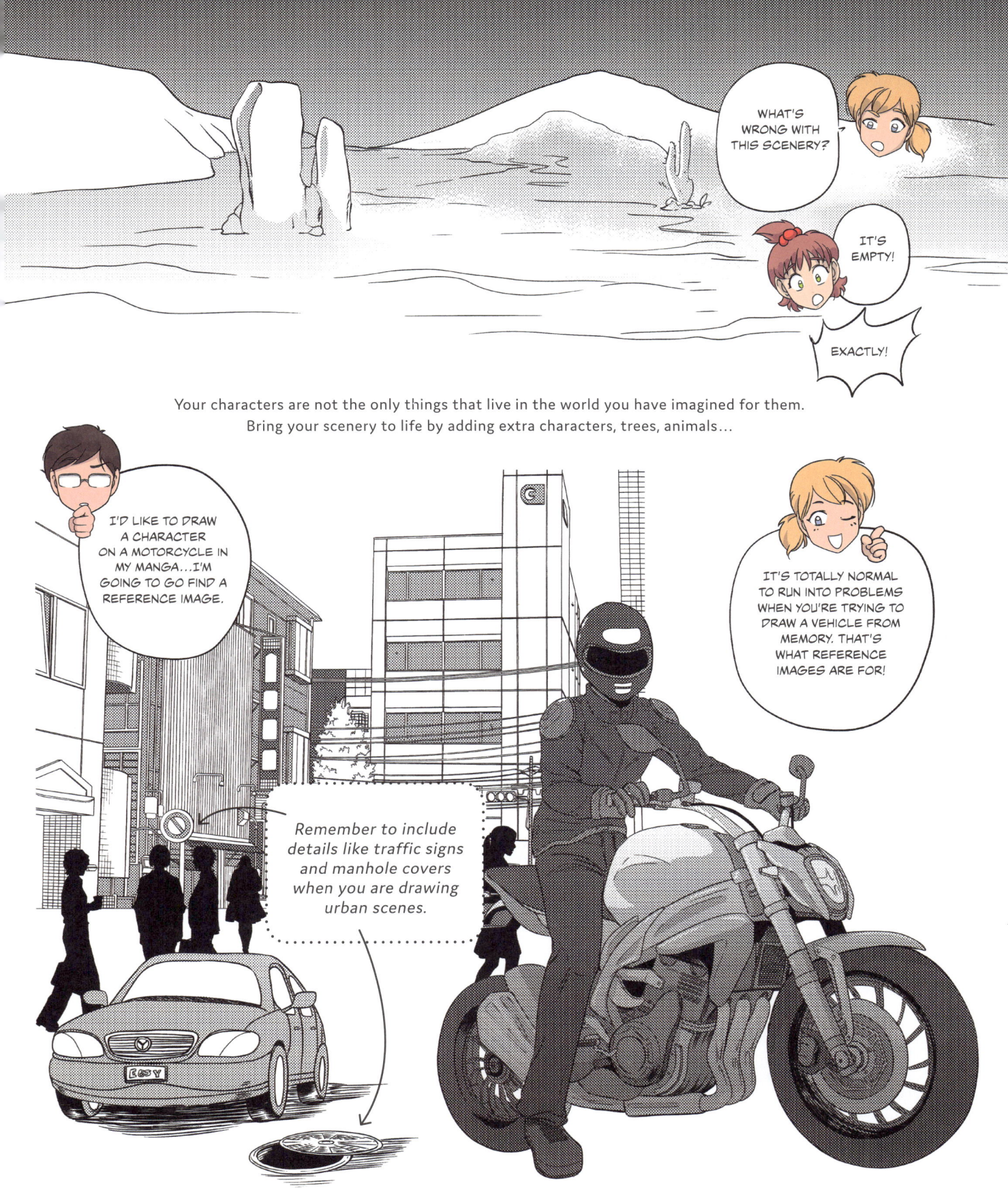

Your characters are not the only things that live in the world you have imagined for them. Bring your scenery to life by adding extra characters, trees, animals…

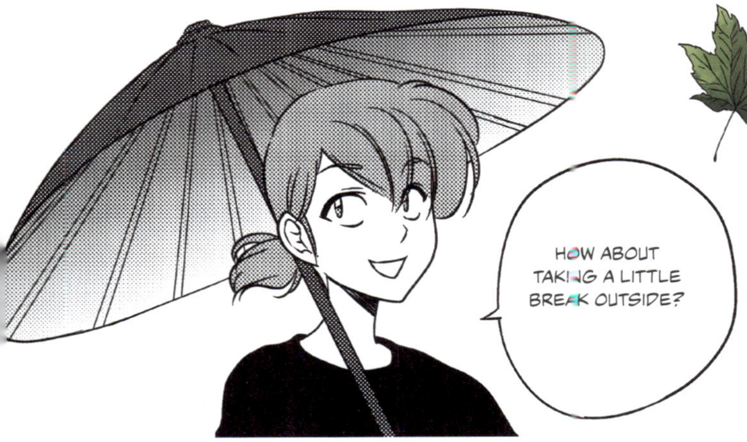

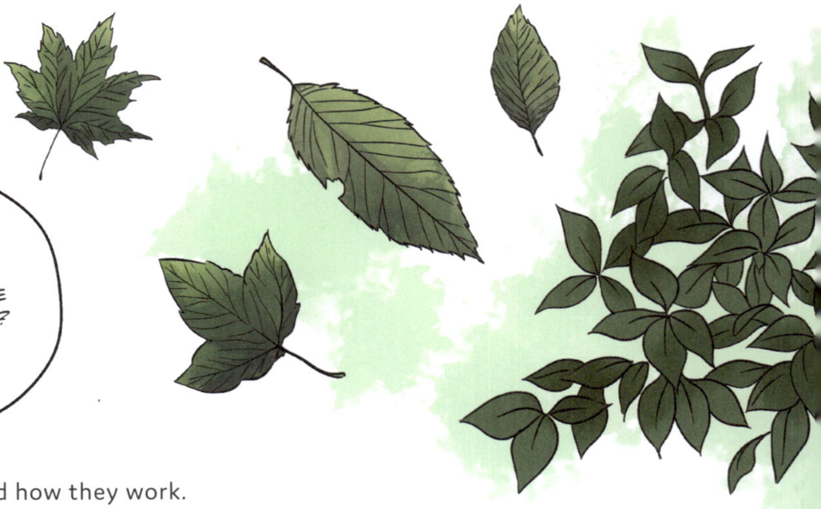

Plants are very pleasant to draw once you understand how they work.

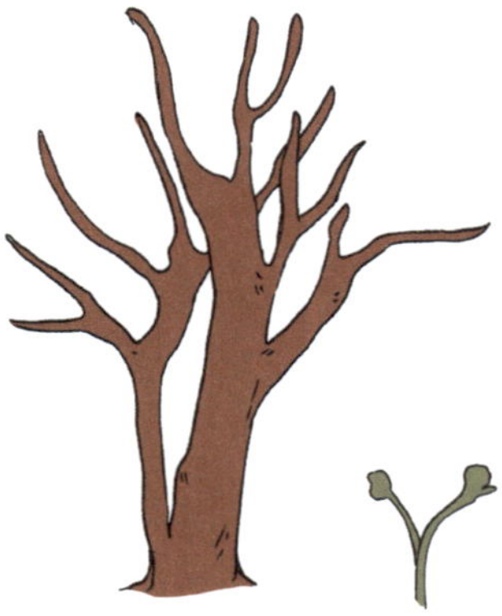

1 Start by drawing the shapes of the trunks and branches (of a tree) or the stems (of plants).

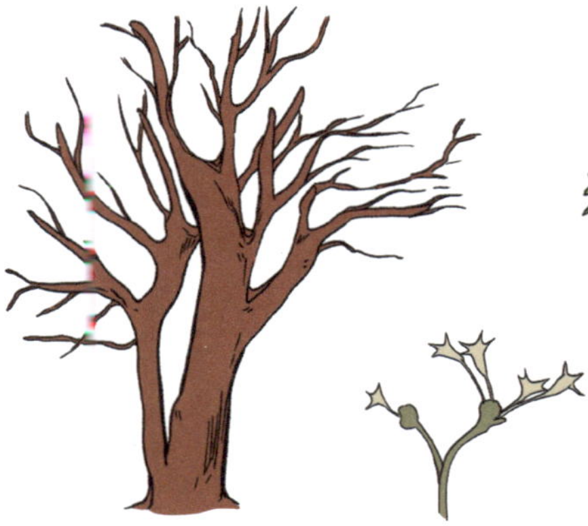

2 Add offshoots.

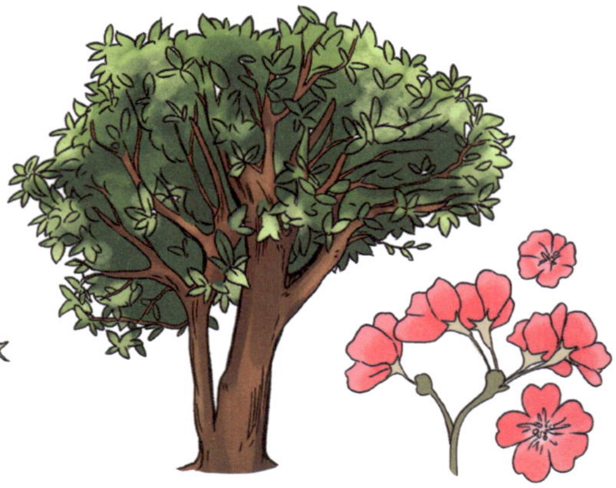

3 Finish up by adding the leaves and/ or flowers.

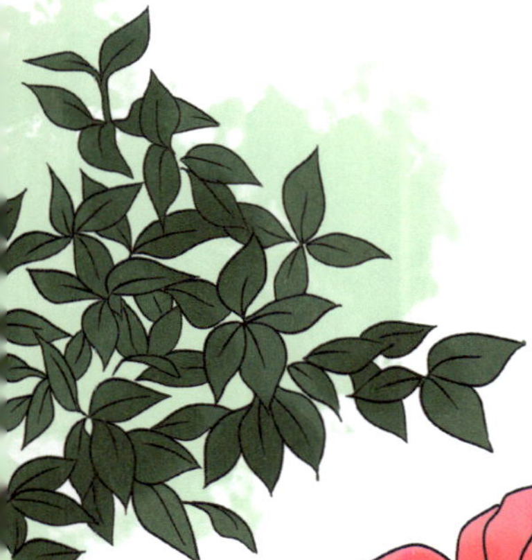

Tree trunks have ribbing that is sometimes drawn horizontally and sometimes vertically.

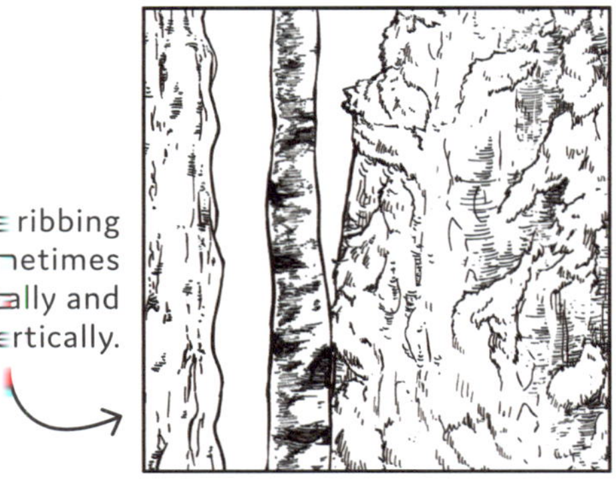

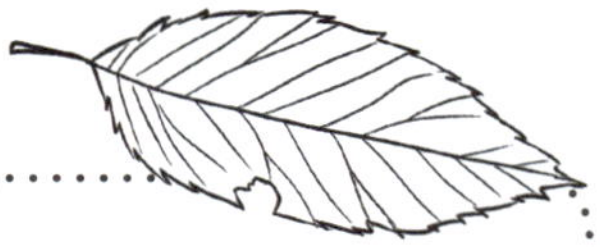

Remember to vary the thickness of your lines when you are doing the inking in order to give your surfaces and foliage some texture.

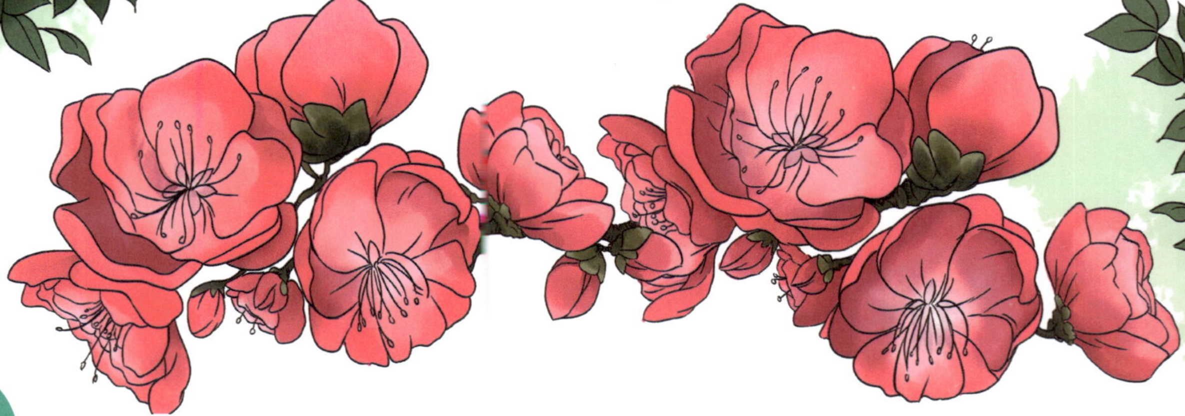

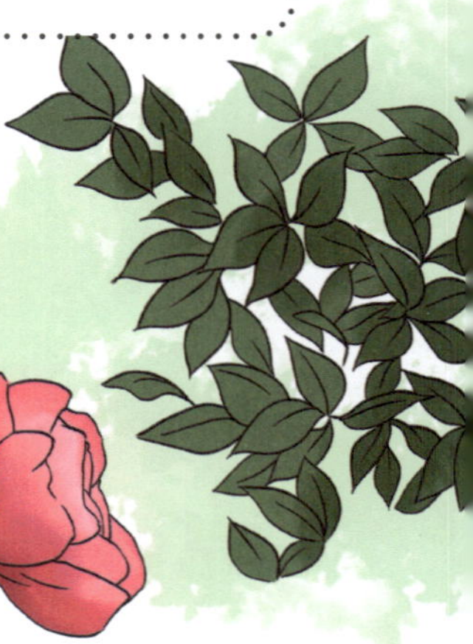

It is also interesting to represent **natural elements**.

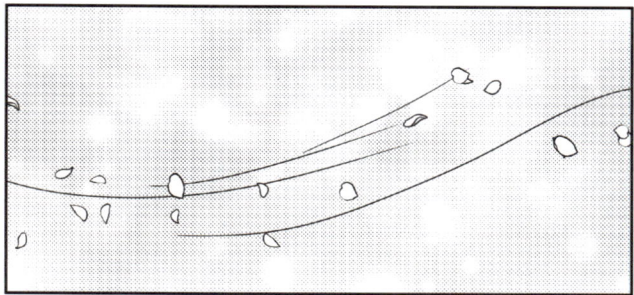

▲ Air is invisible. It can only be represented when it is in motion, through lines or through small, light objects that it carries along.

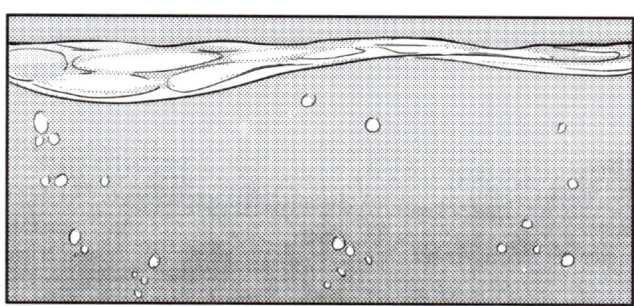

▲ Water is a liquid substance that can be enclosed in a container, like this panel. When it is in movement, its surface shows undulations.

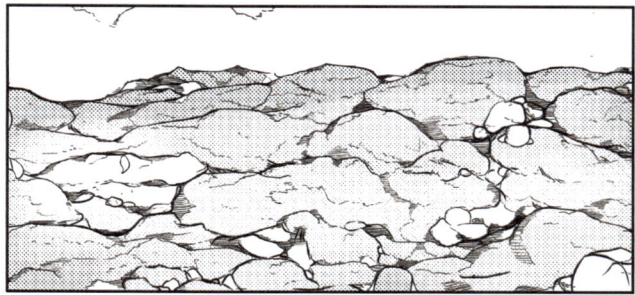

▲ The earth can be either compact or rocky. Draw small piles of gravel on the ground to situate the characters so that they will not appear to be floating.

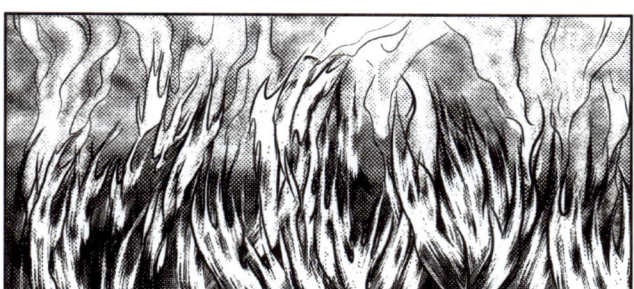

▲ Fire and smoke go together. Wavy, fluid, and irregular lines are ideal for representing these unpredictable elements.

▼ Snow falls in flakes and covers the ground and objects with a white mass.

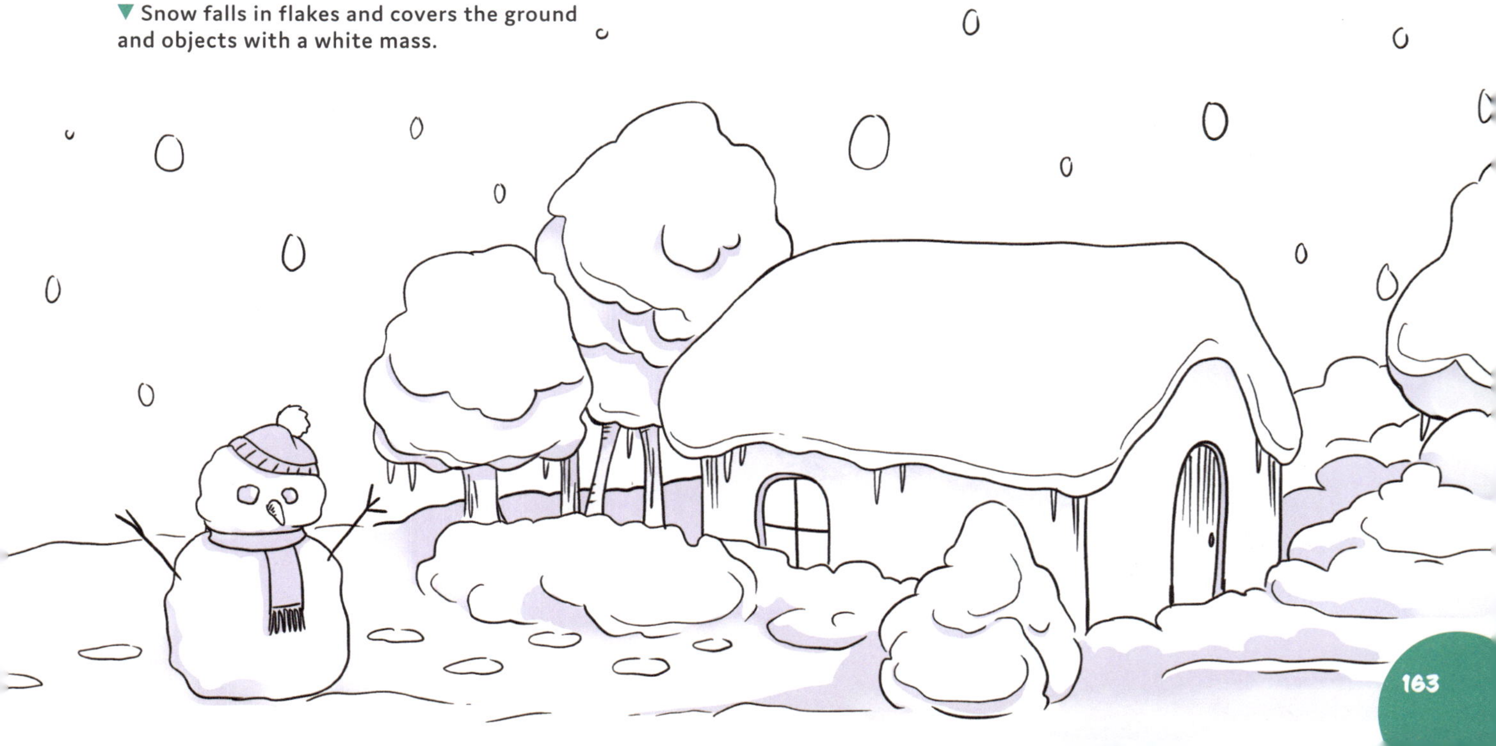

PSYCHOLOGICAL EFFECTS

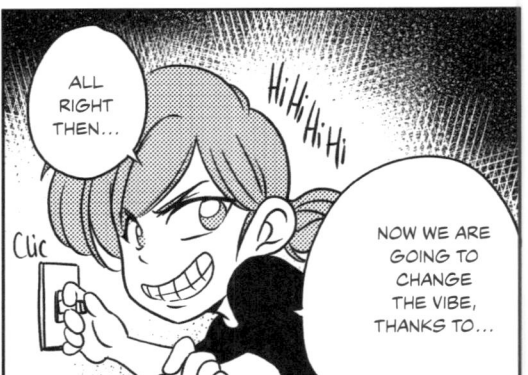

ALL RIGHT THEN...

Hi Hi Hi Hi

Clic

NOW WE ARE GOING TO CHANGE THE VIBE, THANKS TO...

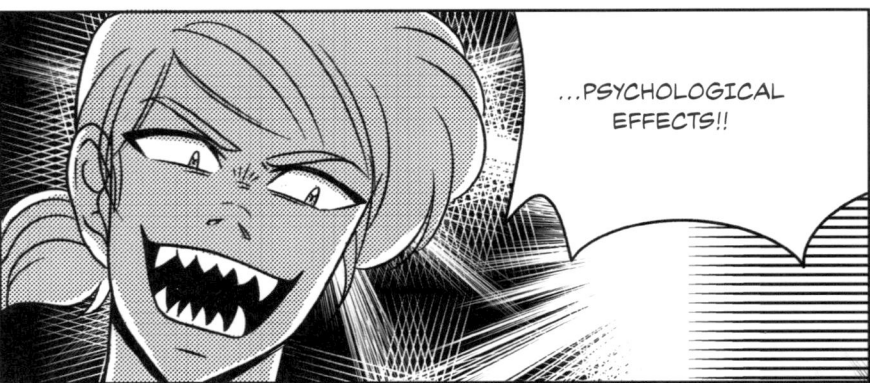

...PSYCHOLOGICAL EFFECTS!!

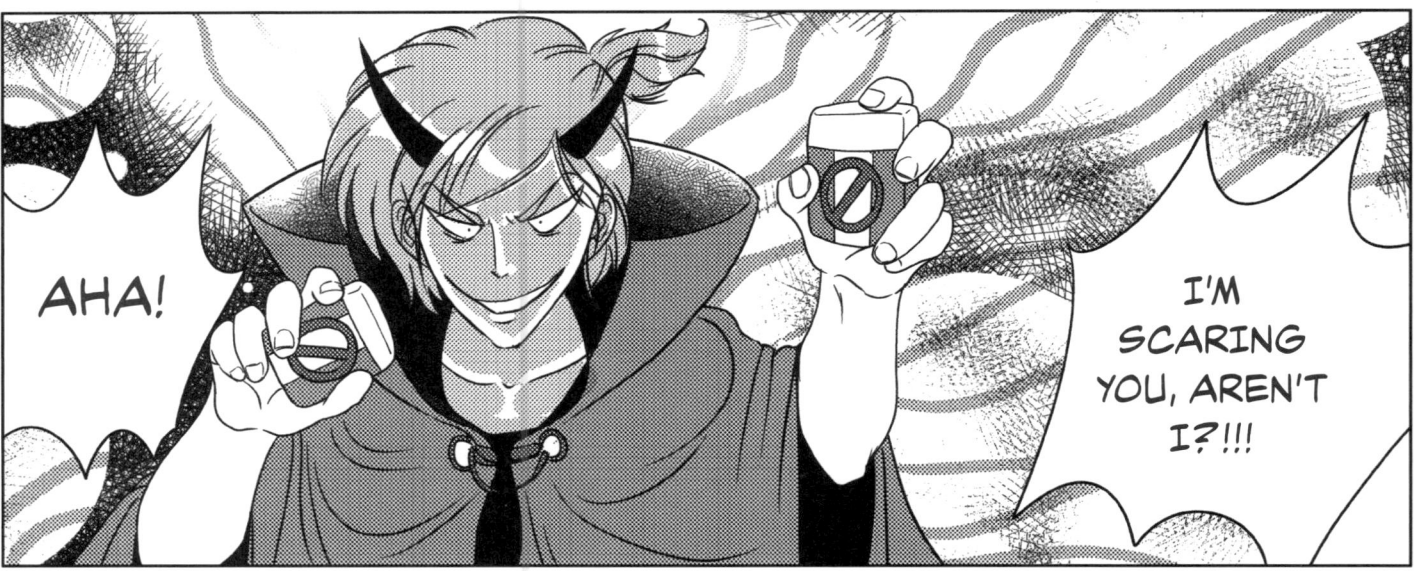

AHA!

I'M SCARING YOU, AREN'T I?!!!

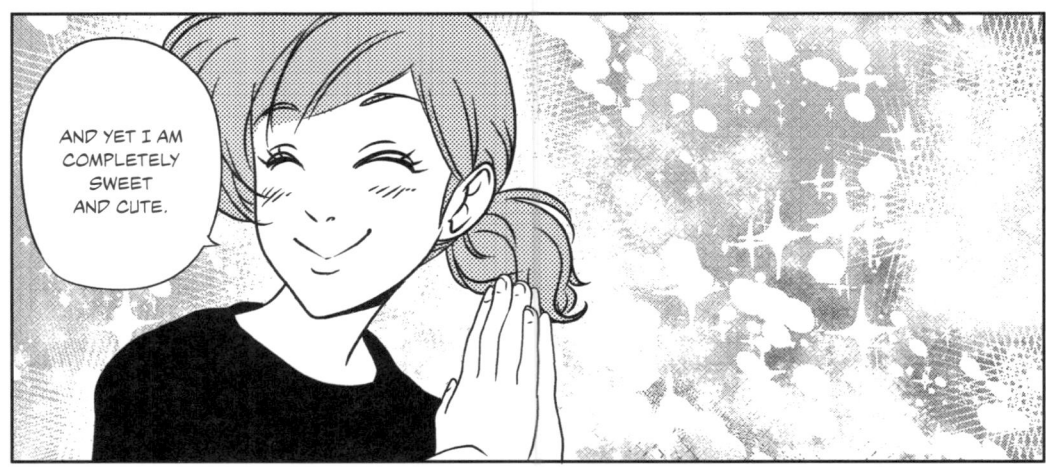

AND YET I AM COMPLETELY SWEET AND CUTE.

It is only the background and the exaggeration of characteristics that change the feel of the panels.

Here are some examples of psychological effects:

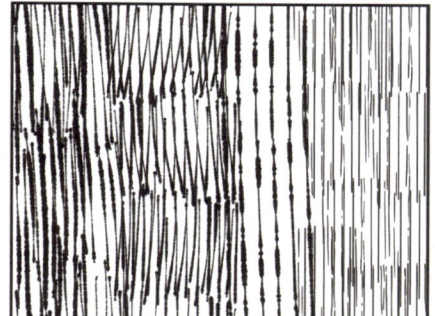

▲ Vertical lines: tension, discomfort, falling

▲ Horizontal lines: speed, dawning awareness

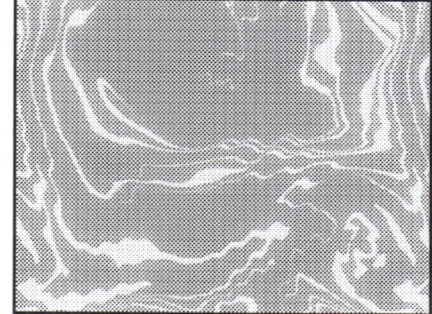

▲ Zigzags and waves: tension, dizziness, confusion

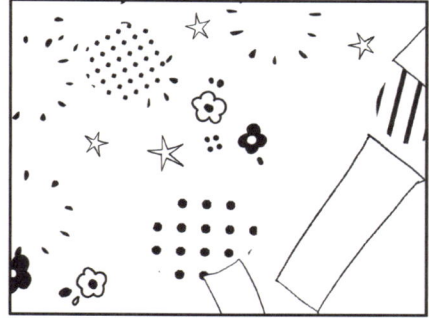

▲ Symbols: each one of these represents a different vibe

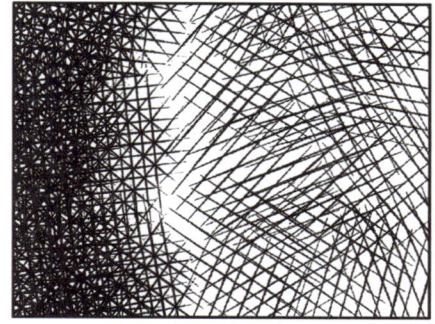

▲ Hatch marks: noise, intensity, shadows

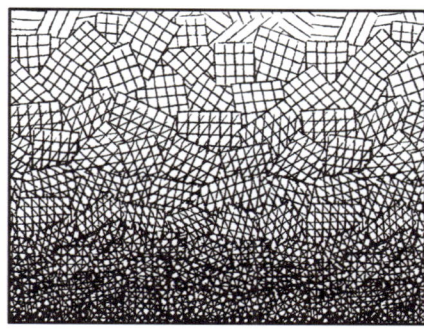

▲ Square hatching: shadows, intensity

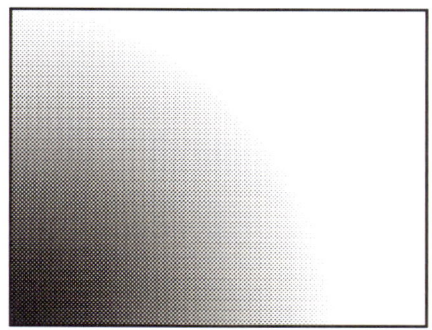

▲ Gradations of shading: transition, intensity

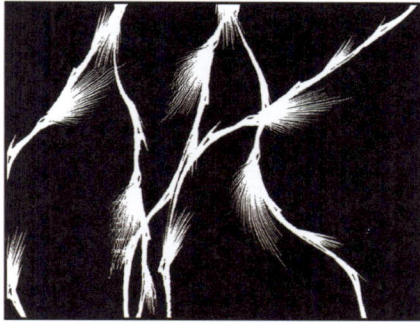

▲ Flashes and lightning bolts: anger, tension, horror

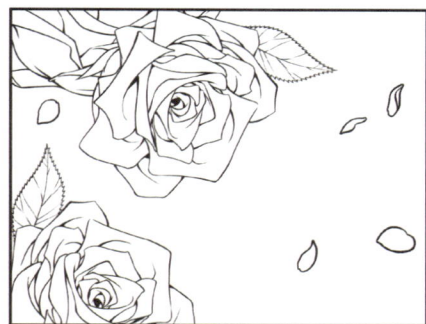

▲ Flowers: love, happiness

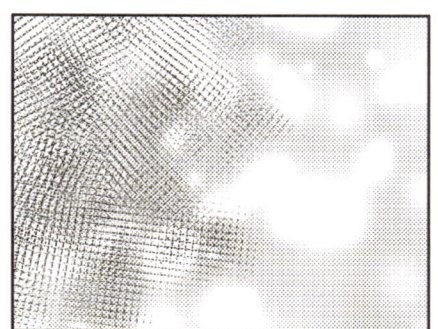

▲ Clouds of dots: enchantment, love, magic

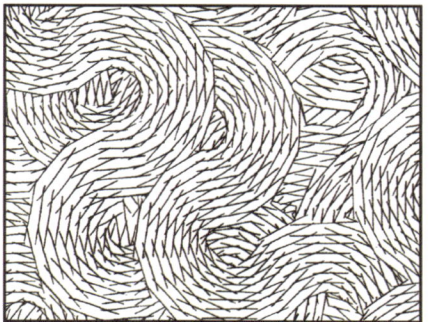

▲ Serpentine lines: unease, movement

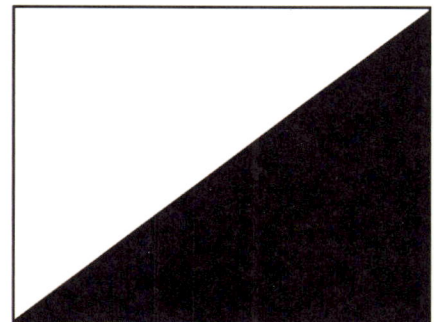

▲ Black and white: emptiness and fullness

SPEED LINES

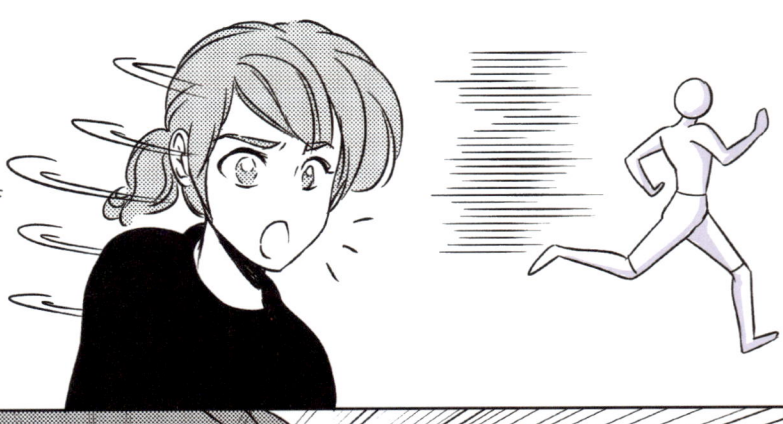

Speed lines and tension lines are part of the set of psychological effects, but they can also illustrate movement.

Horizontal and diagonal lines can accompany characters' movements.

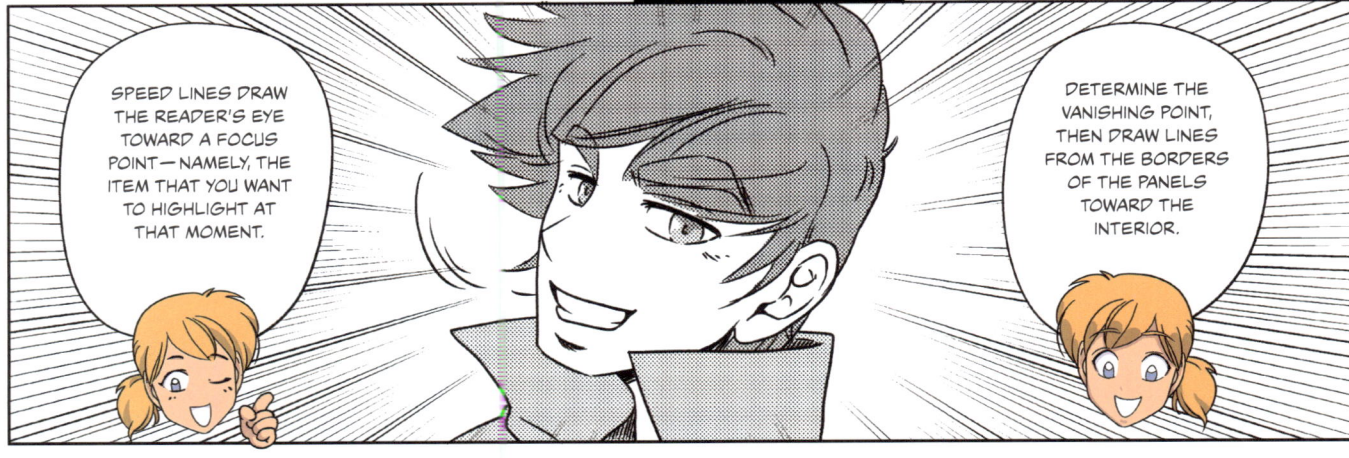

SPEED LINES DRAW THE READER'S EYE TOWARD A FOCUS POINT—NAMELY, THE ITEM THAT YOU WANT TO HIGHLIGHT AT THAT MOMENT.

DETERMINE THE VANISHING POINT, THEN DRAW LINES FROM THE BORDERS OF THE PANELS TOWARD THE INTERIOR.

While the lines of your background and scenery can sometimes be drawn freehand, speed lines are usually drawn using a ruler for more stability.

To draw concentric speed lines, place a vanishing point at the desired location and then draw lines from the borders of the panels toward the vanishing point.

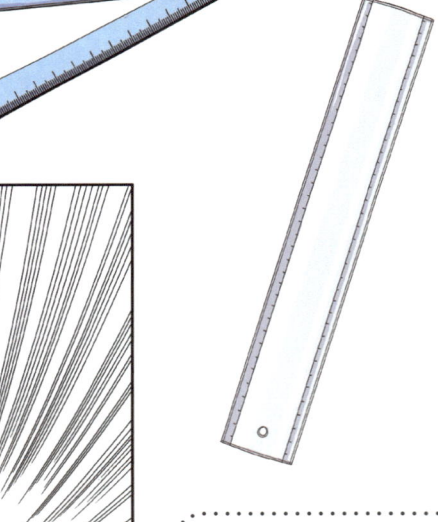

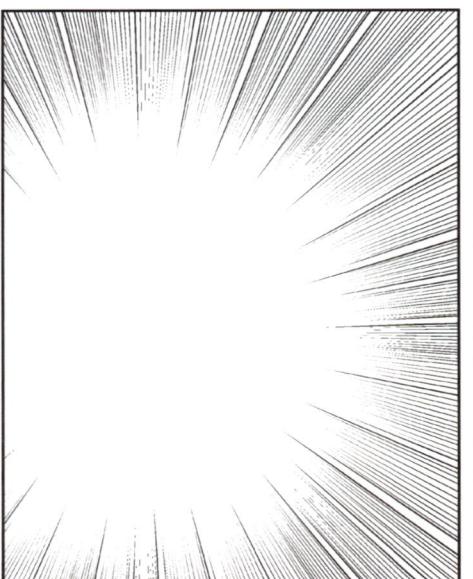

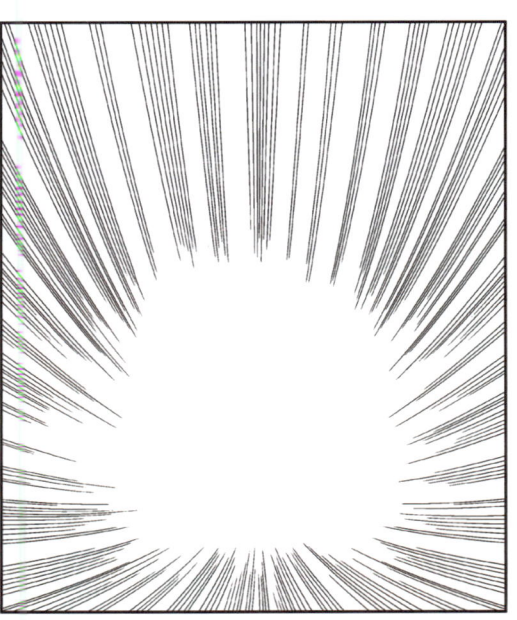

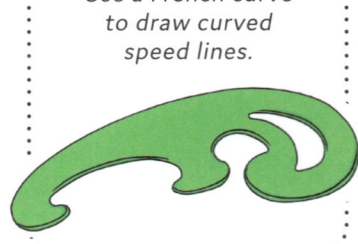

Use a French curve to draw curved speed lines.

HATCHING AND DOTS

Vertical lines imply a certain amount of tension, like a weight on the person's shoulders

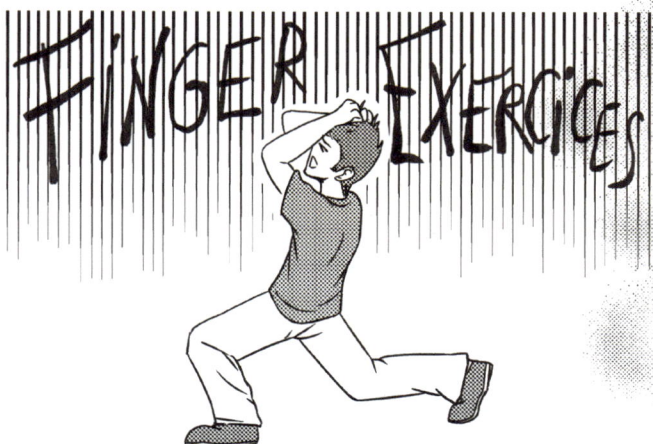

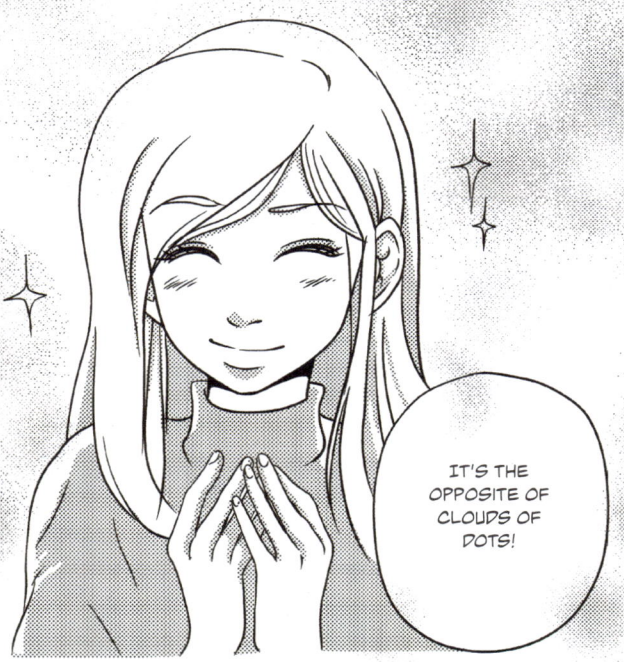

IT'S THE OPPOSITE OF CLOUDS OF DOTS!

Very fine points and dots give a feeling of lightness and softness.

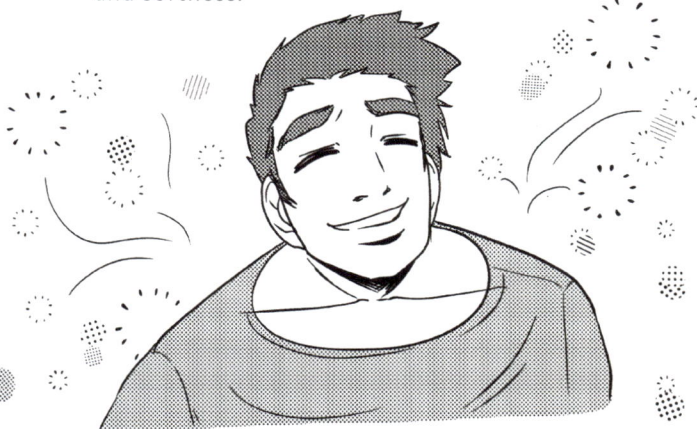

Regular hatching is useful for creating background patterns, but hatching has an even greater impact when it is arranged randomly or on a gradient.

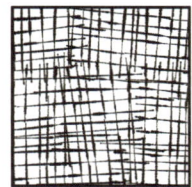 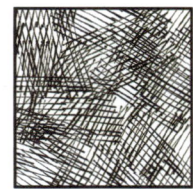 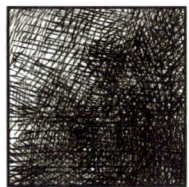

The thickness and number of lines can change the feeling of a drawing.

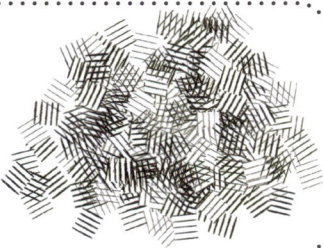

Overlap your lines to create a transition effect going from light to dark.

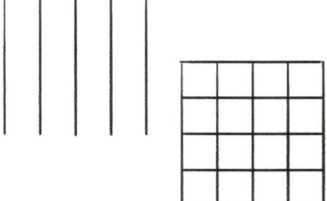 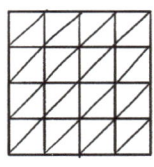 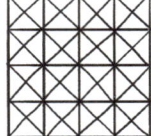

A TRICK

Match the lines of your patterns to the shapes that you're drawing to give your drawings more depth.

167

SOUND EFFECTS

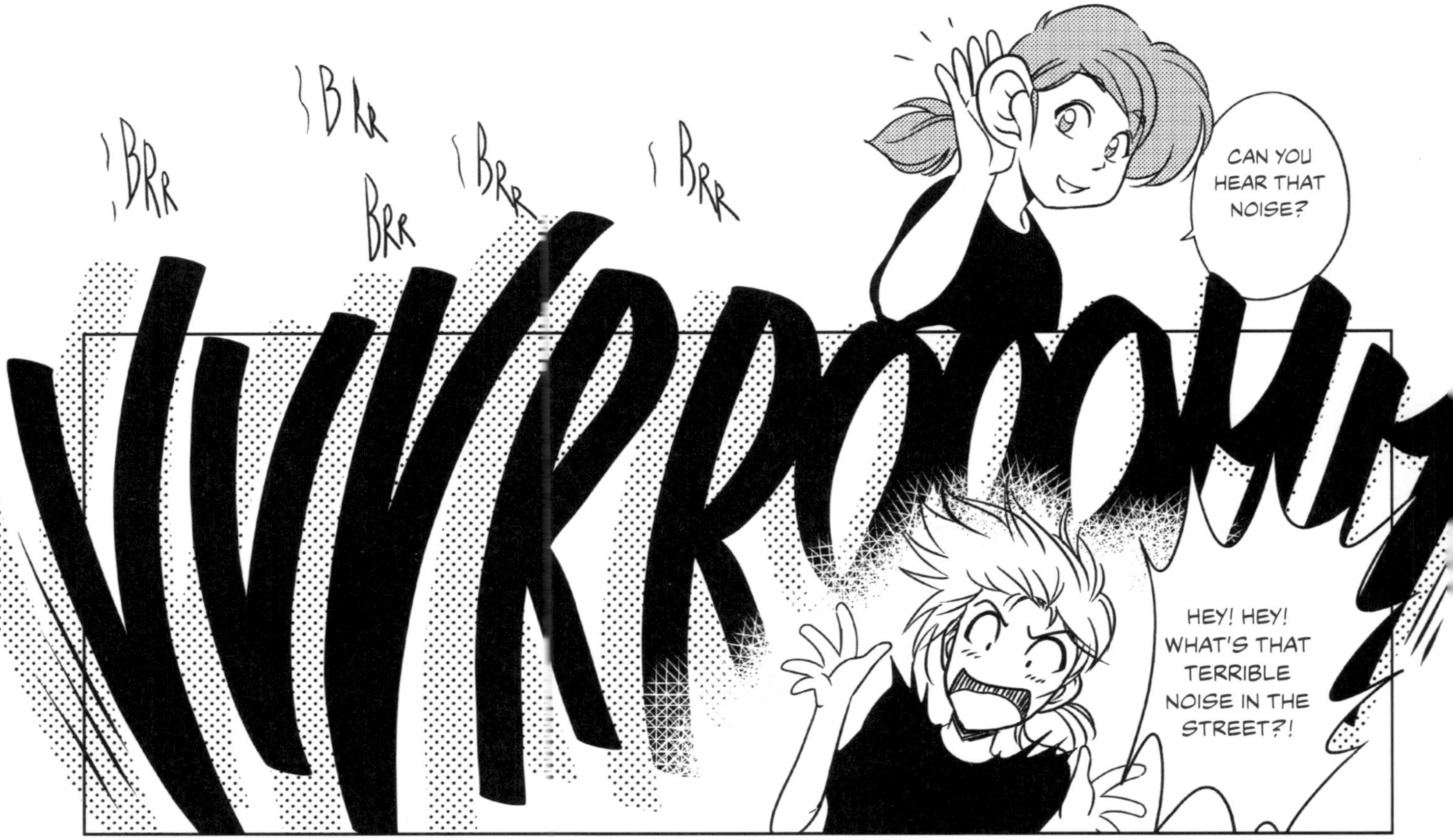

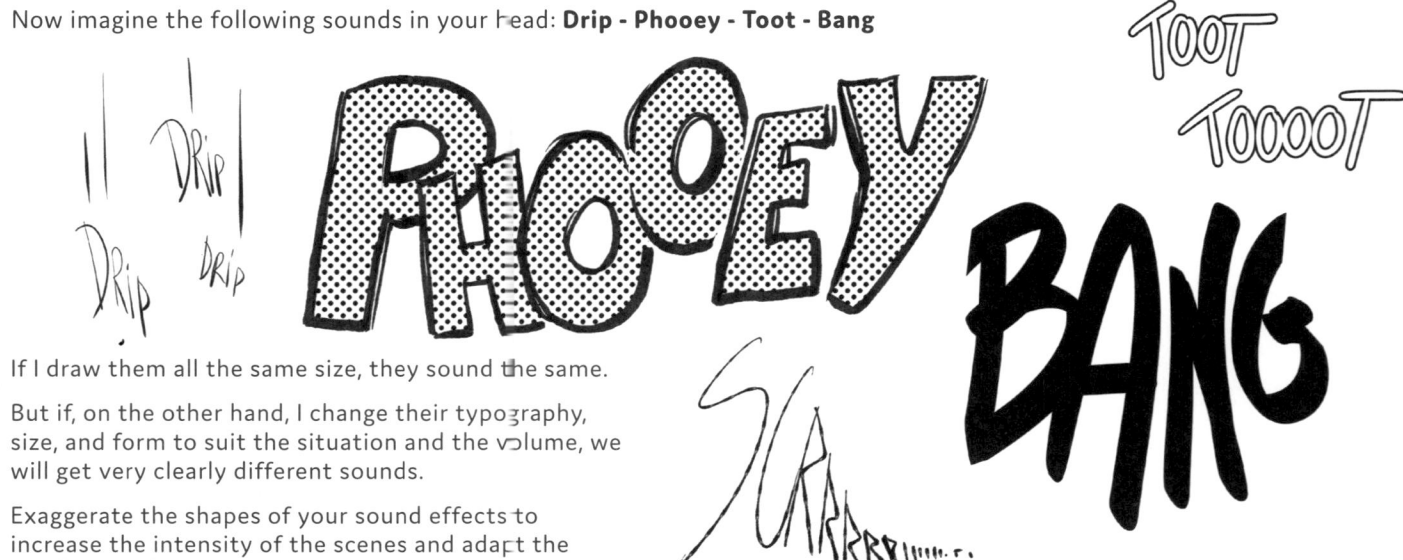

BRR BRR BRR BRR BRR

VVVRROOOMM

CAN YOU HEAR THAT NOISE?

HEY! HEY! WHAT'S THAT TERRIBLE NOISE IN THE STREET?!

When we read a comic book or graphic novel, our brain imagines and "creates" the voices of the characters. Noises are crucial for us to be able to immerse ourselves completely in the story, and we interpret them based on what our eyes see on the page.

Now imagine the following sounds in your head: **Drip - Phooey - Toot - Bang**

DRIP DRIP DRIP

PHOOEY

TOOT TOOOOT

BANG

SCRRRRIIIIIII

If I draw them all the same size, they sound the same.

But if, on the other hand, I change their typography, size, and form to suit the situation and the volume, we will get very clearly different sounds.

Exaggerate the shapes of your sound effects to increase the intensity of the scenes and adapt the graphics to the context.

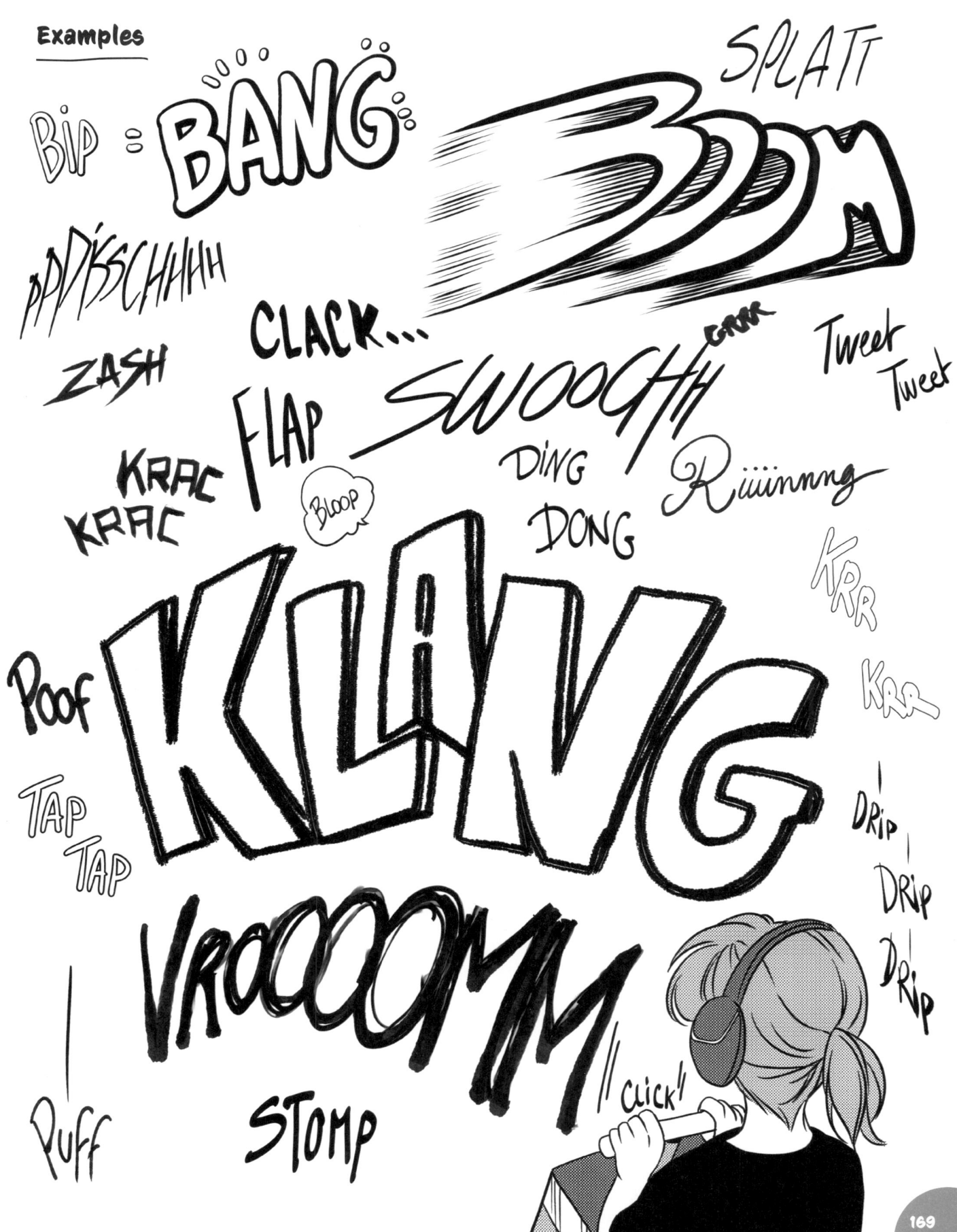

SCREENS

On page 26, I briefly showed you what a screen is.

There are all kinds of screens: with dots, gradients, lines, patterns...

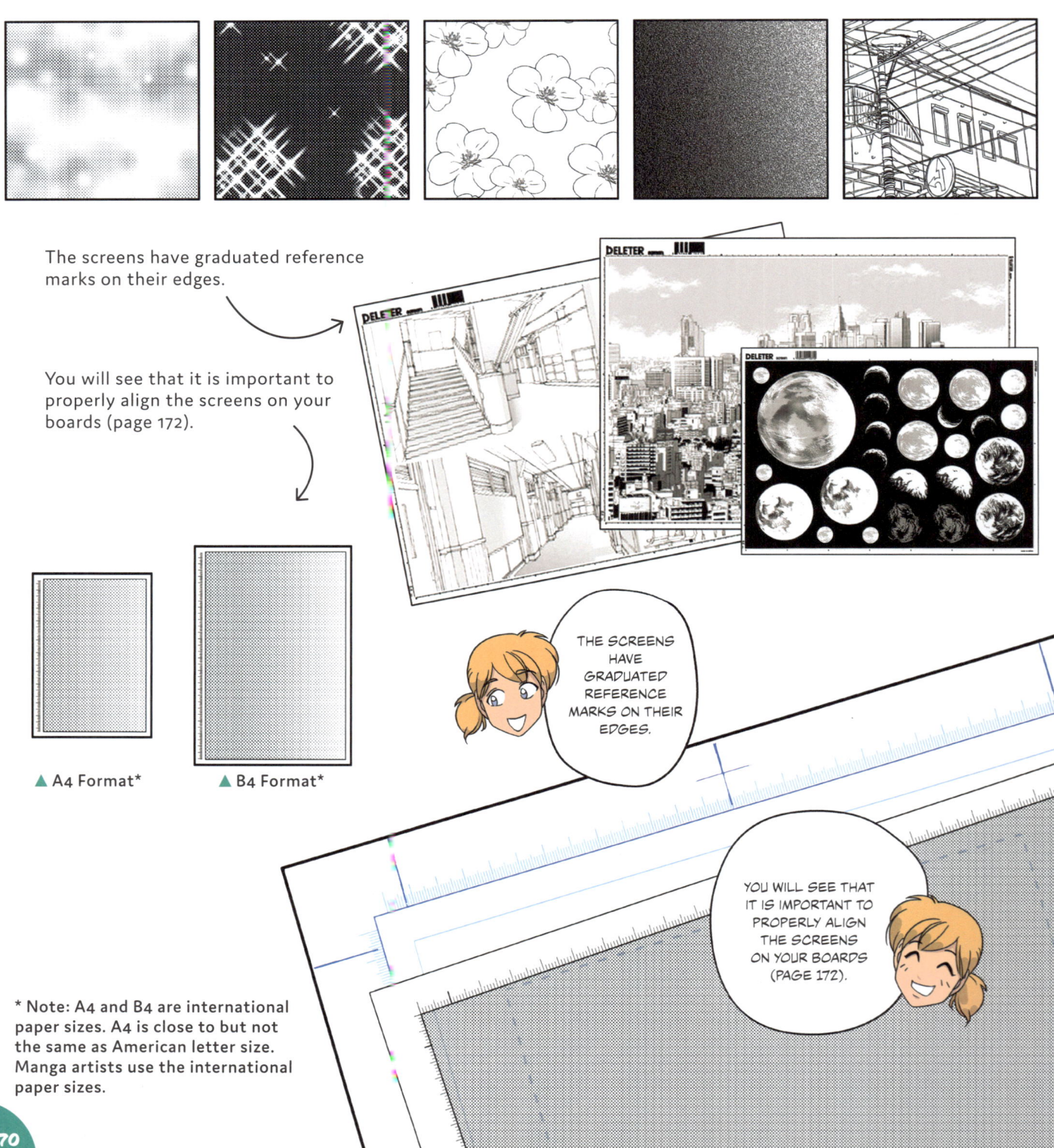

The screens have graduated reference marks on their edges.

You will see that it is important to properly align the screens on your boards (page 172).

▲ A4 Format*

▲ B4 Format*

THE SCREENS HAVE GRADUATED REFERENCE MARKS ON THEIR EDGES.

YOU WILL SEE THAT IT IS IMPORTANT TO PROPERLY ALIGN THE SCREENS ON YOUR BOARDS (PAGE 172).

* Note: A4 and B4 are international paper sizes. A4 is close to but not the same as American letter size. Manga artists use the international paper sizes.

Before you start working with the screens, make sure that the inking is completely finished and dry and that your boards are nice and clean. You should have erased all the pencil marks and brushed away all the eraser residue and dust from your page.

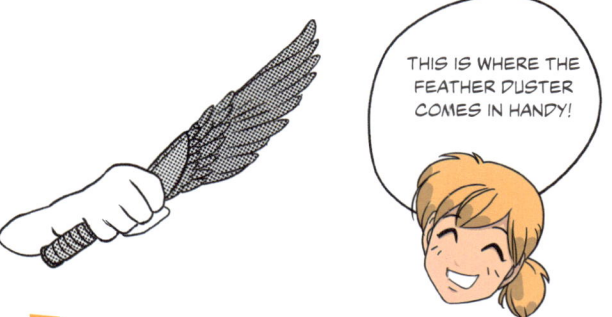

THIS IS WHERE THE FEATHER DUSTER COMES IN HANDY!

1 Choose your screens and determine which areas you are going to use them in on your pages

2 Place the screen sheet on your board and roughly cut out the piece that you need, leaving a little bit of margin for the final cuts.

3 Remove the protective film and lay the screen onto the work area using a spatula (Tone Hera). Handle the peeled screen sheets as little as possible so as not to get them dirty or damage the adhesive.

4 Use the rounded edge of the spatula to push out any air bubbles that may have gotten lodged between the paper and the screen by rubbing outward from the center.

5 Pay close attention to how much pressure you are exerting on the blade.

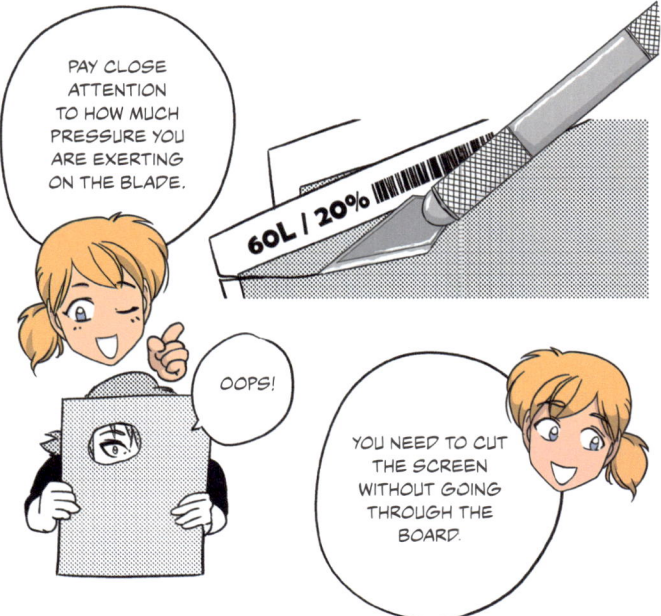

PAY CLOSE ATTENTION TO HOW MUCH PRESSURE YOU ARE EXERTING ON THE BLADE.

OOPS!

YOU NEED TO CUT THE SCREEN WITHOUT GOING THROUGH THE BOARD.

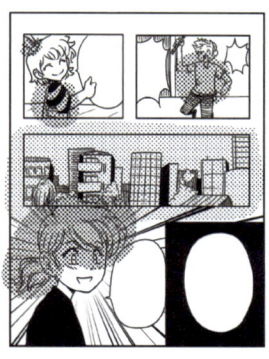
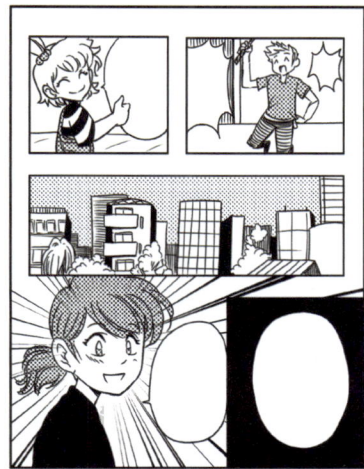

The screen can be used to fill in an element in the drawing or, on the contrary, to enclose an area that is left unfilled.

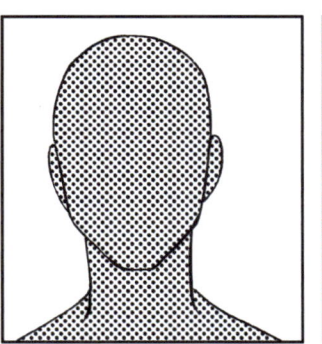
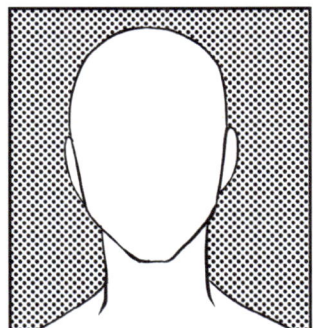

6 Once the pattern is correctly cut out, you can fix the screen in place by rubbing with the spatula to chase out any last air bubbles and activate the adhesive through the friction of the rubbing.

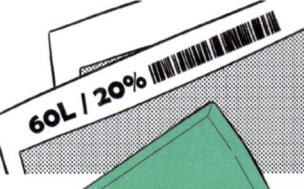

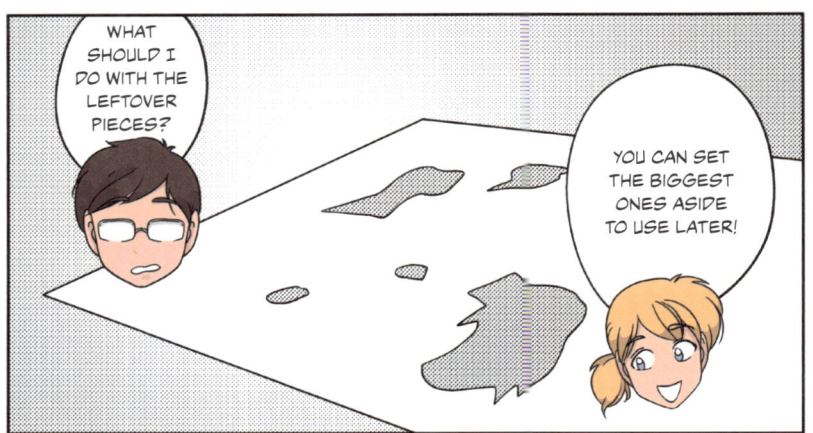

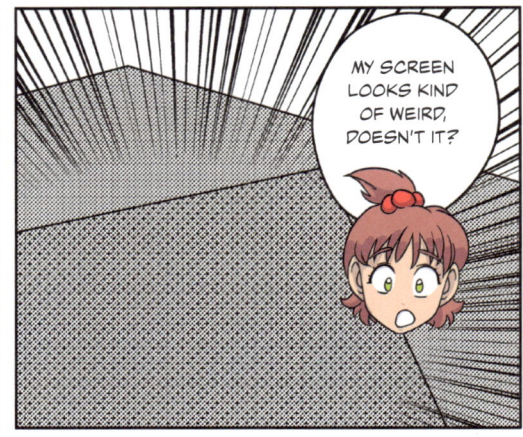

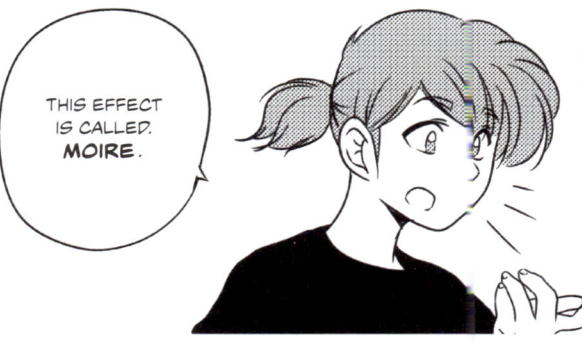

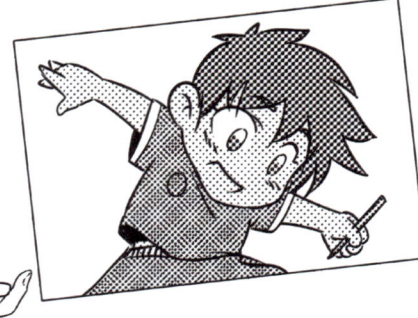

Screens are lines of dots arranged in rows spaced the same distance apart.

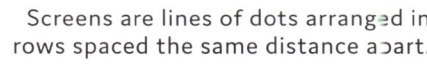

To avoid the moire effect, choose screens that have the same line spacing for your boards (see page 26).

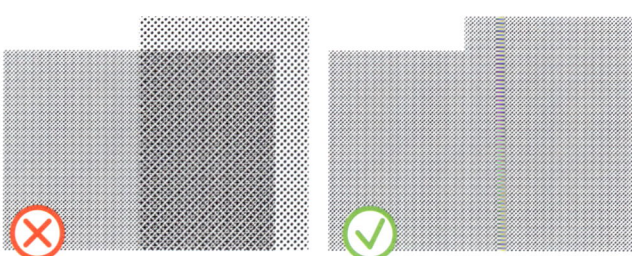

If you superimpose two screens with the same line spacing, you also have to keep the dots aligned with each other on both sheets.

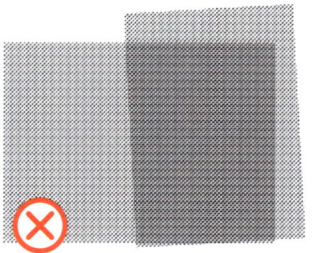

The dots are usually **set at a slope of 45°** with respect to the edge of the page. This is why the ruled markings along the edge of the screen sheets are useful. They can be aligned with the markings on the sheet of paper.

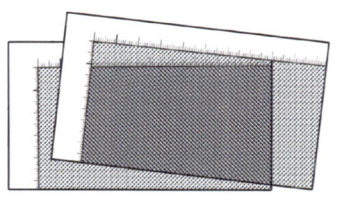

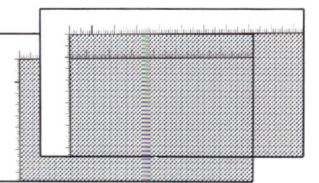

TIP

Start by using just one screen on your drawings. Once you are comfortable with the technique, you can increase the number of screens that you use per board.

THE DIFFERENT USES OF SCREENS

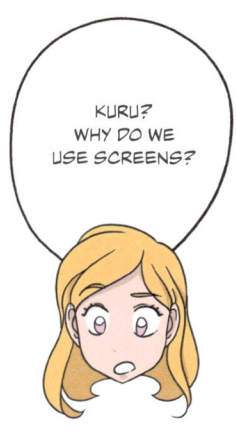

KURU?
WHY DO WE
USE SCREENS?

Screens have several different functions. They are primarily used to **fill in shaded areas**.

We use screens with lines or dots and gradients to represent darker or lighter shaded areas.

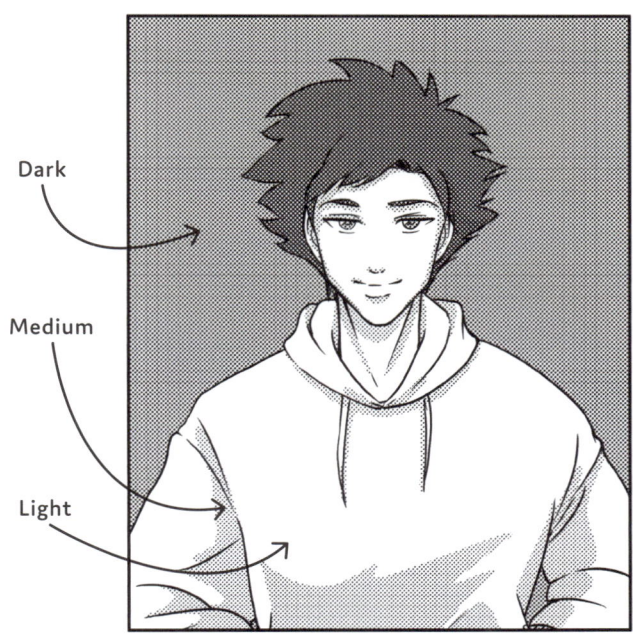

Dark

Medium

Light

They **also represent colors** (60L screens).

White: no screen	Yellow/Blue: 0% to 20%	Green: 15% to 50%	Red/Brown: 30% to 100% (or gradient)	Black: inked

Screens with patterns and textures save artists time. There are screens with **scenery**, with **gradients**, with **objects**, with **accents**, and with **natural effects**.

For some mangaka, using screens is a real headache, because it takes a long time to add them. There might be only one or two screens, or even none at all, in an entire manga volume.

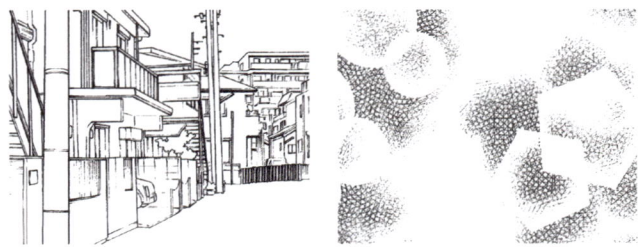

TIP

In any case, use screens in moderation. Think about the distribution of white, black, and gray throughout your manga when you are adapting the ambiance to the scenes.

Sometimes, a mangaka will use clever workarounds to find quick and inexpensive alternatives for drawing black-and-white shadows and textures on their boards:

- Black hatching
- Flat black areas
- More or less diluted black wash
- Flat gray areas
- Patterns

173

ILLUSTRATING IN COLOR

THE COVER ILLUSTRATION

This is the first image that your readers will see. It's both a summary of your story and an invitation to discover it inside the book.

This illustration conveys information about both the contents (**the choice of characters, scenery, symbols**) and the form (the **choice of composition, graphic style, inking, colors, fonts,** etc.) of your manga.

To create a cover illustration, we start with some preliminary sketches to find the composition that best reflects the tone and style of our manga. These first drafts are like a single-page storyboard, which will serve as a model for drawing a sketch of the illustration.

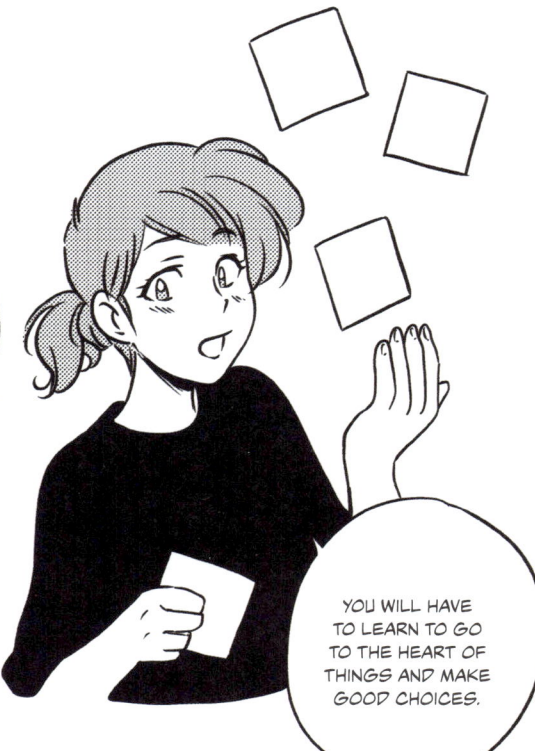

JUST LIKE WITH WRITING DIALOGUES OR COMPOSING YOUR BOARDS...

YOU WILL HAVE TO LEARN TO GO TO THE HEART OF THINGS AND MAKE GOOD CHOICES.

1 = Background

2 = Character

3 = Emotion

4 = Action

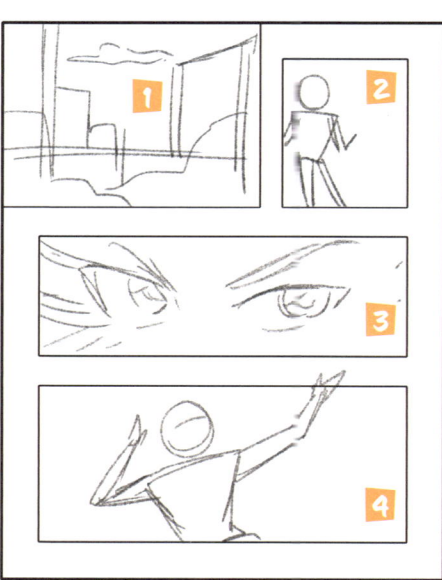

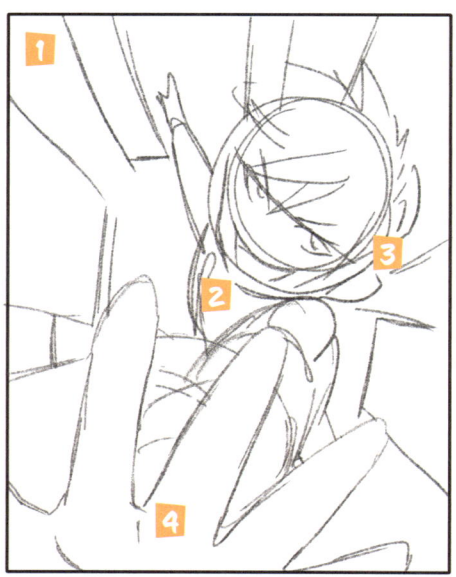

It's the cover image that invites the reader to open the book and leaf through it. It has to present enough information so that the reader will understand what it's about.

After having gone over the outlines of the elements of the illustration in black or in color, we remove all of the pencil sketching, using an eraser, to make way for the addition of color.

ILLUSTRATING YOUR IDEA IN ONE IMAGE

Once you have defined the theme of your illustration, choose the essential elements of your message: the character, symbols, background, style, and text, if relevant.

Also choose the format of your illustration.

▼ Landscape

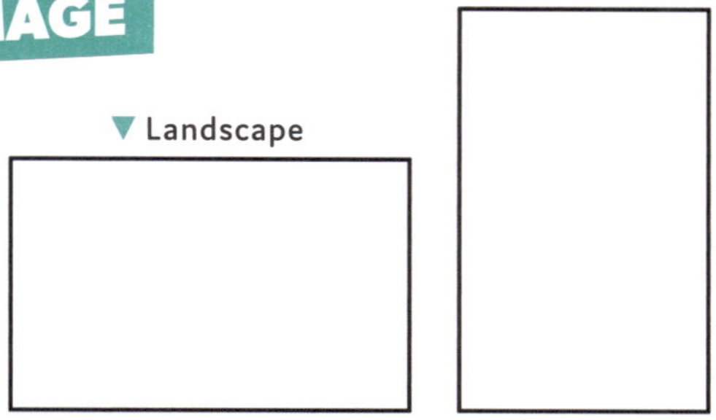

◀ Portrait

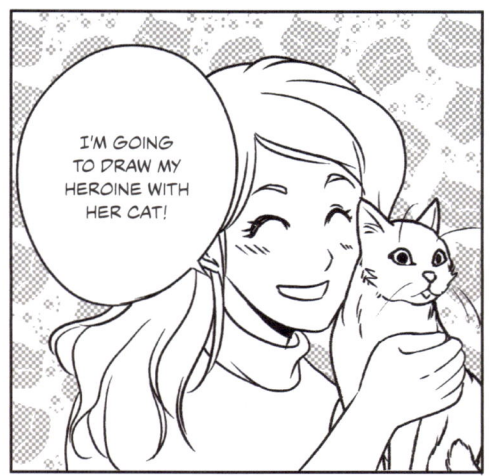

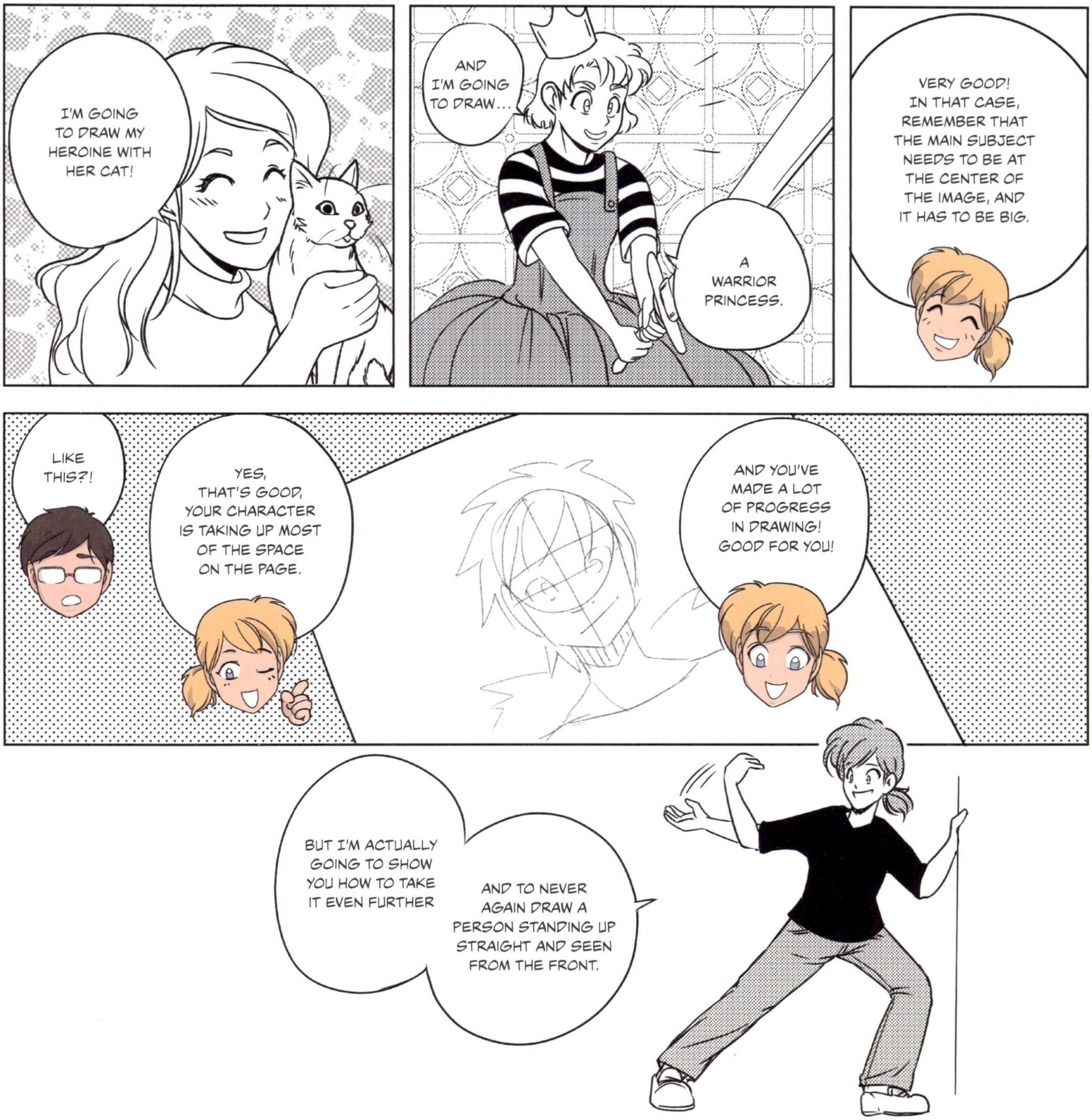

I'M GOING TO DRAW MY HEROINE WITH HER CAT!

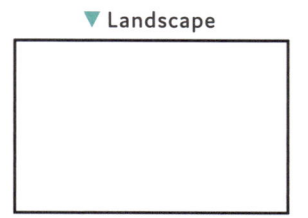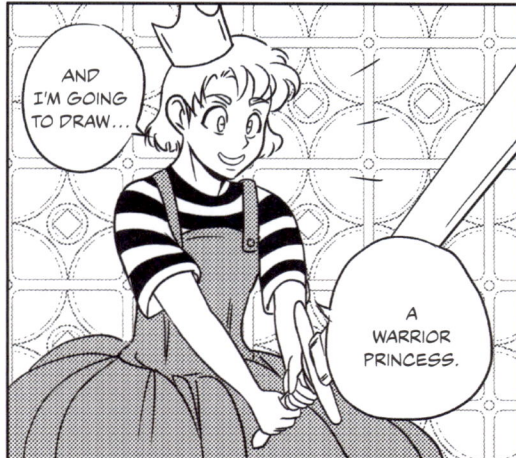

AND I'M GOING TO DRAW...

A WARRIOR PRINCESS.

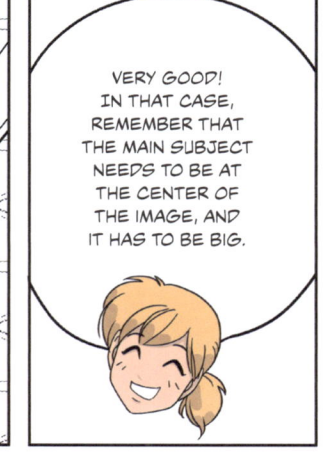

VERY GOOD! IN THAT CASE, REMEMBER THAT THE MAIN SUBJECT NEEDS TO BE AT THE CENTER OF THE IMAGE, AND IT HAS TO BE BIG.

LIKE THIS?!

YES, THAT'S GOOD, YOUR CHARACTER IS TAKING UP MOST OF THE SPACE ON THE PAGE.

AND YOU'VE MADE A LOT OF PROGRESS IN DRAWING! GOOD FOR YOU!

BUT I'M ACTUALLY GOING TO SHOW YOU HOW TO TAKE IT EVEN FURTHER

AND TO NEVER AGAIN DRAW A PERSON STANDING UP STRAIGHT AND SEEN FROM THE FRONT.

COMPOSITION

Illustration is the art of conveying information with just one single image.

This one will be read in a very specific order, just like a manga page.

Composition allows us to guide the reader's eye and to cause them to read the image in the most optimal way.

There are several ways to help the reader's gaze.

1 The simplest is the **rule of thirds**.

An image is divided into three equal parts both horizontally and vertically.

Our gaze is naturally directed to the four intersections, in a Z shape. So those points are where we should place the important elements of the illustration.

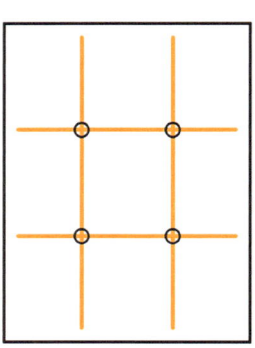
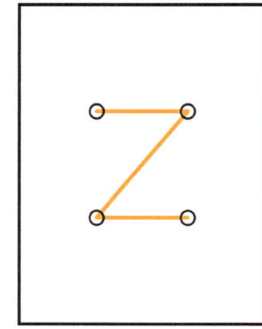

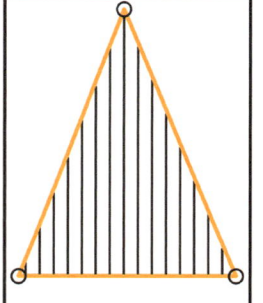
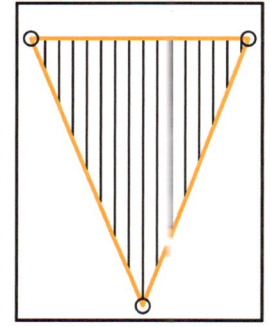

2 Another very common composition uses **geometric shapes** like triangles.

The important elements of the image are placed inside or at the ends of the triangle.

3 **Spiral** composition draws the gaze to a specific point in the illustration. It is essential to place the central element of the drawing at the center of the spiral.

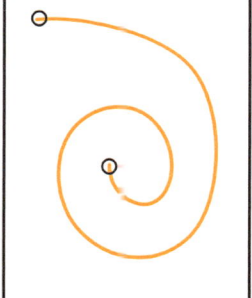

4 Single or intersecting **diagonal** lines add a lot of dynamism to an illustration.

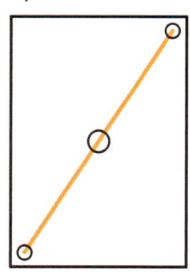
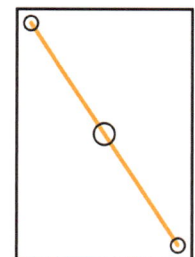
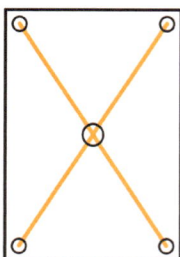

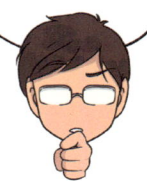

CAN YOU PUT SEVERAL SHAPES INTO THE SAME COMPOSITION?

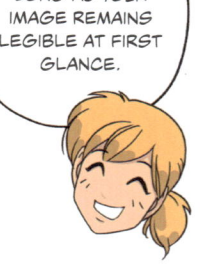

YES, AS LONG AS YOUR IMAGE REMAINS LEGIBLE AT FIRST GLANCE.

SOME EXAMPLES OF COVER COMPOSITION

Here are some sketches of this book's cover illustration.

The same elements are arranged on the page in such a way as to suggest several different readings.

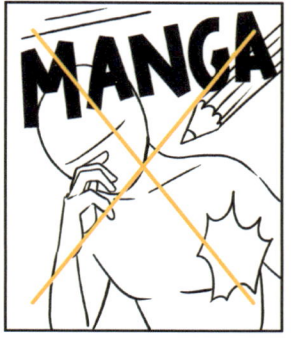

▲ Lines and a cross

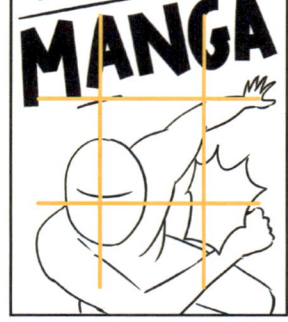

▲ Rule of thirds

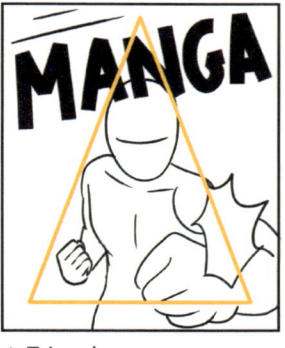

▲ Triangle

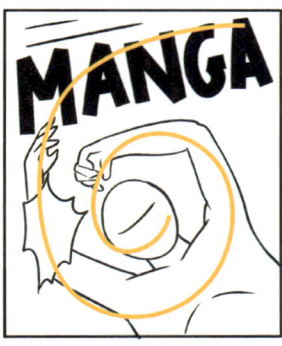

▲ Spiral

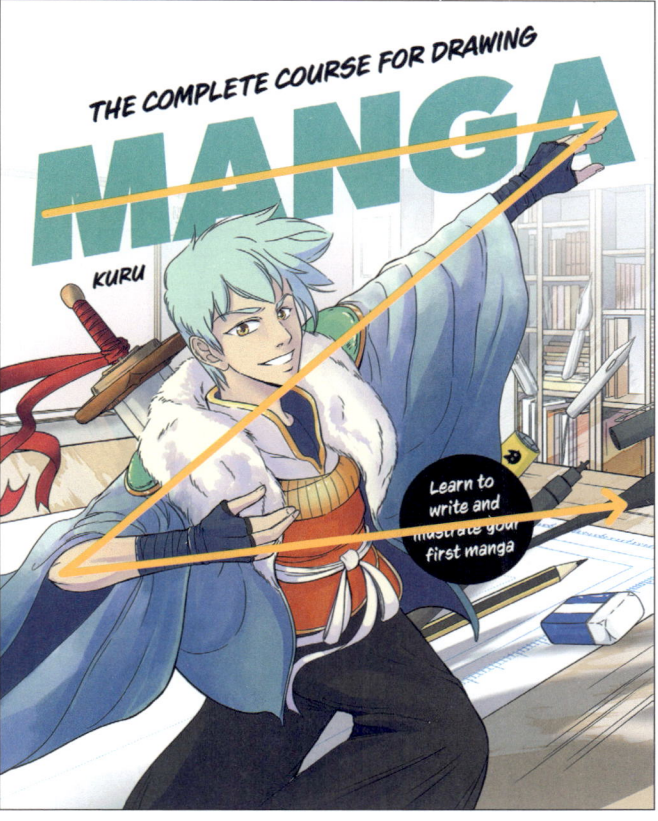

Remember to include the title in how you think about your composition.

PRACTICE

Try Out Several Different Compositions

To practice drawing illustrations using different compositions, all you have to do is take an A4 sheet and fold it into quarters. This will give you four miniature thumbnail areas in the A6 format on each side of the page.

Choose two or three key elements of your illustration (characters, symbols, background elements) and arrange them in different configurations to see how you can create several variations of the same illustration.

Go back and forth between portrait and landscape formats until you find the composition that will allow for the best presentation of your message.

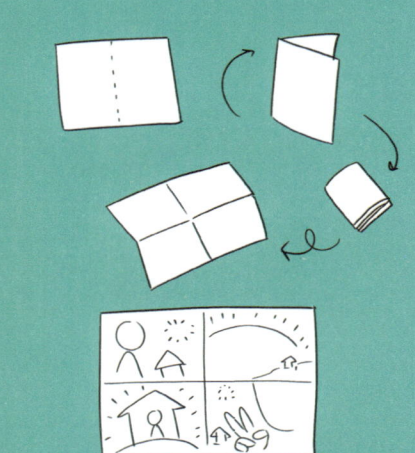

COLOR

The word "color" can have several different meanings. It can be used to mean our **perception of a light**, of the **look of a surface**, or of the **pigments** used in art for painting.

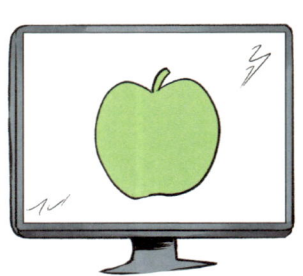
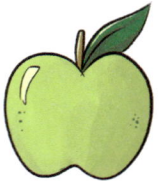
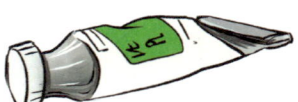

THE COLOR WHEEL

Here are the main colors, grouped around a **color wheel**. Here we find:

The **primary** (1) colors: yellow, red, and blue.

The **secondary** (2) colors: orange, purple, and green.

And in between those, the **tertiary** (3) colors.

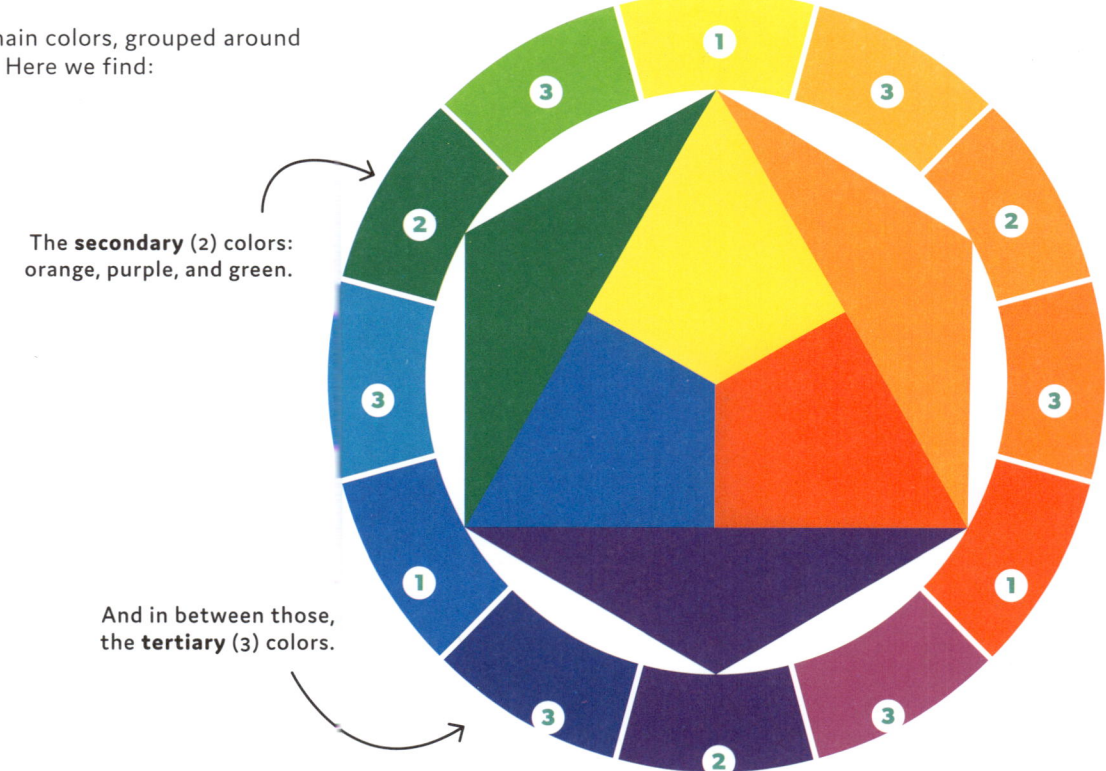

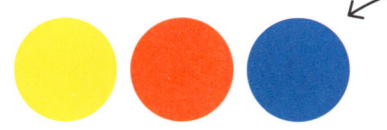

By mixing the three primary colors, we can obtain all of the other colors.

If we mix two primary colors in equal parts,
we get secondary colors.

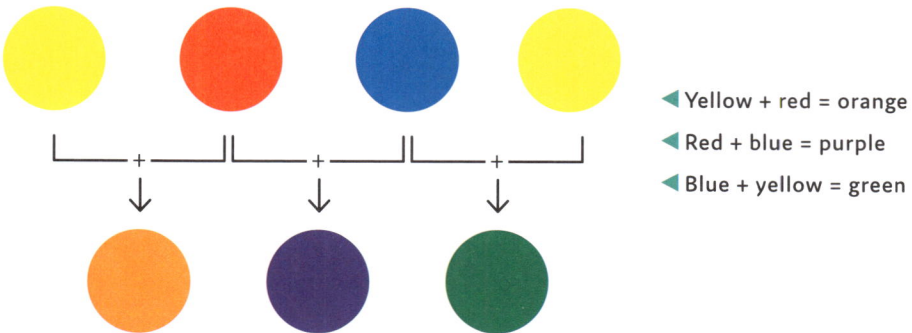

◀ Yellow + red = orange

◀ Red + blue = purple

◀ Blue + yellow = green

The tertiary colors are the result of the mixture of primary and secondary colors.

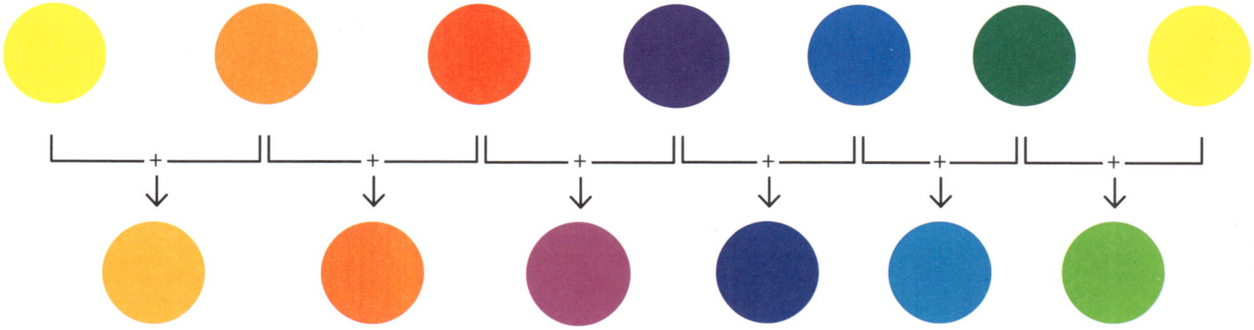

▲ Yellow + orange = orangish yellow

▲ Orange + red = orangish red

▲ Red + purple = violet red

▲ Purple + blue = violet blue

▲ Blue + green = blue-green

▲ Green + yellow = yellowish green

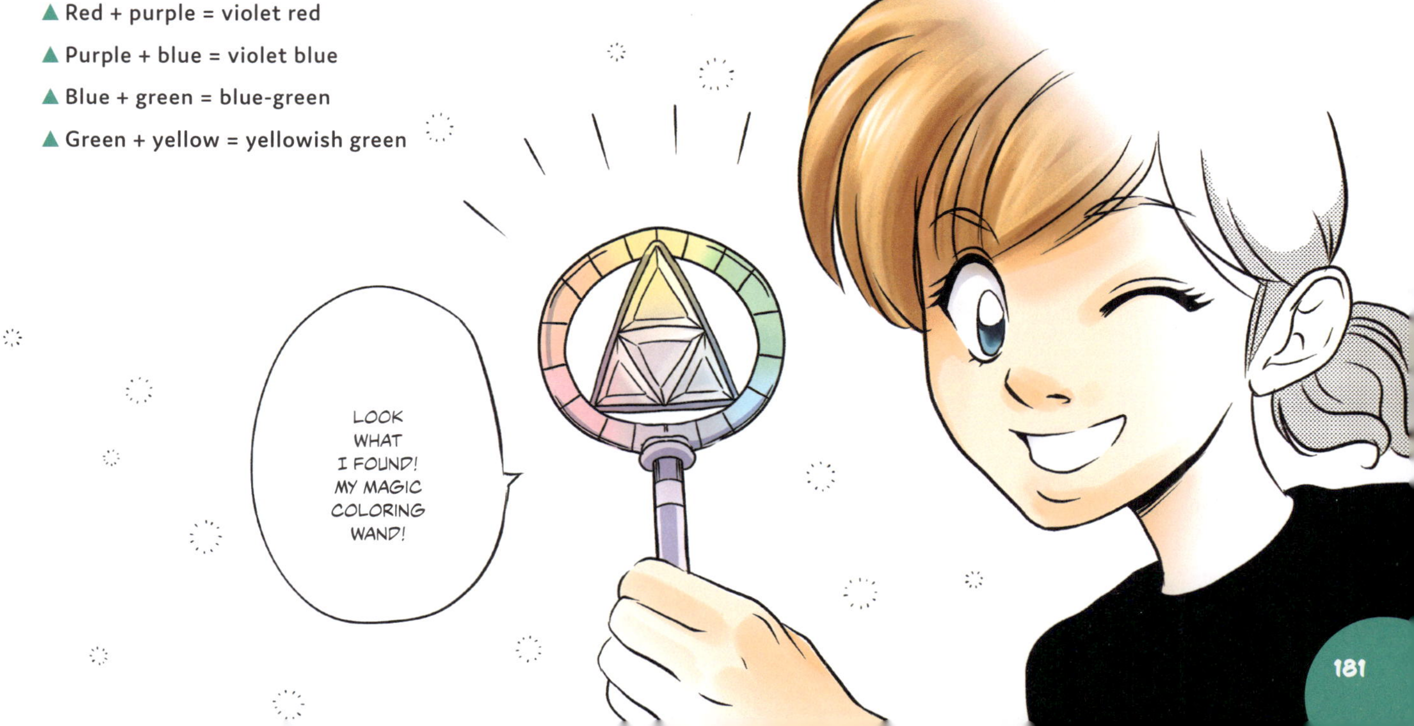

LOOK
WHAT
I FOUND!
MY MAGIC
COLORING
WAND!

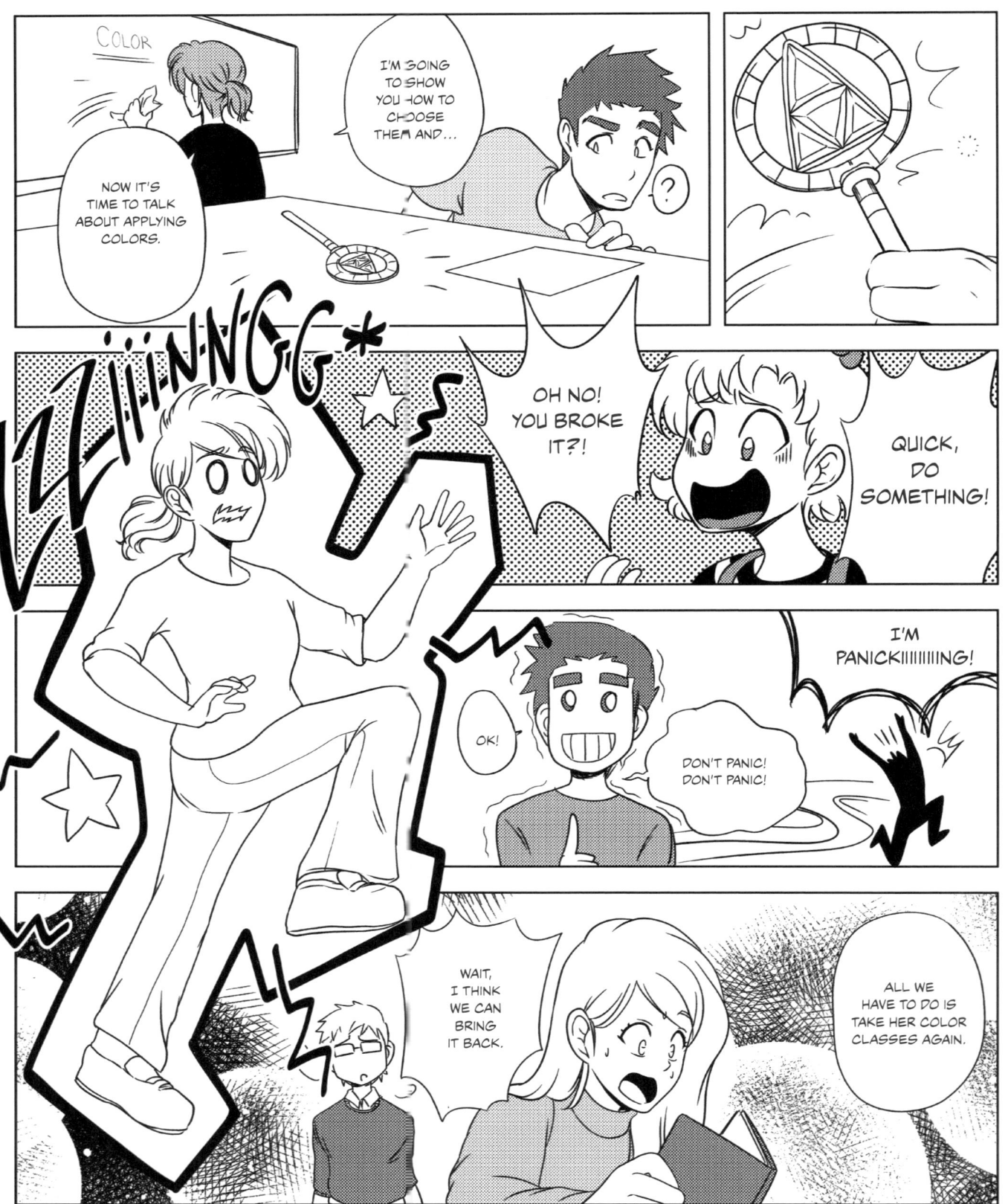

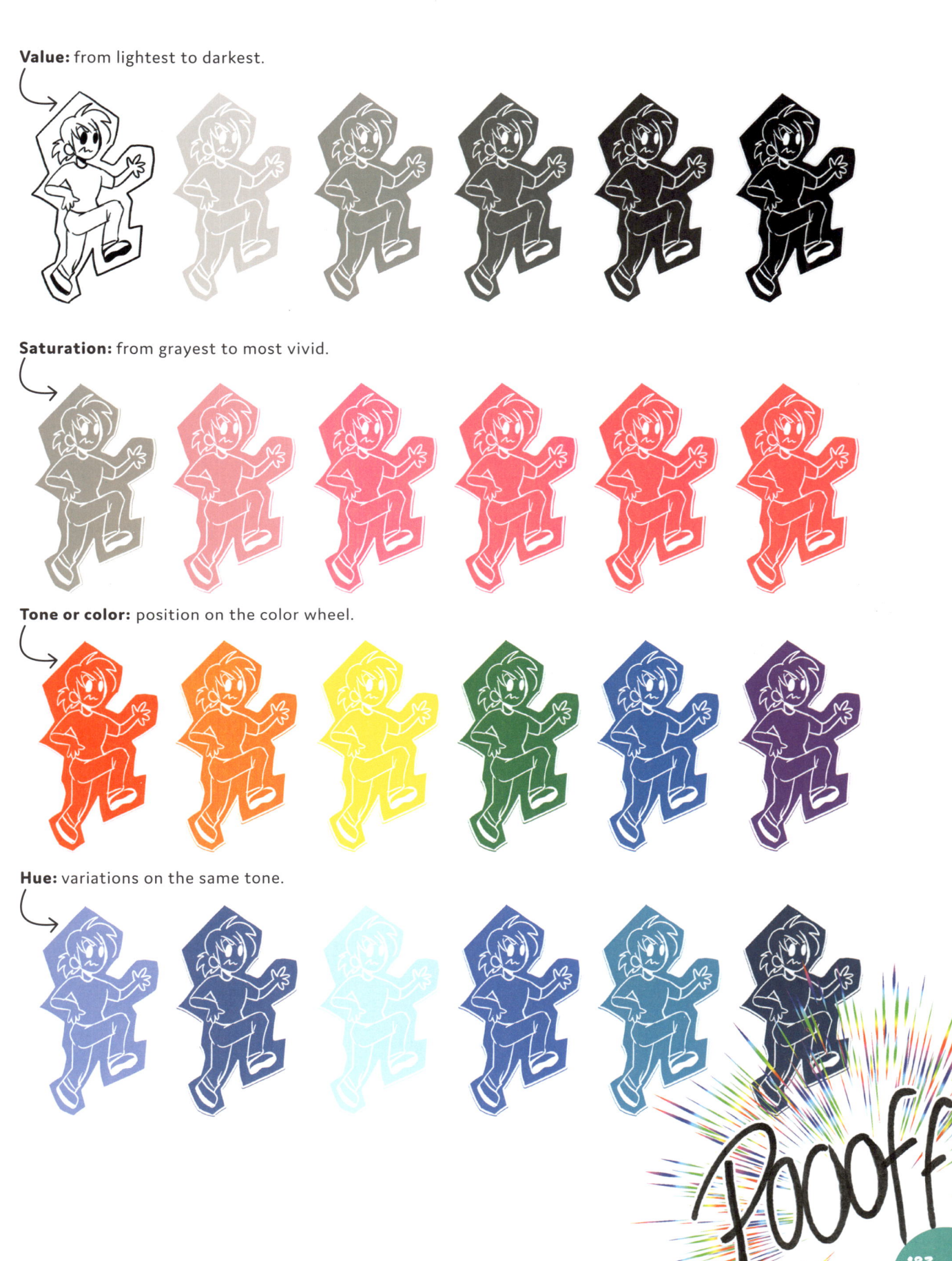

Value: from lightest to darkest.

Saturation: from grayest to most vivid.

Tone or color: position on the color wheel.

Hue: variations on the same tone.

Poooff

183

WHEWWW!!

WOW!

THANK YOU, KIDS!

NOW WHERE WAS I?

? ? ?

YOU WANTED TO TELL US HOW TO CHOOSE COLORS.

OH RIGHT...

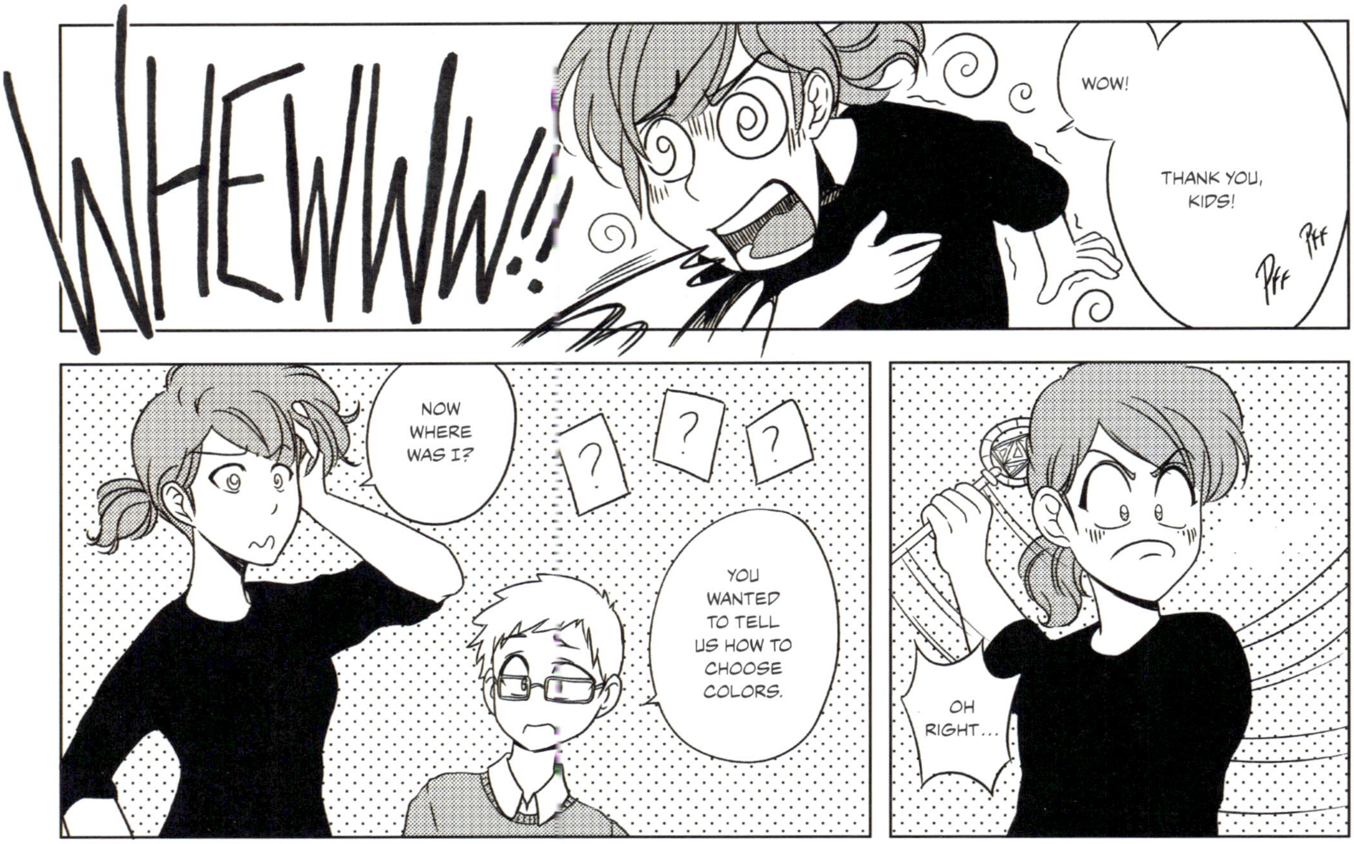

Some colors are called **complementary**, which means that they enhance each other and, taken together, give us a feeling of harmony. They are opposite each other on the color wheel—like orange and blue, red and green, yellow and purple.

If we mix two complementary colors with each other, we get a colored gray.

The warm colors are opposite the cold colors. The temperature of the colors allows us to represent a variety of ambiances.

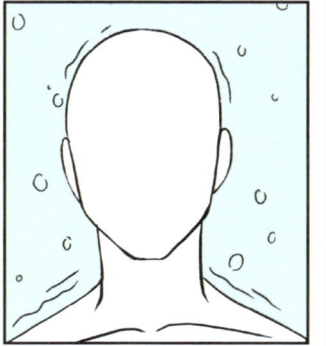 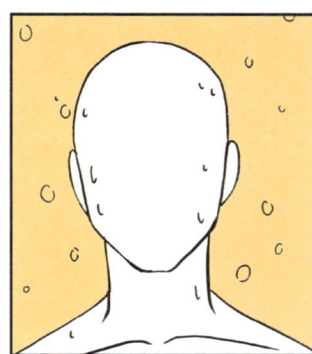

Some colors adore each other, while others don't like each other that much.

You can choose to use only complementary colors to color your drawings, so that your final result will be balanced. The colors that are next to each other along the color wheel generally go together well too.

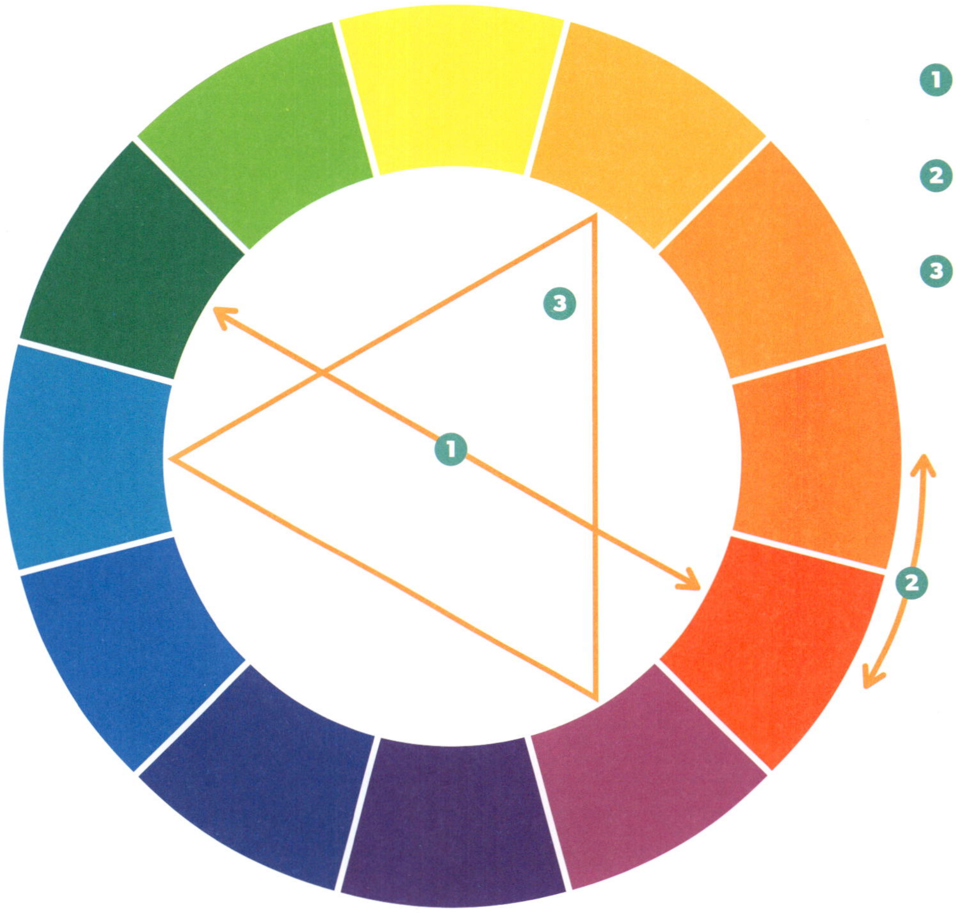

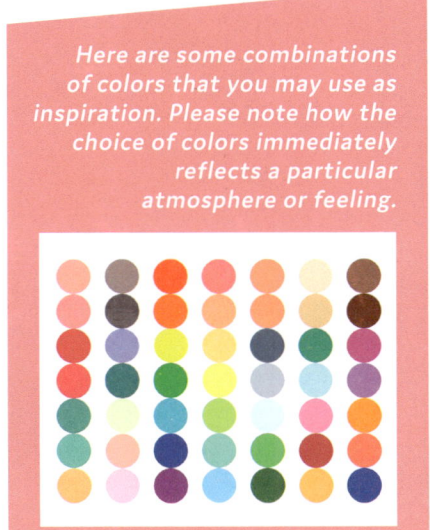

1 **Complementary colors:** facing each other

2 **Analogous colors:** side by side

3 **Triadic colors:** separated from each other on the color wheel by a regular interval

Another good way of coloring harmoniously is to choose colors of the same value or saturation. If you choose colors that are too different from each other to use in your palettes, you will create a **contrast**. In some cases, this can be useful for emphasizing one element in the drawing. But it is also possible that the contrast will distort the reading of the image.

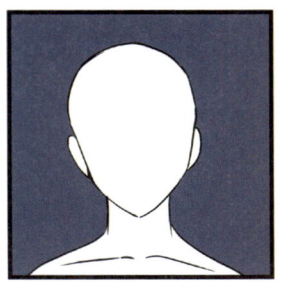
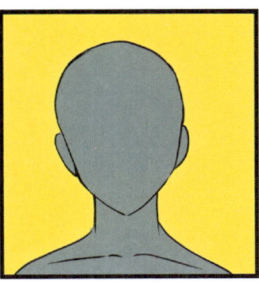
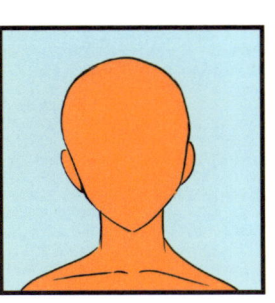

TIP

Here are some combinations of colors that you may use as inspiration. Please note how the choice of colors immediately reflects a particular atmosphere or feeling.

COLORING

Traditionally, alcohol markers have been used to color manga cover illustrations, but you can also color your drawings using colored pencils, paint, classic school markers, or even digital tools.

Each technique provides a different result. It's up to you to choose which one suits your work best.

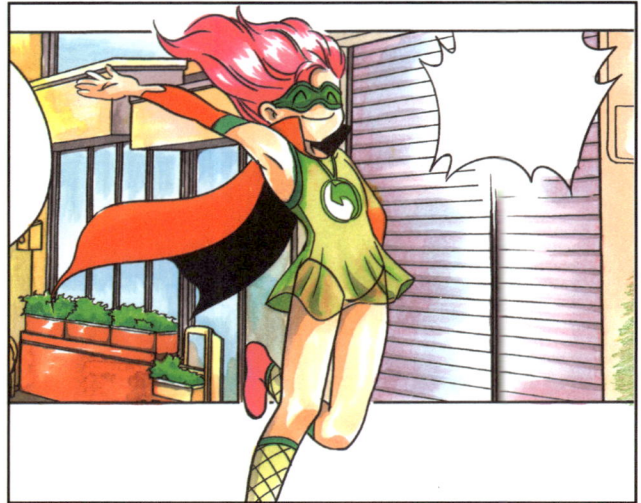

▲ Alcohol markers

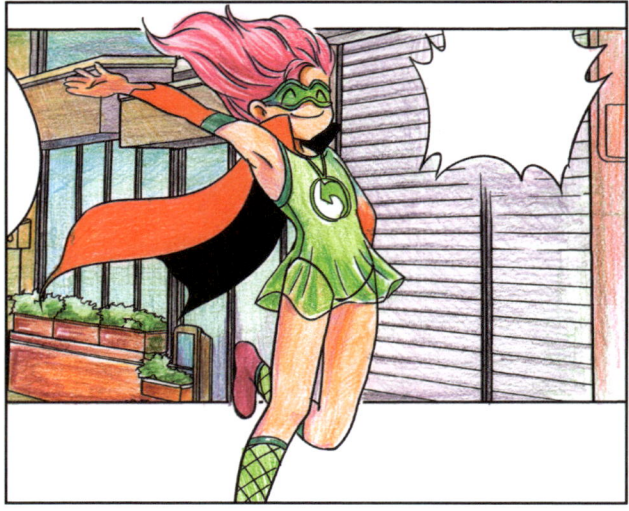

▲ Colored pencils

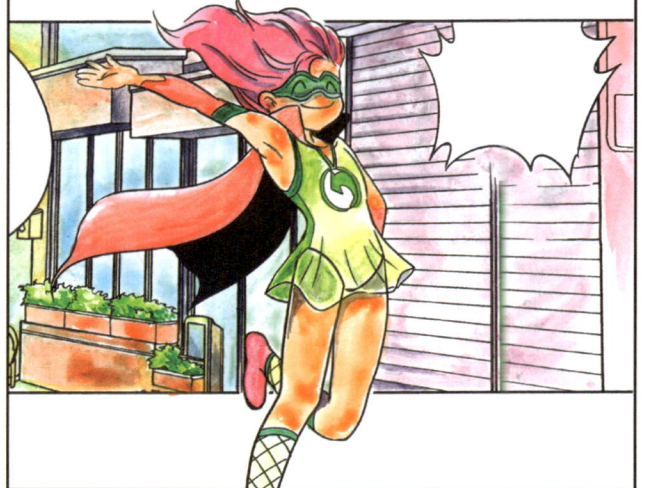

▲ Watercolors

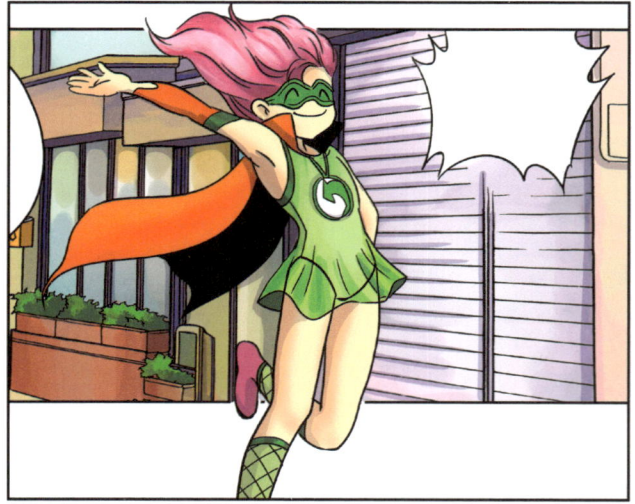

▲ Digital tools

On the following pages, I am going to show you how to color with alcohol markers.

METHODOLOGY

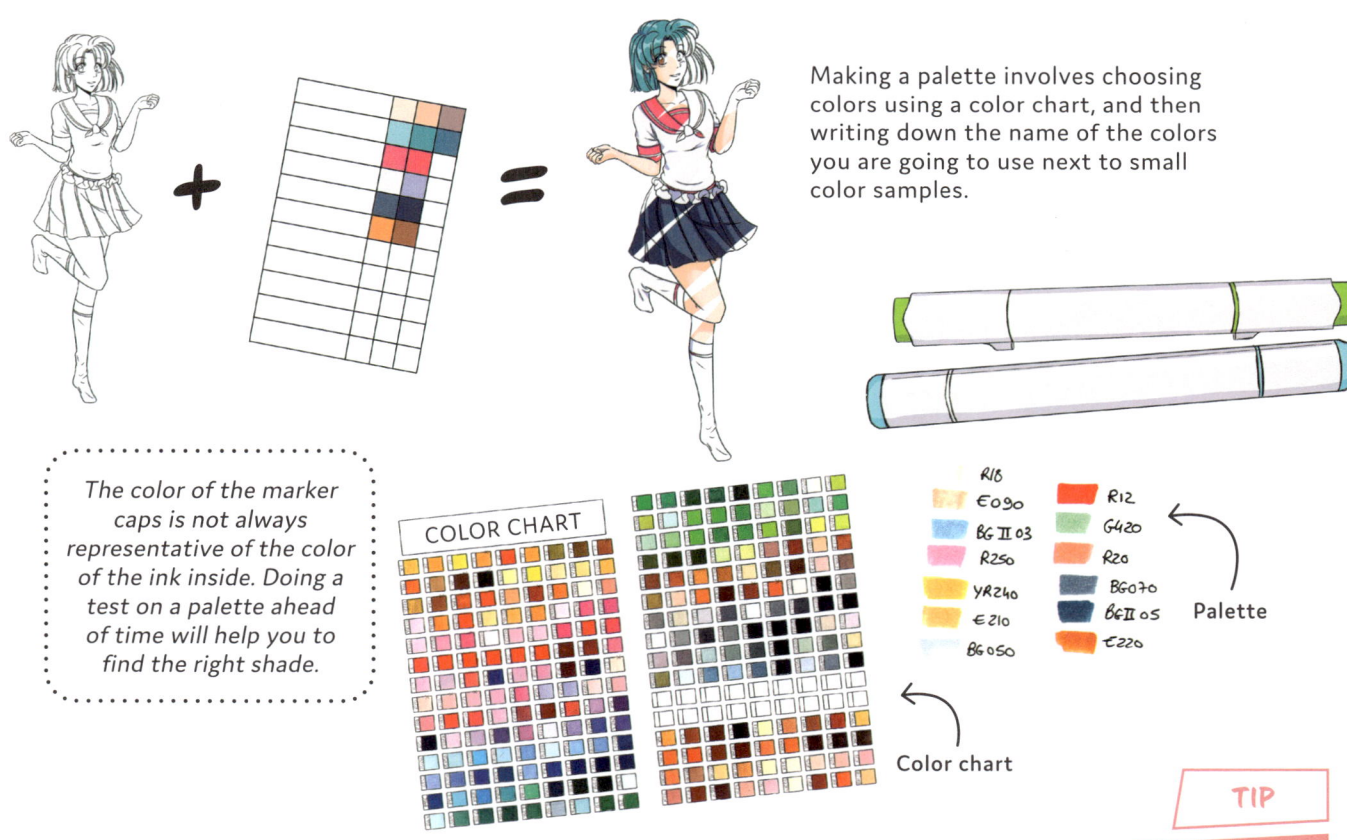

HERE IS A DRAWING THAT WE ARE GOING TO COLOR TOGETHER.

COOL! WHERE SHALL WE START?

WITH PALETTES!

Coloring with alcohol markers happens in several stages.
First, choose the colors that you're going to use, and then add them to the drawing.

Making a palette involves choosing colors using a color chart, and then writing down the name of the colors you are going to use next to small color samples.

The color of the marker caps is not always representative of the color of the ink inside. Doing a test on a palette ahead of time will help you to find the right shade.

COLOR CHART

R18
E090
BG II 03
R250
YR240
E210
BG050

R12
G420
R20
BG070
BG II 05
E220

Palette

Color chart

In choosing your colors, keep in mind the harmony of colors and everything that we have discussed so far.

The palettes will give you a preview of the feeling of your final illustration.

TIP

For every element of your drawing, choose two or three colors from among the light, medium, and dark colors.

Solid Areas

There are several ways of applying colors. To create solid areas—in other words, areas of color filled in uniformly—I suggest several different methods:

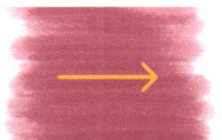 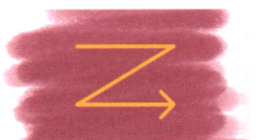  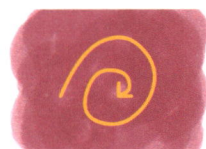 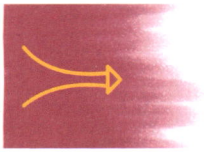

▲ Parallel strokes　　▲ Zigzag strokes　　▲ Crossed strokes　　▲ Spiral strokes　　▲ Strokes that are pressed down and then released

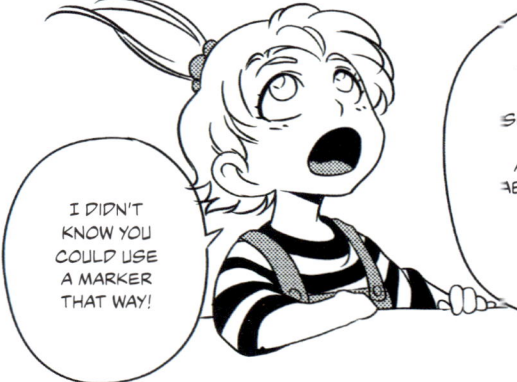

I DIDN'T KNOW YOU COULD USE A MARKER THAT WAY!

WITH EVERY TECHNIQUE, YOU WILL ALREADY SEE A DIFFERENCE IN THE RESULT, AND YOU WILL BE ABLE TO PUT THESE INTO PRACTICE IN YOUR NEXT COLORING.

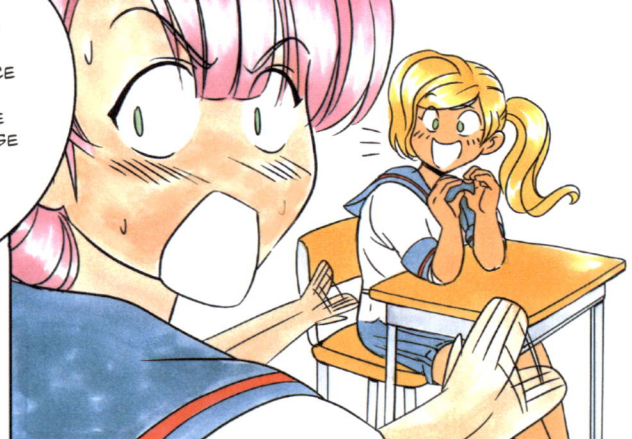

Start by applying the lightest colors. Color in the direction of the textures: for hair, for instance, from the roots to the tips.

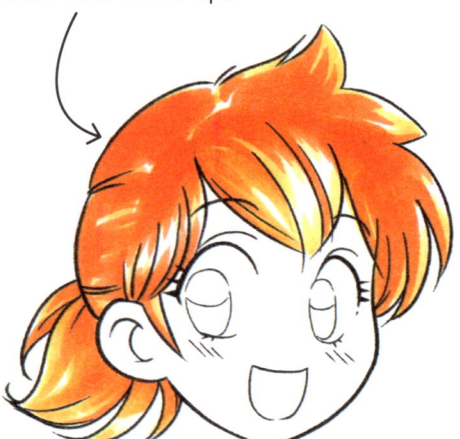

Gradients

By paying attention to how much pressure you exert on the tip of the marker, you can create gradients using just one marker. This technique is useful for drawing shadows, for example.

 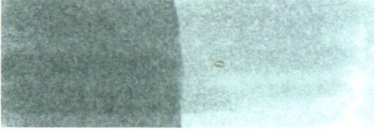

Go over the same area several times to add more color and deepen the drawing.

Mixing Colors

The ink of alcohol markers allows you to mix the different colors with each other.

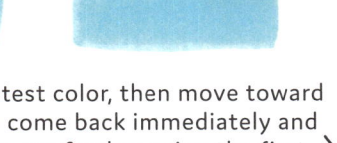
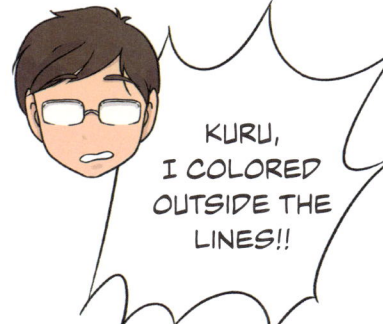

First, apply the lightest color, then move toward darker colors. Then come back immediately and stretch the pigment out further using the first light-colored marker.

Use this technique on certain parts of your drawing.

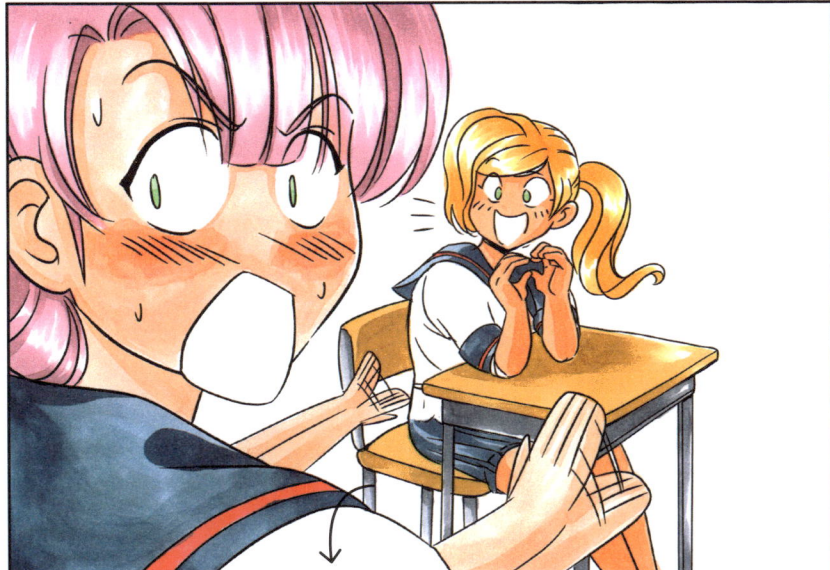

KURU, I COLORED OUTSIDE THE LINES!!

If you have just gone outside the lines by a little bit, it's possible to make the color come back inside the lines using a colorless **blender**.

Whatever technique you're using, I recommend that you always start with the lightest color. You can add color, but you can't take it away!

This particular marker does not contain any pigment. If you tap lightly with the colorless marker around the area of the excess paint, the paper will become moist and the pigments will be pushed back.

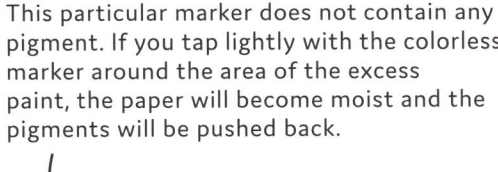

To avoid going outside the lines, all you have to do is first draw the outlines of the area to be filled in, or stop just a little bit before you get to the edges of the character.

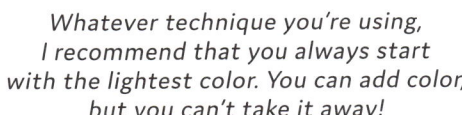

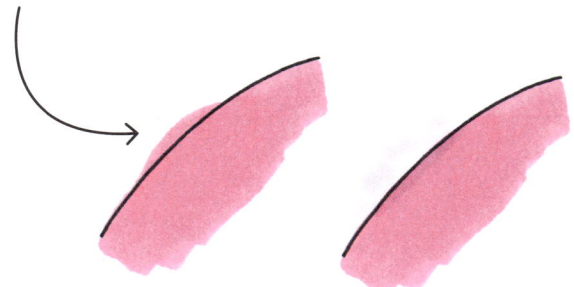

LIGHT AND SHADOWS

With **light and shadows**, you can add volume and depth to your drawings. Shadows are the result of light rays meeting an obstacle.

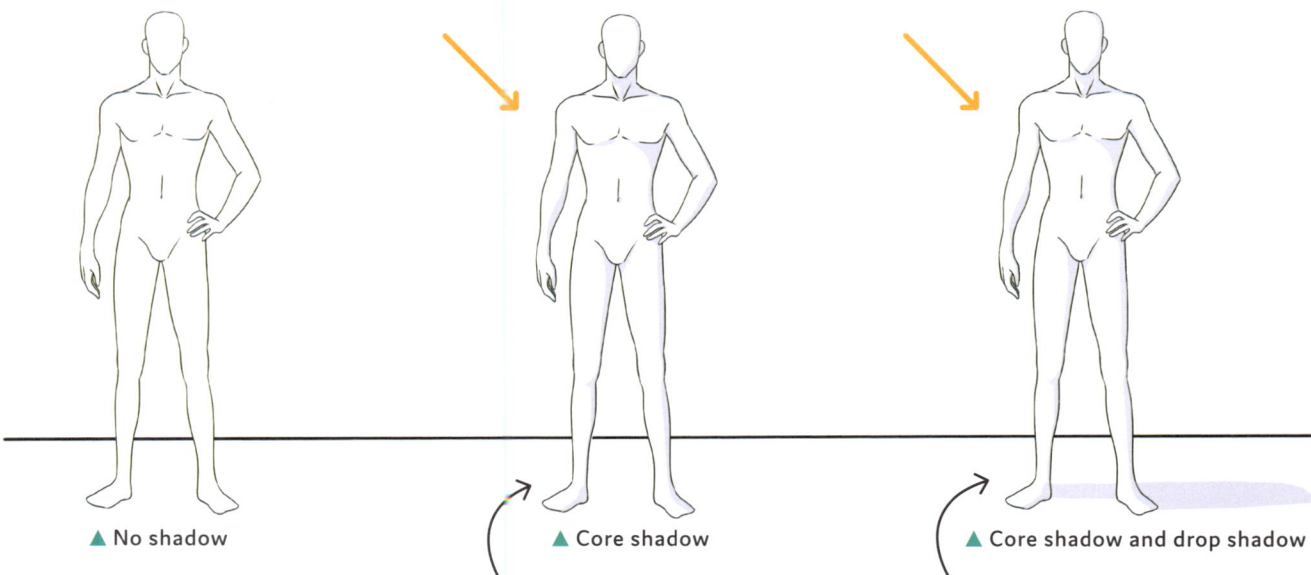

▲ No shadow   ▲ Core shadow   ▲ Core shadow and drop shadow

Sometimes, an object creates a shadow on itself, because the source of the light only lights one of its sides at a time, and in that case, we speak of a **core shadow**.

If this same object is then placed on a surface or in front of a second object, it will keep the light from passing through and project a shadow beyond itself—this is the **cast shadow**.

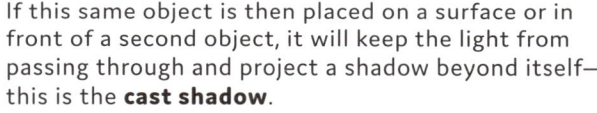

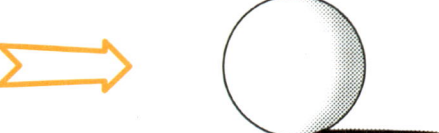

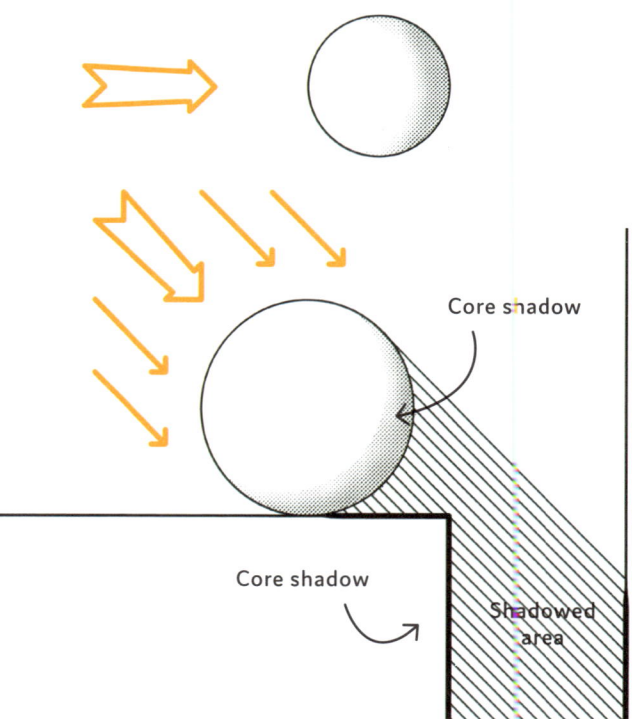

Core shadow

Core shadow

Shadowed area

We use a technique similar to perspective to draw cast shadows.

The light is represented by rays that emanate from a light source. The farther away that light source is, the more parallel the lines will appear to be.

The shadows on the character above immediately give the character an additional dimension. By projecting the character's shadow onto the floor or the wall, we are integrating it into a space.

It is helpful to learn how to position shadows to go from two to three dimensions.

DEFINING THE DIRECTION OF THE LIGHT

To draw shadows on an object or a character, you have to first identify the light source.

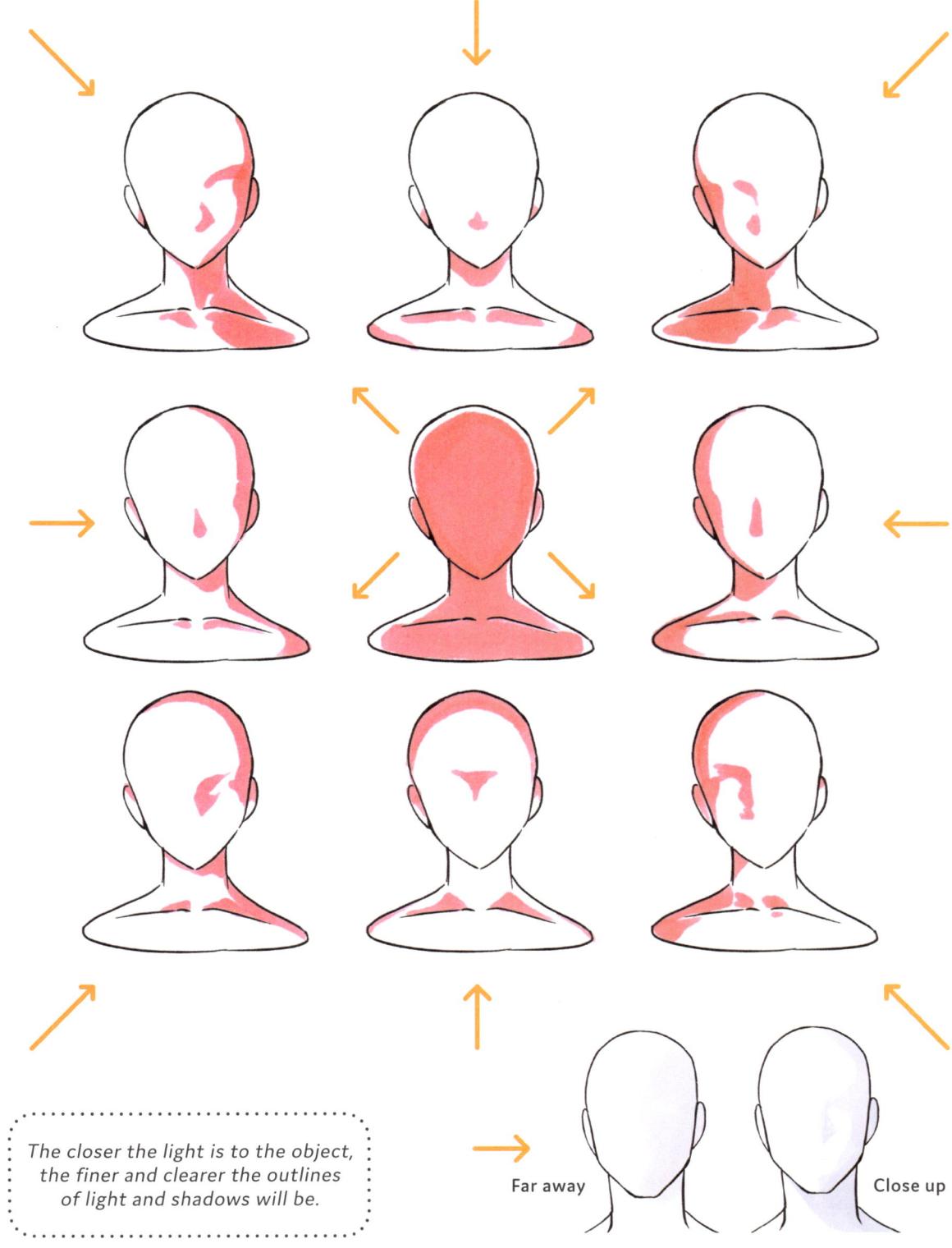

The closer the light is to the object, the finer and clearer the outlines of light and shadows will be.

Far away   Close up

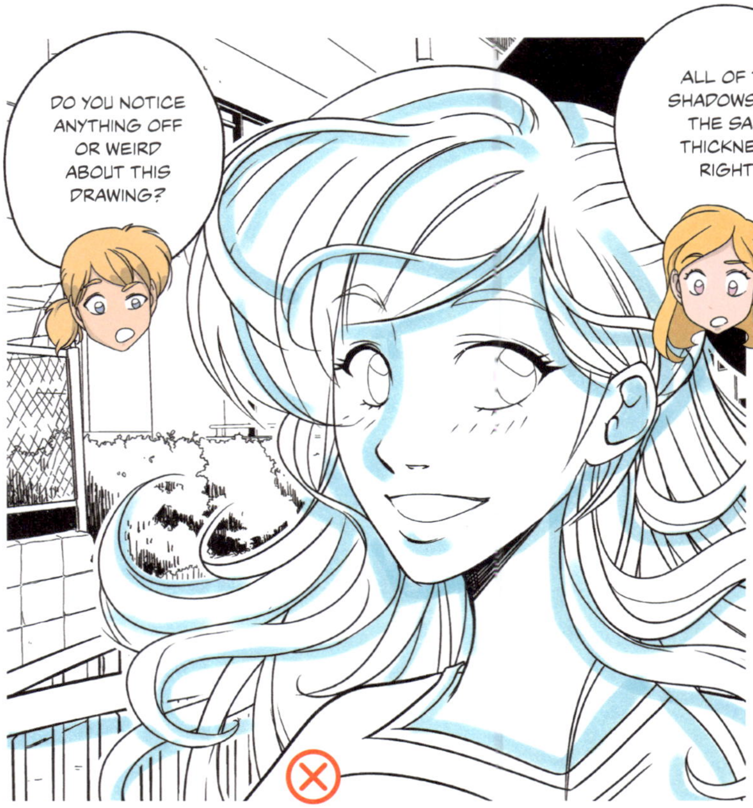

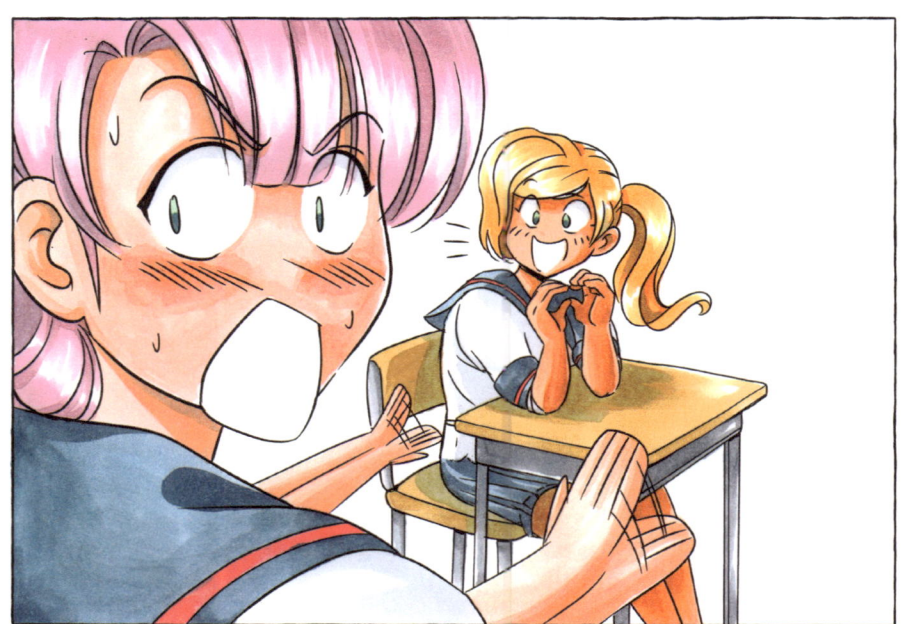

DO YOU NOTICE ANYTHING OFF OR WEIRD ABOUT THIS DRAWING?

ALL OF THE SHADOWS ARE THE SAME THICKNESS, RIGHT?

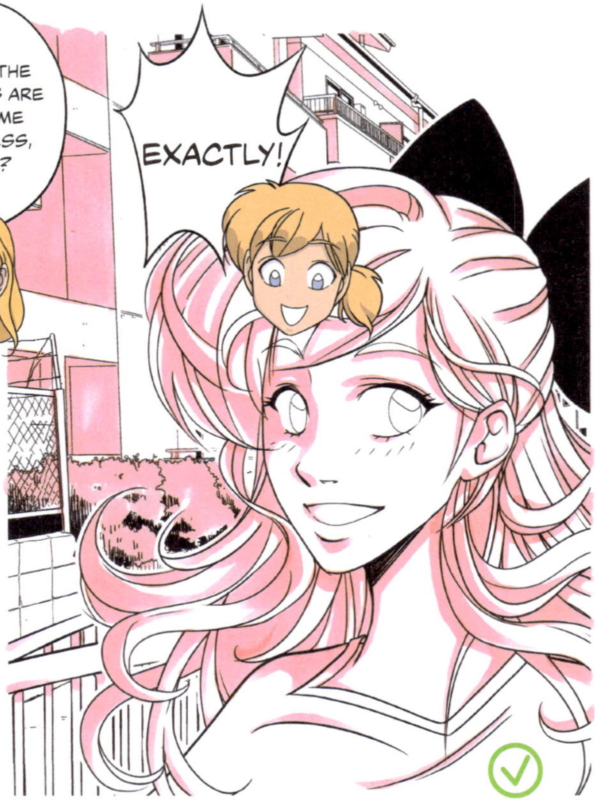

EXACTLY!

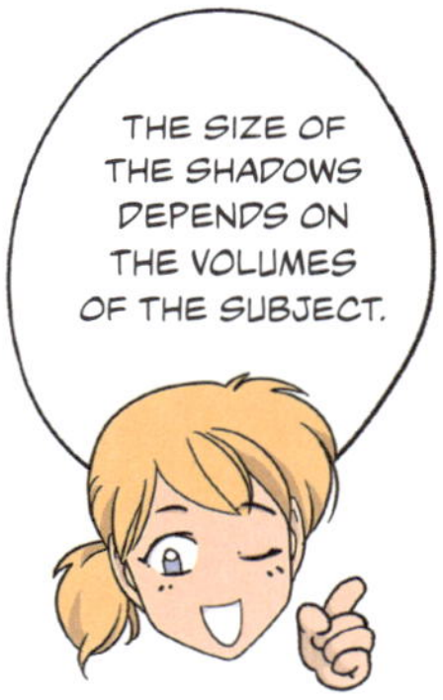

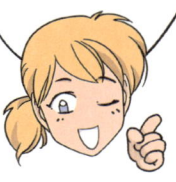

THE SIZE OF THE SHADOWS DEPENDS ON THE VOLUMES OF THE SUBJECT.

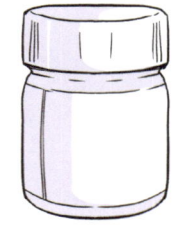

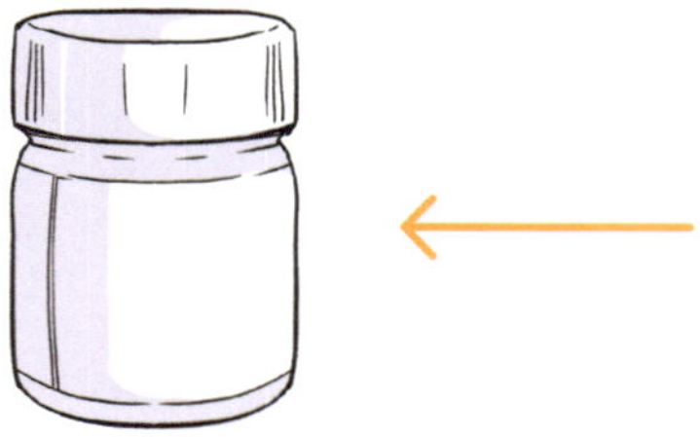

It's possible to use one single color for all of the shadows in the same drawing: a gray, a blue, a pink, a green, and a purple, for example.

TIP

Always pay attention to the volumes that you want to shade, and don't forget to use references to inspire you and get the details right!

Shadows and light reflections are part of the finishing touches and are thus added to your drawing last, depending on the direction of the light.

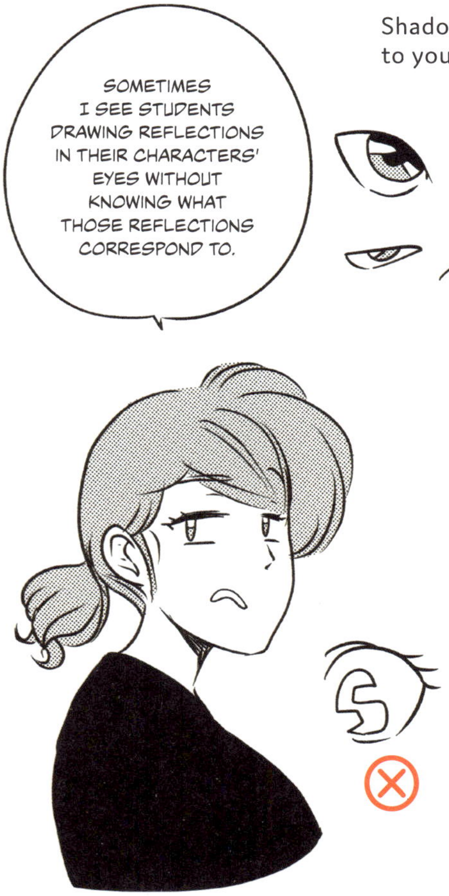

> SOMETIMES I SEE STUDENTS DRAWING REFLECTIONS IN THEIR CHARACTERS' EYES WITHOUT KNOWING WHAT THOSE REFLECTIONS CORRESPOND TO.

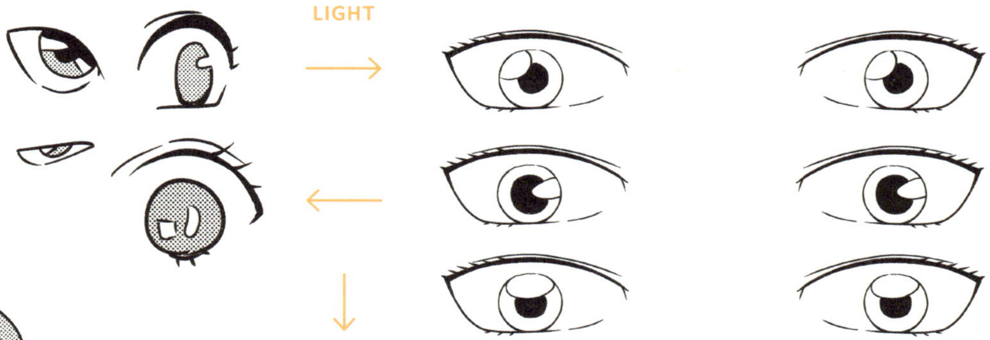

LIGHT

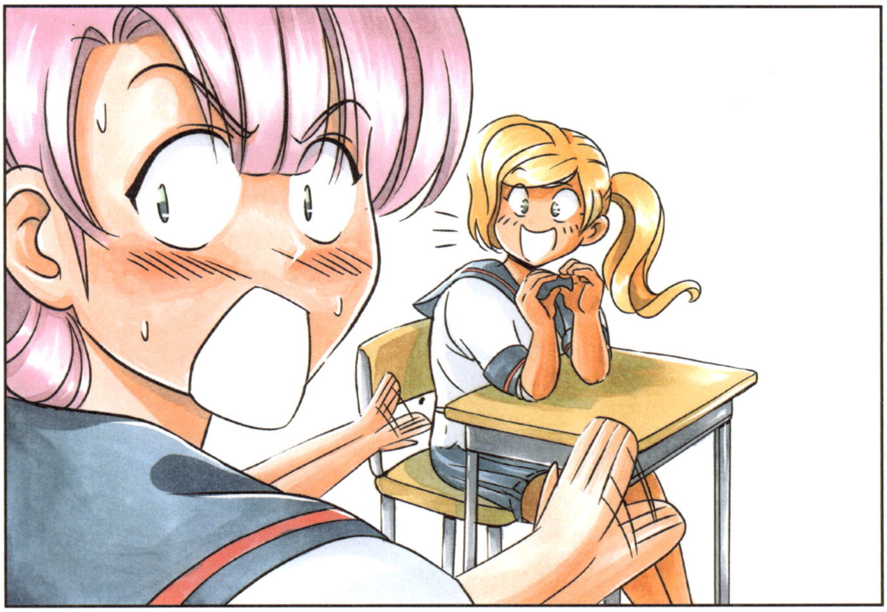

To finish my coloring, I add highlights using white ink.

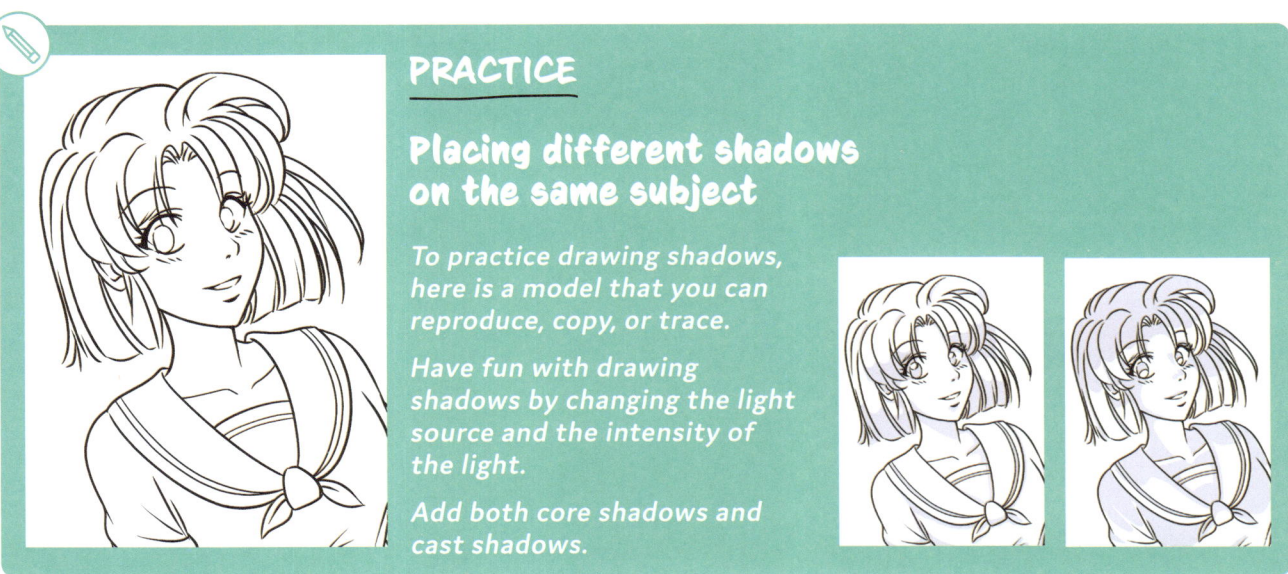

PRACTICE

Placing different shadows on the same subject

To practice drawing shadows, here is a model that you can reproduce, copy, or trace.

Have fun with drawing shadows by changing the light source and the intensity of the light.

Add both core shadows and cast shadows.

DIGITAL DRAWING

More and more artists are turning to digital tools to create their manga. Drawing software is equipped with tools that imitate traditional manga drawing techniques: drawing pens, markers, paint…

The drawing is usually done on a graphics tablet using a stylus. The drawing appears instantly on the screen.

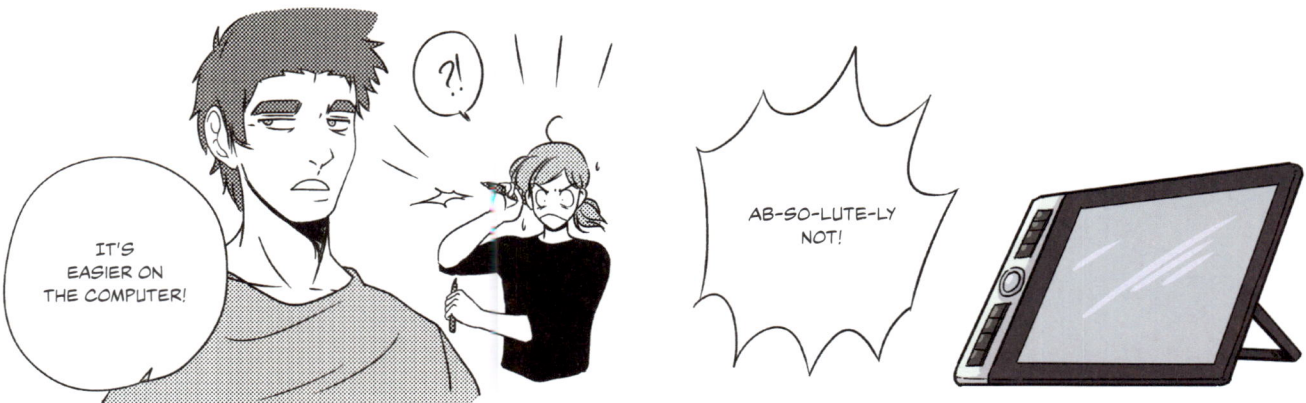

Whether it's on paper or on a computer, you're still the one doing the drawing.

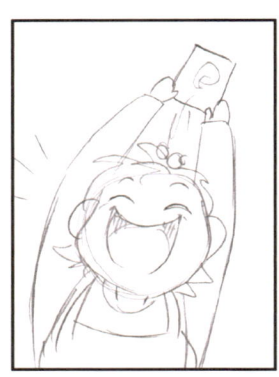 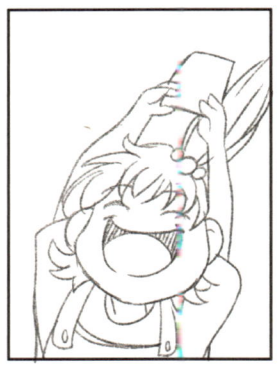 

For every new document, you start out by drawing on a first layer. You can draw things on each layer that will then be assembled to make a whole image. You'll add new layers to separate out the sketch from the inking, for example.

Most different kinds of drawing software have the same features.

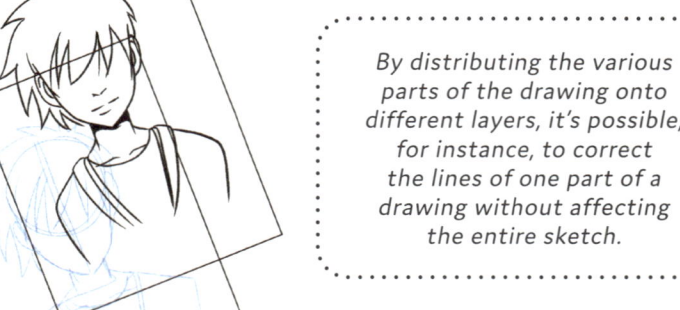

By distributing the various parts of the drawing onto different layers, it's possible, for instance, to correct the lines of one part of a drawing without affecting the entire sketch.

TECHNIQUES

There are different techniques for coloring using digital tools.

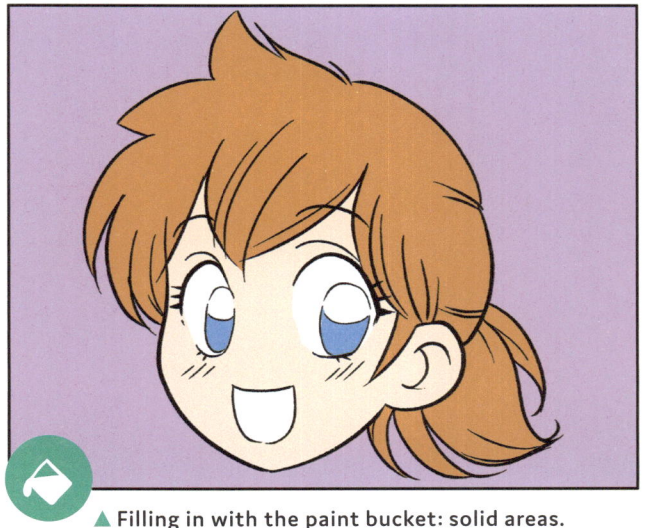

▲ Filling in with the paint bucket: solid areas.

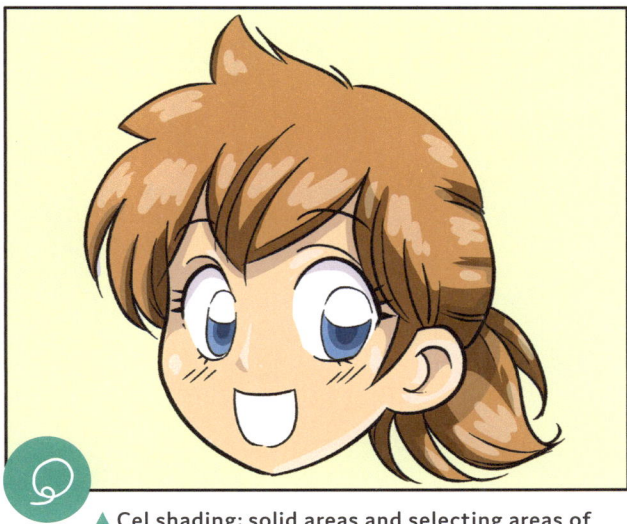

▲ Cel shading: solid areas and selecting areas of sharp shadow.

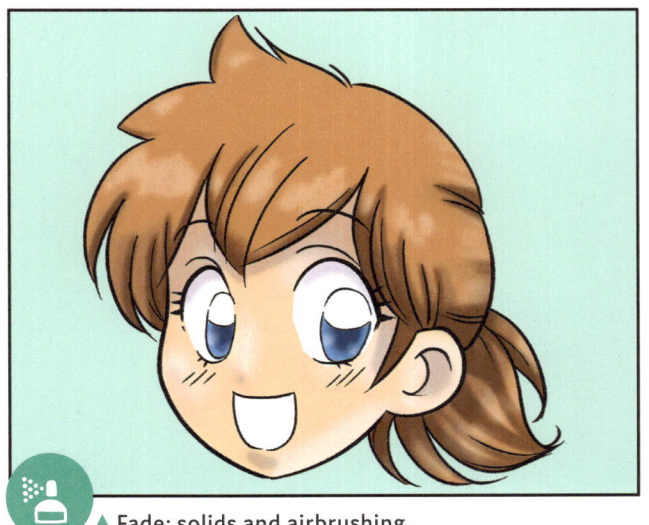

▲ Fade: solids and airbrushing.

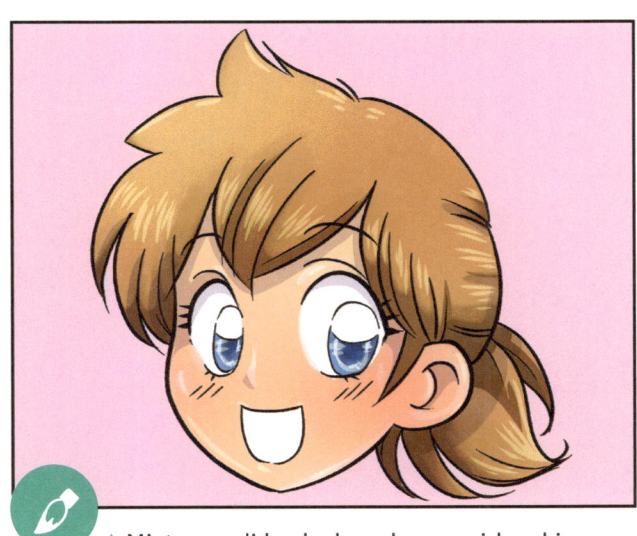

▲ Mixture: solids, shadowed areas, airbrushing, fades.

If you want to create your color version using drawing software, I encourage you to keep the habit of working with a palette of colors.

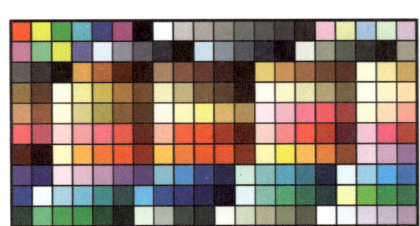

The pipette tool is used to choose a color so that you can use it immediately.

FINAL TIPS

FINDING YOUR RHYTHM

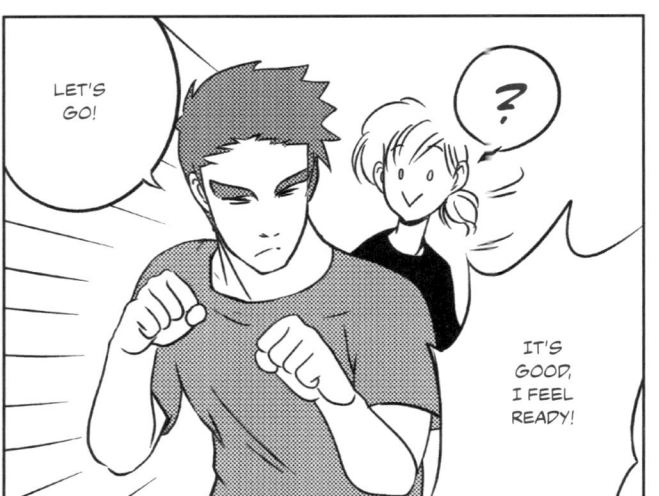

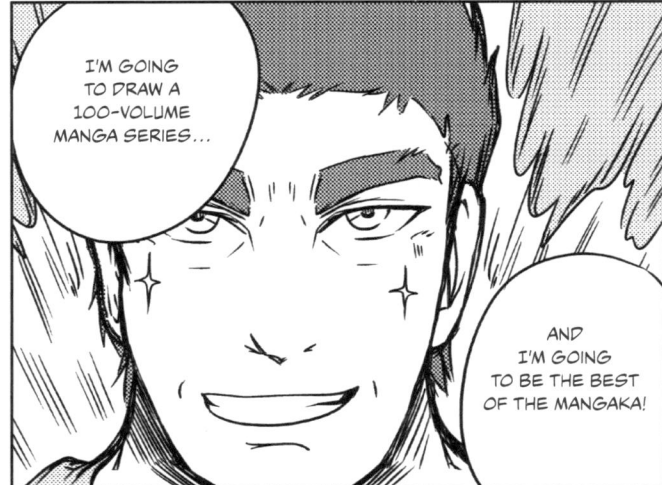

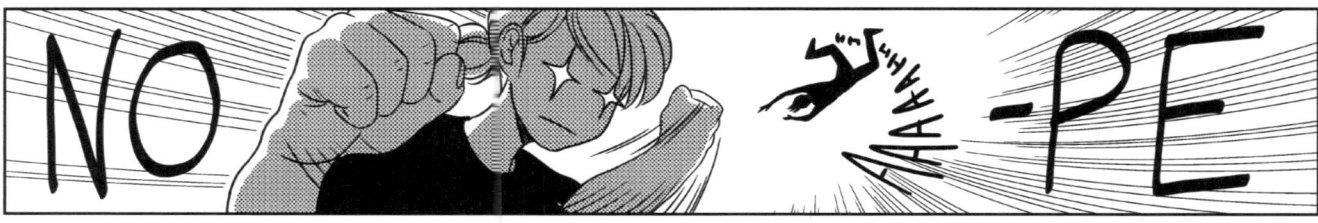

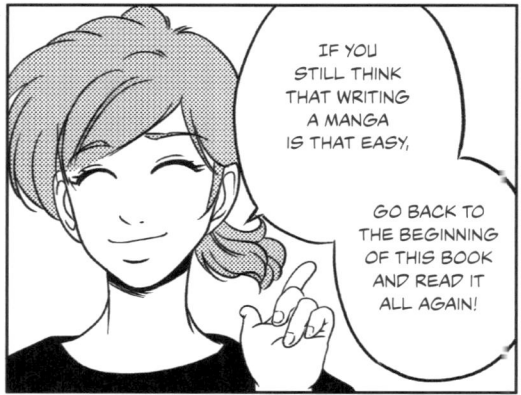

If your goal is to work with a publishing house, you will not be able to choose how many volumes your project will have. The success of a series determines how long new volumes will keep being published, so work on giving it your very best!

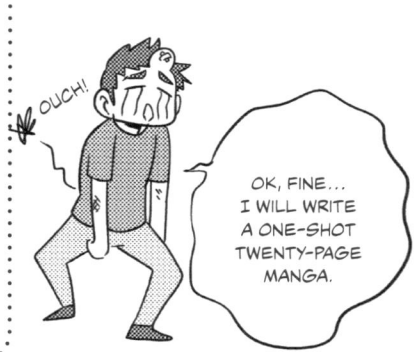

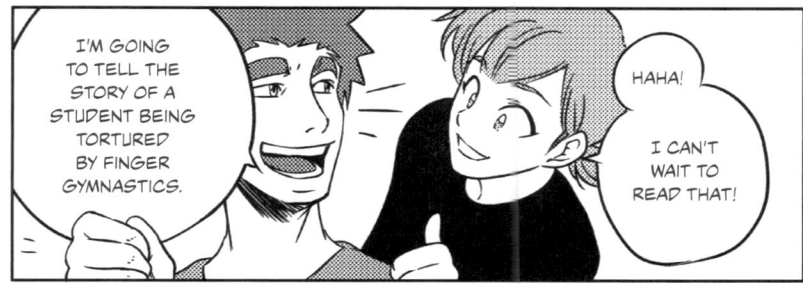

Like Rowan, start with short stories so that you can become familiar and comfortable with all of the steps of creating a manga, and then increase the difficulty by adding more pages or creating more complex worlds!

GETTING SUPPORT

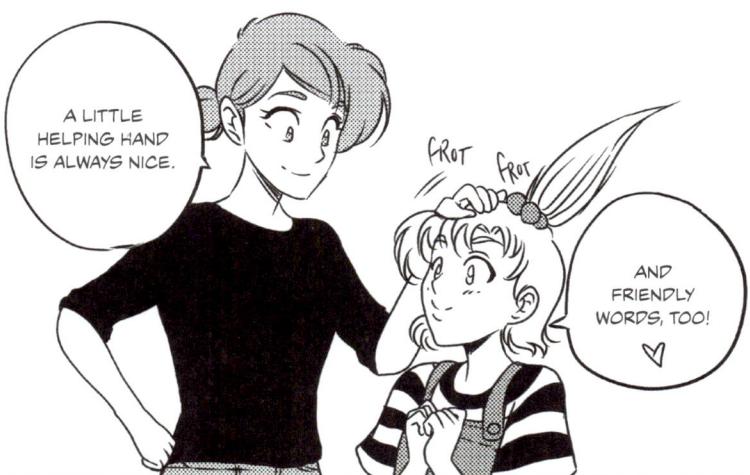

Drawing manga is not an easy thing. In fact, I would say that it's very hard.

When we start drawing manga, whether it's just for fun or in the hopes of making it into a career, nothing says that we have to do it alone.

We all have phases when we're feeling really motivated and other times when we doubt ourselves, and there is no reason not to get help and support.

Manga can turn into large-scale projects, and the support of our loved ones is then very important.

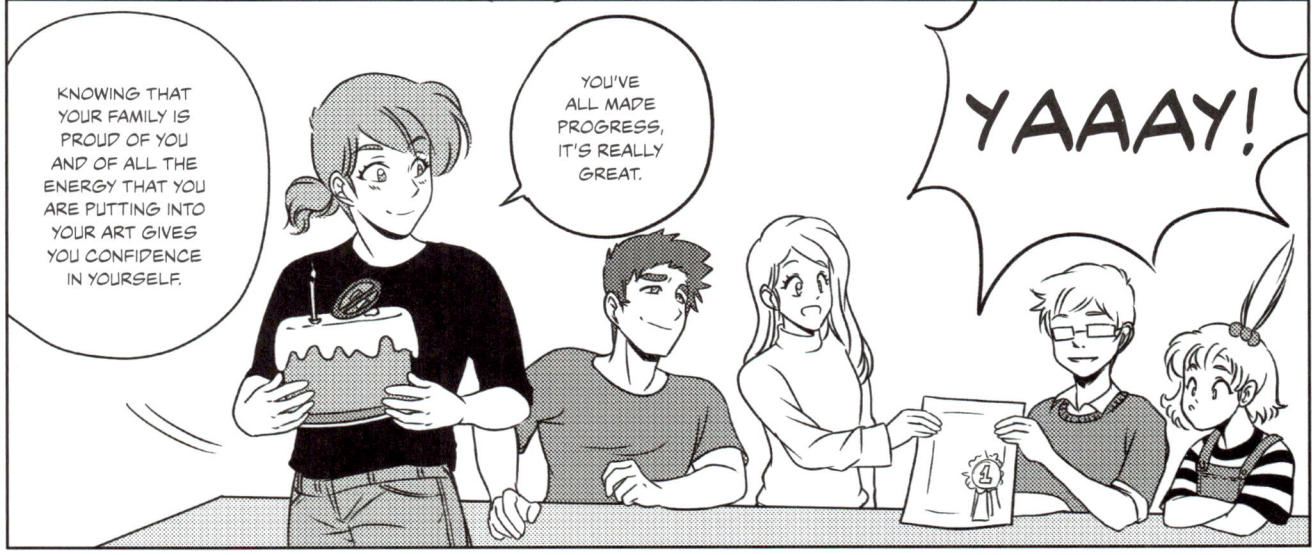

You can get a lot of advice from professionals by reading books like this one, watching online tutorials, or taking courses within specialized systems on all levels, like workshops, community education classes, or professional training.

You will discover that there are more and more mangaka from all over and that you can learn a lot from their careers. Follow them on social media to discover their worlds and see how they work. You can even meet them in person at signing events!

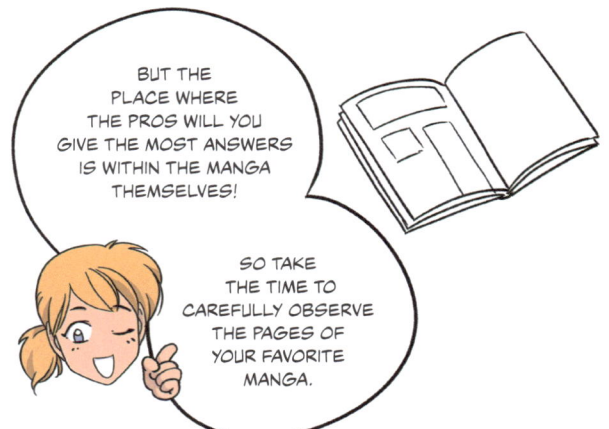

TEN IMPORTANT POINTS

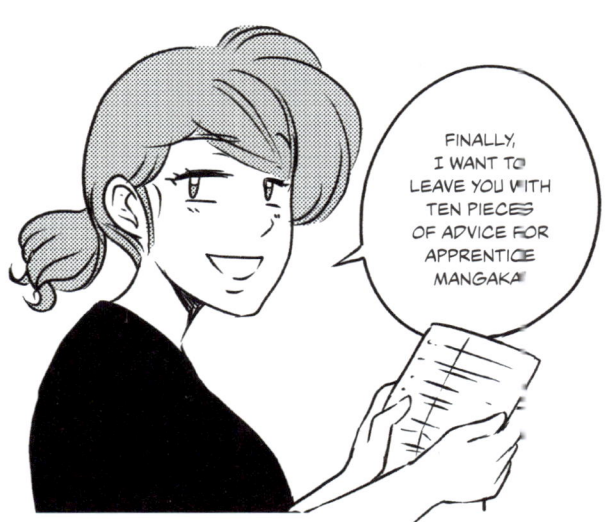

FINALLY, I WANT TO LEAVE YOU WITH TEN PIECES OF ADVICE FOR APPRENTICE MANGAKA!

1 Start Drawing Right Now

Get going! It's very easy to find excuses to avoid drawing even though you really want to do it. Sometimes, this reluctance comes from a fear of doing it wrong. But who cares if you're not "good" at drawing yet? We learn by doing, so be messy, make mistakes, but always keep going forward.

2 Get Organized

Define clear objectives that match your particular situation. Decide on a plan of action with deadlines and hold to your pace and schedule!

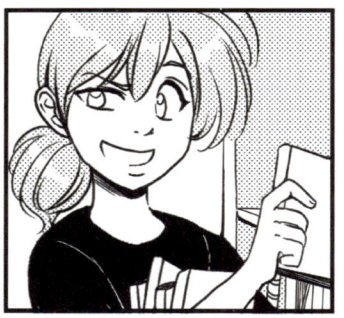

3 Do the Research

Read! Observe! Go get all the information you need for your project to succeed: advice on drawing, exercises on perspective, reference, inspiration…

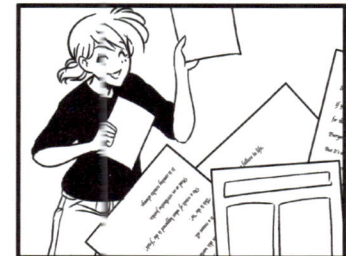

4 Get the Gear You Need

The material does not make the artist! Find the brands and materials that work best for you.

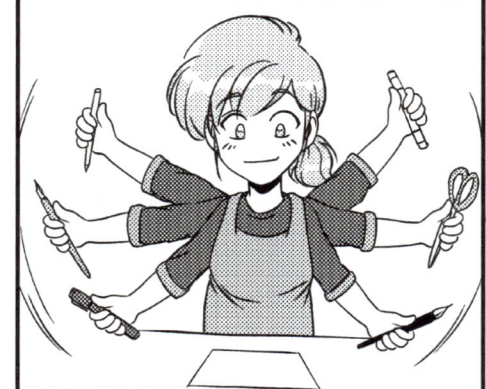

5 Challenge Your Limits

Push beyond your comfort zone! Nothing is more effective for making progress than practicing drawing things that seem impossible. Draw a background in perspective, then another one, then another one…Add a vanishing point, add in more elements, and they will get easier and easier to create.

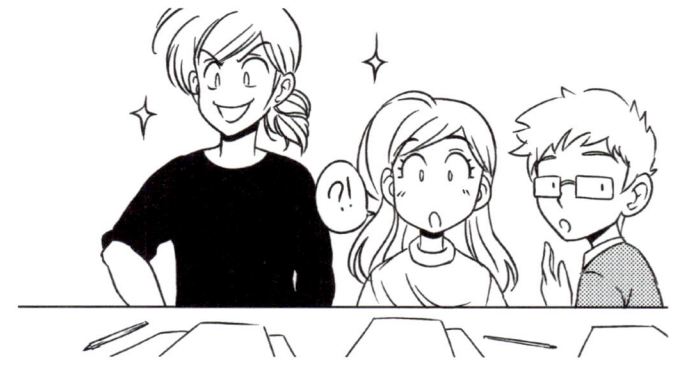

6 Work on a Regular Schedule

Practice will make you into an expert. Every new drawing will teach you something! If one step in the process feels particularly hard to you, don't give up! Take a break, then come back to face the obstacle, which is not that insurmountable after all!

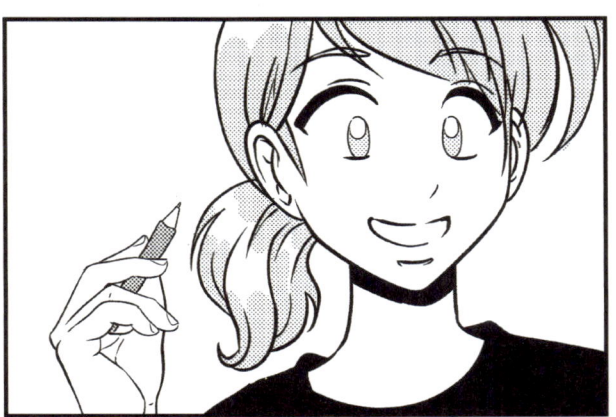

7 Share Your Emotions

Your drawings, your stories, and your worlds represent you. They make it possible for you to share ideas, values, and especially emotions through your characters. Tell your stories with passion and you will touch your readers' hearts.

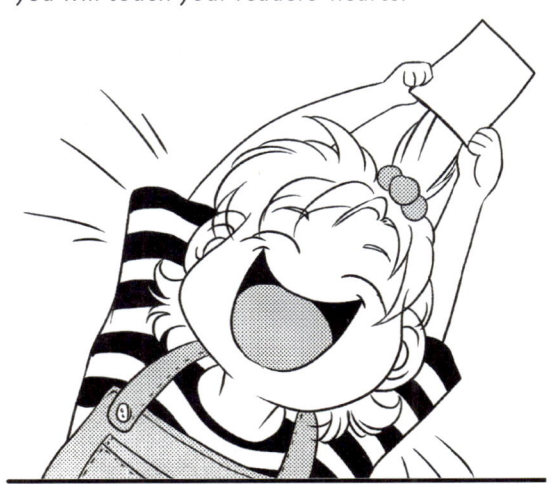

8 Believe in Yourself

Drawing manga is a complex process. Don't be afraid to ask for help from your friends, your loved ones, and even from the pros!

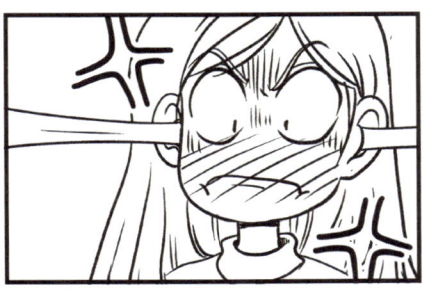

9 Accept Help

For a seed to grow into a fruit, it takes time, sun, and water. But just like not every fruit grows at the same speed and doesn't have the same flavor, every artist progresses at their own rhythm toward their own destination.

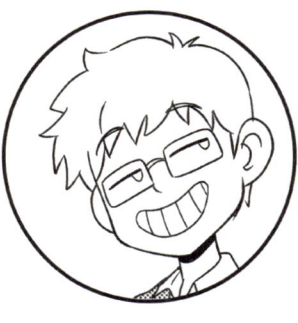

Don't compare your work to other people's work, especially if you're just starting. Get into the good habit of only comparing yourself to yourself. Take advantage of every new drawing to learn something! Go full speed ahead toward your goals and, just like your hero, become a better version of yourself!

10 Have Fun

Whether you're drawing manga for fun or to make it your career, keep in mind your primary objective: being happy. Take pleasure in expressing your ideas through the pages of your manga.

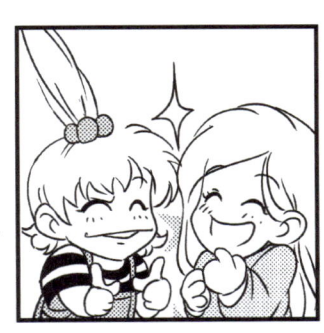

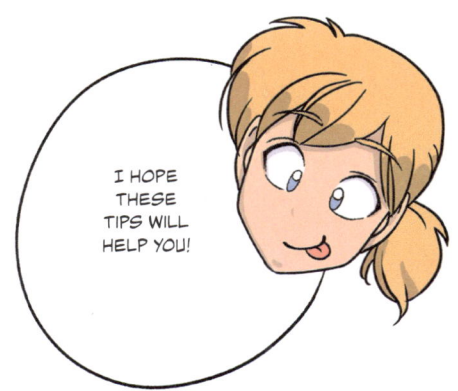

I HOPE THESE TIPS WILL HELP YOU!

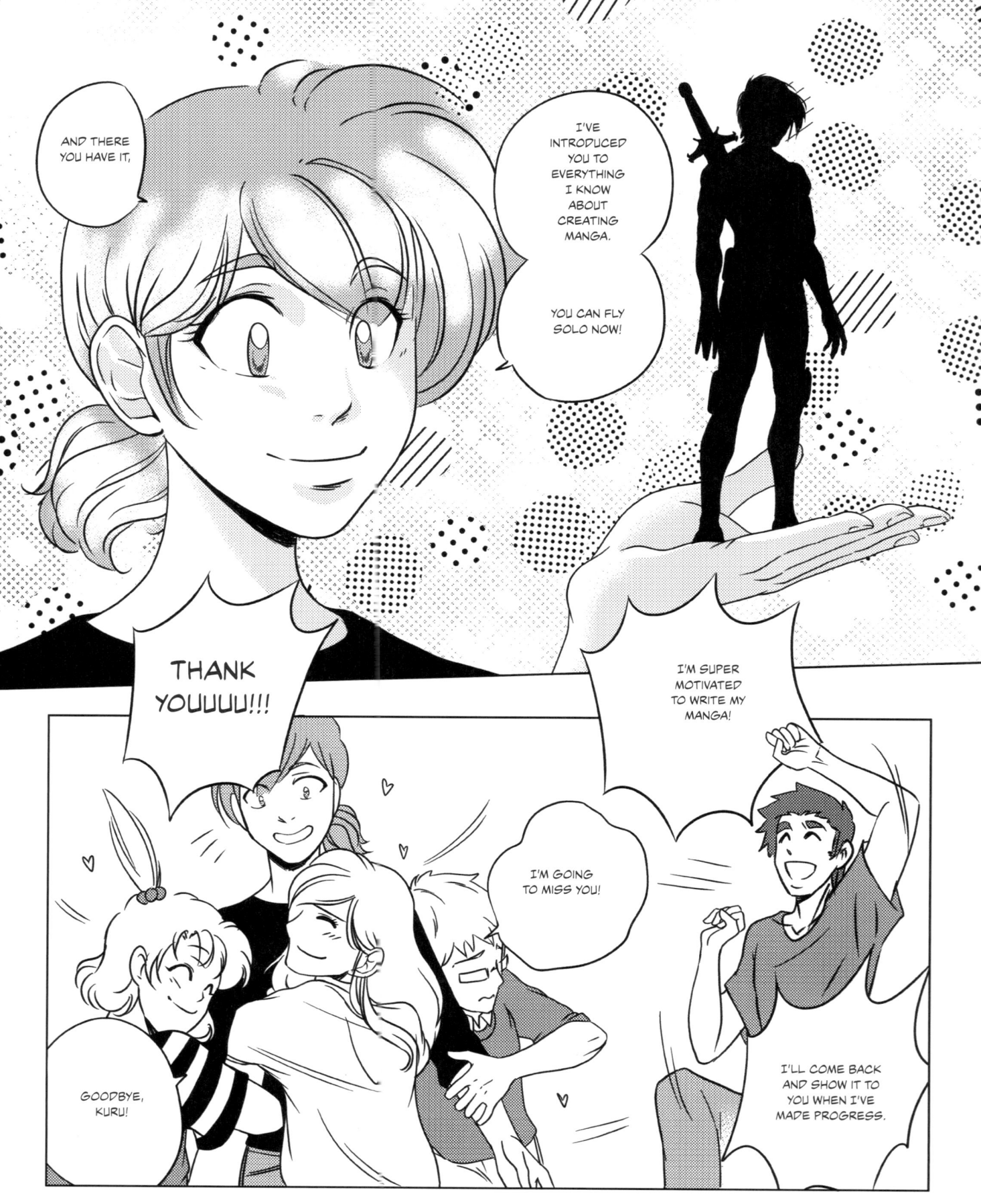

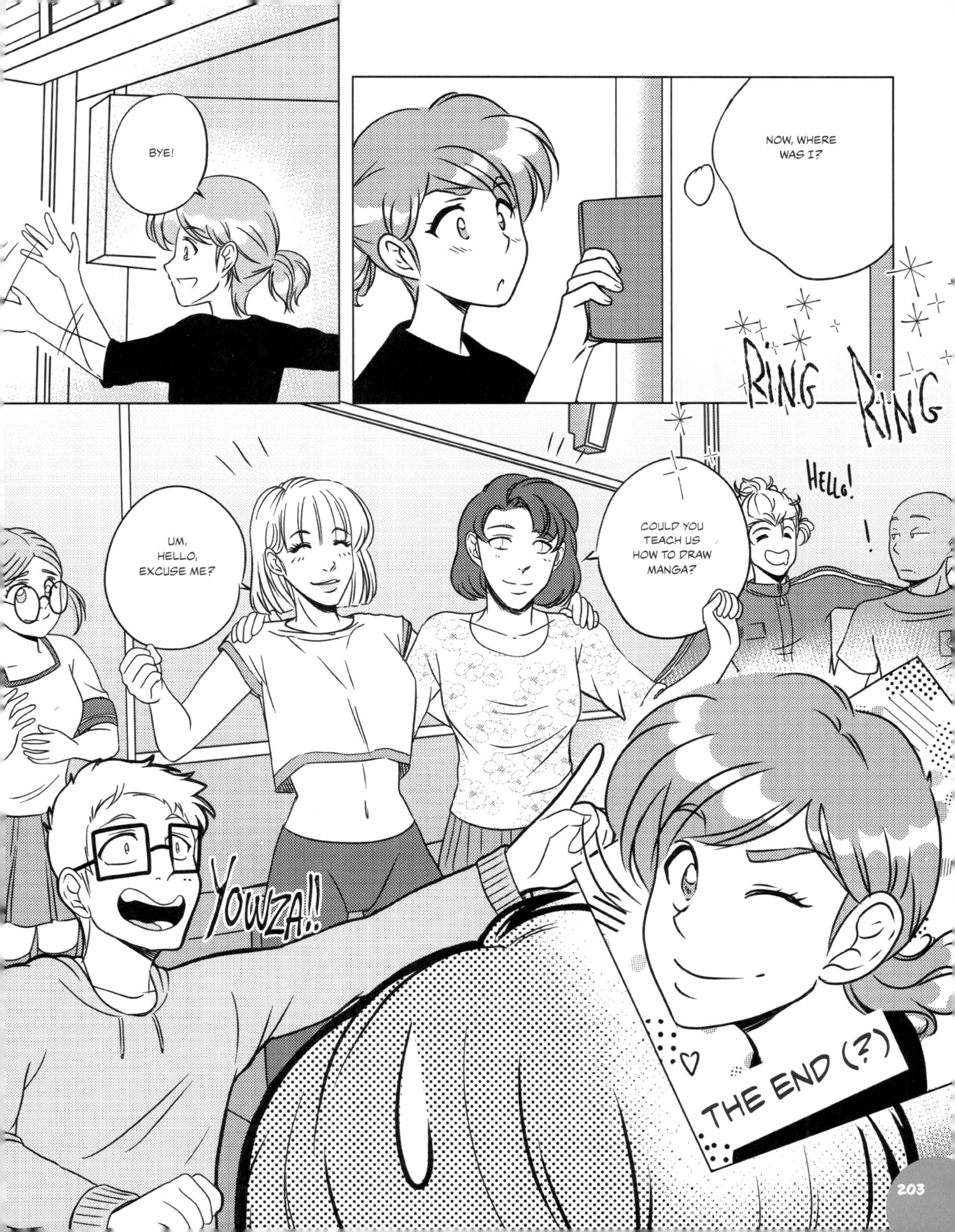

GLOSSARY

#

180° line: Imaginary line connecting two characters that the camera must not cross because otherwise it will distort what we see.

A

Action line: A path that the readers follow on a drawing or a manga page.

Allegory: The use of a concrete idea in a story to evoke an abstract idea.

Anatomy: The organization of structures and shapes that make up a living being.

B

Board: Drawn page of a comic book, graphic novel, or manga. The board is also the sheet of paper on which the pages are drawn.

C

Cast shadow: Shadowed area that a lighted object projects onto a surface or another object.

Character design: The conception of a character or the drawing presenting a character with their traits and attributes.

Chibi: Small, cute character or caricaturized version of a character with childlike attributes.

Climax: The most intense moment in the plot.

Color: The perception of a light on the surface of an object.

Color wheel: Catalogue of the hues of one or more colors.

Composition: Organization of the elements of an illustration or a board according to action lines in order to direct the reader and aid comprehension.

Construction lines: Geometric lines and shapes used as guidelines for a drawing.

Contrast: The opposition of two values in order to highlight an important piece of information.

Core shadow: Shadowed area on a lighted object.

D

Dialogues: Lines of text attributed to the characters.

E

Ellipsis: Jump in time to allow for a transition between two scenes.

Established narrative: Preexisting narrative scheme.

F

Flashback: A scene that happens in the past with respect to the rest of the story.

Framing: The choice of the distance and the angle of view for a scene in a panel.

Full-length view: A full-length view shows a whole character, from head to toe.

G

Gijinka: Anthropomorphic character that has some of the attributes of an object or of a concept. For instance: a fire-boy, a moon-girl…

Grain: The texture of the surface of a sheet of paper.

Graphic overlaps: Disturbing visual effect produced when the outlines of elements on two different planes connect on the same line.

Gutter: Empty space between the panels of a comic book, graphic novel, or manga.

H

Horizon line: A line placed at the height of the camera that is filming the scene or the height of the reader's gaze. This line corresponds to the place where the ground meets the sky.

Hue: Variations on the same color.

I

Inking: A drawing made in ink. This stage follows the pencil sketch stage and fixes the drawing in its definitive version.

K

Kawaii: "Cute" in Japanese.

Kemonomimi: Anthropomorphic character that has some of the attributes of an animal. Examples: a catwoman, a siren...

L

Layout: Organization of a sequence into panels of various shapes and sizes on the pages of the manga.

M

Mangaka: Manga artist and/or author.

Manpu: Symbol that allows you to express and/or emphasize emotions.

Mecha: Anthropomorphic character with robotic attributes.

Moire: Unpleasant visual effect that sometimes results from a misalignment of screens.

N

Narrative scheme: More or less detailed outline of a storyline, presented in a series of key steps.

O

Offscreen: In framing, what is offscreen corresponds to everything that is outside the field of action and that we therefore cannot see.

One-shot: Short story that is finished within one chapter or one volume.

P

Palette: Selection of colors and hues to be used in coloring.

Panel: Drawing area, defined by a full border (or not), showing a moment in the story.

Pencil sketch: Drawing in pencil. In manga, this is the first stage in drawing the boards.

Perspective: Drawing technique that allows you to represent a three-dimensional view of a scene or object.

Posture: The way a character stands or holds themself.

Proportions: The relationship among several elements of a whole.

Protagonist: Main character of a story.

Psychological effects: Drawings or textures produced to create a particular feeling on the pages of the manga.

R

Reverse shot: In framing, the reverse shot is the view directly opposite the shot of the starting viewpoint.

S

Screen ruling: Number of dots per inch on a screen sheet.

Screens: Collection of black dots, distributed uniformly or in a pattern. The self-adhesive sheets that these patterns are printed on are also called screens.

Sensei: Teacher in Japanese.

Sequential art: Term invented by Will Eisner to designate the artistic practices in which a succession of images results in a graphic narration.

Shot: Choice of the distance at which to represent a character, an object, or a scene within a panel.

Solid: Filling in a surface in a uniform way.

Sound effect: Words that are part of the drawing that represent sounds.

Speech bubbles: Shapes containing dialogues, usually rounded, and with a border around the outside.

Storyboard: Sequences of the story, drawn in panels, page by page, acting as a draft for sketching the boards.

Storyline: Text describing the progress of a story and the dialogues.

Stylization: Representing a subject (object, character, or scene) in a simplified manner for a decorative effect.

Symbols: Visual or narrative clues that help in understanding the work.

T

Theme: The main subject of the story.

Timeline: A succession of events presented in the order of their occurrence in time.

Tone: The way the story is told, depending on the intended audience.

V

Vanishing line: Line drawn in such a way as to connect the edge of an object with a vanishing point on the horizon line.

Vanishing point: Point on the horizon line at which the vanishing lines meet.

W

Weight: The thickness of a sheet of paper.

Y

Yonkoma: Mini manga in four panels, read from top to bottom.

ACKNOWLEDGMENTS

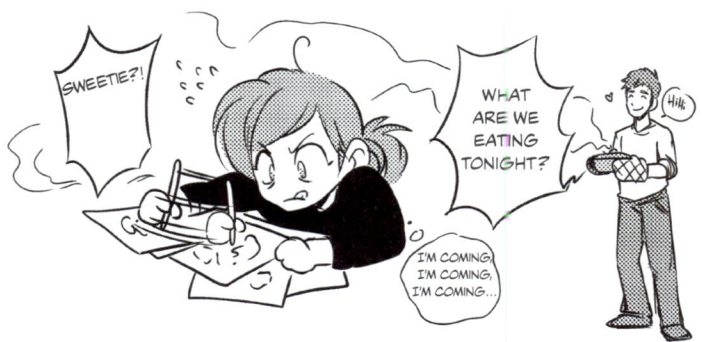

A great big thank you to Fabien for his constant support throughout this entire project.

Thank you to my editors for my first white hairs… but also and especially for their patience! And thank you to Sonia.

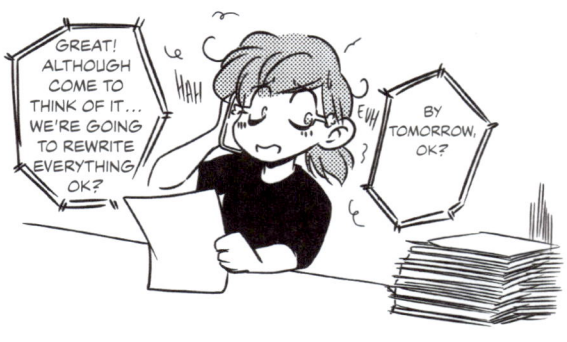

200 pages

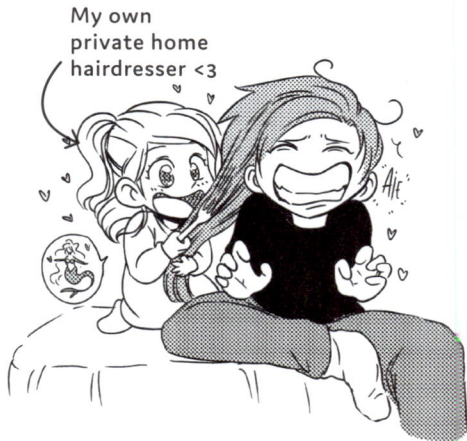

My own private home hairdresser <3

Thank you to my daughter and her cleverness in removing those same white hairs!

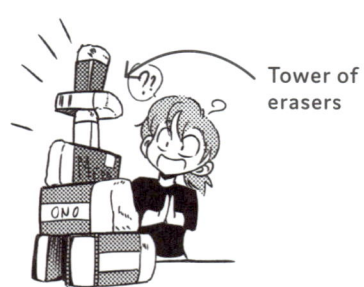

Tower of erasers

Thank you to my family and to my students, inexhaustible sources of inspiration!

And finally, my thanks to you for having bought this book. I'm hoping you'll share with me the progress you've made!

@ateliermangadekuru
@kuru_mbc